Movies as History

Movies as History
Scenes of America, 1930–1970

MARIE L. AQUILA

McFarland & Company, Inc., Publishers
Jefferson, North Carolina

LIBRARY OF CONGRESS CATALOGUING-IN-PUBLICATION DATA

Aquila, Marie L., 1948–
  Movies as history : scenes of America, 1930–1970 / Marie L. Aquila.
      p.   cm.
  Includes bibliographical references and index.

  ISBN 978-0-7864-4637-7 (softcover : acid free paper) ♾
  ISBN 978-1-4766-1465-6 (ebook)

  1. Motion pictures—United States—History. 2. Motion pictures and history. 3. United States—Civilization—Sources. I. Title.
  PN1993.5.U6A68 2014
  791.43'0973—dc23   2014009389

BRITISH LIBRARY CATALOGUING DATA ARE AVAILABLE

© 2014 Marie L. Aquila. All rights reserved

No part of this book may be reproduced or transmitted in any form or by any means, electronic or mechanical, including photocopying or recording, or by any information storage and retrieval system, without permission in writing from the publisher.

On the front cover: Slim Pickens as Maj. T.J. "King" Kong in *Dr. Strangelove or: How I Learned to Stop Worrying and Love the Bomb*, 1964 (Columbia Pictures/Photofest)

Printed in the United States of America

McFarland & Company, Inc., Publishers
  Box 611, Jefferson, North Carolina 28640
  www.mcfarlandpub.com

For Dick

Table of Contents

Preface: Movies as Primary Sources	1
Introduction	5
Part I: Hard Times and Hollywood Hope, 1931–1939	15
The Public Enemy (1931)	22
I Am a Fugitive from a Chain Gang (1932)	27
Lady for a Day (1934)	30
You Can't Take It with You (1938)	34
Stagecoach (1939)	38
Part II: War and Peace Around the Globe, 1937–1956	45
Prewar Era Movies	
Grand Illusion (1937)	61
The Lady Vanishes (1938)	65
Sergeant York (1941)	70
War Era Movies	
Casablanca (1942)	75
The More the Merrier (1943)	79
Rome, Open City (1945)	84
Postwar Era Movies	
The Best Years of Our Lives (1946)	88
Bicycle Thieves (1948)	93
The Third Man (1949)	97
Godzilla, King of the Monsters (1956)	102
Part III: Red Fears and Nuclear Anxieties, 1939–1966	109
Red Fears	
Ninotchka (1939)	118
Notorious (1946)	123
My Son John (1952)	127
Invasion of the Body Snatchers (1956)	131
The Manchurian Candidate (1962)	135

Nuclear Anxieties
- *Kiss Me Deadly* (1955) — 139
- *On the Beach* (1959) — 144
- *Dr. Strangelove or: How I Learned to Stop Worrying and Love the Bomb* (1964) — 149
- *From Russia with Love* (1963) — 153
- *The Bedford Incident* (1965) — 158
- *The Russians Are Coming, The Russians Are Coming* (1966) — 162

Part IV: Images of Women through Good Times and Bad, 1933–1969 — 169
- *Dinner at Eight* (1933) — 186
- *His Girl Friday* (1940) — 190
- *Christmas in Connecticut* (1945) — 195
- *Born Yesterday* (1950) — 199
- *Picnic* (1955) — 204
- *Tammy and the Bachelor* (1957) / *Gidget* (1959) — 210
- *The Thrill of It All* (1963) — 221
- *True Grit* (1969) — 227

Appendix — 235

Notes — 237

Bibliography — 245

Index — 251

Preface: Movies as Primary Sources

Movies as History: Scenes of America, 1930–1970 illustrates how popular movies can enhance the study of the history of the 20th century. Educational research demonstrates that different types of materials can appeal to different learning styles and that primary sources broaden and illuminate our understanding of events. Movies were a dominant form of popular entertainment throughout the last century, and they contain clues to an audience's thoughts and beliefs. Using popular movies as primary sources is an effective, winning strategy that can support the study of a particular historical event or issue. It can also help students become aware of the subtle messages to which they are exposed in all types of mass media.

Movies as History begins with a brief history of the moviemaking industry and a General Movie Analysis Guide designed to help students determine a movie's main plot and any special themes, information, or cultural attitudes it presents. The topics covered are related to the Great Depression, the home fronts here and abroad during World War II, the early decades of the Cold War, and images of women in movies from the early 1930s to the late sixties. Each section begins with an overview of the history of the topic and references significant movies related to it. Representative movies are then analyzed in depth. Suggested Discussion Questions that place each movie in its historical context and reinforce the topic or other issues, including gender, race, or social concerns, follow the analyses.

This book focuses almost exclusively on movies made between 1930 and 1970 for a variety of reasons. The sheer volume of movies made in the 20th century, which number in the tens of thousands, made it necessary to limit the study to a manageable time period. There are many extraordinary movies made before the advent of the "talkies," but encouraging student interest in old movies is one of the book's aims, and silent movies would be a hard sell to today's young people. By the end of the tumultuous 1960s, on the other hand, the movie industry was changing quite rapidly. Movies became far more explicit after the Production Code, which circumscribed movie content, especially content that involved nudity, sex, profanity, race, or violence, was scrapped in 1968. The mature content of many historically significant movies made after 1970 makes those films more problematic for classroom use. In addition, many of the movies made before 1970 are now relatively unknown to contemporary audiences, including many teachers born after 1970. Some may even dismiss those films as simplistic and dated. Today's moviegoers, for example, would probably find the controversy over the use of "damn" in *Gone With the Wind* quaint at best, if not downright silly. Yet, movies produced before 1970 offer a treasure trove of historical information. They present remarkable opportunities to observe social behaviors, political attitudes, gender or racial issues, and reactions to historical events that were current when the movies were made.

An important goal of this book is to familiarize readers with some forgotten movie gems that can illustrate issues and topics as well as offer great entertainment. The representative movies may or may not be about a real character or event. *Sergeant York* is based on the early life and military career of Alvin York, a World War I Medal of Honor winner. York was a sincere conscientious objector, and he grappled with whether or not to register for the draft in 1917. But the movie was made in 1941 and celebrates York's heroism at a time when many Americans were reluctant to get involved in another conflict in Europe. The Suggested Discussion Questions focus on the movie's portrayal of York's pacifism and combat experiences and how they may have reflected or influenced the debate in 1941 about what role America should play in Europe's new war. *Lady for a Day*, on the other hand, is fictional, but it addresses real issues regarding the relationship between America's rich and poor in 1933, at the start of President Franklin D. Roosevelt's New Deal. The Suggested Discussion Questions explore the costs and benefits of aiding the poor at a time when government programs were helping millions of desperate, out of work Americans.

Other books advocate using movies as teaching tools, but many are aimed at more sophisticated classroom use than those offered in this volume. Books that are aimed at secondary teachers—including *The History Teacher's Movie Guide* by Richard Di Giacomo and Jerry Di Giacomo, and *Teaching History with Film* by Alan S. Marcus, *et al.*—offer helpful guidelines about how to use movies as classroom tools. But much of their focus is on historical movies that portray an event rather than on movies as primary sources from the times in which they were produced.

Movies as History emphasizes when the movie was made and its connection to the times. It does not critique movies from an aesthetic perspective, nor does it emphasize directing or acting techniques or focus on specific directors, actors, or actresses—except in a few instances. Although some of the movies discussed have won or received nominations for Academy Awards, artistic quality is not the book's primary concern. Its main purpose is to demonstrate how popular movies can be used as primary sources and to guide middle and secondary school teachers in the use of movies for classroom discussion. All of the movies analyzed in this volume are readily available on DVD or other formats. (See the Appendix for information on copyright guidelines and fair use.)

The idea for this book grew out of my own teaching experiences and my love of old movies. I would often see something in a movie that directly reflected historical events or attitudes from the period when the movie was made. For example, Americans' deep fears about the possibility of Communist subversion during the Cold War frame the 1956 science-fiction classic, *Invasion of the Body Snatchers*. World War II was an all-consuming international experience, and the section on the war covers life on the home front in America and also includes movies from France, Italy, England, and Japan. Understanding how people from other countries viewed an event of such magnitude can help students recognize and evaluate differing international views about contemporary issues.

I could never have completed this book without the support of colleagues, friends, and family. When I was young, my aunt, Claudia Kobilsek, made sure I never missed a movie musical, new or reissue, or an important Disney event. Ken Stuart, a truly gifted teacher at the Indiana Academy for Science, Mathematics, and Humanities, set a high standard for teaching excellence and innovation. For more than 40 years, good friends and fellow teachers Ken and Trudy Feltges have shared their love of teaching and movies. My daughter, Valerie, son, Stephen, and his wife, Meredith, were willing to try an endless list of old movies, and their inspired suggestions introduced me to some great new titles. My husband, Dick, established the model and cheerfully encouraged and celebrated this ever-expanding project. He alerted me to movies that might work and endured some real lemons as I searched for more.

What surprised me as I went along was how much more historical evidence I discovered in old movie favorites I thought I knew well. When viewed from an historical perspective, these familiar (and sometimes not so familiar) movies become important, nontraditional sources that offer new ways of looking at the past. Placed in their proper historical context, they can expand students' understanding of the complex forces that shaped the history of the 20th century. They offer fascinating glimpses of the values, beliefs, and actions of their audiences during America's first one hundred years "at the movies."

Introduction

A Brief History of the American Movie Industry

Movies have captivated audiences for more than a century. The term itself is shorthand for "pictures that move," and the public was enthralled when inventors created the early technologies that used still photographs to show motion. At first, the novelty was so great that people would pay money just to see action. They did not expect a story.[1]

Once the novelty wore off, audiences became more demanding, and moviemakers added storylines and made technological improvements in order to keep selling tickets. By the early 1900s, movies began to feature dramatic narrative plots that focused on heroes and villains and women in distress. Companies devoted to movie production also emerged and soon migrated to California, partly to take advantage of the climate and scenery and partly to avoid conflict with Thomas Edison's own production company, which had an exclusive agreement with Kodak for motion picture film stock.[2] Directors, often with training in the theater, became important influences as they developed techniques that took advantage of the opportunities offered by the new medium. At first, "players" were not identified by name, but by 1910 producers had launched the "star system," which meant that a popular actor or actress playing in a movie was often as big a draw as the movie itself, occasionally even bigger.[3]

By the end of the first decade of the twentieth century, all the basic elements of the modern motion picture industry were in place: a central site that served as a market for talent, ideas, and deal making; companies that would finance and guide production; an emphasis on technological innovation; and stars and stories that would attract the ticket-buying public. Thousands of movies of varying quality were made over the next century. Many would be badly scripted, poorly acted, and filmed without any discernible style.

Others, however, are significant for their artistry and for the affect they have had on audiences over the years. These movies can often be identified by their ticket sales and the awards or accolades they have earned. But their value extends beyond these measures. Movies represent the times in which they are made, and they often reflect—and may even help shape—audience attitudes, interests, and concerns. Therefore, they are also valuable as historical sources. Movies can reveal important information about continuity and change. Themes emerge and evolve, plot elements shift from one construct to another, and serious social issues, such as the anxieties that resulted from the Cold War or attitudes toward gender relations, are addressed and thrashed out in movies just as they are in real life.

In 1903, Edwin S. Porter sent a cast of cowboys and crooks on a chase through the New Jersey countryside in his seminal nine-minute Western, *The Great Train Robbery*. Much has changed in America and the rest of the world since then. A careful study of movie content, including plot, theme, and characters, can uncover changes in attitudes and behaviors that offer insights into historical trends and developments. For example, the good guys in Porter's movie were easily identifiable. By 1956, the distinction between good and bad was not nearly so clear in John Ford's *The Searchers*. The female characters in *The Great Train Robbery* were distraught and nearly helpless (the little girl in the red cloak) or there for a good time (the dancehall women). These images have little in common with the riveting, almost primal conflict that drove characters played by Joan Crawford and Mercedes McCambridge in *Johnny Guitar* (1954) or with Kim Darby's portrayal of the resourceful, relentless daughter determined to avenge her father's death in *True Grit* (1969).

In addition to demonstrating social change, movies often shine a light on issues that offer insights into people's thoughts and actions at various points in history. The Civil Rights struggles of the 1960s created enormous social tensions. Old movie stereotypes of African Americans did not immediately disappear, but during that era new roles emerged that served to counter earlier cowardly, criminal, or subordinate characterizations. In *Sergeant Rutledge* (1960), Woody Strode plays a powerful, dignified soldier on trial for the rape and murder of a young white woman, a crime for which many black men, especially in the South, were tried and briskly convicted by all-white juries. Rather than a rush to judgment, Rutledge's trial proceeds with judicial fairness to an unexpected conclusion. The theme of racial and ethnic understanding received added support the following year from *West Side Story* (1961), which focuses on Puerto Rican immigrants but reinforces the same message of tolerance. Sidney Poitier played strong, forceful characters in a string of major films from the late fifties into the sixties, including *Blackboard Jungle* (1955), *The Defiant Ones* (1958), *A Raisin in the Sun* (1961), *The Bedford Incident* (1965), and *Duel at Diablo* (1966). In 1964 he became the first African American to win an Academy Award in the Best Actor category for his performance in *Lilies of the Field* (1963). In 1967, Poitier took on the role of Virgil Tibbs, a polished, urbane homicide detective from Philadelphia, who finds himself stuck in a small Southern town in *In the Heat of the Night*. The movie was a blunt attack on Southern racism, and it won the Academy Award for Best Picture. Roles like these by Poitier and others reflected (and perhaps guided) changing public perceptions of racial issues.

Movies reflect social change partly because the most successful movie writers, directors, and producers are usually those who can relate to the attitudes and concerns of the movie audience. Some cultural critics argue that objects of consumer consumption, including movies, are created by producers and marketers who have little regard for the needs or desires of the public. This theory makes the producer the dominant force in the exchange and argues that audiences have little choice over where and on what to spend their money. However, other cultural criticism supports a more balanced relationship between producer and purchaser, and there is substantial evidence to support this interpretation.[4] Had producers simply been able to direct the market, widely publicized and thoroughly rejected products such as the Ford Edsel, the Sack Dress, and New Coke would have succeeded. The long list of movies with strong advance publicity and all the right elements in place (director, script, and stars) that have failed at the box office also supports the notion that consumer enthusiasm cannot be guaranteed by following reliable formulas or by well-financed advertising campaigns.

The historical and entertainment value of movies, therefore, make them an important primary source. Great movies demonstrate how audiences viewed issues decades ago and what kinds of stories received the support of the ticket-buying public. They allow us to explore common attitudes from then and now, discover what myths persist and what myths change over time, and observe how certain issues rise to the fore and then fade or are transformed as a result of social, cultural, or political change. Using stories, images, and themes from the movies of the 1930s through the 1960s to study history and social issues can help students broaden their understanding of events and attitudes and can lead them to a greater appreciation of the connection between popular culture and history.

This book surveys historical eras and issues, considers various movies, compares and contrasts their content, and places them within an historical context. It explores issues of race, ethnicity, and gender and suggests ways to use movies to enhance discussions in history and social studies classrooms. The General Movie Analysis Guide and Suggested Discussion Questions will help students analyze individual movies.

Understanding how to analyze movies from an historical perspective will enable students to think more critically, not only about movies, but also about social media and other forms of contemporary mass media. As an added bonus, once students understand how to analyze movies historically, they will be more likely to watch one of the many excellent movies that predate the latest multiplex release, despite the fact that the newer models often come complete with product tie-ins, game options, and computer-generated graphics. Once they become familiar with some of the wonderful movies made in the early to middle decades of the 20th century, at the very least, it may be possible to begin watching an old movie without hearing someone ask, stunned and dismayed, "It's in black and white?"

Terminology and Structure

In order to evaluate movie content it is important to have a common understanding of terms for discussion. The general arc of a movie plot contains the same elements as that of the short story or novel. Most movie plots involve a *conflict* between two or more people or groups. The *protagonist* is the character audiences most often identify with and who will, they hope, achieve a positive resolution to the conflict. The *antagonist* is the character who, for some reason, is not destined to succeed. Audiences may feel some pity for this character, but they support the protagonist. Depending on the scope of the movie, there may be secondary characters and conflicts, but they generally reinforce the main conflict and its resolution. As the plot progresses the conflict intensifies until the *climax*, the point where the conflict is at its most intense and some decisive action occurs. The *resolution*, usually brief, wraps up any loose ends. This structure is the basic outline for the vast majority of commercial movies.

Many plots share common elements. Plots have common traits because they must attract audience interest, and audiences may find it difficult to support a plot in which destruction reigns, evil triumphs over good, or the villain does get the lovely young girl. When these events do occur in movies, there is usually some punishment rendered the evildoer in order to balance this outcome. Plots that do not reward the good are sometimes designed as satire or irony or as a warning of the dangers inherent in some behavior or attitude. For example, *Romeo and Juliet* and *West Side Story* end tragically and deliver a similar message of generational forgiveness. *On the Beach* from 1959 and *Miracle Mile*, made 30 years later, illustrate the pointless death and destruction that are the inevitable result of atomic war.

In addition to audience expectations, there is another reason pre–1970 movie plots conformed to generally accepted patterns of behavior. In the first three decades of the twentieth century, there were few restrictions on what could be shown on screen or who would be admitted to theaters. As a result, movies grew more explicit, and socially unacceptable behavior was sometimes rewarded. By the late 1920s, Hollywood was forced to reconsider this type of movie content because of public pressure, especially from religious groups who objected to behavior they found offensive. As public condemnation increased, the industry decided to police itself in order to avoid the imposition of government controls. In 1930, Hollywood established a *Production Code*, sometimes referred to as the *Hays Code* after Will H. Hays, the man who designed it. The code circumscribed movie content and required that "no picture should lower the moral standards of those who see it."[5] Scripts were submitted for review and sometimes altered in order to receive code approval. However, the code was not strictly enforced until 1934 when Joseph I. Breen became director of Code Administration. It remained in effect until the late 1960s. Among the forces that undermined it were competition from television, competition from foreign movies to which the code did not apply (and which were often much more sexually explicit than American movies), and social and cultural changes within the United States.

Movies that share common themes or plots are frequently classified by *genre*. There are many different genres and sub-genres. Some familiar examples are crime dramas, romantic comedies, musical romantic comedies, Westerns, horror movies, *film noir*, Biblical epics, and science fiction. Genres follow the same general formula and share similar plots, themes, and conventions. A Western, for instance, is usually set somewhere west of the Mississippi River. The location is important because the frontier is an area of contention. The main conflict in many Western movies often involves a confrontation between new arrivals and older inhabitants. A person or group—ranchers, Native Americans, criminals—may already be there, but their claim to the area will be challenged. This confrontation may happen outside the jurisdiction of a legal authority or, in some cases, the legal authority will be corrupt. In the absence of a legitimate authority, the protagonist, often with one or more trusty associates, must make decisions or take actions that would not be necessary or even acceptable in an established, civilized territory. Characters struggle to come up with a reasonable and just response to conflict in movies like *Stagecoach* (1939), *Shane* (1953), and *Ride the High Country* (1962) because there is no enforced law to guide them.[6] Women feature prominently in many Westerns, and they often play strong, influential characters. But for the first half of the twentieth century, the real fighting in Western movies was left to men.[7]

Film noir requires a brief explanation. This genre developed in the late 1940s. It features plots that usually center on some criminal act and depict people and behaviors that are morally ambiguous. These movies make use of darkened or shadowy shots taken at odd angles that can leave viewers as confused as the main character, who often exhibits an attitude of helplessness in the face of unknown or powerfully corrupt forces.[8] Success for any character comes at a cost and is not a clear triumph of good over evil. As a result, audiences often come away with a conflicted sense of resolution at the movie's end.

Movie content can also be categorized by *theme*. Some common themes are love lost and regained, crime solved or criminals apprehended, and the dangers of technology run amuck, technology that is sometimes brought back under control—and sometimes not. Mickey Mouse's near catastrophe with the brooms in *Fantasia* (1940) is a forceful demonstration of the problems that can occur when a character unleashes technology (in this case, cartoon magic) without a healthy respect for the knowledge and humility necessary to control it. *Dr. Strangelove or: How I Learned to Stop Worrying and Love the Bomb* (1964) and *The Bedford Incident* (1965) explore this same theme but are set in the real world of the Cold War era.

Common plot elements reflect *cultural myths*. Myths are usually associated with stories of gods and goddesses from the mythologies of the ancient world. But the term has a much broader meaning. A myth is a reflection of the core beliefs and assumptions shared by a group. For example, one important core American assumption is the superiority of the common man or woman. Other beliefs and assumptions shared by Americans include the value of the individual, the expectation that virtue will be rewarded, the belief that the vulnerable should be protected by the strong, and the right of everyone to pursue a dream, no matter how improbable. These myths play out again and again in movies. As a result, even though plots may sometimes portray scenarios that run counter to the myths described above, they do not *celebrate* the triumph of wealth or power at the expense of the poor or the weak (*The Petrified Forest, The Little Foxes, Five Graves to Cairo*), the defeat of the reasonable individual by the group (*Mr. Smith Goes to Washington, To Kill a Mockingbird, 12 Angry Men*), or the hardworking common folk bested by the upper class (*Stagecoach, The Grapes of Wrath, The Apartment*). And if the girl is truly beautiful and virtuous, she would rather die—or its equivalent for most of the 1900s, remain unmarried—than submit to evil, to the unworthy, or, as is sometimes the case, to the wealthy but dull (*It Happened One Night, His Girl Friday, The Philadelphia Story, An Affair to Remember, Picnic*).

The structure of these shared beliefs generates specific character types. If common folk are to triumph over the elites they should be virtuous in some way. The virtue that enables the protagonist to succeed may be obvious greatness, stubborn determination, cleverness, or just a pure heart (see Dorothy in *The Wizard of Oz*, Father Flanagan in *Boys Town*, Longfellow Deeds in *Mr. Deeds Goes to Town*, or Maria in *The Sound of Music*). Intelligence and scientific knowledge are important personal virtues, but only very rarely will formal education have greater value than street smarts. Entire movie franchises are built upon this premise, including those featuring Nick and Nora Charles (*The Thin Man*), Mike Hammer, James Bond, and Dirty Harry.

The powerful may be powerful for a legitimate reason, and power itself is not a flaw, as the FDR biography, *Sunrise at Campobello* (1960), demonstrates. The powerful must have some fault, such as arrogance or greed, that will justify their defeat. Orson Welles's much-celebrated 1941 movie, *Citizen Kane*, offers a masterful illustration of this construct. Another popular flaw is a character's lack of appreciation for the resources that he or she has in abundance. The resources can be personal (appearance or physical strength), social or political (family status, an organization's support), or financial (unearned wealth or sudden good fortune). When people take these resources for granted or abuse the power they confer, they demonstrate their unworthiness, and the structure of their flaws will often explain how they will be defeated.

If the individual is to succeed against the group, he or she should be a strong character, willing to go it alone if necessary. This character type has always found an especially welcoming place in Westerns. And the heroine, whether rescued from evil or from boredom or from an uninspiring suitor, must be worthy of the hero's devotion and effort. Beauty, by itself, is not enough. Heroes are sometimes led astray by undeserving beauty, but, in the end, they return, wiser and repentant, to the girl who is smart, devoted, loyal, and sometimes living right next door.

The broad requirements for characters featured in movies often result in *archetypes*, characters that represent the attributes described above in such pure form that they literally define the type. Men do not get much more "common" than Gary Cooper's portrayal of the poor, unsophisticated Appalachian farmer in *Sergeant York* (1941), a story made all the more compelling because it is based on the life of reformed drunkard and born-again Christian Alvin York. Using the skills he learned hunting turkeys in the backwoods of Tennessee, York earned the Medal of Honor, the nation's highest military award, in World War I, and Cooper earned a Best Actor Academy Award for playing him. Jack Palance, the black-hatted gunslinger in *Shane* (1953), is so distant, evil, and menacing that he defined the Western bad guy in movies for a generation. Margaret Hamilton's scene-stealing performance in *The Wizard of Oz* (1939) came to personify the evil witch. And Debbie Reynolds's star turn as Kathy Selden, an earnest, slightly plain Jane with talent who steals Don Lockwood (Gene Kelly) right out from under the possessive, self-important, platinum blonde, and clearly untalented Lina Lamont (Jean Hagen) in *Singin' in the Rain* (1952) gave hope to every girl who wanted to make it in Hollywood on tap-dancing lessons alone.

Sometimes, the characters that audiences are likely to support do not fit so easily into a category, and the resolution to the conflict does not guarantee a positive outcome. In *Picnic* (1955), Madge (Kim Novak) is undecided about marrying the rich young man who wants her. She suspects that he values her only because she is the most beautiful girl in town. But her mother wants her to accept him so that Madge's future will be financially secure. The man Madge prefers is from a poor background. He has problems holding a job, and he is clearly lacking in virtue. He is also the more virile and dangerously attractive alternative. Even though William Holden's Hal may be the sentimental favorite, the audience can be forgiven for thinking that Madge will probably regret choosing him.

Each section in this book begins with an overview of movies related to the topic. The movies mentioned in the overview have been selected because they illustrate the historical evolution of the era or topic. Representative movies are analyzed, and questions that relate to movie content and historical issues follow the analyses. The movies selected for analysis were chosen primarily for their historical and cultural significance, production values, and potential to appeal to young audiences. A few of the movies in the section on World War II are foreign, with English subtitles. They are included because they represent international issues from the war years and offer a broader understanding of that era. Many of the selected movies won or were nominated for Academy Awards for Best Picture, and they should have wide appeal and interesting applications for teachers and students in the history classroom.

Note to Readers: At the conclusion of each movie analysis, a paragraph, occasionally two, describes either how the movie ends or sets up the ending. If you don't want to know how a movie ends, you can skip the last paragraph before the discussion questions. The Suggested Discussion Questions contain information about the end of the movie as well.

General Movie Analysis Guide

Title:
Director:
Year Released:
Lead Actors and Actresses:
Major Awards:
1. Describe the protagonists. Include any important characteristics.
2. Describe the antagonists. Include any important characteristics.
3. Describe the conflict.
   a. What themes does the conflict explore?
   b. Describe any significant secondary conflicts. Do these support the main conflict? If so, how?
4. Describe the setting, both geographic location and interior and exterior sets.
   a. Does the setting affect the conflict and if so, how?
   b. How do the location and sets support the movie's message?
5. How do the musical score and/or songs contribute to the overall effect of the movie?
6. Does the plot incorporate gender issues? How do they affect the outcome of the plot?
7. Do any of the movie characters represent specific ethnic or racial groups?
   a. How are they portrayed and how do they relate to the plot?
   b. How do they reflect attitudes from the time period in which the film was made?
8. Describe any other important elements that contribute to the movie's overall effect (i.e., elaborate special effects, use of real film footage, a plot based on an actual event or person).
9. How is the conflict resolved?
   a. Who wins and who loses?
   b. How do you feel about this resolution?
10. How does the plot's resolution reflect, or not reflect, American values?
11. Describe anything about the movie that you found particularly meaningful or significant and explain why you think it is important.

PART I
Hard Times and Hollywood Hope, 1931–1939

Overview

The "roar" of the Roaring Twenties was no mere descriptive metaphor. It emanated from the technological advances of the times—radio, moving pictures, automobiles, and airplanes foremost among them. Illegal liquor, liberated women, and easy money kept raising the volume.[1] Prohibition made lawbreakers out of many upstanding citizens and created empathy for others who disobeyed the law. Motor vehicle registrations grew from 468,000 in 1910 to 15 million by the mid-1920s, and the growing popularity of cars offered new opportunities for young people to spend time together without adult supervision, which pushed gender relations and the issue of birth control into the spotlight.[2] Meanwhile, Wall Street operated like a stock casino with little government oversight, and the resulting, much publicized financial gains lured many new investors into the market.

The decade's exuberance was not without justification. Modern inventions and new attitudes generated an excitement for new things, and the era's economic upturn created the expectation that they were attainable. The inventions themselves generated their own economic momentum. Pittsburgh station KDKA broadcast the first commercial radio programming in 1920.[3] By the middle of the decade, the medium had become so popular that one out of every three homes in the country had a radio.[4] One of the most exciting and widely celebrated events of the decade was Charles Lindbergh's 1927 solo flight across the Atlantic, an impressive technological feat for the time. Lindbergh, a lanky, modest young man, captured the world's imagination and instantly became an American hero.[5] (In 1957, the story of his flight was made into a movie, *The Spirit of St. Louis*. It starred James Stewart, a former Army Air Force colonel who flew 20 bombing missions in Europe during World War II and had a modest, straightforward approach to acting.[6]) Another significant innovation of the twenties was the coming of "talking" pictures. Audiences were amazed and thrilled in 1927 by *The Jazz Singer*, a "talkie," starring Broadway entertainer Al Jolson. The decade seemed to be one exhilarating up-ride on a roller coaster.

In September 1929, seven months into his presidency, President Herbert Hoover called a group of social scientists to the White House to discuss the country's future. America had experienced substantial economic growth in the previous decades, and he was confident that he and his fellow Americans were ready to define the future on their own terms.[7] A month later the stock market crashed. The stunning swiftness and severity of the financial collapse were difficult to comprehend. Its scope staggered the country. The Great Depression deepened steadily throughout Hoover's presidency. He had won the presidency, in part, based on his reputation as an expert administrator. The American people had been impressed by Hoover's handling of relief for starving Belgians during World War I. But Hoover could not or would not translate that experience into a comprehensive relief program for beleaguered Americans.[8]

Events in Europe and elsewhere exacerbated America's financial crisis. Long-standing empires in Germany, Austria-Hungary, Russia, and the Middle East had collapsed during or after World War I, and the resulting political chaos created openings for opportunists. The times proved especially receptive to those who were willing to build political movements on wounded national pride and the desire for revenge. Germany's first postwar government, the Weimar Republic, was undermined by the weight of a punishing peace settlement imposed upon Germany by the Treaty of Versailles. The treaty limited the size of the German military, redistributed German territory to other nations, demanded reparations, and included a "war guilt" clause. It led immediately to public fury and, ultimately, to economic collapse.[9] As the Weimar government struggled to cope with Germany's problems throughout the 1920s, many Germans were eager to find someone to blame for their humiliation and some way back to power within Germany and within the European community as well. By the early 1930s, Adolf Hitler was able to attract millions to his efforts to revitalize and remilitarize the country and create a "pure" German race.

Other nations struggled to regain political stability as well. A civil war roiled Russia in the early twenties as it emerged from tsarist rule and further postponed its recovery from the devastation of World War I. After the end of the Qing Dynasty in 1911, China unraveled politically, slowly at first and then more rapidly after President Sun Yat-sen's death in 1925. In the early 1930s the Japanese military attempted to expand the area it controlled in northern China, which further contributed to China's woes. China would spend the rest of the twentieth century putting itself back together again.

America's internal focus during the Great Depression left the country with little political energy to deal with developments overseas. The breadth and depth of the economic catastrophe were bewildering to Americans. Between 1929 and 1933 stocks lost three-quarters of their value, another $7 billion in investments evaporated with the failure of 5,000 banks. The gross national product fell by half, and 600,000 people lost their homes. People hedged their bets on the future. Over the same period, the marriage rate fell by 22 percent, and births fell by 15 percent.[10] With unemployment running at 50 percent in Cleveland and 80 percent in Toledo, men who had once brought home pay checks were without work and had no realistic chance of finding any.[11] The Depression widened and deepened during Hoover's presidency, and the reality of these statistics altered the lives of millions of Americans. Families fell apart when members left to try to survive on their own. By 1932, there were 15 million unemployed out of a labor force of 45 million.[12]

Women suffered as well as men, whether through lost jobs, lost husbands, or lost futures. The 1920s began with the passage of the 19th Amendment giving women the right to vote. This success and the passage of child labor laws during the Progressive Era encouraged a new set of expectations for women. At the beginning of the century, the Gibson Girl offered an active, athletic, outgoing model for young women as they ventured out of the protected environment of the Victorian Era. By the twenties, that model had become outmoded and was replaced by the Flapper, an educated, possibly employed woman who wore her skirts shorter, drank illegally, used makeup, and sought amusements once barred to her on the basis of propriety.[13] The Depression changed this trajectory, and women and men had to negotiate new roles and responsibilities. As Sara M. Evans writes in *Born for Liberty*, the hardships facing male breadwinners meant that women would have to be "grownups, partners in the struggle for survival in a way the culture had not acknowledged for well over a century."[14]

There was a special cruelty in this fate. Even though it came after three years of grueling and tremendously costly efforts by British, French, and Russian armies, the American success in World War I had generated a sense of national triumph and confident expectations for the future. The high-flying economics and technological accomplishments of the 1920s seemed to validate these expectations. In no small part, the economic cataclysm caused by the Depression left Americans confused because they had accepted the progress and successes of the postwar decade as their due and believed themselves blameless in this new crisis.

Over time, economists, historians, and others would study the era and assess blame. But early on, the best summation of the country's pervasive sense of the Depression's unfairness comes through the lyrics of the unofficial anthem of the era, "Brother, Can You Spare a Dime?" The song was a number-one hit for both Bing Crosby and Rudy Vallee in late 1932, making it the most popular song in the country at the same time that Franklin D. Roosevelt was challenging Herbert Hoover for the presidency.[15] Vallee sings a surprisingly upbeat, almost jaunty version that seems to contradict the meaning of the lyrics. Crosby's interpretation is a much more melancholy vocal by a down-on-his-luck Everyman whose story encompasses much of the story of the 1920s. The singer describes how he worked hard and did what was expected of a good citizen. He clearly believes that he is deserving of some reward or at least some fairness from fate, and he cannot quite believe that he has been brought so low. He asks finally, plaintively, "Brother, can you spare a dime?"

The Depression was depressing. Movies offered an escape from the dreary reality, and they were a good deal for the money. By the end of the 1930s, a ten- or 15-cent ticket bought moviegoers cartoons, newsreels, short subjects, movie trailers, and a double feature.[16] Those feature-length pictures often delivered a story plus a sprinkling or more of real entertainment. In *Lady for a Day* (1933), the audience gets to watch glamorous Glenda Farrell shimmy and vamp her way through "I Want a Man" and May Robson's Apple Annie magically transform from a crude, sloppy, alcoholic street vendor into a regal beauty at the center of a New York City fairy tale. Busby Berkeley choreographed lavish dance numbers for dozens of chorus girls swathed in even more lavish costumes in *42nd Street* (1933) and four *Gold Diggers* movies (1933, 1935, 1937, and 1938). In *Roberta* (1935), Fred Astaire sings, Ginger Rogers sings, Fred and Ginger dance alone and together, and Irene Dunne sings "Smoke Gets in Your Eyes." There is a nightclub scene with elegantly dressed diners and a fashion show resplendent with gorgeous dresses and furs. There is even a sparkly tiara, worn by a member of Russian royalty. Astaire and Rogers co-starred in a series of movies throughout the thirties that were heavy on glamour, comedy, romantic complications, snappy dialogue, and even snappier song-and-dance numbers. Movie plots such as these were frothy and barely believable, but they were entertaining and affordable, and they offered moviegoers temporary escape from the era's economic troubles.

High on the list of popular themes during that decade was sudden, miraculous financial gain by sometimes foolish but always deserving ordinary people. Money or good fortune often fell from the skies for the most unlikely of reasons. A rich benefactor unexpectedly bestows wealth in *City Lights* (1931), *Gold Diggers of 1933* (1933), *Mr. Deeds Goes to Town* (1936), and *Little Lord Fauntleroy* (1936). Or the reason for unearned wealth may be much more mundane, as in *The Good Fairy* (1935) and *Dinner at Eight* (1933), wherein rich older men find themselves attracted to younger women. People work hard and are ultimately rewarded in *Dodsworth* (1936) and *Drums Along the Mohawk* (1939). But sometimes they just play the angles and move up the social ladder like Barbara Stanwyck does in *Baby Face* (1933).

Marrying someone with wealth was a standard plot device in many movies. Men marry or pursue wealthy women in *It Happened One Night* (1934), *The Richest Girl in the World* (1934), *Merrily We Live* (1938), and *There Goes My Heart* (1938). Women try that approach in *Double Harness* (1933), *Baby Face, Gold Diggers of 1933,* and *Gone With the Wind* (1939). In *Personal Property* (1937), both the guy and girl seek financial enrichment through marriage. These movies were all made after 1933 and support the message mandated by the Production Code—such pursuits can only bring happiness when based on true love.

Other movies focus on the joys of little or no money. *The Divorcee* (1930) clearly shows that money will not bring happiness and true love is worth sacrifice. The title character in *Tarzan the Ape Man* (1932) never has much, just a hut in a tree and a chimp for a sidekick. But Jane finds him very attractive, and he makes living off the land seem so effortless. Robert Montgomery plays a sophisticated city hoodlum who succumbs to the charms of Maureen O'Sullivan and the simple country life in *Hide-Out* (1934). Money is low on the list of priorities for Ann Harding's bohemian artist in *Biography of a Bachelor Girl* (1935) and for the Martin Vanderhof family in *You Can't Take It with You* (1938). A princess learns to appreciate the joys of caring for seven sloppy men in a forest dwelling filled with rustic furniture in *Snow White and the Seven Dwarfs* (1937). It was the first full-length animated movie and became a critical and box-office triumph for producer Walt Disney. Shirley Temple found success in a string of box-office hits in the 1930s by playing poor but cheerful children who are rewarded because they rarely complain about their meager circumstances.

Rapid-fire dialogue, absurd misunderstandings, and bizarre plots made screwball comedies another popular, upbeat, escapist movie genre of the thirties. Audiences were amused and often confused by the antics in *Nothing Sacred* (1937), *The Awful Truth* (1937), *Bringing Up Baby* (1938), and *Merrily We Live*. The Marx Brothers' brand of screwball zaniness was a genre unto itself. Groucho and his brothers appeared in some of the most successful comic hits of the decade, including *Animal Crackers* (1930), *A Night at the Opera* (1935), and *A Day at the Races* (1937). One of their less commercially successful movies, *Duck Soup* (1933), has gained a reputation in the years since its release as a pointed and very timely political satire.[17]

Not all Great Depression movies were escapist. Sometimes audiences sought reality at the picture show, perhaps as a way to put their own lives in perspective. Movies that feature the complications, anxieties, and outright pain of being poor and scraping to get by also did well at the box office. The background for Barbara Stanwyck's conniving corporate climber in *Baby Face* includes a very grim life with her father, a mean drunk who prostitutes his teenage daughter to lure customers to his bar. Fay Wray's character in the Depression-era blockbuster *King Kong* (1933) is near starvation when she is rescued by a director who offers her an acting job. Desperate for work, she accepts the job without really knowing what is involved and willfully ignores some obvious early warning signs. No matter what may be hiding behind that wall on Skull Island, she finally has a job. Sensational crime dramas such as *The Public Enemy* (1931), *Manhattan Melodrama* (1934), and *Angels with Dirty Faces* (1938) focused on the tough lives of men who often found themselves with no other options but crime. One of the darkest crime films from those years, *I Am a Fugitive from a Chain Gang* (1932), had the added attraction of being based on a true story.[18]

Even comedies tapped into the era's economic woes. In *Gold Diggers of 1933*, savvy, wise-cracking showgirls steal milk for breakfast and scramble to cobble together one decent outfit for a friend's job interview. During the depths of the Depression, the audacity of its bouncy opening number, "We're in the Money," must have surprised audiences. Supported by a chorus line in costumes made from gold coins, Ginger Rogers rehearses lyrics that mock the Depression. Reality soon intrudes when the police arrive to close down the rehearsal because the producer cannot pay his bills. The hero is finally persuaded to save the show by thinly veiled references to prostitution, an even harsher reality the showgirls may face if the show does not go on.

Young people shared the fears and burdens of poverty. Director William Wellman paints a threatening picture of the perils adolescents face when they try to strike out on their own in *Wild Boys of the Road* (1933). Unlike Shirley Temple, who had great luck finding softhearted help, Wellman's characters suffer serious consequences at the hands of inept, disreputable, or mean-spirited adults as they tramp about in search of work and food. The movie is also interesting for its presentation, however limited, of integration among the teenage group. *Boys Town* (1938) focuses on the Nebraska home for abandoned boys established by Father Edward J. Flanagan in the early 1900s. Spencer Tracy played the role of Father Flanagan, and Mickey Rooney starred as a tough teenager who refuses to renounce his gangster brother and accept the assistance and security Boys Town offers until a crisis gets his attention.

The election of Franklin D. Roosevelt in 1932 showed that, hungry for hope, the American people were willing to put their faith in an exuberant optimist who practiced politics with enthusiasm and promised a better, brighter future in the middle of America's darkest days. During his first one hundred days in office, FDR sent a torrent of legislation to Congress to address various elements of the Depression. Some of it worked and some of it did not, but he kept at it. His leadership energized the country, and his New Deal programs slowly began to turn things around.

As if to emphasize that the going would not be easy, Roosevelt assumed the presidency just in time to deal with the Dust Bowl, a devastating environmental disaster. John Steinbeck's novel *The Grapes of Wrath* tells the story of this economic and agricultural catastrophe through the lives of the Joad family of Oklahoma and the cruel fate they meet with fear, determination, and humble dignity. The difficulties that the Joads face and the familial devotion they exhibit paralleled the complicated circumstances facing millions of Americans during that decade. The book won a Pulitzer Prize, and the movie based on the book is considered an American classic. It picked up two Academy Awards. John Ford won as Best Director, and Jane Darwell took home Best Supporting Actress for her portrayal of Ma Joad as the archetype of unyielding motherhood.

As the 1930s dragged on, the Depression lingered in America while war clouds gathered in Europe and Asia. Through aggressive military action or political manipulation, Germany and Japan had amassed ever broader territorial gains at the expense of their neighbors. Germany introduced conscription in 1935 and increased the size of its army to 500,000, five times greater than allowed by the Treaty of Versailles.[19] When the world community offered no forceful opposition, the Germans proceeded to establish an *Anschluss* (union) with Austria and begin the dismemberment of Czechoslovakia.[20] Japan was also on the march. As it moved to expand its control of China, Japan attacked the city of Nanking (Nanjing) with horrifying brutality in December 1937. Americans and Europeans living there captured evidence of the attack against a largely civilian population on film. John Magee, an American missionary, smuggled the film out of the country in 1938 and went on an extensive speaking tour in the United States to report on what became known as the Rape of Nanking.[21] For any Americans who were paying attention, these were ominous signs of the future.

In 1939, amidst growing international tensions and one year before the end of FDR's second and presumed last term in office, Hollywood produced a flood of outstanding movies. The uncertain times seemed to inspire imaginative greatness from the movie industry in classics such as *Gone With the Wind, Gunga Din, Mr. Smith Goes to Washington, Ninotchka, Stagecoach, The Wizard of Oz, The Women, Wuthering Heights,* and *Young Mr. Lincoln*. In 1988, Congress established a National Film Registry in an effort to preserve films and prevent changes to them that would affect their historical as well as artistic value. Some 25 "culturally, historically, or esthetically significant" films were to be selected annually for inclusion in the registry.[22] All of the movies listed above are in the registry, making 1939 one of the most well-represented years in the list.[23] *Gone With the Wind* was the year's biggest success. Based on the wildly popular Civil War novel by Margaret Mitchell, it won ten Academy Awards. The award for Best Supporting Actress went to Hattie McDaniel for her portrayal of Mammy and marked the first acting Oscar for an Africa American, an accomplishment that would not be repeated until Sidney Poitier's Best Actor Award twenty-four years later. The movie remained the all-time box-office leader until *The Sound of Music* in 1965.[24]

Many of the movies listed above feature optimistic characters who fight against overwhelming odds, odds that are an integral part of some established system, whether it be the politics of Washington, D.C., or the Soviet Union; power dynamics in the Land of Oz or in the post–Civil War South; or the legal system of the American West. In each case, women either strongly support those efforts or, in *Gone With the Wind, Ninotchka, The Women,* and *The Wizard of Oz,* are the major forces in the plot. The frivolous, helpless women of so many earlier movies had finally become "grownups" on screen as they had in the real world of the Great Depression. The powerful movies produced at the end of the 1930s reflect the changing mood of the nation and increasing optimism that the country's greatest economic crisis was coming to an end.

Representative Movies

***The Public Enemy* (1931)**

(84 minutes) *Director:* William A. Wellman; *Stars:* James Cagney, Jean Harlow, Edward Woods, Joan Blondell, Leslie Fenton, Robert Emmett O'Connor, Murray Kinnell, Mae Clarke.

Prohibition sets the stage for William Wellman's 1931 classic, *The Public Enemy*. But the movie's full meaning cannot be understood without appreciating its connection to the deeper changes that were straining the American social fabric during the early 1900s. The rise of urban areas and the spread of industrialization created a variety of stresses and tensions in American society.

By the late 1800s workers were demanding better working conditions and wages. Their efforts, and the work of muckraking journalists during the Progressive Era of the early 1900s, resulted in legislative reforms, including child labor laws inspired in part by the photographs of Lewis W. Hine. As child labor decreased, education spread more broadly through the population with an especially dramatic rise at the secondary level. High school enrollments went from 200,000 in 1890 to 2.2 million in 1920, an increase of 1000 percent over a 30-year period.[25] Young men who once might have been able to get work only as laborers became high school graduates and had better opportunities and pay available to them. As radios, telephones, moving pictures, and cars became more common, the changes they generated in travel and communication increased the pressure to be able to afford them. When these same young men found themselves out of work during the Depression, they faced the temptation to acquire these items illegally, and the criminal organizations that emerged in the 1920s in response to Prohibition provided established avenues for professional advancement to anyone willing to accept the risk.

Women were also affected by these broad social changes. Mothers who did their courting in the parlor or at church socials in the late 1800s watched their more educated daughters enter the workforce, earn money to support their own interests, and meet men independent of parental control.[26] This independence undermined the prevailing "cult of domesticity" that glorified the home as an expression of a woman's "maternal gifts."[27] New attitudes encouraged women to expand their social lives and expect greater things for themselves, things that, in time-honored fashion, many women still expected men to provide. The passage of the 19th Amendment granted women the right to vote, and was one more affront to traditionalists. These changes created tensions within families as well as within communities as young people pursued lives that were markedly different from those of their parents' generation.

The ethnic profile of the American population also underwent tremendous change during this period. Immigrants from southern and eastern Europe began arriving in ever-greater numbers from the end of the nineteenth through the first two decades of the twentieth century. Many Americans of northern European ancestry believed that these new immigrants were the cause of various social problems that arose as industrialization expanded and urban areas became more crowded.[28] Religion was a major component of the tensions generated by these newcomers. Italians were predominantly Roman Catholic, and their obedience to the Pope seemed to threaten the American concept of self-rule. Their numbers added to the Irish, an earlier wave of Catholic immigrants, many of whom had left home because of the Potato Famine in the 1840s. Many Polish and Russian immigrants were Jewish. Most of these immigrants settled in large northeastern urban areas, and the consumption of alcohol was traditional among them. The image of the city as a center for un-American immigrant influence—social, political, religious, and alcoholic—took hold. It was a major factor in the rebirth of the Ku Klux Klan, which enjoyed vastly expanded support in the early 1920s, primarily in rural America, because of its reputation as a defender of traditional Protestant American values. It also led directly to the quotas enacted in the Immigration Act of 1924.

Change is not easy. It requires that people rethink the way they function at home, at work, in relationships, and as citizens. However, there was no going back to some of the old ways. Cars, moving pictures, telephones, and immigrants were here to stay. Women would not give up the vote, and because they had it, men could no longer vote it away from them. Broad access to education was a benefit to the nation's youth even as it profoundly altered their expectations. But something could be done about alcohol, and many Americans fastened on that as a way to halt or slow the changes that seemed to overwhelm them.

Alcohol abuse was a serious social problem, and women's groups in particular had tried for many years to get laws passed to control it.[29] They only achieved success, however, when the rest of the country had a good reason to join them in the effort. By 1919, this "good reason" came with the arrival of large numbers of non–Protestant, non-northern European ethnic groups with relaxed attitudes toward the consumption of alcohol. But whatever its inspiration, the results of the passage of the 18th Amendment (also known as the Volstead Act, named for Republican congressman Andrew John Volstead) in 1919 were clearly not what its supporters had intended. Widespread disregard for Prohibition made enforcement difficult, which made the law that much easier to disregard. Criminal gangs took control of the illegal distribution of alcohol, and some of them grew rich and famous as a result.

The Public Enemy reflects attitudes toward prohibition as well as many of the deeper social and cultural changes then facing the United States. The movie begins in 1904 with scenes of beer being poured into buckets for sale, a drunk stumbling across a street, and two young boys sneaking a drink. The plot follows the boys as they grow into a life of crime that becomes increasingly organized, lucrative, and violent. The early scenes establish the characters. Tom Powers is the born leader and chief troublemaker, and Matt Doyle is his devoted sidekick. Tom's older brother, Mike (Donald Cook), takes life much more seriously and lectures Tom for stealing. Tom's father observes this scene and leads Tom into the bedroom for a whipping. The audience gains greater insight into Tom's character when he reaches for his belt buckle and asks his father with a sneer, "How do you want 'em this time, up or down?"

The boys contact a local club house leader, Putty Nose (Murray Kinnell), and ask him to fence some watches they have stolen. As they negotiate the sale, it becomes clear that even though he claims he is protecting their interests, Putty is really trying to cut them a bad deal. But he does promise to set them up with something big someday. When that someday comes, Tom (James Cagney) and Matt (Edward Woods) are teenagers and old enough to be skeptical of the risks involved in the warehouse robbery Putty proposes. He lures them into it with a gift of guns. Tom and Matt are used and abandoned when the plan falls apart.

A few years later Tom and Matt team up with Paddy Ryan (Robert Emmett O'Connor), a local Irish bar owner who seems to have a better set of criminal ethics. Prohibition determines their career course. They distribute beer illegally for Paddy and become wealthy as a result. When the owner of a large brewery asks Paddy to take on his wares, Paddy invites a bigger operator, "Nails" Nathan (Leslie Fenton), into the deal. Nails has a wider criminal franchise that will allow Paddy to expand his business. Tom and Matt become enforcers for Nails as he tries to undercut the Burns gang, his main competition. In the world of organized illegal opposition to Prohibition, Paddy and the boys have hit the big time.

Edward Wood was originally assigned the role of Tom and James Cagney was going to play Matt, but Cagney's performance was so dominant in the early stages of production that the roles were reversed.[30] Cagney brought a malicious, wounded ferocity to his portrayal of Tom, and audiences were both repelled by and attracted to his character. Tom's brother, Mike, is his antithesis, and Tom frequently makes fun of him. At one point Tom says Mike is in school, "learning to be poor." The movie uses a number of techniques to help the audience track the boys' success. Their clothes and vehicles go from scrubby to work-related to flashy. They visit more expensive night clubs. They have little trouble finding women. Matt's relationship with Mamie (Joan Blondell) seems somewhat genuine, but when Tom's girl, Kitty (Mae Clarke), pouts over breakfast about Tom's lack of interest, he smashes a grapefruit in her face. He soon moves on to Gwen Allen (Jean Harlow). Harlow plays the glamour girl in the movie, complete with platinum hair, luxury furs, formfitting satins, and sophisticated charm.

Ethnic stereotypes are central to the depiction of the characters. Tom, Matt, and Paddy are Irish, and the audience would recognize "Nails" Nathan as Jewish. By focusing on these ethnic groups, the movie suggests that immigrants, not real Americans, are the cause of the trouble. The Immigration Act of 1924 reflects this representation. Prohibition, however, is the central force in the plot and the inspiration for the increasing criminality of the era. In his run for president a year after the movie was made, Franklin Delano Roosevelt announced his intention to end Prohibition, a promise he kept in 1933.

Tom becomes ever more violent as the story progresses. Matt seems to be less sure of their course, but he remains Tom's true friend. Paddy provides them with illegal but steady employment. When personal animosity and warfare over territory break out between Paddy, Tom, Matt, and the Burns gang, the violence they live by spirals out of their control.

Suggested Discussion Questions

1. Analyze Tom's early misbehaviors. Do they give any indication that he will become a violent gangster or do they fall into the normal range for adolescent mischief?

2. Analyze the scenes in the movie that occur the night Prohibition begins. Who is involved? How do they behave? What does their behavior suggest about future enforcement of the law?

3. Explain Tom's relationships with Mike, Putty Nose, Paddy Ryan, and "Nails" Nathan. Which of these men does he admire, and why? Explain Tom's use of the term "ding, ding."

4. How and why does the robbery at the fur warehouse fail? How does Putty respond?

5. How is Putty able to convince Tom and Matt to participate in the fur heist? How does "Nails" Nathan figure in the murder of Putty? What do these two incidents suggest about Tom's character? Why is this type of manipulation effective?

6. The boys' first bootleg delivery was very sneaky, involving men climbing in a window and siphoning alcohol into a truck marked "gasoline." The Leehman Brewery is in a large, clearly labeled building that had been closed. What does it suggest about Prohibition that the brewery is being reopened? Why are Tom and Matt able to go into a bar and order a beer?

7. Compare Mamie, Kitty, Gwen, Jane, and Molly, Matt's sister. Do they have anything in common? Do they have anything in common with Ma? How are they representative of the Flapper era? How do they fit into the economic circumstances of the Depression?

8. Tom rubs a grapefruit in Kitty's face and slaps Jane hard. Analyze these acts in relation to Gwen's comment, "The men I know ... they're so nice, so polished, so considerate.... But you're so strong. You don't give, you take. Oh, Tommy, I could love you to death." How do you believe audiences of both genders would respond to her remark in 1931? How would they respond today?

9. The movie plays off ethnic and gender stereotypes. How would American audiences of different genders, regions of the country, and ethnic backgrounds react to these characters in 1931? How have issues related to the major immigrant groups of the early 1900s been resolved?

10. Does the country face any significant immigration issues today, and if so, how is it responding? Do past experiences with immigrant populations offer any guide as to the best way to deal with immigrant issues, and if so, what are they?

11. How effectively does the movie deliver its message that crime does not pay? Why is "Nails" Nathan's funeral so well attended?

12. Did Prohibition improve American society? Should President Roosevelt have ended it or left it in place?

I Am a Fugitive from a Chain Gang (1932)

(93 minutes) *Director:* Mervyn LeRoy; *Stars:* Paul Muni, Glenda Farrell, Helen Vinson, Allen Jenkins, Edward Ellis.

As the Great Depression dragged on, hopes for a recovery faded. Men and women suffered equally in the failing economy, but they experienced the effects of the Depression in different ways. Mervyn LeRoy's *I Am a Fugitive from a Chain Gang* vividly depicts the effects the hard economic times had on a generation of American men.

Despite the social and political advances in women's lives during the first two decades of the century, men were still the principal providers for their families. Men in their thirties and forties had come of age just as America had come of age on the international stage. Like the country as a whole, they had experienced rising expectations and had met them on the battlefield and in the workplace. As job losses mounted in the early years of the Depression, these same men were often unable to meet the expectations of family and society. As Hoover's first term in office came to a close, a view of the Depression as unfair to people who had worked hard and deserved better became a frame for the times.

Desperation sometimes drove people to commit crimes. Some criminal behavior was organized and on a large scale, but much of it was simply a convergence of need and opportunity. In addition, laws on vagrancy made criminals out of the many drifters who were forced out onto the road as a result of lost jobs and lost homes. (A scene in *Wild Boys of the Road* shows young people scrambling from boxcars before the train comes to a full stop so they can avoid the police who are waiting to grab any tramps found "riding the rails" when the train reaches the station.)

People often found themselves trapped in the criminal justice system. In some cases, law enforcement officials were corrupt.[31] In the South, some prisons rented out convicts as chain gangs, either for public projects or to private interests.[32] Progressives had raised public awareness of corruption involving prisoners earlier in the century, but Robert E. Burns's 1932 autobiography, *I Am a Fugitive from a Georgia Chain Gang*, propelled the issue back into the spotlight. Burns's book describes his World War I experiences and his later life of crime, imprisonment, and escape. It was quickly turned into a movie and released that same year.[33]

The movie features Sergeant James Allen (Paul Muni), a character based on Burns, as a World War I veteran Everyman. The war has changed him. It has given him confidence and ambition, and he has plans for better things when he returns home. But family pressures force him back into the "factory grind." When he finally does leave home to pursue his dreams, he begins a long slide into failure. He is smart, eager, and affable and does not appear to be responsible for his joblessness, a situation many in the audience could relate to in 1932. He unwittingly becomes involved in a five-dollar robbery in Georgia and is sent to prison.

The character's ties to World War I veterans are more than just an element from Burns's book or a plot device. The country had become convinced that something was broken at the national level. People were willing to work, and they needed food. But farmers could not make money on what they produced. In order to raise prices, some even went so far as to prevent their products from getting to consumers.[34] People needed other goods as well, but it was as if all the gears that made up the American economy had disengaged from one another, and there was no way to reconnect them and get things going again. The government had played a limited role in American life up to this point. Its role did expand in the Progressive Era. But, by and large, most Americans preferred that the government stay out of their way. The failed experiment with Prohibition reinforced this view. The immensity of the Great Depression, however, caused many people to look to the federal government for help because it was the only agency large enough to tackle the problem. Among those who believed they had an especially strong claim to federal help were World War I veterans.

When the war ended in 1918, the government gave veterans a bonus, payable partly in bonds that would mature later. In the summer of 1932, the severity of the Depression inspired eleven thousand veterans to descend on Washington, D.C., in order to pressure Congress to pay this bonus immediately. The protesters, labeled the Bonus Army, established a messy but orderly camp along the Anacostia River, but President Hoover wanted them removed. The United States Army complied vigorously, driving the marchers away and torching the tent city. Newsreel footage of the ouster of these veterans enraged audiences across the country.[35] The Depression may have been a cross many had to bear, but most Americans believed that this was no way to treat veterans. James Allen was not part of the Bonus Army, but he was one of the men whose efforts and enthusiasm had been rewarded by triumph in World War I and by the successes of the 1920s. Allen's suffering in the 1930s resonated with veterans and others who believed the government was unwilling to champion their cause or provide even basic human protections.

The scenes connected to Allen's prison experiences are startling in their brutality. Ankle chains, beatings, grueling hours of work, and inedible food are typical components of his prison life. The people who fail Allen most, however, are representatives of government agencies. He is lied to and abused by those whose job is to be impartial, just, and humane. The movie raises questions about personal and government responsibility. What do citizens owe the state and what does the state owe its citizens? Is life "poor, nasty, brutish, and short," as Thomas Hobbs declared, or could people expect—even demand—more from their lives and from the governments they elect? These issues were not just theoretical to millions of people, including veterans, in 1932. *I Am a Fugitive from a Chain Gang* offered audiences an object lesson to clarify the debate over the role of government in helping those in need.

Allen escapes from prison and manages to establish an honest, successful life for himself in Chicago under an assumed name until his landlady discovers his true identity and blackmails him. Eventually, he and the legal representatives of two states must confront his past and come to some sort of resolution. The heart of the movie revolves around what constitutes justice for Allen and whether he will be willing to pay the cost.

Suggested Discussion Questions

1. As he sentences Allen, the judge remarks, "I see no reason for leniency since the money was found on your person." Does this conclusion seem fair? Why, or why not? Compare the appearance of Berton Churchill, the actor who plays the judge, with a photograph of Herbert Hoover. Why use this actor for this role?

2. What kind of man is Allen? What kind of mistakes does he make? What does he get right? Why is he able to succeed in Chicago? How does he fit the image of a good citizen?

3. Like Allen, the Depression left many people in financial crisis. How should government at any level react to people in circumstances such as this? How would Americans in the 1930s be likely to respond to this question?

4. Describe the prison scenes. Why include the image of the mules? Explain the significance of the scene when Barney is released and the camera follows him as he walks out of prison.

5. Sebastian, an African-American prisoner, helps Allen escape. How does the movie present African-American characters? How do Sebastian's skills fit stereotypes about African Americans? Why does another character assert that Sebastian will never be released?

6. The police at the barbershop and train station do not realize who Allen is but do go after a vagrant they suspect is Allen. What do these scenes suggest about law enforcement, images of criminals, and Allen's cleverness? Explain "profiling" and discuss whether it is ethical for law enforcement to use it in the exercise of their duties.

7. Allen uses a fake name when he is hired in Chicago. Why is he able to get away with this? Would he be able to do so now?

8. Describe Marie and Helen. How do they fit into gender stereotypes of that era?

9. The governor of Illinois is still debating whether to extradite him when Allen agrees to return to face the charges against him. Why does the governor of Illinois have this power? Do states still have the power to deny extradition to other states? Why would refusing to extradite a wanted person to another state be a good or bad idea?

10. The prison board chairman refutes Allen's claims about the chain-gang system. He declares that "punishments must be hard" and "discipline must be strict," and claims that this system made Allen into the decent hardworking citizen he is now. The board decides that Allen must still serve hard time. Does the chairman's argument seem reasonable, and would people in the 1930s likely support it? Why do you support or oppose it?

11. The Depression raised questions of who deserves society's help, an issue that resonated at the national as well as the family level. Based on their behavior, who qualifies as Allen's "family," and why?

12. Is there anything the judicial system could have done differently that might have resulted in a better outcome for Allen and for society?

Lady for a Day (1933)

(96 minutes) *Director:* Frank Capra; *Stars:* Warren William, May Robson, Glenda Farrell, Ned Sparks, Nat Pendleton, Guy Kibbee, Jean Parker, Walter Connolly.

Frank Capra's *Lady for a Day* explores issues of poverty and gender during the early 1930s and offers a subtle comparison of the different approaches taken by Presidents Herbert Hoover and Franklin D. Roosevelt. The Great Depression soon overwhelmed the usual sources of charity and relief, but Hoover believed that individualism was the foundation of a democracy, and he attempted to let the system correct itself as much as possible. He used the federal government sparingly to improve conditions. The enormity of the crisis quickly outran the efforts of government at all levels to assist people in need just as it did all other sources of assistance.[36]

Roosevelt took a different approach. When he became president he inserted the government into the nation's problems in multiple ways. He declared a Bank Holiday and passed the Emergency Banking Act just a few days into his term to shore up the crumbling banking system. He submitted legislation to aid farmers, to regulate securities and business practices, to protect depositors, and to provide direct relief to those in need. Not all of these measures succeeded, and he had his share of critics. His response to failure and critics alike: "The country needs, and unless I mistake its temper, the country demands, bold, persistent experimentation."[37]

Roosevelt's actions brought the issue of government intervention to the public's attention. How far should the government of a free society go to aid people in need? Should it do anything at all? In a broader sense, what did Americans owe one another? People's views often depended on how financially secure they were. However, the Hoovervilles (campsites, often in urban areas, that were filled with the poor and unemployed) that sprang up across the country and the poverty that afflicted so many could not be ignored. Were the poor solely responsible for their circumstances? Or did the government with its vast resources owe something to those less fortunate?

Lady for a Day ruminates on these issues with all the effervescence of fine champagne served up in an old coffee mug. The story takes place in a part of New York City that seems to glow with modern nightclub razzmatazz and Old Dutch charm. Although it is set in the 1930s, much of the movie has a misty, fairytale quality that lends a touch of timelessness to the plot and ties it firmly to its Cinderella roots.

In the opening scene, Apple Annie (May Robson) wanders through a reasonably well-dressed sidewalk crowd, trying to peddle her wares. She has little luck, but she generously advises other neighborhood panhandlers and street musicians that there might be better pickings at another site. Later that evening she waits at the side door of the elegant Marbury Hotel to pay a friendly bellhop for the guest stationery he steals for her each week, and she catches up with a steady customer, Dave the Dude (Warren William), a wealthy gambler and gangster who believes her apples bring him luck. He admonishes her for not being around the previous week, and he does not believe her claims that she had been ill rather than drunk.

The first few scenes establish a familial camaraderie between Annie, her street friends, and her wealthy customers. They also establish an atmosphere of urban sophistication and energy. New York City was then and remains an international gateway for commerce and culture. The great port city started as a free-wheeling Dutch trading center, and its vibrant commercial character has endured. New York never succumbed to the self-righteous influences of its Puritan or Quaker neighbors, the earnest civic concerns of the nation's capital, the manufactured glamour of the West Coast, or the focused industry of Midwestern cities like Chicago or Detroit. The city never lost its enthusiasm for robust commerce, legitimate or otherwise, and the profits to be made from it either. Dave the Dude is just a fictional representation of the many creative entrepreneurs who have made it very big in the Big Apple.

The crisis occurs when Annie receives a letter from her daughter, Louise (Jean Parker), a daughter she has kept secret from everyone. Louise has grown up in a Spanish convent believing that her mother is Mrs. E. Worthington Manville, a wealthy socialite who lives in a fancy hotel. Annie maintains this fraud through the letters she sends Louise on the stolen stationery. Now a young woman, Louise writes that she and her fiancé will soon be arriving in New York City by ship. Also arriving is Louise's fiancé's wealthy father who wants to meet Mrs. Manville before he will approve of the marriage. It quickly becomes apparent that Annie's whole existence has been organized around providing for and protecting her daughter. When Annie believes that her carefully structured plan is about to unravel and ruin Louise's chances for happiness, she becomes frantic with grief. Her street friends immediately turn to Dave the Dude for help because he is the one person they know who has the resources to help Annie. Dave, who feels indebted to Annie for all the luck her apples have brought him, agrees to lend a hand. The rest of the movie follows the machinations of Dave and Annie's other friends as they scheme to keep Louise, her fiancé, and his father from discovering the truth.

The movie is based on the Damon Runyon short story, "Madame La Gimp."[38] Runyon wrote about Broadway and the colorful characters in and around that slice of the city in a style so idiosyncratic it was labeled "Runyonese." Many of his stories were turned into movie or stage productions.[39] Runyon viewed gangsters, gamblers, and crime through a soft-focus lens. His Depression-era gangsters are less threatening than they are calculating and grumpy. Their crimes reflect the simple needs of simple people who have somehow gotten crosswise with life, and who never seem to be able to figure out how to untangle themselves without first creating even greater entanglements. Their command of the English language combines antique phrasing with streetwise philosophy and produces observations such as gambling is fundamental, dames are always working an angle, love is a trap to be avoided, marriage is an even bigger trap, falling in love is inevitable, and marriage happens. *Lady for a Day* covers all these bases.

The fundamental decency of most of Runyon's characters plays out in this movie. Dave is solicitous of Annie even before her letter from Louise. He references a doctor that she has seen more than once at his insistence. Dave's girlfriend, nightclub owner Missouri Martin (Glenda Farrell), and one of his associates, Shakespeare (Nat Pendleton), are willing co-conspirators in Dave's plan to fabricate a believable life for Annie as a New York socialite. Even the "Judge" (Guy Kibbee), a pool hustler and con man with a sophisticated vocabulary who agrees to play Annie's husband, comes through with creativity and enthusiasm.

The brief glimpses of what Annie must have been like in her younger years would have resonated with audiences. Many people who once enjoyed grander ambitions and opportunities found themselves living in reduced circumstances as a result of the Depression. Annie puts a record of classical music on the turntable when she returns to her shabby room, and her neighbors, equally poor, listen to it appreciatively. As an apple peddler, Annie had crudely thumbed her nose at one of Dave's associates. But when she is cleaned up and dressed up, her manner becomes elegant and gracious and hints at a better upbringing than suggested by her earlier behavior. The entire premise of the story is based on Annie's concern for the well-being of her child, a concern shared by many parents at the time.

The fraud Dave creates for Annie grows bigger and more complex, and he must take bigger risks and bring in more conspirators to pull it off. The gangling, escalating enterprise comes to the attention of the city newspaper editors, the police chief, the mayor, and eventually even the governor. They become convinced that Dave is up to something, probably something criminal, and the more complicated his scheme becomes, the more they harass the next man down the line to arrest him. Despite the elaborate, earnest efforts of the diverse group who go to work on Annie's behalf, catastrophe looms. If Dave cannot salvage the plan, Annie will have to face her daughter and the truth about her past, no matter what the consequences.

Suggested Discussion Questions

1. Annie appears crude and pushy at first. But she is solicitous of some. Explain her behavior in terms of those she scorns and those she aids. Why is she not gracious to everyone?

2. Is Dave the Dude acting solely out of compassion? If he has any ulterior motives, do they undercut the merits of his efforts on Annie's behalf?

3. Describe examples of various characters who act in someone else's best interests. Why would they do this? How does their behavior fit in with the times in general and with the philosophy behind the New Deal? Apply the concept of family to Annie's acquaintances. Who qualifies as her "family," and why?

4. The New Deal required the government to expend greater resources than ever before in an effort to fix what was broken and aid those in need. Some voters did not support it, but Roosevelt was re-elected in 1936 by a landslide, losing only eight electoral votes. What would motivate people to accept such an enormous expansion of the role of government?

5. Opponents of big government often criticize it, using terms like "Big Brother" and "the Nanny state." Analyze the positive and negative implications of these terms. Choose some important political figures from today and describe how they would view the New Deal in 1933.

6. Almost every major character is playing some sort of con game. Is this unethical or is it simply how business gets done? Is fraud ever morally acceptable?

7. Do Apple Annie and Missouri Martin qualify as liberated women? Defend your answer.

8. Happy McGuire (Ned Sparks) offers a cynical counterpoint to Dave's philanthropic impulses. Why is he annoyed when Dave insists on helping Annie? Does he ever approve of Dave's generosity? What is the likelihood that Annie will need to be rescued like this again?

9. At one point Annie admits with embarrassment that she and Louise's father never married. The movie, therefore, is championing a woman who has sinned. Why would the Production Code permit this plot element? Is Annie a morally acceptable protagonist?

10. As the mayor, police chief, newspaper editors, and governor discuss the plan to help Annie, they apologize to one another for any offenses or criticism that may have gone on among them in their pursuit of Dave the Dude. What causes their anger in the first place, and why apologize now?

11. Choose one of the following phrases and explain why it best describes the movie's message: (a) Sin does pay; (b) Redemption is possible; (c) It is better to give than to receive. What choice do you believe a Depression-era audience would make, and why?

You Can't Take It with You (1938)

(127 minutes) *Director:* Frank Capra; *Stars:* Jean Arthur, Lionel Barrymore, James Stewart, Spring Byington, Ann Miller, Edward Arnold, Eddie Anderson, Donald Meek, Halliwell Hobbes, Dub Taylor, Samuel S. Hinds, Harry Davenport, Charles Lane.

The economic crisis of the 1930s rippled broadly through the American social landscape. It affected people's confidence and their expectations for the future. It was no longer possible to become a high-rolling high flyer in the style of the 1920s. That era was over. People needed some other model for their futures and for America's future. But if the goal of a life of extravagance and excess was no longer realistic, what would replace it? *You Can't Take It with You*, directed by Frank Capra, pits two different visions of personal responsibility and public behavior against each other. In its simplest terms, the movie asks whether we are here to help our neighbors or to fleece them.

President Franklin D. Roosevelt recognized the need to rethink values and reconfigure personal plans, and he offered Americans his vision for these changes in his first inaugural address. He used a Biblical metaphor to make his point, referencing "money changers" in the "temple of our civilization." He added:

We may now restore that temple to the ancient truths. Happiness lies not in the mere possession of money; it lies in the joy of achievement, in the thrill of creative effort. The joy and moral stimulation of work no longer must be forgotten in the mad chase of evanescent profits.[40]

The new president was trying to lessen the link between money and happiness, which had become so strong during the Roaring Twenties, and to strengthen the link between work, creativity, and joy. *You Can't Take It with You* offers a compelling illustration of Roosevelt's remarks. Based on a Pulitzer Prize-winning Broadway play from 1937, the movie showcased a marvelous performance by Lionel Barrymore as family patriarch and guiding spirit Martin Vanderhof. The film's powerful message and excellent production values helped it win the Academy Award for Best Picture, and for Frank Capra as Best Director.

Alice Sycamore (Jean Arthur) and Tony Kirby (James Stewart), son of businessman Anthony Kirby (Edward Arnold), have fallen in love. Tony's father is planning a business monopoly that requires control of a block of real estate, but one homeowner, Alice's grandfather Martin Vanderhof, will not sell. If Anthony Kirby cannot get Grandpa Vanderhof to sell, he cannot go forward with his plan, which will save the homes of all of Grandpa's neighbors as well. Grandpa Vanderhof appears at Kirby's offices at the start of the movie to discuss the sale, but he has no real interest in selling, and as he waits to see Kirby, he begins chatting with a meek, submissive office accountant, Mr. Poppins (Donald Meek).

Grandpa operates on intuition, and he senses that Poppins is not happy in his job. When he presses him about what he really likes to do, Poppins shows him a charming mechanical toy he has created. Grandpa invites Poppins to his home where "everybody ... does just what he wants to do." Poppins is alarmed by this lack of responsible behavior and fiscal seriousness, and he asks who takes care of them. Grandpa replies, "The same One that takes care of the lilies of the field, Mr. Poppins. Except that we toil a little and spin a little and have a barrel of fun." As Poppins picks up his toy and follows Grandpa out the door, he comments helplessly, "The die is cast. I'm a lily."

At the Vanderhof home Poppins meets a variety of loopy, friendly, cheerful people who are doing whatever they want and experiencing various levels of success. The household includes Vanderhof's daughter, Penny Sycamore (Spring Byington) and her husband; their two daughters, Alice and Essie (Ann Miller); Essie's husband, Ed Carmichael (Dub Taylor); and assorted other folk, some of whom come and go, others of whom came once and simply never left. Initially Poppins is taken aback by the group, but he soon blends in beautifully. Amidst all the earnest effort, ambition, and conviviality, Penny mentions that there is a letter for Grandpa from the Internal Revenue Service, but she cannot seem to remember where she put it.

The essential conflict in the movie is defined by the scene between

Grandpa and Mr. Poppins and the scene just before it in which Mr. Kirby demands that his agent get possession of the Vanderhof property. Tony Kirby's father personifies the callous businessman who seeks to crush all opposition in order to increase his profits. A subplot involves another businessman, Ramsey (H. B. Warner), over whom Kirby senior is determined to triumph. When Ramsey bitterly confronts him, their meeting reveals Kirby's moral bankruptcy. Grandpa also challenges Kirby's behavior, but he does so in a much gentler fashion. The one time that Grandpa takes Kirby to task, he immediately apologizes for his remarks.

The mislaid unpaid tax bill is another plot element, and it ultimately brings in agents of the federal government. However, they are not portrayed as brutal or abusive but rather as bureaucratic and functional, just doing their jobs. In this movie, unlike *I Was a Fugitive from a Chain Gang*, government agents are not unscrupulous and vengeful. The movie presents the demands of government as an unpleasant but necessary part of a functioning society that Grandpa Vanderhof will have to find some way to accommodate.

By 1938, the general perception of the Depression had shifted. It no longer appeared to be a freak economic disaster that a cruel, unfeeling government allowed to continue unchecked. After Roosevelt's election in 1932, the government had taken an active, expansive, and highly visible role in tackling the Depression, a role that received solid voter affirmation in Roosevelt's 1936 re-election landslide. (Roosevelt received 523 electoral votes; his opponent received 8.) But the results of an investigation by the Pecora Commission, which was set up by the Senate to investigate the role that banking had played in the economic collapse, showed that the actions of banks were clearly instrumental in precipitating the crash and worsening its effects. Banks and big business were handy scapegoats for the economic problems people faced by 1938, and the movie portrays them with scathing contempt.[41]

Tony and Alice's engagement, which Tony's mother strenuously opposes, prompts the Kirbys to visit the Vanderhofs for dinner. The confrontation between their families is a disaster. The IRS eventually catches up to Grandpa, and things seem destined to fall apart for the whole Vanderhof clan. As a result, Mr. Kirby is about to get title to the Vanderhof home. Things are looking grim for everyone, but especially for Alice and Tony.

Suggested Discussion Questions

1. The movie's opening shot is of a bustling city street with the caption, "Wall Street." How might an audience in 1938 respond to this image? What other elements of the first few scenes would affect their response? How would an audience of today respond?

2. Analyze these four plot devices: Mr. Kirby's need for bicarbonate of soda, Mr. Blakely's twitching eye, Mr. Ramsey's illness, and Mr. Vanderhof's broken foot. Why include them? How did they happen and what do they represent?

3. How are Reba and Daniel treated by the Vanderhofs? Does either one fit into any African American stereotypes? Describe other images of African Americans in the movie. Do they support or offer a counterpoint to typical African American stereotypes of that era?

4. What product will be produced by the conglomerate Mr. Kirby is putting together? How does the product reflect national and international concerns in 1938? Compare profit figures from 1938 and 1945 for General Electric, Dupont, Ford Motors, and McDonnell Douglas. Were Kirby's product plans unrealistic? Were they appropriate or ethical?

5. Privately owned companies are one of the cornerstones of capitalism. How does the movie portray capitalism in relation to the Kirbys and the Vanderhofs? Is the Vanderhof lifestyle essentially capitalist or Communist? Would you want to live there?

6. The movie has a strong religious component. Describe the Vanderhofs' (a) vision of God; (b) view of others; and (c) view of what people owe one another. Are these views compatible with traditional Christianity? Explain the style of Grandpa's blessings. Are they compatible with traditional Christianity?

7. How does the movie view the role of women in business and family life? Describe any instances in the movie where women or men act with intelligence and courage. Which gender comes out ahead?

8. Describe Tony Kirby's character. In what ways is he worthy or unworthy of Alice? How does he relate to Alice's parents and to his own? Compare his speech on his business plans with the Roosevelt quote about the "joy of creative effort."

9. In the movie's darkest scene, Ramsey excoriates Kirby for his greed. Most of the scene is shot from behind Ramsey and focuses on Kirby and his associates as they watch him. Why would the director choose to structure the shot this way?

10. How does Grandpa view the relationship between citizens and government? How does the government view Grandpa? Which political party would he probably belong to today, and why?

11. How does the movie view corporate culture? Give examples. Does the plot of the movie support, directly or indirectly, more government oversight of corporate behavior or does it accept the unimpeded application of market forces that will improve a corporation's profits as the best way to help the economy?

12. Research the Wagner Act (1935) and the securities provisions of the Glass-Steagall Act (1933). How does the movie's point of view match up with the actions of government toward business and labor during the Depression?

13. For whom does Grandpa reserve his deepest hatred? How does this reflect national and international concerns at the time? Explain any parallels between then and now related to this issue. Are there any people or groups who would make it onto Grandpa's list now?

Stagecoach (1939)

(96 minutes) *Director:* John Ford; *Stars:* Claire Trevor, John Wayne, Thomas Mitchell, John Carradine, George Bancroft, Andy Devine, Donald Meek, Berton Churchill, Louise Platt.

Stagecoach, John Ford's classic western from 1939, offered audiences an exciting saga of cowboys, Indians, good guys, bad guys, cavalry charges, and women in distress. It was also a masterful allegory of the Great Depression.

Even though the economy was no longer in a steep decline when the movie was released, the Depression dragged on and the economy continued in a state of flux. As a result of the financial crisis, the government had undergone a tremendous expansion throughout the 1930s in order to mitigate the hardships and sufferings of the American people. By the end of the decade it was difficult to know exactly what normal looked like. The glamorous, freewheeling twenties seemed distant and frivolous and did not offer an adequate blueprint for American success. After enduring such upheaval and loss, what could and what should people aspire to?

At the same time, international events also threatened to undermine American stability. Germany had grown from a disgruntled military failure to an aggressive continental power. Hitler's Third Reich controlled a large swath of central Europe by the late 1930s and threatened other nations with aggression. World War II would begin in September 1939 with the German invasion of Poland. Japan was flexing its muscles and grabbing more territory in north China. Many Americans opposed getting involved in these conflicts, and the Neutrality Acts of the late thirties were expressly designed to keep the United States out of another foreign war. But the fact that Congress felt the need to pass the acts was clear evidence of the growing fear some Americans had that the country would be dragged into these escalating international conflicts. The uncertain times affected the nation's economic situation as well. Despite the country's reluctance to become involved abroad, President Franklin D. Roosevelt secured funds from Congress to enhance America's defenses.

As the decade drew to a close, America's future seemed to hold both promise and threat. The expectation that Roosevelt's presidency was coming to an end added to the unsettled outlook. He had been a strong and trusted guide through terrible times as well as a powerful and tremendously effective communicator. His leadership and rhetoric, especially the famous line from his first inaugural address, "We have nothing to fear but fear itself," had framed the challenges the country faced at a very dark time and implied that Americans could succeed if they had the courage to do so. Roosevelt's actions spoke as loud as his words. His New Deal programs, political appointments, and Fireside Chats gave his remarks added power and inspired downtrodden Americans across the land.

Many of the great movies from 1939 offered similar inspiration. They showed audiences a way forward that acknowledged the flawed past and the complicated present but offered hope for the future. The storylines in movies like *Drums Along the Mohawk*, *Gone With the Wind*, *Mr. Smith Goes to Washington*, *The Wizard of Oz*, and *Young Mr. Lincoln* were both grand and personal. They all celebrate courage in the face of daunting obstacles. But the beleaguered group of travelers who crowded onto a dusty, unsteady *Stagecoach* may have spoken most directly to Depression-era audiences. The characters in Ford's Western are a varied and seriously flawed lot. Four members of the group are failures by any measure. They carry significant emotional and legal baggage, which under ordinary circumstances should have denied them any kind of future happiness or success. Their flaws bring them together, but it is their shared crises that unite and ultimately redeem them.

The stagecoach of the movie's title has stopped in the small town of Tonto to change horses and add new passengers on its way to Lordsburg. It is headed across difficult country. There are dangers ahead. Sightings of Geronimo have been reported in the area, and the Ringo Kid (John Wayne) has escaped from prison and may be headed to Lordsburg as well. Driver Buck (Andy Devine) is unsure whether to go on. But the town marshal, Curley Wilcox (George Bancroft), believes that Ringo is probably headed to Lordsburg, and he insists that the stagecoach continue. Curley announces that he will ride along for security, and a company of United States cavalry will also be traveling with the stage for part of the trip.

The willing passengers include Lucy Mallory (Louise Platt), a determined but apparently unwell young woman who is eager to be reunited along the stagecoach route with her husband; Mr. Peacock (Donald Meek), a timid whiskey salesman who carries with him a case of his samples; and Hatfield (John Carradine), a brooding gambler and ex–Confederate soldier who is extremely solicitous of Mrs. Mallory. The unwilling passengers are Dallas (Claire Trevor), a prostitute forced out of town by the self-righteous members of the Ladies Law and Order League, and the man who gallantly if drunkenly offers her his arm, Doc Boone (Thomas Mitchell, in an Academy Award-winning performance). Boone, a penniless, convivial alcoholic, has also been sent packing against his will by the locals. As the stagecoach nears the edge of town, Mr. Gatewood, the town banker (Berton Churchill; see also *I Am a Fugitive from a Chain Gang*), hurriedly boards, carrying a small valise.

The stagecoach heads out, and director Ford raises the tension early on by emphasizing the dangers it must endure just in terms of the road and the weather. There is peril ahead even without the dual threats of Geronimo and the Ringo Kid. The camera follows the stagecoach as it climbs a hill, wobbling precariously as the horses struggle up the grade. Ford uses wide-angle camera shots of Monument Valley to emphasize the insignificance of the stagecoach and the vulnerability of its passengers. Biting cold and dust afflict them. At one point on the trail the passengers must construct a makeshift raft to enable the stagecoach to ford a stream, a treacherous enterprise that requires a focused effort by all of the passengers. A camera shot from the driver's seat during this scene and the outstanding work of stuntman Yakima Canutt add to the sense of danger.

Andy Devine portrays driver Buck as insecure, bumbling, and loquacious. He grouses at length about his wife and her Mexican family, and at every stop he is reluctant to continue. His unease is assuaged little by the presence of the cavalry, which will eventually part ways with the stagecoach to travel to a different destination. But Curley demands that they go on because he is intent on capturing the Ringo Kid, and he is soon rewarded.

As the stagecoach rounds a bend, the camera zooms in on one of the great iconic images in American cinema, the Ringo Kid, standing tall, clutching his saddle, and twirling his rifle, a dramatic gesture previously confined to the simple six-shooter. But everything about Ringo is larger than life—his hat, his stride, his dignified surrender, and his all–American face, a face that displays a fluid combination of modesty, grace, and power. He has lost his horse and now finds himself Curley's prisoner. Curley asks him to turn in his rifle just as the cavalry catches up to them. Ringo complies respectfully, but he points out that he and it may soon be needed. He describes a house fire that he has just seen, information that implies an Indian threat in the area.

Many actors and actresses are attractive, but looks alone do not determine their appeal. The most successful among them connect with the public because audiences can somehow relate to them or to the roles they play. Every once in a while, an actor or actress comes along who represents something real that people can believe in. He or she is able to capture the moment and the public's affection. John Wayne is a perfect example of this phenomenon. He brought a strong, clearly defined vision to the pictures he made, and his characters continued to earn the affection of audiences for four decades. Writer Joan Didion describes the clarity of Wayne's screen presence in her essay, "John Wayne, A Love Song."

> [In a world] characterized by venality and doubt and paralyzing ambiguities, [Wayne] suggested another world, one which may or may not have existed ever but in any case existed no more: a place where a man could move free, could make his own code and live by it ... there at the bend in the river, the cottonwoods shimmering in the early morning sun.[42]

John Wayne's Ringo Kid becomes the moral center of *Stagecoach*, and the passengers and plot revolve around him. As the stage rolls on, his story unfolds. He has escaped prison to go after the Plummer brothers who murdered his father and brother and framed him for another death. Crowded with the others into the stagecoach, Ringo demonstrates unexpected civic tendencies and becomes the referee for various conflicts that erupt. Curley may be officially in command, but Ringo is the leader who will shepherd them through their crises.

Initially, Ringo and the prostitute Dallas are shunned by the others. Hatfield assumes the role of Mrs. Mallory's protector with exaggerated Southern gallantry and attempts to shield her from any contact with Dallas. Ringo becomes Dallas's defender in turn. He treats her like a lady and insists that others do so as well. When he asks her to marry him it is not clear if he realizes that she is a prostitute. Dallas is torn over his proposal, but she eventually agrees to join him at his ranch if he will give up his plan to go after the Plummers at Lordsburg.

The stagecoach journey forces these nine travelers to depend upon one another whether they like it or not. At each stop, Curley invites them to vote on whether to continue, and each person has reasons for wanting to turn back or go on. They are a small, conflicted democracy, but once the cavalry rides away, they must rely on one another to outwit or outfight future foes and survive future threats.

Three members of the group represent positions of social respectability and power, Marshal Curley, Doc Boone, and the banker, Gatewood. Curley exercises official authority fairly. He offers them all a chance to participate in decisions about the trip. He is never abusive or dismissive toward Ringo, even though he has arrested him, and he is carefully neutral toward Dallas. Doc is a slobbering, pathetic alcoholic, but he can still claim professional skills that set him above the others. When various crises demand it, the travelers turn to him and he comes through. The banker Gatewood is another representative of authority, but he exercises it belligerently. He consistently resists any efforts to turn back, and he delivers a lengthy speech critical of the government for not providing a cavalry escort for the entire trip. The irony, already known to the audience, is that Gatewood is a thief. He has skipped town with a payroll stashed in his valise, and he must get to Lordsburg before the telegraph wires are repaired and can alert officials there of his crime.

Though set in the Old West, John Ford's *Stagecoach* offers timely social commentary about the 1930s and the Great Depression. The movie's overriding conflict forces the marshal to arrest the Ringo Kid, an honest man of good character and humble background who has been victimized by forces beyond his control, while the banker who occupies a respected social and professional position is guilty of a crime he will very likely get away with. The traits these characters exhibit and the challenges they face parallel the Depression, the public's view of the role played by the banks, and the tribulations so many people had experienced during the past decade. The movie shows common people joining together for the common good, and fighting against external enemies and corrupt elites.

There are multiple conflicts that need resolution at the movie's end. Can the murderous Hatfield salvage some small shred of his former Southern gallantry? Ringo is determined to go after the Plummers, but he is a prisoner, and Curley will be the one to decide if Ringo gets a chance to avenge his family's deaths. Mrs. Mallory's health takes a dramatic turn. Can a drunk as far gone as Doc still function professionally? Dallas has fallen in love with Ringo, but he is going back to prison, and her past may make their future together impossible whenever he gets out. And Gatewood is on track to get away with the money. The stagecoach passengers must grapple with challenges that test their bravery and character, just as the Depression tested the bravery and character of the American people.

Suggested Discussion Questions

1. Why are Doc and Dallas sent packing, and by whom? How does each one respond to this treatment?

2. Describe various representations of ethnic minorities. How are they portrayed? Do they exhibit any positive traits? Does the movie respect any of these characters? How does Ringo respond to these characters?

3. What kind of reputation does Hatfield have? How does he treat Lucy Mallory, and why? Why is Hatfield prepared to shoot Lucy with his last bullet? How would a Southern audience at that time view him? Explain the probable meaning of his last line.

4. Why is Dallas so reluctant to accept Ringo's marriage proposal?

5. The greatest danger faced by the stagecoach passengers as a group is the Indian attack. They are rescued by the United States cavalry. Relate this example of federal action to the role of government that emerges during

Franklin Roosevelt's presidency. What should people expect from their government?

6. In the longest speech in the movie, Gatewood lambasts the federal government for intruding into business affairs. "Why, they're even talking now about having 'bank' examiners. As if we bankers don't know how to run our own banks!" Compare his comments with the findings of the Pecora Commission. How would a Depression-era audience view his remarks in 1939? Consider, also, recent American banking crises. Should the government regulate banking? If so, to what degree? If not, why not?

7. How are women portrayed in the movie? What stereotypes of women does the movie exploit? Does it show women who do not fit stereotypes, and if so, how are they portrayed?

8. How would a Depression-era audience respond to Dallas's comment, "Ya' gotta live, no matter what happens?" Consider the kinds of difficulties Americans faced during the Depression years. Describe any parallels you can detect between the things people endured during the Depression and the lives of the characters on the stagecoach.

9. Curley is the formal representative of the government in the group. It is his duty to bring Ringo in. Explain his relationship with Ringo. Why does he agree to let Ringo go after the Plummers?

10. How is Curley, the agent of government, portrayed in this movie? (Compare his role to that of the government agents in *I Am a Fugitive from a Chain Gang* and *You Can't Take It with You*.) How does this reflect society's perception of the government during the Depression?

11. Ringo's confrontation with the Plummers results in a shootout that leads to deaths. Curley does not make any arrests as a result. Is this outcome just? Defend your answer.

12. The Production Code specifically rejected movie plots that offer positive outcomes for promiscuous women. Relate this requirement to the way things turn out for Dallas? Does the movie defy the Production Code or support it?

13. How does the end of the movie reflect American attitudes as the Depression was coming to a close? What are the chances that (a) Doc will stay sober?; (b) Ringo and Dallas will achieve happiness?

14. Is justice served at the end of *Stagecoach?* Explain your answer.

PART II
War and Peace Around the Globe, 1937–1956

Overview

World War I devastated Europe. Battles lasting months and involving hundreds of thousands of men gutted the countryside. The Battle of Verdun, for example, raged for ten months and resulted in more than half a million casualties, including more than 300,000 dead.[1] (By comparison, the Battle of Gettysburg lasted for three days and involved a combined total of 165,000 Union and Confederate troops.) On the western front, which ran through France and Belgium, both sides quickly adopted trench warfare to protect their positions. "Trench" implies a simple ditch, but the term is misleading. These were elaborate, reinforced earthworks with cross trenches connecting the frontline trench to two or three reserve and supply trenches in the rear. The entire system was often more than a mile deep and faced a comparable system on the other side of the battlefield.[2] In addition to purely physical damage, the war caused political devastation. During or immediately after World War I empires collapsed from Europe to Russia to the Middle East.

However, the most unanticipated and worrisome result of the war may have been summarized best by General John J. Pershing, the man who led the American Expeditionary Forces to Europe in 1917. He believed that the war had not been a decisive military defeat for Germany. As a result, Pershing said, "They never knew they were beaten in Berlin. It will have to be done all over again."[3]

Prewar Era

By the late 1930s Europeans and eventually Americans as well realized that another war, begun by Germany, was almost certainly coming. When, where, and how were unclear. But the German drumbeat for war became increasingly impossible to obscure, as Germany occasionally tried to do.[4] Nor could it be ignored, as other nations who were appalled by the costs of World War I attempted to do when confronted by German aggression. The photograph of British Prime Minister Neville Chamberlain standing at a microphone waving a sheet of white paper just after the 1938 Munich Conference is the ultimate manifestation of these appeasement efforts.[5] The document in his hand surrendered half of Czechoslovakia to Germany in exchange for "peace in our time." Not surprisingly, the Germans mistook the document for a white flag and proceeded accordingly.

After the end of World War I, many countries signed various treaties or joined organizations designed to avoid war. President Woodrow Wilson's primary goal in promoting the League of Nations was to establish a method for settling international disputes before they led to warfare. But despite the support of other nations, he was unable to convince the United States to join, which seriously undermined the league's effectiveness. In the early 1920s, multi-nation naval treaties placed limits on battleship construction in order to prevent countries from engaging in financially ruinous and potentially dangerous competitions to build ever-bigger ships. In 1928, 62 nations signed the Kellogg-Briand Pact outlawing war even though—or perhaps because—the pact "contained loopholes for all occasions."[6] The economic crises of the early 1930s diverted national concerns from foreign threats to economic survival for a while, but by the end of the decade aggressive actions by Germany, Italy, and Japan had ratcheted up war worries once more.

Different countries experienced World War I in different ways, ways that were critical in determining how they responded to the rising international tensions of the late 1930s. Deeply unhappy over their defeat and governed from 1933 on by a militant expansionist, the Germans re-armed and prepared to re-assert themselves among their European neighbors. The French built the Maginot Line, an enormously costly defensive fortification that ran from Switzerland to the Belgian border. They were desperate to avoid another war and especially another Verdun, so they convinced themselves that this bulwark would stop another German invasion. They believed this even though the main thrust of the German attack in 1914 had come through Belgium, and the Maginot Line left that avenue still undefended.

American soldiers had gone to Europe in 1917 exuberantly singing "Over There." They were ready and eager to tackle the Germans and win the war. But by the late 1930s, they were older and wiser and no longer so easily lured into battle by the promise that this would be the "war to end all wars." Many Americans were determined to revert to their isolationist traditions and stay out of the coming conflict. The Neutrality Acts passed in the late 1930s and the America First Committee that emerged in 1940 were designed to strengthen America's resolve to stay out of the conflict. Other Americans accepted or eagerly supported an interventionist approach. This debate finally ended in December 1941 when the Japanese attacked Pearl Harbor.

Movies offer additional insights into national attitudes toward war. German author Erich Maria Remarque's novel, *All Quiet on the Western Front*, offered a depressing, fatalistic vision of the life of a German soldier in World War I. Remarque delivered a powerful anti-war message, but the book was published in 1929 before the resurgence of the militant nationalism of the Nazi era. When the Nazis took over they publicly burned the novel, banned the 1930 movie version, and drove Remarque into exile.[7]

The German government was more enthusiastic about other movies, however. Adolf Hitler was aware of the potential that propaganda offered to affect political outcomes, and he used movies as a way to promote Nazism. Two historically important German movies from the 1930s, *Triumph of the Will* and *Olympia*, both of which were artfully directed by actress and director Leni Riefenstahl, highlight the accomplishments of the Third Reich. Hitler personally commissioned Riefenstahl to create a movie celebrating the annual Nazi Party Rally at Nuremburg in 1934, but *Triumph of the Will* also had another, grander aim. According to Richard J. Evans, its main purpose was "to convey a choreographed image of new-found spiritual unity through a series of gargantuan displays of huge masses of men moving and marching in unison...; and it was Hitler and [Joseph] Goebbels's intention to convey it not just to Germany, but to the world."[8]

Riefenstahl opens the movie with a shot taken from an airplane as it flies above the clouds. The picture frame gradually descends through the clouds to encompass soaring views of the medieval city of Nuremburg, images that bring to mind Germany's glorious Teutonic past. Carefully crafted scenes of disciplined party members, massive military marches, and fawning supporters are interspersed with shots of adoring citizens, some in regional folk dress, and cheerful, well-fed boys and girls. Riefenstahl's camera often lingers on the faces of children, and they are an effective visual device. As is true of children everywhere, they offer hope for the future and demand commitment from the present. After the humiliation and economic chaos of the 1920s, their vibrant good health offered physical evidence of the success of Nazi rule. Riefenstahl's documentary unselfconsciously highlights the frenzied, fanatic devotion Nazi leaders and common people alike had for Adolf Hitler.

In 1936, Berlin hosted the Olympics, and Riefenstahl was again given the task of filming the event. Using techniques similar to those in *Triumph of the Will*, the opening sequence in *Olympia* (1936) ties the games to history and myth. Nude athletes carry the Olympic torch from an ancient Greek setting through the mists of time and geography (and the discrete addition of a track suit) to the modern stadium in Berlin where the games would be held. Nazi Germany carefully erased any evidence of its already robust anti-Semitism and welcomed the world community with open arms. The movie makes no mention of the absence of any German-Jewish athletes, an issue that almost prompted the United States to boycott the games.[9] Riefenstahl shows crowds of enthusiastic spectators, Germans and other national groups as well, dedicated athletes, and fair and open competitions.

Riefenstahl used her camera in ways that almost caress her subjects and emphasize athletic ardor and artistry, especially through the use of slow-motion shots. The beauty of the human form is a prominent feature of her work. Sequences like the diving competitions and morning exercises appear almost ballet like. She often focuses on racially mixed groups, and for the most part her coverage of athletes appears to be based on their successes and stature in the sports world rather than on their racial or ethnic heritage. Riefenstahl gave considerable screen time to African American Jesse Owens, winner of four gold medals and the unofficial hero of the games, as well as other non-white athletes, which demonstrates a respect for other racial groups that is strongly at odds with Nazi ideology. Given the movie's scope and length—nearly four hours—images of Hitler do not seem excessive. In some scenes Hitler exhibits the reasonable reactions of a home-team enthusiast. He is delighted by Germany's victories and dismayed by her failures.

Both movies were public-relations successes for the Third Reich. After the disastrous, expansionist war launched by Germany in 1914 and the chaotic economic and political times that followed, *Triumph of the Will* generated an overriding impression of discipline, power, and national resolve. *Olympia* demonstrated that the country had recovered and regrouped and seemed eager to be accepted as a responsible member of the world community. As a testament to its renewed national and political vigor, German athletes won more Olympic medals that year than any other country. The movie presents scenes of athletic struggle and victory where athletes are given the spotlight they have earned, and German officials run fair competitions (a water obstacle in an equestrian event is a glaring exception) and conscientiously monitor events or assist exhausted competitors. Riefenstahl bracketed the athletic events with footage of grandly extravagant opening and closing pageants. The movie's ultimate message is a compelling vision of German efficiency, good sportsmanship, and triumph.

These potent pro-Nazi movies contributed to the growing fears of other European nations that German aggression would lead to war once again. The evidence mounted during the second half of the decade. In 1935, the citizens of the Saar Valley voted to rejoin Germany in a plebiscite, and in 1936 the

Germans remilitarized the Rhineland. In 1938, Austria acquiesced to the *Anschluss* (although not all Austrians were pleased; see Georg von Trapp in *The Sound of Music*), and the Sudetenland was surrendered by the Munich Agreement.

Like other European nations, the British observed these events with growing alarm but did nothing to oppose them. However, war worries did begin to filter into British movie plots and themes as the 1930s went on, and they were not complimentary to the Third Reich. The sinister German with evil intentions became a stock character in many movies from the decade. *Dark Journey* (1937) and *Night Train to Munich* (1940) feature nefarious German intelligence agents who mislead women with whom they are romantically involved in order to accomplish their goals. The British have had a long love affair with detectives and detective stories, and English writers have created some of the world's best-known literary sleuths, including Sherlock Holmes, Father Brown, Miss Marple, and Hercule Poirot. By the late 1930s characters like these begin to appear in movies that depict Germans as secretive, dangerous aggressors who are thwarted by clever, unlikely, and often underestimated opponents. British director Alfred Hitchcock turned plots about espionage into a virtual cottage industry with *The 39 Steps* (1935), *The Lady Vanishes* (1938), and, after moving to the United States, *Foreign Correspondent* (1941) and *Saboteur* (1942). (Hitchcock continued this theme after the war in *Notorious* from 1946 and *The Man Who Knew Too Much* in 1956.) All these movies present a consistent message: ordinary Brits and Americans are more than a match for emerging world threats, no matter how cleverly concealed or malevolently executed.

Because of France's long border with Germany, the French understood that another war almost certainly meant another invasion. World War I had settled into a four-year stalemate in Europe on a line that curved through France from Switzerland to the Belgian border. Tremendously costly battles and extensive trench construction by both sides had deeply scarred the land and her people. French filmmakers reminded viewers of the horrors of World War I, which killed 1,700,000 Frenchmen[10] and created 600,000 widows and nearly 1,000,000 fatherless children.[11] Two notable French World War I movies, *I Accuse* (*J'accuse!*, 1919) and *Wooden Crosses* (*Les croix des bois*, 1932), offer grim visions of life at the front. In his 1937 classic, *Grand Illusion* (*La Grand Illusion*), writer-director Jean Renoir stepped back from the carnage and despair of frontline combat and concentrated instead on four characters as they navigate the world of German prisoner of war camps. Each of them exhibits weary sorrow laced with irony, and the movie is permeated by the sad conviction that the same costly tragedy is about to happen again.

Many of the earliest American movies about World War I also dealt realistically with the horrors of war. *The Lost Battalion* (1919) uses soldiers who had actually been lost in the Argonne Forest to depict that harrowing episode.[12] *The Four Horsemen of the Apocalypse* (1921), *The Big Parade* (1925), *Wings* (1927), *Hell's Angels* (1930), *All Quiet on the Western Front* (1930), and *A Farewell to Arms* (1932) are all major studio productions that emphasize the war's sadness rather than its military triumphs. Audiences were receptive to this view. *Wings* won the first Academy Award for Outstanding Picture, and *The Big Parade* was a huge hit. It earned millions of dollars at the box office, and ran for 96 weeks at the Astor Theater in New York City.[13] As a new war spread around the globe, however, two World War I movies from 1940 and 1941 celebrated the heroism of ordinary American soldiers. They were major successes, and both were based on actual events. *The Fighting 69th* added a troubled fictional character to the celebrated Irish regiment from New York City that first achieved fame in the Civil War. *Sergeant York* showcased the courage of an ordinary American, Medal of Honor winner Alvin C. York, in a movie of redemption and triumph against overwhelming odds.

The American public was aware of the Nazi government's repression of the rights of German Jews and of overt acts of aggression toward them. Even before America entered World War II, Hollywood had begun to focus on the growing threat that Nazi Germany presented to its Jewish citizens and to Jews throughout the rest of Europe as well. Fritz Lang, Billy Wilder, Marlene Dietrich, Peter Lorre, Hedy Lamarr, and Paul Henreid were among the many directors and actors who fled Germany after the Nazis took power in 1933, and Germany's escalating anti–Semitism was a major motivation for some of them.[14] Although the true extent of the Holocaust did not become apparent until after the war, Hollywood stepped up and condemned the Third Reich early on.

Confessions of a Nazi Spy and *Idiot's Delight,* both from 1939, were early efforts to draw attention to the danger Germany presented to Europe and the United States. In *Confessions of a Nazi Spy,* German-Americans within the United States try to drum up support for the Nazi cause. In the latter movie, a group of international travelers becomes trapped at an Alpine inn when a war begins and countries close their borders. The stranded guests express various views of the conflict. Among them are Norma Shearer, playing a mysterious European *femme fatale,* and Clark Gable as the leader of an all-girl touring vaudeville troupe. At one point, as the war closes in around them, he and his chorus line entertain the inn's guests with an impressive floor show to "Puttin' on the Ritz," and a graceful Gable tap dancing in top hat and tails is the highlight of the movie.

Sometimes the pro-intervention message came in an unlikely package. *Destry Rides Again,* also from 1939, is representative of the offbeat Western musical comedy, a very limited genre. It stars James Stewart as Tom Destry and Marlene Dietrich as Frenchy. Destry has come to town to help out the local sheriff, but he refuses to carry a gun. He prefers to disarm with charm and stern admonishments. By the end of the movie it becomes evident that he cannot stop evil without the use of force, and Destry finally straps on his guns to defeat the bad guys. The movie sends a clear message: sometimes it is just not possible to avoid a fight. The presence of Dietrich, a world-famous celebrity and recent German émigré, served to drive home the point. Dietrich would later become celebrated for her work with the USO during the war, often entertaining American troops very near the frontlines.[15]

World War II

War began in Europe on September 1, 1939, when the Germans invaded Poland. War was no longer a much-feared possibility. It was real, and moviemakers altered their storylines accordingly. Comedian and director Charles Chaplin tackled the Nazi threat with Little Tramp-style humor in *The Great Dictator* (1940). Chaplin depicts Hitler's attacks on German Jews and brilliantly satirizes Hitler and Benito Mussolini. But Chaplin's entire production was made more complicated by the fact that the war was unfolding as he filmed the movie. The thrust of events forced him to adjust his plot as he went along because his humor kept getting undercut by reality.[16] *Mortal Storm* (1940), starring James Stewart, Margaret Sullavan, and Frank Morgan, explores the corrosive effects of Nazi racial policies on Jews and on other Germans who do not share their government's anti–Semitic views. In *All Through the Night* (1941), American gangsters led by Gloves Donahue (Humphrey Bogart) confront Nazi infiltrators in New York City. The movie includes an oblique reference to Dachau, already one of Germany's most notorious concentration camps. Murderous Nazis track Alan Thorndike (Walter Pidgeon) through the streets of London in *Man Hunt* (1941) because they suspect that the suave English big-game hunter had attempted to kill Adolf Hitler. As his chief pursuer closes in, Thorndike excoriates him and Hitler for their crimes against humanity.

These movies were all produced before the United States entered the war, and the movie industry's consistent condemnation of Nazi Germany caused concern among those who opposed American intervention in the conflict. In 1941, Senators Gerald P. Nye (D-NE) and Burton K. Wheeler (R-IN) initiated an investigation into what they believed was Hollywood's strong pro-intervention bias. Senator Nye blasted movies as "the most gigantic engines of propaganda in existence," and he called Hollywood "a raging volcano of war fever. It swarms with refugees. It also swarms with British actors."[17] Pearl Harbor ended the debate, and Hollywood's cinematic support became a popular element of the country's all-out effort to win the war.

To Be or Not to Be (1942), directed by Ernst Lubitsch, was perhaps the funniest movie made about the Nazis during the war years. Carole Lombard (in her last movie) is glamorous and droll; Jack Benny is pompous, insecure, and droll; and the fast-paced plot is part bedroom farce and part mistaken identity caper. It centers on the German invasion of Poland, which is not a subject that normally lends itself to humorous interpretation, and proceeds with a zaniness the Marx Brothers would have envied. Using comedy to address such a serious issue generated some criticism at the time, but comedy is one way to get viewers into a theater.[18] The movie manages to remind audiences of the plight of the Jews by presenting William Shakespeare's famous speech from *Merchant of Venice*, "Hath not a Jew eyes," twice, first as comedy and then as tragedy neatly averted. In this setting, at least, the Germans are outmaneuvered, overwhelmed, and relentlessly upstaged.

Naïve American Kathie O'Hara (Ginger Rogers) is newly married to a Nazi official in *Once Upon a Honeymoon* (1942). She learns the truth about his politics from reporter Pat O'Toole (Cary Grant), and together they attempt to stop her husband as he travels around Europe promoting Nazism. At one point they are rounded up with a group of Jews awaiting deportation, one of whom begins to sing in Yiddish. Even though the song's meaning is unclear, its haunting message of heartbreak and loss comes through. In *Watch on the Rhine* (1943), German national Kurt Muller (Paul Lukas) and his American wife, Sara (Bette Davis), seek sanctuary for their family in America. Kurt is working against the Nazis, but his efforts are threatened by an unscrupulous Nazi sympathizer. Lukas's role in that movie was powerful enough to win him a 1943 Best Actor Academy Award over Humphrey Bogart in *Casablanca*. *The Seventh Cross*, from 1944, is set in 1936 and follows seven concentration camp escapees as they try to make their way to safety in Holland. The camp commander erects seven crosses where he intends to put each one to death when they are captured. Along with *Mortal Storm* and *Watch on the Rhine*, it is one of the few wartime movies to include characters who are "good Germans."

Once the United States entered the war, Americans had to cope with enormous changes, and the country expanded its military forces and industrial production to meet them. In addition to 15,500,000[19] military personnel, an estimated 15,000,000 other Americans (out of a wartime population of about 140,000,000) crossed county lines for reasons related to the war.[20] These dislocations strained families, relationships, and communities as people adjusted to the new normal. Expanded employment opportunities for women and minorities, fewer men of marriageable age, less supervision for children, rapid industrial expansion into unprepared communities, and the rationing of food, clothing, gasoline, and rubber complicated people's daily lives and added to the overriding concern for loved ones at war.

The movie industry also had to deal with changes coming from all directions, and in most cases it rose to the challenge with gallant patriotism. Many movies at the start of the war celebrated support for the war in any form. The changing roles of women in American society suggested many new plot possibilities. *The More the Merrier* and *Government Girl* (both from 1943) feature women who deal competently with the responsibilities of their war-related jobs, almost too competently in the latter case. Both movies also touch on wartime shortages of housing and men and include amusing scenes of women aggressively pursuing male companionship. As if to highlight how inappropriate this behavior is, the men are made uncomfortable by the attention, which suggests that once the war is over this reversal of traditional male-female interaction will have to stop. In *The Miracle of Morgan's Creek* (1944), too many men arriving at a new military base cause perfectly predictable complications for a pretty, outgoing seventeen-year-old.

Men also faced challenges to their perceived roles in society. Joining the war effort was expected. Comedians Bud Abbott and Lou Costello took a humorous approach to enlistments in *Buck Privates* and *In the Navy*. The enormous popularity of these movies made Abbott and Costello the lead box office attraction in 1941.[21] Men who did not join up were viewed by others (and often by themselves) as not doing their part. In *Casablanca* (1942), tough guy Rick Blaine (Humphrey Bogart) refuses to get personally involved with the spies and refugees who congregate in his bar. Like many Americans before Pearl Harbor, he does not want to get dragged into another war, and he says repeatedly, "I stick my neck out for nobody." But as he becomes better acquainted with both sides of the conflict, Rick changes his tune.

Other men suffer because they do try to stick their necks out. An embarrassing health problem gets Marine Woodrow Lafayette Pershing Truesmith (Eddie Bracken) sent home before he even gets into the fighting in *Hail the Conquering Hero* (1944). In a moment of weakness, he compounds this humiliation by pretending to be a hero. Director Preston Sturges builds a funny, pointed social satire around Woodrow's overblown and undeserved hometown reception. (Bracken experiences a similar problem in *The Miracle of Morgan's Creek*, also directed by Sturges.) An older, henpecked Edward G. Robinson gets the chance to demonstrate his patriotism and return to his wife a hero in *Mr. Winkle Goes to War* (1944).

The widespread eagerness to be part of the war effort even extended to B-Westerns. Before the war started they were already commenting on the conflict and picking sides. In *The Night Riders* (1939), for example, the Three

Mesquiteers (John Wayne, Ray Corrigan, and Max Terhune) take on a villain who tries to establish an empire out West using a private army, a storyline clearly meant to evoke Hitler and his storm troopers. Once the war began, contemporary cowboys thwarted Nazi saboteurs and Japanese espionage agents in movies like *Wild Horse Rustlers* and *Texas to Bataan*, both from 1943.[22]

During the war, the Bureau of Motion Pictures (BMP), a federal agency under the authority of the Office of War Information (OWI), was established to influence movie content so that it supported the broad aims of the war. OWI published a "Government Information Manual for the Motion Picture Industry," and the BMP opened an office in Hollywood to encourage moviemakers to incorporate its recommendations. Although the federal government did not directly dictate movie content, it did strongly suggest ways that Hollywood could aid the war effort by featuring patriotic characters and plots. The aim was to have movies show "people making small sacrifices for victory—making them voluntarily, cheerfully and because of the people's own sense of responsibility ... accepting ... tire and gas rationing cheerfully,... riding in crowded buses and streetcars."[23] OWI wanted movies to present a unified, democratic image to wartime audiences. Scenes of class conflict, racial discrimination, crime, and poverty were to be avoided.[24]

The United States and Britain were close allies during World War II and shared a common heritage and language. As a result, the two nations readily exchanged movies made during the war, and their respective audiences were supportive of stars from both countries. British movies often exhibited jaunty stoicism, the standard national response in times of crisis. Britain had a long history of survival against various enemies, a tradition of muddling through with plucky good humor, and great confidence in the protective barrier provided by the seas surrounding her and her powerful navy. Britain would deal with this war as it had with so many other wars before it. But despite their bravery, the British were not immune to the ordinary stresses that came with the extraordinary loss of life, devastating bombing raids, and endless privations brought about by the war.

The British realized that morale was important and movies could help raise it. Popular British actor Leslie Howard, who had played Ashley Wilkes in *Gone With the Wind*, returned to England and directed, produced, or acted in six movies that feature Nazi defeats or champion British resolve. (Howard was killed in an air attack in 1943.) One of his movies, *The 49th Parallel* (1941), focuses on the German military threat to Canada. The movie was released before Pearl Harbor, and this clever plot element moved the danger closer to the United States, which had not yet joined the war. It is a compelling story as well as a compelling piece of propaganda. Greer Garson was another Brit whose movies did much to contribute to the war effort. Garson was a major star during the 1940s. She was nominated for an Academy Award in 1939, and again every year from 1941 to 1945, a record matched only by Bette Davis. Three of her most successful movies, *Goodbye, Mr. Chips* (British, 1939), *Mrs. Miniver* (1942), and *Random Harvest* (1942), are set in England and reference either World War I or II. Garson plays a devoted, adoring support for her husband and, by extension, her country in each of them.

Mrs. Miniver was nominated for 12 Academy Awards and won six, including Best Picture, Best Director (William Wyler), Best Actress (Garson), and Best Supporting Actress (Teresa Wright). At one point in the movie a downed German pilot seeks safety in Mrs. Miniver's kitchen, and she must calmly and singlehandedly defend her country because Mr. Miniver (Walter Pidgeon) has sailed off in a small boat to help rescue the British army at Dunkirk. The movie's last scene takes place in a church. The minister concludes his sermon with a stirring call to action: "This is the people's war! It is our war! We are the fighters! Fight it then! Fight it with all that is in us, and may God defend the right." As the congregation begins to sing "Onward, Christian Soldiers," the camera pulls back to reveal that the church is roofless, the result of a recent bombing raid. Across the open sky a formation of RAF planes flies overhead. It was an overly sentimental production, and it included subplots that hinted to American audiences that the class-conscious British were about to become democrats with a small "d." It was also the year's biggest hit.[25]

Sometimes, movie content had to be calibrated so that it did not become too political. Britain discovered that too much focus on war could generate audience apathy.[26] But the war was a fact of life, and people struggled to cope with its daily realities. One issue that arose again and again in British movies— as it did in real life—was whether to marry while the war went on or wait for it to end. *In Which We Serve* (1942), *Mrs. Miniver*, and *Johnny in the Clouds* (1944; American title, *The Way to the Stars*) all tackled this topic. They supported marriage rather than waiting, despite the fact that choosing marriage in all of them offered no protection from heartbreak.

English movies were not alone in dealing with this issue. *Rome, Open City* (*Roma, Citta Aperta*, 1945), one of the great Italian war movies, struggles with it as well. Like the British movies above, it also includes a couple who plan to marry even though the fighting goes on. Set during the German occupation of Rome, the heartbreak in this movie is especially cruel. American movies such as *Casablanca*, *The Human Comedy* (1943), *The More the Merrier*, *A Guy Named Joe* (1943), and *Since You Went Away* (1944) struggle with the same question and also affirm the importance of love, no matter how complicated it becomes.

The Human Comedy, based on the novel of the same title by William Saroyan, takes a particularly unusual approach. It is set in the small California town of Ithaca and features brothers Homer and Ulysses. These names tie the story to *The Iliad* and *The Odyssey*, epic poems from ancient Greece that relate tales of the hero in war and of those who wait for his return. The movie fits these ageless themes into a World War II setting. Homer's father, who has recently died, narrates the movie as a kind of benevolent ghostly observer. His mother (Fay Bainter) appears lost without her husband. She does not seem to be firmly anchored in the real world. But teenage Homer (Mickey Rooney in an Academy Award-nominated performance) is quite firmly anchored in the present and must deal with multiple issues. Some are the result of his age and circumstances. Others are a direct outcome of the war. Unlike his mother's drift between past and present, Homer seems caught between the present in Ithaca and the "present" of the ongoing war. This complex perspective challenges Homer's ability to cope. His classmates, his job, the financial needs of his family, Ulysses's simple childhood anxieties, and the looming combat experience facing older brother Marcus (Van Johnson) all demand his attention. Homer gallantly tries to be the grownup in these critical times, but his responsibilities and personal crises almost overwhelm him. The love and support of family and friends ultimately binds them together and binds up their sorrows. The movie's ethereal blend of the here and the hereafter transforms a simple story about small-town life into a sweet, somber rumination on the meaning of family.

The strong focus on children in *The Human Comedy* was unusual among war movies. In *Man Hunt*, the British child star Roddy McDowall has a brief but important scene with Walter Pidgeon, and older children are part of a general family perspective in *Since You Went Away*, but children are more likely to need rescue or care in war movies, as in *Mrs. Miniver*, than to be strong forces in movie plots. *Rome, Open City* is an exception to this rule. In it, children's independent actions advance the plot and the war effort.

Even though children did not play major roles in most movies about the war, movies did find a way to bring children into the overall picture in stories that celebrate national values but have no overt connections to the war. *Lassie Come Home* (1943) stars child actors Roddy McDowall as Joe Carraclough and 11-year-old Elizabeth Taylor as Priscilla, the granddaughter of the Duke of Rudling. But the true star of the picture is Joe's dog, Lassie. She is separated from Joe and taken to the remote Scottish Highlands. As she attempts to return to him, the resourceful animal must overcome many obstacles, including an attack by German shepherds. Lassie helps or is helped by others along the way, all of whom part with her sadly as she leaves to continue the long, hard trek back to her Yorkshire home. Although the story is about a boy and his dog, it would be difficult to view the movie in 1943 and not see parallels to the British war effort in Lassie's brave struggles.

The following year Elizabeth Taylor starred in *National Velvet* as overeager, adolescent horse enthusiast Velvet Brown. The role earned her stardom that would last a lifetime. Velvet enters a contest and wins a horse. She is overjoyed to discover that it is a fast runner and a strong jumper. Ex-jockey Mi (Mickey Rooney) signs on as the horse's trainer, and, with help from her family, Velvet and Mi enter the horse in England's Grand National Sweepstakes. Complications challenge her ambitions, but despite class, gender, and age bias, Velvet perseveres and achieves an unlikely victory.

Vincente Minnelli's *Meet Me in St. Louis* (1944) is another movie that featured determined youngsters and highlighted national pride. Judy Garland plays Esther Smith in this extravagant MGM musical, and Margaret O'Brien plays younger sister Tootie, the most exuberant of the four Smith daughters. The seven-year-old O'Brien more than holds her own among the strong adult cast. A precocious civic booster, Tootie is amazed that of all of the cities in the world she had the great good luck to be born in St. Louis, her favorite. It is 1903 and the city is preparing to host the upcoming World's Fair. The whole family has gotten caught up in the excitement. When their father announces his job transfer to New York City, it sets off entirely predictable heart-wrenching disappointment among his daughters and sets up one of the war years' most memorable contributions to Christmas music, "Have Yourself a Merry Little Christmas."

Lassie Come Home, *National Velvet*, and *Meet Me in St. Louis* resonated with wartime audiences because they celebrate everything the Allies were fighting for—hopes and dreams, family ties, fair play, and the joys of the rolling hills, small towns, and bustling cites of home. Along with promoting cherished national values, these movies gave audiences some truly great moments and memorable characters. The delightfully unsophisticated family in *National Velvet* featured Anne Revere in an Academy Award-winning performance as Velvet's mother, and introduced a young Angela Lansbury. Lassie went on to star in a string of movies and enjoyed a career on American television as well. And Judy Garland's "Trolley Song," a grand, buoyant ensemble number, epitomized the MGM musical style and lifted moviegoers' war-weary spirits.

Postwar Era

When the war ended in 1945, the world was forever changed. There would be no going back to simpler days. A new social and political era was on the cusp, and the future was uncertain. Most of Eastern Europe was under the control of the Soviet Union, although it was still not clear how this situation would play out. Much of the infrastructure of Europe had been wrecked, and countries struggled to rebuild. Many of the continent's major cities lay in ruins. England, nearly bankrupted by the war, struggled to deal with the demands of her far-flung empire. The Holocaust had decimated the Jewish population of Europe and Russia, wiping out whole communities that dated back centuries. Japan faced a long hard road to economic and political self-reliance, a process that would be overseen by an American army of occupation until 1952. China was embroiled in a civil war that would not end for another four years.

Among the major powers, only the United States emerged from the war relatively unscathed. The fighting had not reached America's shores; therefore, its cities and industrial centers were still in good shape. Its economy was booming by comparison with other nations, winners or losers, and despite the shock of Roosevelt's death in April 1945, America's political institutions still functioned effectively. Americans had hoped that once the war ended they would be able to return to some kind of normal or even good times. What they got instead were the inevitable challenges and complications of the postwar era. The United States soon realized it would have to provide leadership in this chaos. Social, political, and economic instability threatened to undermine the establishment of democracy in newly liberated countries in Europe. The rising tide of nationalism sweeping through colonial territories in Africa, the Middle East, and Asia hinted at other wars to come. The frightening implications of the Soviet Union's aggressive promotion of Communism in Europe and elsewhere loomed ominously over the postwar world.

Europe's situation was particularly troubling. The physical damage Europe suffered during the war made jobs scarce and slowed economic recovery. In addition, the war created millions of refugees, and their dislocations placed added demands on the resources that were available. In the first years after the war ended, much of Europe faced a serious threat of starvation. These conditions created fertile ground for Communist propaganda. The Soviet Union's attempts to expand further into Europe and institutionalize its power there strained relations with the United States, Great Britain, and France. Adding to the confusion and chaos, many people were unsure whether Hitler had survived and if he would try to return. Hard times and political tensions such as these set the stage in postwar movies for the ambitious plotters in *Notorious* (1946); a father and son's anxious search for *Bicycle Thieves* (*Ladri di Biciclette,* Italy, 1948); and the black market opportunities that drive *The Third Man* (British, 1949).

Japan had suffered as well, but its damage—structural and psychological—was made significantly worse by the atomic bombs that fell on Hiroshima and Nagasaki. In addition to dealing with the humiliation of defeat, the Japanese had to contend with the effects of a new and devastating weapon. Five years after Japan's surrender, director Akira Kurosawa produced one of the world's most acclaimed movies, *Rashomon* (1950). It presents multiple, conflicting perspectives on an incidence of rape and, in doing so, questions the validity of everyone's truth. Although the movie won numerous critical awards, it was not a commercial success in the United States. That honor went to another Japanese production with a decidedly more popular appeal—*Gojira* (1954), an over-the-top monster movie with a nuclear twist. The movie was dubbed into English with characters and scenes added and released in the United States in 1956 as *Godzilla, King of the Monsters*. A huge, hulking iguana-like creature, Gojira/Godzilla emerges from his ocean home as a result of an atomic test and threatens Japan with destruction. In this fictional contest between the forces of good and evil and nuclear danger, Japan aligns itself with the forces of good and finally triumphs over a nuclear threat. The movie became one of the classics of the monster genre and spawned a successful franchise.

Once the war was over the reality of the Holocaust became apparent, to the horror of the civilized world. Photographers were there to document the scene when the United States Army liberated Buchenwald concentration camp in April 1945. Their photographs of the dead and near dead appeared in the May 7 issue of *LIFE Magazine* and gave Americans their first real understanding of the Nazis' "final solution."[27] Although a substantial number of grim combat-related movies were produced in the years during and after the war, movies that focus specifically on the Holocaust are few. Actual scenes of the camps, real or staged, are even more rare. *The Stranger* (1946), which uses brief images from newsreel footage to illustrate the Holocaust, is one exception to this rule. Most of the early movies about the Holocaust depict people who are trying to avoid internment, like *The Rake's Progress* (British, 1945; American title, *Notorious Gentleman*) and *The Diary of Anne Frank* (1959), or they deal with the aftermath of the Holocaust as in *The Search* (1948) and *Exodus* (1960). *The Search* was filmed in occupied Germany, and many scenes were shot in streets still filled with the rubble of war. The plot involves a mother's efforts to find her son after she is released from a concentration camp. The United Nations Relief and Rehabilitation Administration plays an important role in the story, which allows the movie to emphasize the desperation and destruction that still existed in postwar Europe as well as the need to resettle the overwhelming number of displaced persons who were left homeless and often country-less by the war. An important scene involves the relocation of Jewish orphans to Palestine. *Judgment at Nuremburg* (1961) and *The Pawnbroker* (1964) are two of the earliest movies to include scenes of the camps, but most of their content centers on the postwar period.

Movies that prominently feature representations of life in concentration camps do not appear in the United States until after 1970. Among the best examples are *The Hiding Place* (1975), *Sophie's Choice* (1982), *Schindler's List* (1993, Academy Award for Best Picture), and *Life is Beautiful* (*La Vita e Bella,* Italy, 1997; Academy Award for Best Foreign Language Film). *The Last Days* (1998), an Academy Award-winning documentary, uses interviews, photographs, and newsreel footage to track the lives, then and now, of five Auschwitz survivors. By comparison with combat movies, which appear throughout the war and after, this delay in giving substantial screen time to images of concentration-camp experiences may be a reflection of how hard it would have been for audiences to confront the reality of the Holocaust in the immediate aftermath of the war.[28]

Although the United States had not suffered significant physical damage during the war, Americans on the home front also faced adjustments after it ended. Millions of men were coming home. Some would have permanent and, in some cases, disabling injuries. What would life be like for them and for those who had waited for them once they returned? Industry had its own readjustment problems. Companies had retooled to produce war-related products. Now they had to revert to peacetime production, and until that happened, jobs would be scarce. Women had gone to work or had taken on new roles in the home while their husbands were away. What would peace mean for these women and the roles they had assumed during the war years?

Mildred Pierce (1945), a bleak, tense *film noir,* seems to anticipate the pressures married women would face when men finally returned. It illustrates the inevitable tragedy that awaits Mom (Joan Crawford in an Academy Award-winning performance) when she decides to leave Dad and make serious money on her own. *Christmas in Connecticut* (1945) offers a much more light-hearted take on the financial independence working women experienced during the war. This movie's clear message is that even though women may have enjoyed their money-earning ways for a while, once a real man appears, love will triumph over employment and women will be happy to return to the home. If these two movies did not convince post–World War II female audiences that submitting to marriage, housewifery, and child rearing was the right thing to do, a movie from 1948 made the point even more bluntly. *Every Girl Should Be Married* details the painfully obvious campaign devised by Anabel Sims (Betsy Drake) to get Dr. Madison W. Brown (Cary Grant), an unwed (!) pediatrician, to marry her. She finds lots of local support for the idea. No one seriously questions the merits of her plan except Dr. Brown, and he eventually succumbs. The movie demonstrates what seemed self-evident at the time—strategizing for marriage and maintaining a home are all the career fulfillment even the smartest, most ambitious woman will ever need.

Returning veterans faced their own set of problems. They may have hoped for an uncomplicated, arms-open welcome when they got back, but their adjustments were rarely so smooth. They needed to leave behind the intense, male-dominated, combat-focused military life and reconnect with families, communities, and civilian work, and doing so was not always easy. William Wyler's acclaimed drama, *The Best Years of Our Lives* (1946), follows three returning veterans as they navigate the social, emotional, and psychological minefields of home. The movie was enormously popular with audiences. The complications and difficulties faced by both its male and female characters reminded audiences that they were not alone as they struggled to leave the war behind and fit into post–World War II America.

The war was a cataclysmic event that created political, economic, and personal chaos on a scale never before seen. When it was over, people had to cope with all that had happened and all that remained. Movies tracked the events leading up to it, tried to come to terms with the complications of the war years, and explored new realities that emerged in its wake. They gave audiences a chance to measure their own experiences against what others had endured. Fiction may not have matched up perfectly with reality, but these movies were able to offer points of reference for millions of people as they coped with the tremendously unsettled times.

Prewar Era Movies

Grand Illusion (1937)

(*La Grande Illusion;* French, 117 minutes) *Director:* Jean Renoir; *Stars:* Jean Gabin, Marcel Dalio, Pierre Fresnay, Dita Parlo, Erich von Stroheim.

Germany's aggressive behavior in the late 1930s caused great anxiety in France and Belgium. Other countries were concerned as well, but few of them based their fears on such depth of experience. No German army landed in England during World War I. The German invasion of Russia eventually drove the Russians to sign a separate peace treaty in March 1918, but their capitulation was partly the result of incompetent leadership and the ongoing revolutionary upheaval that soon overwhelmed their country.[29] Italy had also suffered greatly in World War I. But by the 1930s Benito Mussolini was reconsidering Italy's options and did not fear Hitler as much as he hoped to emulate his fellow fascist.[30] In terms of territory, France and Belgium had borne the brunt of the German military effort in the West and would very likely do so again if another war came. French writer-director Jean Renoir's masterful *Grand Illusion* explores social class divisions among French and German combatants during World War I and gave 1937 audiences an understanding of the attitudes and events from the era that set the stage for the coming of World War II.

The Treaty of Versailles that ended World War I was designed to punish Germany so thoroughly that it would be impossible for the country to go to war again. It did not work. From 1933 on, evidence mounted of Germany's rising militarism. Furthermore, many Germans believed the treaty had been a terrible wrong, insulting and unfair, and that their country had been betrayed by its leaders at the end of the war. Adolf Hitler insisted that this betrayal had been orchestrated by Jews, and he made avenging it part of his political program. In addition to theories about racial purity, Hitler firmly anchored Nazi anti-Semitism to the idea that Jews were complicit in Germany's defeat and postwar humiliation.[31]

In 1910, Englishman Norman Angell published *The Great Illusion*. In it he argued that war was no longer a sane option. The interdependent nature of world commerce dictated that war would harm the victor along with the vanquished. Therefore, Angell wrote: "[I]f conquest is not to be self-injurious it must respect the enemy's property, in which case, it becomes economically futile."[32] By 1913 his book was in its third edition and had been published in most European languages, plus Russian and Japanese.[33] It was a big hit, especially in Britain, where Lord Esher, a liberal British politician, gave lectures based on the book, reinforcing Angell's point that modern economic ties between nations make war "unthinkable."[34]

World War I demonstrated that Angell's *Great Illusion* was itself a great illusion. Renoir's title for his movie reminds audiences of Angell's theory, and other allusions to the book ripple through the movie. The opening scenes show groups of French and German soldiers in two different bars. The bars share many similarities—music, joking patrons, posters that encourage safe behavior. Renoir makes the similarities between combatants a running theme throughout the movie. Both sides complain about food or the length of the war or express their irritation with senior officers.

The movie follows the experiences of two French pilots who are captured by the Germans in the early months of World War I. Captain de Boeldieu (Pierre Fresnay) and Lieutenant Maréchal (Jean Gabin) are shot down over Germany during a reconnaissance flight. The pilot who shot them down, Captain von Rauffenstein (Erich [billed as Eric] von Stroheim), invites them to a meal. He and the other German officers at the table are polite and respectful toward their enemies. For example, Maréchal has suffered an injury to his arm, and as the meal begins, a German offers to help him cut his food. Someone carries a burial wreath into the room as they eat, and Rauffenstein apologizes for the awkwardness of the moment. The wreath is for another downed French flyer. All at the table rise as Rauffenstein toasts the dead pilot: "May the earth lie lightly on our valiant enemy." The two Frenchmen are soon sent to a series of German prisoner-of-war camps, and the main thread of the story picks up again many months later when they meet Rauffenstein in one of the camps.

Renoir emphasizes several themes throughout the movie, particularly social class distinctions and the futility of war. In the first camp, Boeldieu and Maréchal get to know one another better, but it is clear that Boeldieu is of a higher social class than Maréchal, who was a mechanic before the war. Boeldieu seems to wear his upper-class status rather wearily, and he accepts his place in the group out of what seems like *noblesse oblige* modified by a mild democratic impulse. In one scene shortly after they arrive, Maréchal's arm is still in a sling, and Boeldieu washes his feet. Another scene focuses on a poster celebrating the German capture of Douaumont (February 1916), one of the major French forts guarding Verdun. Some months later, the prisoners plan a musical review for their own entertainment, and the Germans camp guards are invited to the performance. When they arrive, the Germans taunt the French about the lost fort by singing "La Marseillaise." But, during the show, word arrives that the French have retaken Douaumont (October 1916), and the prisoners sing it back to the Germans triumphantly. (The French national anthem seems tailor made for scenes of soul-stirring patriotism aimed at overreaching Germans; see also *Casablanca*.)

The Battle of Verdun is of particular importance in World War I and for Renoir because of its enormity and also because it is emblematic of the carnage and futility that was typical of many major battles of the war. The city of Verdun is historically significant for the French, but its location made it hard to defend. The German general in command of the battle, Erich von Falkenhayn, believed that an attack against Verdun would succeed because the French could not successfully defend it without incurring enormous losses.[35] But the French put up a tremendous resistance. The battle raged from February to December of 1916, and, in the end, Falkenhayn's plan to "bleed [the French army] to death" ended up costing 377,000 French and 337,000 German casualties, with no significant territorial gains for either side.[36]

Boeldieu and Maréchal become friendly with another prisoner, Lieutenant Rosenthal (Marcel Dalio), a French Jew. He receives frequent food parcels from home and shares his gifts with the others in their barracks. He explains that he is a naturalized French citizen with Danish and Polish parents, and he is happy to fight for the country that allowed his family, owners of a major bank, to become so wealthy. The obvious parallel is to the Rothschild family of bankers who had long figured prominently in French political and economic history, but featuring a Jewish soldier in the movie served another purpose as well. Anti-Semitism was on the rise in Europe in the late 1800s.[37] In the 1890s France had suffered through the Dreyfus Affair, which centered on charges of treason against a Jewish army officer. This divisive controversy included accusations of military fraud, political intrigue, and anti–Semitism and strained France's relations with its Jewish citizens. The nation became obsessed with the scandal, and the contentious issue dragged on in court and in public opinion until well into the new century.[38] The easy friendship that develops between Rosenthal and the two other Frenchmen demonstrates that they have moved on and offers an example for others to follow as well.

Boeldieu, Maréchal, and Rosenthal are transferred to other camps and separated for a while, but they eventually meet again at a camp housed in a magnificent old cathedral situated on the top of a steep mountain peak. Its walls are 50 feet high in places, and big menacing dogs are part of the prison guard. Rauffenstein, who is recuperating from combat injuries, is the camp commander. He greets Boeldieu and Maréchal as old friends when they arrive but warns them, "Gentlemen, I respect your patriotism and your courage, but no one escapes from this fortress." Rosenthal, who is already at the prison, has been working on an escape plan that will get them out of prison, out of Germany, and back into battle. The question they face is how to pull it off under such well-guarded and challenging conditions.

Boeldieu comes up with an idea that will enable Maréchal and Rosenthal to escape. He refuses to join them, despite Maréchal's encouragement. As Boeldieu proceeds with his plan to help them, Rauffenstein is at first puzzled and then almost hurt by Boeldieu's behavior. Maréchal and Rosenthal attempt their escape, but they encounter difficulties that threaten to ruin their plans and destroy their friendship.

Suggested Discussion Questions

1. Describe the social class status of Boeldieu, Maréchal, Rosenthal, and Rauffenstein. Explain Rauffenstein's views of warfare, of his role in the war, and of Boeldieu.

2. How does Boeldieu respond to Rauffenstein's gestures of friendship? Compare Boeldieu's and Rauffenstein's views and attitudes toward warfare and the aristocracy's role in it.

3. When Boeldieu says that Maréchal and Rosenthal are also officers, he implies that they are his equal. Analyze Rauffenstein's response: "Charming legacy of the French Revolution."

4. How are German soldiers portrayed in the movie? Describe specific instances where they behave in a helpful or non-threatening manner. Explain the incident with the harmonica. Why would a French director include these scenes in a movie about World War I?

5. How is anti–Semitism presented in the movie? Explain Rosenthal's

ancestry. Why is he willing to fight for France, which is at war with Austria, the country of his birth? How does he determine his citizenship?

6. Class differences affect relationships between various characters. Analyze the conversation Boeldieu, Maréchal, and Rosenthal have about different diseases. What kind of social change do they believe is taking place?

7. Explain what happens when the Russians receive the crate from the Tsarina. What were conditions like in Russia from 1915 to 1917? Compare the attitudes and expectations of the Russian prisoners to conditions in Russia in late 1917.

8. Why does Boeldieu refuse to join the escape? As Maréchal and Rosenthal prepare to escape, explain Rauffenstein's reactions to Boeldieu's diversion when (a) it is happening; (b) he learns of Maréchal and Rosenthal's escape; and (c) Boeldieu is dying. Why is Boeldieu so forgiving of Rauffenstein?

9. Why does the German widow take in the two escaped prisoners? Why do they trust her?

10. The German widow shows them pictures of her husband and brothers and identifies the battles in which they were killed. All are major German victories. Although he is a Jew, Rosenthal helps build the Christmas crèche for her little girl. Why would Renoir include these two scenes?

11. The story ends in the winter of 1917. What would an audience watching the movie in 1937 expect to happen to Maréchal and Rosenthal just after the movie ends? Assume that the two men survive the war, what might their lives, attitudes, and expectations be like in 1937?

12. Analyze Renoir's choice of a title for the movie. What is the "grand illusion?"

The Lady Vanishes (1938)

(British, 97 minutes) *Director:* Alfred Hitchcock; *Stars:* Margaret Lockwood, Michael Redgrave, Paul Lukas, Dame May Whitty, Googie Withers, Cecil Parker, Linden Travers, Catherine Lacey.

Alfred Hitchcock's thriller, *The Lady Vanishes,* serves as an excellent metaphor for Europe's determination to ignore aggressive Germany militarism in the years before World War II. Rebounding from World War I had not been easy for any of the countries involved. The losers struggled to rebuild and restructure themselves. The winners assessed the cost of the war and recoiled. The dated battle tactics still in use throughout the war were designed for rifle, cavalry, and lance, and proved catastrophic for infantrymen confronting machine guns, barbed wire, and artillery. World War I was a "blood-letting, man-killing, nation-eating nightmare of unprecedented horror," wrote historian David Kennedy. "All [the nations involved] were determined to avoid its recurrence."[39] In addition, the economic collapse of the 1930s left few countries with the financial resources to invest heavily in armaments.

Adolf Hitler understood the mood of Europe, and, like a crafty poker player gaming the table, he used the widespread fear of another war to advance Nazi power and expand German territory.[40] For example, national self-determination was one of the goals of the Treaty of Versailles. But newly created nations like Poland and Czechoslovakia and territorial adjustments in areas like the Rhineland left substantial numbers of German citizens outside Germany's borders. Hitler aggressively exploited these circumstances in the 1930s. He used subterfuge, political pressure, and violence to accomplish his goals of territorial expansion while at the same time pretending his only interests were "justifiable revisions" to the new national borders established by the treaty.[41]

England, France, and America looked the other way time and again as Hitler violated the spirit of the treaty or the sovereignty of other nations, sometimes blatantly. Shortly after becoming chancellor of Germany in 1933, Hitler orchestrated the passage of the Enabling Act, which gave him the unlimited powers of a dictator. In 1935, he issued the Nuremburg Laws designed to codify Nazi anti–Semitism and severely restrict the rights of German Jews. That year he also reoccupied the Rhineland, expanded the army, and announced the hitherto secret existence of a 28,000-man air force, all clear violations of the Treaty of Versailles. In 1937, Hitler offered military aid to the fascist forces of Francisco Franco in the Spanish Civil War, and a German air strike on a small village became infamous as the first use of air attacks against a civilian population. (In just a few months Pablo Picasso had channeled the town's agony into his abstract masterpiece, *Guernica*.[42]) In February 1938, Hitler coerced Austria into signing the *Anschluss*, which established a political union between them.[43] In addition, Germany signed treaties with Italy and Japan in the mid–1930s that prefigured the Axis alliance in World War II.

Germany's aggressive posturing, Italy's invasion of Ethiopia, and Japan's actions in China prompted President Roosevelt to argue in late 1937 that "aggressors" should be "quarantined." His idea was strongly opposed by isolationists and others who feared such actions might provoke war with Germany. Many British leaders were also reluctant to take action against German aggression. However, the appalling Nazi attacks on Austria's Jews in the aftermath of the *Anschluss* were widely reported and finally prompted some to support Winston Churchill as he sounded the alarm in Parliament about the danger of Nazi power and the unpreparedness of Britain's defenses.[44] Member of Parliament Harold Nicolson, greatly distressed by Britain's weak response to Germany, complained that Prime Minister Neville Chamberlain had the intellect of a "clothes-brush." Nicolson was concerned about the worsening situation in Europe and the response of Britain's upper class. Members of the "governing classes," he wrote, "think only of their own fortunes, which means hatred for the [communists]. This creates a perfectly artificial but at present most effective secret bond between ourselves and Hitler.... I go to bed in gloom."[45] (The 1993 Merchant-Ivory movie, *The Remains of the Day,* illustrates the tie Nicolson described between Nazism and the British upper class.)

The stubborn desire of non-interventionists in Great Britain and the United States to stay out of another war became increasingly difficult to defend in the face of ever-more menacing international militarism. Hitchcock made this disconnect between reality and response the central theme of *The Lady Vanishes* (British, 1938), a story about the mysterious disappearance of an elderly woman on a train and the passengers who willfully refuse to acknowledge that she was ever on board.

The movie opens at an inn in a small mountainous country near Germany. Iris Henderson (Margaret Lockwood) is there on vacation with friends. Another guest, Miss Froy (Dame May Whitty), had been working in the country as a governess and has stopped at the inn on her way back to England. Other travelers become stranded at the inn because of an avalanche along the train tracks. That night, Iris gets into an argument with Gilbert (Michael Redgrave), a poor, enthusiastic, and very noisy musicologist staying in the room above hers. By the next day the tracks are cleared of snow, and Iris, Miss Froy, and Gilbert board the train along with the stranded passengers to return to England.

Iris and Miss Froy share a train compartment with others and visit the dining car for tea. Miss Froy insists to the waiter that he make it with her own exotic blend. When the tea is served, she asks Caldicott and Charters, two cricket-besotted Englishmen at a nearby table, if she may borrow their sugar bowl. After their tea, the women return to their compartment, and Iris drifts off to sleep. When she awakes Miss Froy is gone, and from then on no one will admit she was ever on the train. Iris was with her when they encountered other passengers, but they all deny having seen Miss Froy. Iris is bewildered, angry, and insistent as she frantically searches the train for her friend. Along the way she meets Gilbert, who gallantly offers to help, as does another passenger, Dr. Haartz (Paul Lukas), a German psychiatrist. Haartz quickly concludes that Iris is hallucinating because earlier that day she had suffered a bump on the head, caused by a falling flower pot. What Iris does not know but the audience does is that the falling flower pot was no accident, and the passengers and train staff have various reasons to refuse to acknowledge Miss Froy's disappearance.

It soon becomes apparent that Haartz has organized a deception to keep

Iris from finding Miss Froy. The other passengers in Iris's compartment include the wife of the German minister of propaganda and an Italian magician with his wife and child. They are part of Haartz's plot as are some of the train staff. The other passengers who will not admit they saw Miss Froy, for reasons ranging from petty to malevolent, are Haartz's unwitting accomplices. Mr. and "Mrs." Eric Todhunter, the upper-class couple in the compartment next to Iris's, are involved in an adulterous affair. An investigation into Miss Froy's disappearance will bring them unwanted publicity. Caldicott and Charters are desperate to return home in time to attend an important cricket match. Searching for a missing passenger will slow down the train. Finally, there is a nun in another compartment caring for a patient. Haartz describes the nun as a deaf mute, but she turns out to be a Cockney lass playing a role for pay.

The passengers offer an interesting parallel to the political situation in late 1938. The Italian is a junior partner on the German's payroll and has no ethical qualms about accommodating Dr. Haartz's demands. Eric Todhunter, a lawyer, refuses to believe that any harm can come to a man of his social stature. Caldicott and Charters are deeply concerned about what is happening to England, but only in the sports world. They seem oblivious to the real one. The woman impersonating the nun is in it for the money. Gilbert wants to believe Iris, but once he actually figures out most of what is going on, he turns to Dr. Haartz for help. Therefore, the upper-class character does not believe anyone would have the temerity to interfere with his life. The middle-class gentlemen are uninterested in anything outside their personal concerns. The lower-class woman can be bought. And when Gilbert, the smartest of them all, figures out most of what is going on, he promptly turns to the wrong person for help because he is constitutionally incapable of questioning the integrity of someone with prestigious professional credentials. The train is a metaphor for a Europe that either could not or would not comprehend the danger of German militarism, while Gilbert's misplaced trust of the German professional resembles Chamberlain's misjudgment of Hitler at Munich. (*The Lady Vanishes* was released in the United Kingdom on October 7, 1938.[46] The Munich Conference that abandoned Czechoslovakia's Sudetenland to the Germans occurred on September 30, 1938.)

Many scenes in Hitchcock's movie appear to parallel contemporary events. Early on, the hotel manager could just as easily have been talking about the war clouds gathering over Europe when he declares, "Is a bad wind that blow nowhere no good." When Caldicott and Charters make their first appearance, they are gravely concerned about their homeland. Charters remarks, "That last report was pretty ghastly." In other scenes they worry because "England is on the brink," and the two of them are "cut off in a time of crisis." Only later does the audience realize they are discussing cricket and not world affairs. After Iris collapses, Dr. Haartz strongly recommends "peace and rest." When the passengers finally realize the danger they are in, Todhunter announces confidently, "They can't do anything to us, we're British," and declares in words reminiscent of Norman Angell's *The Great Illusion*, 'I'm not going to fight. It's madness."

Only when Haartz shows his true intentions do the passengers realize that by refusing to acknowledge reality they have jeopardized their own lives. Todhunter deserts the group, but the others, including the nun, finally band together to tough it out.

Suggested Discussion Questions

1. Describe Iris's character. Why does she persist in her search for Miss Froy despite the fact that everyone else denies there ever was a Miss Froy?
2. Describe Gilbert's character. Why does he help Iris? Why does he trust Haartz? Why does he forget the melody?
3. Describe the relationship between Groppo, the Italian magician, and Haartz.
4. The movie never explains why the train staff are helping Haartz. Suggest reasons why they would.
5. Describe Charters and Caldicott. What did their behavior at the end of the movie say about them and, by extension, others like them who do not pay attention to anything but their own interests? Explain the joke about the "Hungarian Rhapsody."
6. Why does the nun switch her support from Haartz to Iris and Gilbert?
7. Once the Communists took control of Russia, other European countries were very worried that Communism would spread to their citizens. Communists believed that wealth should be shared by all, not controlled by the few who have earned it. Find Germany and the Soviet Union on a map and analyze the quote by Nicholson regarding Hitler's opposition to Communism (p. 67). Compare Eric Todhunter's behavior to Harold Nicholson's assessment of the British upper class.
8. Miss Froy explains that she has been working as a governess for six years and is returning to England because the children are now grown up. Assume that this information is true but incomplete. What do her actions indicate about the British government's concerns regarding the politics of Europe in the 1930s?
9. Recall the guitar player who was strangled and the incident with the flower pot. How do they connect to Miss Froy's situation and the events on the train?
10. Male and female characters have important roles as Miss Froy's situation

plays out. Does either gender appear more competent or successful by the end of the movie? Does either appear more foolish?

11. Compare the attitudes of the movie's British characters with American attitudes toward escalating world tensions in 1938. Describe any similarities or differences and suggest reasons for them.

12. Condense the central point of this movie into a few words on a 1938 political poster. What is Hitchcock's main message, and who is the intended audience for his message?

Sergeant York (1941)

(143 minutes) *Director:* Howard Hawks; *Stars:* Gary Cooper, Walter Brennan, Margaret Wycherly, Joan Leslie, George Tobias, Stanley Ridges, Ward Bond, Noah Beery, Jr., June Lockhart.

Howard Hawks's classic *Sergeant York* hit movie theaters in the fall of 1941, just months before the United States declared war on the Axis powers. The movie follows the personal struggles of World War I hero Alvin York, and it resonated with moviegoers across the country. Warner Bros.' advertising campaign said it all: "America's Greatest Modern Hero! Timelier today than ever ... thrilling and inspiring story of the kind of men that America is made of!"[47]

World War II began in Europe on September 1, 1939, with the German invasion of Poland. The German army overran the country despite the gallant resistance of her brave cavalry, and Poland surrendered by the end of the month. For a while, however, there was little fighting elsewhere. The German advance stopped on September 30. This lull in the fighting was dubbed the Phony War. It lasted into the spring of 1940 and set the world on edge.

The attack on Poland was a gauntlet thrown at the feet of the Western democracies. France and England took up the challenge and declared war on Germany two days after the invasion began, but the United States did not. Although many Americans, foremost among them President Roosevelt, believed that war was inevitable, many others were determined non-interventionists. Isolationist sentiment ran so high that the House of Representatives almost passed the Ludlow Amendment, which would have limited the government's war-making powers by requiring a national referendum to declare war unless the nation was attacked first.[48] Even after the British declared war, America's ambassador to Great Britain, Joseph P. Kennedy, sent back reports that highlighted British pacifism and encouraged Roosevelt not to offer support to the British because they could not be relied upon.[49]

Americans' enthusiasm for joining the fight remained limited. A Roper poll from 1939 showed that 67 percent wanted the United States to stay neutral, and only 12 percent were willing to send aid to the Allies.[50] Powerful opponents of American intervention such as Senator Burton K. Wheeler of Indiana, newspaper publisher William Randolph Hearst, and nationally syndicated radio commentator Father Charles E. Coughlin spoke out against intervention. Charles Lindbergh also opposed intervention in the war and became a leading spokesperson for the America First Committee. His stature as an American aviation hero gave added weight and publicity to his views, and he vigorously promoted them in radio addresses, Congressional testimony, and articles in national magazines.[51] (Roosevelt was so infuriated by Lindbergh's actions that he told Treasury Secretary Henry Morgenthau, Jr., he believed Lindbergh was a Nazi.)[52]

The pressure on America to join the fight grew as the international crisis deepened. But a constitutional democracy is not designed to move abruptly. Europeans were not alone in their initial reluctance to push back against German aggression after their high hopes for peace—purchased at such staggering cost in the trenches of World War I—now appeared to be disintegrating under the force of another German onslaught. Many questions troubled Americans about this new war. They wondered not only whether it was in America's interest to go to war but also about issues related to the morality of war. Given the inevitable ruin and loss of life that would result, was it right to go to war? Would it accomplish anything lasting?[53]

The Phony War ended in the spring of 1940. On the march again, the Germans quickly overran Norway and Holland. German forces charged through Belgium and into France, slipping around the end of the Maginot Line. Other units rode right over it, straight into the heart of the country. There was little the French could do to stop them. A British Expeditionary Force (BEF) of nearly 400,000 men arrived to support the French, and as the Germans carried the battle westward across northern France, the BEF along with part of the French army became trapped against the English Channel. There, 15 miles from the port of Dunkirk, the Germans halted. Why they did so is still a mystery. Various explanations have been suggested, but because the German tanks did not continue their pursuit across the soft, sandy channel beaches, a rescue of miraculous proportions in June 1940 delivered most of the British army and a portion of the French, nearly 340,000 men, safely back to Britain.

Although the United States had not yet made up its mind to join the fight, international events did make the need to expand the army clear to the American people. By September 1940 Roosevelt was able to get a Selective Service law passed and create a peacetime draft without great argument. Even Wendell Willkie, the Republican candidate running against him for president that year, accepted the need for a draft.⁵⁴ For isolationists, things were starting to unravel.

Isolationism had been an issue during World War I as well. Most Americans were not interested in getting into the war in 1917.⁵⁵ Alvin York, a deeply religious Tennessee sharpshooter, requested exemption from the draft as a conscientious objector, but his request was denied. Ironically, the poor backwoods farmer would later gain fame for his heroism in the war. During the Meuse-Argonne offensive in 1918, where American troops saw heavy fighting, York singlehandedly rescued his company from a German machine gun attack and captured more than 100 German soldiers. Then he and the seven soldiers remaining from his unit captured additional Germans. York and his men led a total of 132 prisoners safely back through an ongoing battle to American headquarters. He received medals from the French, Italian, and American governments and came home a celebrated hero.⁵⁶ His story inspired Americans during the First World War and would inspire them again when it was released as a movie just before the Japanese attacked Pearl Harbor. *Sergeant York* follows Alvin as he evolves from a combative, alcoholic hell raiser to a devout Sunday school teacher and, more to the point for 1941 audiences, from a conscientious objector to a Medal of Honor winner.

Alvin (Gary Cooper) and his mother, sister, and brother live on a rugged, rocky farm in the Tennessee mountains. Ma (Margaret Wycherly) belongs to a small country church led by Pastor Rosier Pile (Walter Brennan). She is proud of all the work Alvin does to support the family but is dismayed by his sinful behavior, and she asks Pastor Pile to speak to him. Alvin is unmoved by the minister's attempts to get him to change his ways, but a series of personal crises leads him to re-evaluate his beliefs and come back to the church. He embraces his faith wholeheartedly and rejects his former rambunctious brawling as sinful. As a result, when the draft is announced, Alvin refuses to enlist. Hoping to keep him out of trouble and also out of the war, Pastor Pile helps him apply for conscientious objector status, but his application fails and Alvin must report for duty. Army officers are aware of his attempts to avoid service, and they keep a close watch on him. However, Alvin's earnest affability and excellent marksmanship eventually win their respect. He is promoted, and during the battle in the Argonne Forest he must lead troops when other senior personnel are injured or killed. Alvin returns home after the war a humble, respected hero.

The first half of the movie centers on Alvin's life in a remote mountainous area of Tennessee. A conversation at the general store between a traveling salesman and some local men highlights the community's insularity and isolationism. They are far from the wider world and not really interested in it. Alvin's personal situation demonstrates his character flaws and his strengths. No amount of hard work is going to improve the family's circumstances. But when he makes up his mind to marry Gracie Williams (Joan Leslie), Alvin sobers up, applies himself, and gambles on getting a better piece of land. His plan fails and he begins drinking again, but a violent thunderstorm prompts him to turn to Pastor Pile's church and abandon his life of alcoholism and fighting.

This part of the story could have been trite, but the quality of the characters, the acting, and the storyline give Alvin, his mother, and Pastor Pile a dignity and blunt sense of humor that elevate their struggles. They are hardworking and smart, but they are also limited by chance and by circumstances beyond their control, problems that would have been familiar to many who had just endured the Great Depression. The quality of the movie is reflected in its award nominations. Cooper won an Academy Award for Best Actor, the movie won for Best Editing, and Brennan and Wycherly were nominated for Best Supporting awards. The movie was also nominated for Best Picture, Best Director, and five other award categories.

Alvin's religion is put to the test when he is drafted into the army. Once his application for conscientious objector status is rejected, Alvin has to reconcile his belief in nonviolence with his role as a soldier. Even the officers who have only known him for a short while understand that he faces a true test of his convictions. His conversations with his commanding officer allow the movie to review and evaluate arguments for and against war. The conflict that Alvin experiences mirrors issues confronting many Americans in 1941. Ultimately, he reaches the conclusion that there are times when a person must "render unto Caesar" (Matthew 22:21). Alvin decides to accept the demands of the government and trust in the Lord.

The second half of the movie covers his military experiences. Rather than present a picture of glorious triumph, it downplays the battlefield heroics. The first combat death Alvin observes is neither dramatic nor heroic. It seems almost accidental. The trenches are poorly constructed and dirty, and the battlefield is a scene of confusion and devastation. At the start of the Meuse-Argonne offensive, a planned artillery barrage that should give Alvin's infantry unit some protection never materializes. When his unit finally moves forward without any artillery cover, they go "down like the long grass before the mowing machine at home."[57] Even Alvin's defeat of the German machine gun position is not recreated in some grand heroic manner. Alvin succeeds because he is a calculating, deadly hunter who hunts men as carefully as he once hunted turkeys in Tennessee.

When he returns with his prisoners, Alvin is not overly impressed by his accomplishments. Instead, he is rather matter-of-fact about them. The ensuing celebrations in Europe and the United States seem a bit overwhelming to him, and he refuses offers to trade on his honors by making endorsements. His true reward waits for him at home.

Suggested Discussion Questions

1. The movie opens with the melody of "America" ("My Country, 'Tis of Thee") playing as a statement appears on the screen. The last line reads: "To their faith and ours that a day will come when man will live in peace on earth, this picture is humbly dedicated." Why would the director use this for an opening? What does the phrasing of the sentence imply about the international situation when the film was released?

2. The men gathered at Pastor Pile's store in the first scene emphasize to the salesman how isolated they are. They are not interested in events outside their community. Is this attitude acceptable in a free society? Is it appropriate in a participatory democracy, and if not, why not?

3. Are Alvin, his family, and his neighbors unsophisticated? Are they reasonably intelligent? Why are they not more economically successful?

4. Describe the relationship between Alvin and his mother. Is Ma a good parent? Is Alvin a good son? How is the family able to survive in such poor circumstances?

5. Alvin initially resists the order to register for the draft. Research how the Selective Service law treated draft resisters in 1917. Can a free society remain free if it lets its citizens refuse to fight? Is it a free society if it punishes those who refuse to fight?

6. Describe the character traits that will enable Alvin to succeed in battle. Suggest how he developed these traits.

7. Evaluate the arguments his commanding officer uses to encourage Alvin to accept his role as a soldier and Alvin's reasons for finally deciding to do so. Are they logical and ethical? Given his religious beliefs, are they valid?

8. Who is Cordell Hull? What role does he play in Alvin's story? What role does he play in World War II?

9. Why does Alvin refuse the very lucrative offers that come to him after he returns home a hero? Was this decision a wise one? What reward does Alvin receive when he returns home?

10. Even though he had offers to sell his story to Hollywood, Alvin refused to do so until 1940, when producer Jesse L. Lasky appealed to his sense of patriotism.[58] What does this timing say about Alvin York, Lasky, and America in 1940? How might a 1941 audience react to Alvin's story? Suggest how an audience today might react after seeing this movie.

11. How is Alvin representative of traditional American values? Describe any current public figures who exhibit these same values.

War Era Movies

Casablanca (1942)

(102 minutes) *Director:* Michael Curtiz; *Stars:* Humphrey Bogart, Ingrid Bergman, Paul Henreid, Claude Rains, Conrad Veidt, Sydney Greenstreet, Peter Lorre, Dooley Wilson, Marcel Dalio, S. Z. Sakall, Joy Page, Helmut Dantine, Curt Bois.

American isolationism evaporated after December 7, 1941. The Japanese attack on Pearl Harbor brought a united country into the war. But the administrative machinery and personnel necessary to organize the military, civilian, and industrial components of the war had not yet been assembled.[59] In the preceding few years America had expanded its support for the British war effort with loans and supplies. After the Germans invaded the Soviet Union in June 1941, it also received American support. But once the United States was officially at war, that support and America's war effort itself would require a tremendous commitment from the American people. *Casablanca,* one of the best-loved American movies of the twentieth century, explores the complications and demands the war made on ordinary people and the extraordinary ways they stepped up to meet them.

The war years saw dramatic increases in jobs and income. In a turnabout from the 1930s, people finally began to see their finances improve as a result of the government's war-time spending. For example, the number of workers in Butte, Montana, mining the copper, zinc, and manganese needed for the war effort went from 800 in 1938 to 9,000 four years later.[60] In 1939, the United States produced 3,807 aircraft. In 1944, the peak year for war production, it produced 96,318.[61] But the requirements of the war economy caused shortages in everything from clothes to food to anything made of metal. In order to buy a new tube of toothpaste, for instance, a customer had to return an empty one.[62] People suffered from reduced or nonexistent supplies of silk and, later, nylon for stockings, coffee, sugar, beef, and shoe leather. In order to save on material, men's lapels got narrower, their suits lost their vests, and women's skirts got shorter.[63]

The economic costs and benefits of the war demanded adjustments, but they were nothing compared to the personal adjustments people had to make. Lives were interrupted, families separated, and loved ones lost. The dislocations, disruptions, and heartbreak further stressed a country that had only recently emerged from an economic catastrophe. No one could know for certain how long the war would last or what its outcome might be, and there were no guarantees that financial hard times would not return once the war ended. Adding to the uncertainties, the United States won no triumphant battle immediately after war was declared. In early 1942 America was unable to mount a significant military assault on Japan, Germany, or Italy, because it lacked the necessary troops and supplies, as well as the means to transport them.[64] America had to build almost everything, including its armed forces, from the ground up. It quickly became clear that the war was going to go on for a while.

In strategic terms, however, the tide of war began to turn in the last half of 1942. Three major battles, at Midway, El Alamein, and Stalingrad, reversed the string of successes that had defined Japanese and German military efforts up until then. But the importance of those three battles was not readily apparent. As a result, the war seemed to loom ahead in 1942, with no end in sight overseas and mounting sacrifices at home.

What Americans needed was a simple, clear vision of their role in a war so huge and all-encompassing that it would engulf the world and demand sacrifices as big as a battleship and as small as a tube of toothpaste. The movie industry soon brought that vision into focus. Senator Gerald P. Nye referred to Hollywood as an "engine" of propaganda, and in late 1942 the movie industry delivered big. *Casablanca* was a call to arms that personified the struggle in characters portrayed by two of Hollywood's most glamorous stars, and it would go on to become one of the most celebrated love stories ever produced. It was nominated for eight Academy Awards and won for Best Picture, Best Director, and Best Screenplay. It features an outstanding international cast and a plot that distills the rationale for the epic conflict into a love affair between cynical American ex-patriot Rick Blaine (Humphrey Bogart) and Ilsa Lund (Ingrid Bergman), the woman who loved him and left him in Paris when the Germans marched into the city.

The movie takes place before the attack on Pearl Harbor. Rick was able to get out of Paris ahead of the Germans in June 1940, and he has opened a nightclub, Rick's Café Américain, in Casablanca, Morocco. In addition to loyal piano player Sam (Dooley Wilson), Rick employs a varied collection of foreign nationals to staff his restaurant, tend his bar, and manipulate his roulette wheel. The café attracts international customers as well. Casablanca is a magnet for these people because the plane that flies out of its small airport every night can, for the right price, transport them to Lisbon in neutral Portugal. From there, those who are brave enough can leave for the United States without legal difficulties or direct interference from the Germans.

Morocco occupied a complex position in the geopolitics of World War II. When Germany defeated France in 1940, it took control of France's entire Atlantic coastline and the northern third of the country. The Germans allowed the rest of the country to be governed by a Franch hero of World War I, Marshal Henri-Philippe Pétain, who was headquartered at Vichy, a town outside the area administered by the Germans. By agreement with the Germans, the Vichy French government would be able to manage France's colonies, including Morocco, as long as the French soldiers stationed there would defend them against Allied attacks. Therefore, Casablanca was under the control of the Vichy French government. Police Captain Louis Renault (Claude Rains) is a local representative of French control. Renault is a frequent customer at Rick's and a man of very flexible ethics. (Both Bogart and Rains were nominated for Academy Awards.)

But the Germans are not convinced of the loyalty of France's colonies so they send Major Strasser (Conrad Veidt) to Casablanca to keep an eye on things and to find and detain a famous hero of the Czech resistance, Victor Laszlo (Paul Henreid). Laszlo has escaped a series of German concentration camps, and he is suspected of trying to get to America in order to lead the Czech resistance from there. He will be able to travel safely if he can acquire letters of transit that were recently stolen from two German couriers. The letters are the equivalent of wartime get-out-of-Casablanca-free cards, and they are for sale on Casablanca's black market. Strasser suspects that Laszlo is after the letters, but he does not order his immediate arrest. Renault, who is eager to accommodate his German visitors, willingly helps Strasser intimidate Laszlo. Renault, Strasser, Laszlo, and Ugarte, the thief who stole the letters of transit (Peter Lorre, in a memorable performance), all arrive at Rick's on the same night. Adding romance to the danger and intrigue, Laszlo has brought with him his beautiful traveling companion, Ilsa Lund.

Much of the movie takes place at Rick's. In an early scene, the camera wanders around the dining room where people from all corners of the globe scheme to get to America. Rick, however, remains aloof. The ultimate cynic, he says more than once, "I stick my neck out for nobody." However, as his past is gradually revealed, it becomes clear that he has a strong record of active support for the principles of fairness and democracy. He is in Casablanca nursing a broken heart and hiding it with fake cynicism. Ilsa's sudden appearance brings all this to the surface and causes him to reminisce about their time in Paris as he drowns his sorrows in a bottle of whiskey.

Paris also has special significance as a setting for the movie. Named after the Greek hero who kidnapped Helen and started the Trojan War, the city has a vibrant romantic and artistic reputation. The German invaders were viewed as regimented, cruel, and inflexible. Their conquest of the city was as big a blow to its image as it was to its inhabitants and to others the world over who cherished the memory or the illusion of Paris.[65] Even before *Casablanca* reached movie theaters, *Lady Be Good,* a lighthearted romantic comedy from 1941, defined how the wider world viewed the German occupation of Paris when it showcased Ann Sothern singing "The Last Time I Saw Paris." The song celebrates the simple pleasures of the city—trees in spring, noisy taxicabs, lovers strolling the streets—and mourns the changes wrought by the war. It won an Academy Award for Best Song.

Casablanca is well known not only for its tragic love triangle and dramatic wartime plot, but also for its memorable dialogue. Lines from the movie are familiar sound bites more than 70 years after its original release. "Play it again, Sam," is perhaps the most famous line, although, ironically, no character says exactly that in the movie. "Here's looking at you, kid," is another common quote from the movie as is "I'm shocked, shocked" said in mock surprise, and the classic, "Of all of the gin joints in all the towns in all the world, she walks into mine." The movie's theme song, which originated in the 1931 Broadway musical, *Everybody's Welcome,* reassures listeners that whatever the future holds, all will be well "As Time Goes By." The song evidently struck a responsive chord with listeners in early 1943 because it went to the top of the music charts and stayed there for four weeks.[66]

The movie's setting was especially timely because Casablanca was one of three principal landing sites for the joint invasion of North Africa by the United States and Great Britain in November 1942. This operation represented America's first major offensive against the Germans. (The movie was released early to take advantage of the public's interest in the invasion.[67]) When French soldiers in Morocco failed to resist the invasion with what the Germans considered appropriate vigor—one French commander complained to the invading American soldiers, "You gentlemen are late"[68]—Germany assumed control of all of France and sent German troops to occupy and defend France's North African colonies as well.

Matters come to a head when Ilsa tries to force Rick to give her the letters of transit so that she and Laszlo can get to America. Complications arise and sacrifices have to be made. The image of Ingrid Bergman's face in the scene at the airport has become an iconic representation of anguished courage. Each character rises to the occasion in a conclusion that manages to be triumphant, hopeful, and heartbreaking all at the same time.

Suggested Discussion Questions

1. The opening scene involves a pickpocket and an arrest. What do these incidents demonstrate about Casablanca?
2. French text on a wall next to a portrait of Marshal Pétain reads, "I keep my promises, just as I keep those of others." Analyze its meaning in the context of the war in France. The police find an image of the Cross of Lorraine on a suspect. What did this represent during World War II? Who were the Maquis and what was their role in the French Resistance?

3. Analyze the conversations at Rick's at the start of the movie. What vision of America is reflected in the aspirations of these characters? Explain the predicament facing the young couple from Bulgaria. How is it resolved?

4. At the beginning of the movie, Rick adopts the attitude of a selfish cynic. Evaluate his views of the people at his café and also of people who are part of his personal life. Analyze Rick's relationship with Ugarte. Based on those he respects and those he rejects, is he selfish and cynical?

5. Renault and Yvonne are French citizens. Describe each one's attitude toward Rick and toward the Germans. France was criticized for not fighting harder against Germany. How do these roles reflect that criticism? Research the German invasion of France in 1940. Is the criticism fair?

6. Sam is played by African American Dooley Wilson. Describe his business and personal relationship with Rick. The role does not require that the actor be African American. Why would the director use Wilson for this role? Explain the deal that Rick cuts with Signor Ferrari (Sydney Greenstreet) regarding Sam. What does it show about Rick and Ferrari's attitudes toward Sam?

7. Explain the roles that Ilsa, Yvonne, and Annina Brandel, the young woman from Bulgaria, play in the movie. Is this an accurate reflection of the roles women played in World War II, or did they contribute in other ways? If so, why would the movie portray them this way?

8. Describe the conflict Ilsa faces. Is she to blame for what has happened, and if not, who is?

9. How does the restaurant crowd respond to "La Marseillaise?" How do the Germans respond? Why does Rick allow the band to play the song?

10. "As Time Goes By" became a big hit as a result of the movie. Research the lyrics. What message does it send about love? Why would it appeal to an audience during wartime?

11. How and why do Renault and Yvonne change by the end of the movie?

12. Research the extended list of actors in the movie and describe any ties they may have had to the war in Europe.

13. What was Victor Laszlo fighting for? What did Rick think of him? Explain Rick's behavior at the airport. Was it a surprise? Why, or why not? How might an American audience in 1942 respond to his actions?

14. Does the movie work as entertainment and propaganda, and if so, why?

The More the Merrier (1943)

(104 minutes) *Director:* George Stevens; *Stars:* Jean Arthur, Joel McCrea, Charles Coburn, Richard Gaines, Bruce Bennett, Ann Savage, Ann Doran, Frank Sully, Grady Sutton.

Changing conditions on the home front, especially those regarding gender relationships, set the stage for George Stevens's timely comedy *The More the Merrier*. The movie highlights the efforts of people eager to do their part for the war effort, an eagerness that sometimes created chaos and confusion even among those far from the battle.

On the frontlines, the Allied war effort was up and running by 1943. The United States had won the months-long battle for Guadalcanal in the Pacific. Along with the British they had taken North Africa and were poised to invade Italy in September. The Russians had defeated the Germans at Stalingrad and turned back a major German tank offensive at Kursk in August. On the home front, industry was operating in high gear, people were back at work, and the complexities of war production were gradually being overcome.

As new jobs opened up and men entered the military, employment opportunities for women expanded dramatically. Women went to work in great numbers and in all areas, including roughly 350,000 who entered the newly created Women's Army Corps and the WAVES (Women Accepted for Voluntary Emergency Service in the Navy).[69] By 1942 government planners realized that all traditional labor sources had been exhausted and shortages still existed. They would have to tap women for industrial work. Rosie the Riveter became the central figure in a public-relations campaign designed to attract women to jobs in defense plants.[70] The initial prejudices of employers and co-workers toward women on the job gradually dissipated as they discovered that women were eager to learn, often better at detail work than men, and usually more willing to ask about what they did not know.[71]

Employment opportunities for women were especially plentiful in Washington, D. C. The government grew exponentially in order to manage the war effort. In addition to expanding and training the armed forces, the United States had to produce its own machinery of war as well as continue to send aid to its British and Russian allies, who were in desperate need of food and military supplies. All of this required allocating American resources to various producers in an orderly fashion so that bullet makers, for example, received the necessary metals to fulfill their quotas, or orange growers were able to process and ship condensed juice to England, where it was needed to stave off scurvy among children.[72] Agencies sprang up in Washington to organize and coordinate American production across an array of industries and agricultural sectors. These new agencies needed to hire new workers, including secretaries, a job category usually filled by women.

Workers, male and female, arrived in Washington, D. C., by the trainload, 70,000 in the first year of the war alone.[73] They were certainly excited by the money they could make, but they were motivated by a determined patriotism as well. The sudden influx of new workers in the nation's capital, however, meant shortages in work space and rooms to rent. The housing situation was so dire that, in some cases, people shared rooms so that those who worked nights could alternate sleep shifts with those who worked days.[74]

In addition to overcrowding, the new agencies grew into a disorganized hodgepodge. In an effort to get things done, the government brought in "dollar a year" men. These men were skilled in a particular product or production method, and they were loaned to the government from private employers who continued to pay their salaries. They were fired up to get things done, but the bureaucracies that sprang up around them often impeded their efforts. Turf wars developed, the result of one person's belief that his particular responsibility was more important and more deserving of scarce resources than any other person's responsibility. It took genius, determination, and no small amount of guile to accomplish anything in such a complex mass of agencies, personalities, limited resources, and pressure to produce.[75]

The More the Merrier combines all these elements into a lighthearted screwball comedy. Connie Milligan (Jean Arthur) is an unmarried but long-engaged government employee. The plot is built around her earnest attempt to help alleviate the housing shortage in Washington by renting out half of her apartment to a suitable roommate. Mr. Benjamin Dingle (Charles Coburn, in an Academy Award–winning performance) has come to town to improve the efficiency of the war effort by building housing for newly arrived workers, but upon his arrival he can find no housing for himself. When he answers Connie's newspaper ad, she protests vehemently that she only intended to rent to a woman. He convinces her that because he is a retired gentleman, he is a much better choice for a roommate, and he describes all kinds of problems a woman roommate would present. Connie reluctantly accepts him on a trial basis. Although their cohabitation hits some snags the first morning, it appears as though they may be able to manage together. The real complication develops when Dingle rents half of his half of her apartment to Joe Carter (Joel McCrea), another recent arrival, who carries an airplane propeller on his shoulder and describes his place of employment as the "Tokyo Baby Carriage Corporation of Burbank, California," makers of "plain and fancy baby carriages for carrying babies to Tokyo."

Their crowded quarters are a perfect setup for comedy, which all three carry off with understated flair. Coburn is especially funny as a clever, seemingly daffy older man who consistently manages to get what he wants by indirect and occasionally dishonest means. His spunk and creativity offer wartime audiences comforting evidence that there are people in charge who can work with or around the system and get results. Because he is retired, he represents the possibility that everyone, including older Americans, can contribute to the war effort. And he is clearly thrifty, thereby alleviating the movie audience of any fears that he has gone to Washington simply to line his pockets. As

Dingle observes Connie with her cautious, uninspired fiancé, Mr. Charles J. Pendergast (Richard Gaines), he concludes that Pendergast is not the right man for her. He becomes convinced that Joe is, and he employs his formidable organizational skills and a good bit of subterfuge to redirect her affections

Joe Carter is plainspoken and forthright, even though he never reveals the exact nature of his military assignment. He is smart, handsome, polite within reason, and somewhat silly—in short, a very likable fellow. He is also a decent guy. When Dingle finds and reads Connie's diary, Joe warns him not to do it. As Dingle reads it out loud, Joe continues to oppose the idea. When Connie discovers them, she is deeply hurt and orders them both to leave. Dingle writes a sincere letter of apology completely absolving Joe of any responsibility for the diary incident, and Joe gives Connie an elegant traveling case with lots of clever cosmetic compartments to make amends, "no strings attached." Connie relents and allows Joe to stay in her apartment for two more days before he must leave for his assignment overseas.

Connie Milligan is the heart of the picture, an uncertain and divided heart. Jean Arthur won an Academy Award nomination as Best Actress for her portrayal of Connie as a determined, competent working woman and also as a confused, love-struck young girl unable to decide between two suitors. When Dingle and Joe meet Connie and Pendergast at a restaurant, Dingle decides to take action. Behaving like a portly, jovial fairy godfather, he steps in and cleverly rearranges everyone's plans.

Although the story is set in Washington, it is reflective of the kinds of attitudes and adjustments people all across the country were experiencing. Audiences could readily relate to the scene at the restaurant and the scenes immediately before and after it. Connie's teenage neighbor, Morton (Stanley Clements), is a thoughtful but not terribly mature young man. When he sees Joe peering out a window with a pair of binoculars, he is quickly overcome by patriotic zeal and enemy phobia and rushes off to report this perceived security threat. The bartender and band members at the restaurant are all female, evidence of the widespread need to employ women in jobs usually filled by men. Connie's girlfriends are aggressively friendly toward Joe, which further demonstrates how the scarcity of men affected traditional gender roles. When Connie and Joe return from the restaurant, they nearly stumble over couples embracing along the sidewalk, the result of the housing shortage coupled with the natural interests of young men and women in war or peace.

A cascade of complications flows from the restaurant meeting. As everything begins to unravel, Dingle keeps his eye on the goal and sticks to his standard approach to solving problems: "Damn the torpedoes, full speed ahead." Prepared for all exigencies and always one step ahead of the next problem, Dingle exhibits the perfect management style, "hot or cold," in a crisis.

Suggested Discussion Questions

1. Explain the tone of the movie's opening sequence. How has the war changed Washington? What do these changes reflect about the country's response to the war?

2. How does Mr. Dingle manage to rent the apartment? What does this suggest about his character?

3. Describe the movie's presentation of the effects of the war on gender roles. How does Connie reflect these changes? In what ways, if any, does she reflect traditional gender roles and behaviors?

4. Describe the dress that Connie wears to the restaurant. Is it appropriate attire for that kind of date? Why would she wear it? How is Joe dressed?

5. Once the United States entered the war, the government had to manage the economy so that essential products would get produced in a timely manner. But the federal government had never undertaken such a huge task. Based just on evidence from the movie, how is it doing? Research the government's role in the economy during the war. Should the government have controlled production more or less tightly? Should it have tried to control it at all?

6. How do Connie and Pendergast react when they discover that the other man in the cab is a reporter? What threat does he present? Describe Dingle's plan to solve this problem.

7. Compare and contrast Joe Carter and Charles Pendergast. How does each one view Connie? How does each one treat her? Depending on whom she marries, is either one likely to encourage Connie to continue working after the war?

8. How does Connie imagine her life after the war ends? Is she likely to want to continue working? How does Joe's attitude toward her change after they are married?

9. The entire movie takes place over a few days. Quick marriages were not uncommon during the war. Should Connie and Joe and others like them wait until the war ends to get married? Why, or why not?

10. Attitudes toward sex and gender have changed a great deal since the 1940s. How would minor plot elements probably be different in a movie with the same basic story as *The More the Merrier* that is set in the present? How would Connie and Joe be different? (For comparison, see *The More the Merrier*'s 1966 remake, *Walk, Don't Run*.)

11. Mr. Dingle keeps singing a song that features a quote from Admiral David Farragut, "Damn the torpedoes. Full speed ahead!" Review the song lyrics and the original quote. Explain possible reasons why the director would use this song and quote in the movie.

Rome, Open City (1945)

(*Roma, Citta Aperta:* Italian, 105 minutes) *Director:* Roberto Rossellini; *Stars:* Aldo Fabrizi, Anna Magnani, Marcello Pagliero, Harry Feist, Maria Michi, Francesco Grandjacquet, Vito Annichiarico, Joop van Hulzen.

Rome, Open City gave American audiences an opportunity to view World War II through the eyes of people caught in a complicated political and moral environment. Roberto Rossellini's dramatic tale was released the year the war ended. It emphasizes the desperation, hard choices, and sometimes brutal outcomes of daily life in occupied Rome.

Adolf Hitler and Benito Mussolini had agreed to an alliance at the start of World War II. Along with Japan, they formed the Axis powers. When German defeats began to pile up in 1943, this partnership became harder for the Italian people to support. Shortly before British and American troops began their invasion of Italy in September 1943, Mussolini was driven out of office and imprisoned by the Italian government in a remote mountain resort. Once Mussolini was out of power, Italy began to waver in its support for the Axis war effort, which presented Hitler with a serious strategic problem. If Italy pulled out of the war, there would be no Italian army to stop the Allies from marching up the Italian peninsula and attacking Germany from the south. Hitler's solution was to have German troops enter Italy and defend it against the Allied invasion. These developments put the Italian government under a great deal of pressure. King Victor Emmanuel III gave Germany assurances that Italy would continue to fight at the same time that Italy's new government was negotiating an armistice with the Allies. On September 8, 1943, as German troops flooded into the country from the north, Italy surrendered to the Allies.[76]

If Mussolini's imprisonment had complicated Italy's official response to the Germans who were arriving in the north just as the Allies were landing in the south, his rescue on September 12 by German paratroopers complicated them even more. Hitler wanted Mussolini in power, but Rome was no longer an option, so he declared Mussolini head of the Salò Republic, a puppet regime headquartered in a small northern Italian town. Not surprisingly, this new government was short lived.[77]

The Germans quickly established their control over most of the Italian peninsula, and they did not extend any gentleness to the citizens of their former ally. In some ways the Italians were treated even more harshly than the citizens of other countries Germany had occupied. The Germans could understand the opposition they faced in conquered countries. But Italy was an ally who had abandoned them, and they could not forgive this betrayal.[78] Their harsh measures invigorated the Italian resistance movement, in particular the Italian Communists, who had their own issues with the Nazis.[79] Therefore, a limited list of the different groups fighting in Italy after September 1943 included American and British troops, the German army, Italian fascists who supported Mussolini, and Italian Communists who opposed him and the Nazis who were keeping him in power. Many Italians were caught in the middle of all of these forces. As the war raged around them, they often had to choose sides. Some chose based on principle; others took easy or opportunistic paths.

The chaos in Italy presented other serious complications as well. Fierce fighting threatened Rome, the Eternal City, site of the historic ruins of the Roman Empire and of the Vatican with all its history, splendor, and worldwide spiritual significance. As Allied forces slowly fought their way up the Italian peninsula, Rome was declared an "open city." In the terminology of warfare, an "open city" will not be defended against an attacking force with the expectation that the attackers will spare the city and its civilian population from destruction. But the term also has other connotations. It implies a political void. If no one will defend the city, does that make all choices equal? Although the Germans were clearly losing ground to the Allies by late 1943, that alone did not guarantee their defeat. Opposition by Italian partisans could hasten the German defeat, but until Allied troops reached Rome, the city would be run by its German occupiers. Anyone who opposed them did so at great risk.

Rome, Open City focuses on the varied ways in which an extended family and their friends navigate Rome's uncertain political and moral terrain. Giorgio Manfredi (Marcello Pagliero) is a resistance fighter who is being pursued by the Germans. He turns up at the home of Pina (Anna Magnani) looking for his friend, Pina's fiancé, Francesco (Francesco Grandjacquet). Giorgio needs Francesco's help to get out of town. Pina lets him in, and sends her son, Marcello (Vito Annichiarico), to let the local priest know of Giorgio's situation while they wait for Francesco's return. The priest, Don Pietro Pellegrini (Aldo Fabrizi), is officially neutral in the war, but he secretly supports the resistance.

The Germans have good information on Giorgio's whereabouts, which they get from his girlfriend, Marina (Maria Michi), a nightclub singer and drug addict who appreciates the better things in life. These become easier for her to come by after she is befriended by Ingrid (Giovanna Galletti), a German staff member who offers Marina favors in exchange for her betrayal of Giorgio. The official Nazi policy defines homosexuality as perversion, and homosexuals were among the groups condemned to concentration camps. Therefore, the scenes between these two women, which imply homosexuality, and the scenes involving Marina and the drugs Ingrid gets for her are designed to demonstrate the depravity at the core of the Nazis' efforts to achieve their goals.

The audience's attention is also directed toward another German, Captain Hartmann (Joop van Hulzen), who criticizes the Nazi war effort. He proclaims drunkenly, "We have sown Europe with corpses ... and from those graves rises an incredible hate, hate, everywhere hate! We are being consumed by hatred." Hartmann's views are representative of the views of some members of the German military. During the war years, one of the few serious internal efforts to rid Germany of Hitler arose in the German military. There were other groups who hoped to drive Hitler out of power from within, but only the organized efforts of the military had any real chance of success.[80] Ultimately, none of these efforts succeeded.

Hartmann's comments also reflect Germany's professional military tradition (as do Captain von Rauffenstein's in *Grand Illusion*), a tradition that was at odds with Hitler's criminal version of warfare. Senior military leaders voiced concerns early in the war that what they were being ordered to do was not warfare but murder, for which they might later be held accountable.[81] After he received instructions for the brutal treatment of Russian prisoners of war in 1941, Major-General Henning von Treskow described the ramifications of Hitler's orders. Treskow, who became one of the leaders of the July 1944 assassination attempt on Hitler, told another officer that the "guilt would fall on the Germans for a hundred years 'and not just on Hitler alone, but on you and me, your wife and mine, your children and my children, the woman crossing the road now, and the boy playing with a ball over there.'"[82]

The movie presents some challenges for contemporary viewers that Italian audiences at the time would not have faced. It does not clearly identify many of the groups who were fighting each other in Italy, even though they are important to the plot. Giorgio is a leader of the National Liberation Committee, an organization with ties to Communism that was fighting an underground campaign against the German occupiers. As a Catholic priest, Don Pietro should be the natural enemy of Communism, which opposes any form of religion, but he offers to help Giorgio. The movie includes references to "Badoglio's men." Pietro Badoglio replaced Mussolini as the leader of the Italian government and negotiated Italy's surrender to the Allies. As the Germans approached Rome on September 8, Badoglio and members of the Italian royal family escaped the city and established a government at Brindisi, a seaport in southern Italy controlled by the Allies.[83] Because the Germans controlled Rome, however, Italian soldiers there are still treated as part of the Axis alliance, and they help German soldiers search Pina's apartment building for Giorgio.

An Austrian deserter from the battle at Monte Cassino also seeks help from Don Pietro. His arrival further complicates the fluid situation as Pina and Francesco's wedding day arrives. There is a bit of comic relief between Don Pietro and Marcello. But the movie quickly takes a tragic turn, and Francesco joins Giorgio as they hide from their Nazi pursuers. Major

Bergmann (Harry Feist), the sadistic German who leads the search for Giorgio, blindly follows Nazi ideology. The major's office connects to a torture chamber, and he occasionally complains because he can hear the screams of his victims. Ingrid is his assistant, and she is his equal in corruption and criminality, especially when it comes to the addicted, cooperative Marina.

When the Germans do capture Girogio and Don Pietro, they pick up the newly arrived Austrian as well. The three are taken to German headquarters where they know they will be tortured. Each one faces his fate with as much courage as he can manage.

Suggested Discussion Questions

1. How do the police sergeant and the sexton react during the bread riot at the beginning of the movie? Are their actions ethical, appropriate, or understandable? How do they react to news of the Americans who have invaded their country?

2. How do the local children respond to the German occupation? What is Romoletto doing? What are the results of their actions? Were their actions helpful or harmful?

3. Describe the relationship between Marcello and Francesco. Why does Francesco, who is not a practicing Catholic, want their marriage to be performed by a priest rather than at City Hall?

4. Describe the living conditions for Pina, her sister, and the others in their apartment. Why is Lauretta disliked? How does Pina feel toward her sister?

5. Explain the role that food plays in the plot. Analyze the scene at the restaurant with the sheep. Why include it? How could it be interpreted as a visual metaphor?

6. War can be dangerous and threatening even for those who are not in combat. Using examples from the movie, what difficulties do ordinary Italians face even though they are not under attack? Some characters make bad choices. What better choices could they have made? How could they have avoided making complicated choices?

7. Many of the characters must deal with ethical dilemmas. Based on how they respond to their circumstances, analyze the ethics of Pina, Lauretta, and Marina. Are Lauretta or Marina in any way to blame for what happens to Pina, and if so, why?

8. Why does Major Bergmann believe that Giorgio will talk if he is tortured? Explain Bergmann's logic. What happens to the philosophical basis for the superiority of the Third Reich if Giorgio does not talk?

9. How do the Germans react when Don Pietro curses them? Why would they care?

10. There are three speeches in the movie in which characters express their view of what is happening around them. Francesco encourages Pina to look to the future with hope, Captain Hartmann excoriates Major Bergmann for the crimes of Germany, and Don Pietro curses the Germans for what they have done to Giorgio. Do any of these men live up to the standards they have defined for themselves and, if so, how? If not, why not?

11. In the final scene, Captain Hartmann commands a firing squad. Explain the squad's behavior and Hartmann's response. Why would Rossellini include children in that scene?

12. How different are the goals of the Communists within Italy from the goals of the American and British forces during the war? Once the war ends, if Germany is defeated, what will the politics of Italy be like? Why would a Catholic priest assist a Communist?

13. *Rome, Open City* is considered the first example of the Italian Realist style of moviemaking. Analyze the movie's "look" and storyline, the style of acting, and the depiction of children. How do they compare with Hollywood productions that were made during the same time period? Research how the movie was filmed. Do the times in which it was produced appear to have any connection to its style and, if so, how?

14. What will become of Marcello? Why will this matter to America?

Postwar Era Movies

The Best Years of Our Lives (1946)

(168 minutes) *Director:* William Wyler; *Stars:* Myrna Loy, Fredric March, Dana Andrews, Teresa Wright, Harold Russell, Virginia Mayo, Cathy O'Donnell, Hoagy Carmichael, Michael Hall.

Americans greeted the end of World War II with jubilation. The war was finally over, and millions of men would be coming home. But as they returned from late 1945 through 1946, many men had to confront unexpected changes, and they had to adjust in ways they had not anticipated. *The Best Years of Our Lives,* released in 1946, brings into sharp focus the post-war problems faced by returning G.I.'s and their families.

Nearly ten million men had been drafted during the war years, more than seven million of them from 1941 to 1943.[84] These figures do not include enlistees who made up the rest of the 15,500,000 American military personnel who fought in World War II. Those who entered the military at the start of the war could have spent nearly five years away from their homes. They may have gotten furloughs, but those brief interludes were often filled with artificial activities that would offer little opportunity to assess the significance of changes on the home front. Changes in the lives of their communities may have been obvious, such as a new factory or more vigorous agricultural production. But the deeper effects of these developments would not be easy to discern in a brief visit.

The changes in women's lives were especially relevant. Women had stepped into new roles with enthusiasm during the war. Many entered the workforce and were able to earn enough money to support themselves on their own, occasionally in a style greater than they had ever imagined possible.[85] But once the war ended and the economy contracted most women lost those jobs, and when the jobs returned, companies hired men to fill them.[86]

The men who returned home had changed, too. In some instances the changes were obvious. Men who suffered lost limbs, blindness, or disfiguring injuries had little hope of stepping effortlessly back into their former lives. But many men changed in less obvious ways. The structure of pre-war society usually limited people to lives lived within the expected norms of their communities. Children often followed their parents into the jobs that were available in local economies, such as mining or the local factory. It was difficult to avoid these patterns because options were so few, especially during the Depression. People may have had dreams for the future, but the reality of the Depression years left many with no opportunity to pursue them.

The war altered this construct in multiple ways. Men who entered the military and who may have had limited social contacts beyond their neighborhoods or workplaces were suddenly required to cooperate with a wide range of unfamiliar types, and do so quickly and effectively. For many, this process would erode the prejudices they had learned at home, and, as a consequence, prompt them to question other accepted truths as well.[87] In the event of combat casualties, they may have had to take on responsibilities above their rank.[88] They may have seen the undeserving promoted or the deserving unfairly denied.[89] Watching the lives of so many men end too soon may have made returning veterans eager to take a chance on their dreams. They had been changed by the war, and they had to determine who they were and what they were they going to do with their lives now that it was over. *The Best Years of Our Lives,* William Wyler's tribute to returning veterans and the women who waited for them, offers no easy answers. Instead, the movie demonstrates that no matter what their pre-war circumstances were or how bravely they had served, every veteran could expect to face complications and adjustments when he returned home.

The movie focuses on three men who had just been released from the military. Fred Derry, Al Stephenson, and Homer Parrish meet on the plane that is taking them all home to Boone City. Fred (Dana Andrews) had been employed at a soda fountain before the war. During the war, he flew bombers and won a Distinguished Flying Cross for heroism. Al (Fredric March, in an Academy Award-winning performance) was a banker with a banker's mindset and a loving family before he served in combat in the Pacific. He is enthusiastically welcomed home by his family and rehired by his old employer, both of whom expect the same old Al back on the job. Homer (Harold Russell), a local high school football hero, returns maimed by the war. He appears casual about his injuries and confidently assures the others that he is able to deal with them. It soon becomes obvious, however, that he cannot deal with other people's reactions to them, in particular those of his fiancée, Wilma (Cathy O'Donnell).

Early in the movie a long sequence observes each man as he returns to his family. Fred and Al watch from their cab as Homer reluctantly steps out to greet family members. His parents try to make his return joyful, but they are seeing his injuries for the first time and are clearly stunned by the reality. The cab stops next at Al's apartment building. He, too, has trouble getting out, and comments, "It feels as if I were going to hit a beach." Fred encourages him, and the camera follows Al to his apartment. He greets his two children silently, hoping to surprise his wife, Millie (Myrna Loy). From another room she suddenly realizes who is at the door. The camera catches all four in a long shot down a hallway as Al and Millie embrace. For both these men their joy at being home is undercut by awkward reunions. Homer sees pity and uncertainty in the welcome he receives from his family and Wilma. Al has trouble reconnecting with Millie and his grown children, Peggy (Teresa Wright) and Rob (Michael Hall). At one point he attempts to show his son some of his souvenirs, but Rob would rather discuss the controversy over the use of the atomic bomb. Al is surprised and dismayed by Rob's attitude because the decision to use the bomb ended the war, which made it possible for Al and millions of other soldiers to return home rather than participate in an invasion of the heavily fortified Japanese mainland.

Fred has achieved the highest military rank of the three, but he returns to the least respectable dwelling, a shack where he greets his father and stepmother in another awkward reunion. They explain to him that his wife, Marie (Virginia Mayo), has moved out so she can get to work easier, news they did not tell him before so as not to worry him. Fred learns that Marie has a job in a nightclub. His father and stepmother do not know the name of the club, but they reassure him they have sent her all his letters and "allotment checks."

A 1946 audience would have understood the meaning behind the phrase "allotment checks." It referred to money paid by the government to the dependents of servicemen. Dependents were also entitled to a $10,000 insurance policy issued by the government and payable in the event of death. These financial inducements caused some women—dubbed "Allotment Annies"—to pursue quick marriages to servicemen. Soldiers heading into battle were especially vulnerable and sometimes found themselves married to women they only knew briefly. Such quickie marriages could become a lucrative career for women who were conniving enough to marry more than one man at a time. Some women even specialized in pilots because they had a higher mortality rate than other branches of the military.[90]

The first night home is not easy for Fred, Al, or Homer. Unable to settle comfortably back into home life, all three men wind up at the same bar. Homer is avoiding his family, Al has brought Millie and grown daughter Peggy out to celebrate, and Fred is looking for Marie. The men's newfound friendship and common bond set the course for the rest of their lives. Each one encounters difficulties as he tries to resume his old life or decides to gamble on some new, uncertain future. Homer struggles to reconcile his loss and his love for Wilma with the love (or perhaps the pity) she feels for him. Based on his experiences on the battlefield, Al has an expanded vision of what men can be trusted to accomplish, in particular, men who do not have easy access to the bank credit that is readily available to the middle class. But his boss wants him to take a cautious approach to granting loans. Al must decide if the new times can accommodate new principles in banking, or if he can accommodate the old ones. Fred has to come to terms with his wife, a woman he knew for less than twenty days before he went overseas, and his growing attraction to Peggy.

The movie offers some very accurate indicators of the changing times in post–World War II America. Fred's former drugstore has adopted new sales techniques to encourage the enthusiasm of the emerging consumer culture. Marie gives up a job she likes to become a housewife again, but Fred's failure to find a job creates friction between them. He has not turned out to be the provider she was counting on, and her work experience has given her the confidence to consider making it on her own. Al's children have drifted away from him and demonstrate by their actions that they are not really all that interested in the wisdom of the older generation, no matter how hard won it may be, a trend that will only accelerate among young people during the 1950s.

The quality of the acting and the look of the movie have drawn much critical praise. In addition to the great onscreen chemistry between audience favorites Myrna Loy and Fredric March, newcomer Harold Russell contributes a wonderful and very natural performance. Russell was not a professional actor, but the injuries he sustained and his courage in facing them made him a good fit for the role of Homer and a great role model for other injured veterans. Russell earned two Academy Awards, one for Best Supporting Actor and one honorary award for his performance. Celebrated cinematographer Gregg

Toland used a technique called "deep focus" to keep near and far objects visible in long shots. This view added emotional resonance to scenes such as Millie and Al's reunion and Fred's phone call to Peggy. The great songwriter Hoagy Carmichael played Homer's uncle Butch, and his musical performances in the movie were another bonus for moviegoers. *The Best Years of Our Lives* was nominated for eight Academy Awards. It won for Best Picture and in six other categories, plus Russell's honorary award.

The men struggle and stumble as they try to resolve the issues they face. The movie sends the message to returning veterans that, just as in combat, they will have to retreat or move forward and accept the consequences of either choice. Homer's confusion over whether to marry Wilma, Al's drinking and work concerns, and Fred's troubled marriage are the final battles they must overcome before each is truly home.

Suggested Discussion Questions

1. Recall images of life in America during the Depression and compare them to the images that greet Al, Fred, and Homer as they ride through town in the cab. Aside from the war itself, how had America changed by 1945, and how do the men respond to what they see?

2. Explain the positives and negatives in each homecoming scene. In what ways, if any, are the men themselves to blame for any awkwardness? How are their families to blame?

3. What motivates the conversation Wilma's father has with Homer about Homer's employment prospects? How do Al and Fred react to Homer's injuries? How does Homer's sister, Luella, respond to him? How does Homer respond to them?

4. As they dance together on his first night home, Al speaks about his "wife" to Millie as if she were someone else. Explain Millie's reaction. Why would Wyler include a scene like this?

5. Describe examples from the movie of people who did not support the war or do not respect the service that these men have given. Offer some possible reasons for their attitudes. What do their reactions suggest about the international political situation at that time?

6. Is Marie to blame for the lack of compatibility between her and Fred? Is Fred? How would an audience of returning servicemen and their wives (or servicewomen and their husbands, a much smaller group) probably react to the Fred-Marie-Peggy plotline?

7. Analyze the kinds of difficulties that Fred and Al have as they try to return to work. In each case, who is at fault? What does each man want for his future? Support your answer with incidents or comments from the movie.

8. Are couples Homer and Wilma and Al and Millie going to make it? Defend your answer.

9. His father does not see the citation for Fred's medal until just before Fred leaves town. Why does Fred not show off his medals or do more bragging about them?

10. The field of airplanes appears in the movie twice and can be viewed as a metaphor for America's production of materiel and servicemen and the end of the war. They are no longer needed. Why does Fred climb into the airplane? How did you expect that scene to end?

11. How do Marie, Millie, Wilma, and Peggy react as the men attempt to adjust to society? Were there other things they could have done when the men first came home that would have made their returns go more smoothly? Was Peggy's behavior ethical? How much blame do Fred, Al, and Homer share for the complications they face in their personal lives?

12. The 1950s and 1960s were a period of economic expansion for America, but in 1946 no one could know for sure what was coming. Based on how the movie portrays life in postwar America, how hopeful should Fred be about his future?

13. Research the G.I. Bill. How could it affect the future of all three men?

14. Extend the storylines for all three couples through the next two decades and incorporate historically accurate events. What might their futures be like?

15. Why would William Wyler put the phrase, "the best years of our lives," the movie's title, in the speech by Marie? Try to imagine how he intended the audience to interpret it. Were they the best years of any of the characters' lives?

Bicycle Thieves (1948)

(*Ladri di Biciclette;* Italian, 90 minutes) *Director:* Vittorio De Sica; *Stars:* Lamberto Maggiorani, Enzo Staiola, Lianella Carell, Gino Saltamerenda, Vittorio Antonucci[91]

Italian director Vittorio De Sica's *Bicycle Thieves* (released in the U.S. as *The Bicycle Thief*) captures the despair of ordinary people and everyday life in postwar Italy. It also illustrates the complications faced by American policy makers after the war ended. Europe had been devastated by the war, and the Soviet Union was eager to move in and pick up the pieces. Before the war, the Soviets had been able to influence the rise of Communist parties in various European countries. After the war, Europe's ruined economies and smashed cities offered ample opportunities to promote Communism as the best way to rebuild. The Soviets understood that they could not take Europe by force, but they might be able to win control through the ballot box in France, Italy, and other countries. The defense of democracy was a fundamental component of America's participation in the war, and to have it benefit the Communists after such great effort and cost was a painful irony.

In the first few years immediately after the war, the United States, Great Britain, and the Soviet Union were positioning themselves within Europe's new geopolitical framework. Some issues were already settled. Germany's immediate political future had been decided at the Yalta Conference in February 1945 as was the basic outline for German reparations, much of which would go to the Soviets. In addition, a process had been adopted to ensure free elections in Poland. But other political outcomes were still in flux, including which political parties would replace the Nazi puppet governments from the war years. The economic problems facing Europe made the Communist Party's position on jobs and the redistribution of wealth appealing to desperate voters in many countries. By 1946, to the dismay of the Truman administration, the Communists were the strongest political parties in France and Italy, and there was a possibility that one or both could be elected to form ruling governments.[92]

In addition, the Soviet Union quickly indicated it would not abide by the Yalta agreements and stand back while each country sorted out its political future on its own. For example, the Soviets orchestrated a *coup d'etat* in Romania once the war ended, and ignored the decisions for free elections in Poland. The Russians refused to include the Polish government-in-exile (then headquartered in London) in Poland's elections. Instead, they conspired to bring a Communist government into power there.[93]

If America simply stood by and did nothing about the volatile political situation in postwar Europe, Communism might well spread across the continent. With the stakes so high, the United States was determined to use its influence to affect outcomes. The question for the Truman administration was how to do it. America had already been drawn directly into postwar European matters by Great Britain, whose dire financial condition undermined her ability to maintain her interests in the Mediterranean. In early 1947, the British requested that America defend and support Greece and Turkey to the tune of $400 million.[94] That same year, American diplomat and Russian expert George F. Kennan proposed a policy of "containment." The central component of the policy was that the United States should seek to counter Soviet expansionism anywhere in the world.[95]

The Truman Doctrine evolved out of these and other factors. Truman declared that America's policy would be to support people who were trying to resist "subjugation by armed minorities or outside pressures."[96] Such activist involvement was new territory for America, but President Truman believed it was necessary. The United States began pumping money covertly into foreign elections. The Italian Communists, for example, were defeated in elections in April 1948 partly because of the financial aid America gave their political rivals.[97]

Bicycle Thieves is a vivid microcosm of the troubling political and economic issues threatening Europe in the years immediately after World War II. The movie opens in a rundown area of Rome where a crowd of men wait for a clerk to hand out work slips. On this particular day only a few are called up. One of them, Antonio (Lamberto Maggiorani), receives a job assignment that requires a bicycle. When he explains that his is broken, the clerk starts to take the assignment back. Antonio hurriedly says he can get a bicycle. In reality, Antonio's bicycle is not broken, it is in hock. When he explains his rotten luck to his wife, Maria (Lianella Carell), she pawns their sheets, a treasured wedding gift, to get it back. The next morning, Antonio drops their young son, Bruno (Enzo Staiola), off at work and sets out on the bicycle to his new job. The bicycle is soon stolen by a gang working together, including one man who misdirects Antonio as he tries to pursue the thief. Antonio is frantic and reports the loss to the police. At the end of the day, he picks up Bruno and heads home without the bicycle. Later that evening he enlists an actor friend, Baiocco (Gino Saltamerenda), to help him search for it.

The heart of the movie takes place the next day. Antonio and Bruno search ever-more desperately for the stolen bicycle. Baiocco and two other men help them hunt through the crowded outdoor market where hundreds of bicycles and bicycle parts are for sale. Father and son follow clues that lead them to a church-run soup kitchen and a brothel. Antonio is alternately determined, distraught, belligerent, and overwhelmed by what he discovers.

Although the movie never makes an overt argument for Communism, it paints a bleak picture of the difficulties faced by the common man. Antonio's struggle is set within a broader context that demonstrates that nothing can be done to solve his problem. Some of the people Antonio turns to make an honest effort to help him. Others are unwilling, unable, or corrupt. His friends cannot find the bicycle. The police do nothing other than require him to file paperwork, which will matter only if the bicycle is found. The Church offers help in return for attendance at Mass. The only real help comes from his young son, Bruno, whom he treats as a child, a companion, and an assistant. When father and son eat at a restaurant, Antonio treats him to wine and says they can do anything they want because "we're both men." Antonio tries to remain cheerful but soon confesses to his son that he fears they will starve if they do not find the bicycle.

The movie is about Antonio's desperate efforts to find the bicycle he needs for his job, but the search proves impossible because forces outside his control—a disorganized and insufficient work economy, thieves, ineffectual police, an ineffectual Church, and people who are even poorer than Antonio—have clearly overwhelmed all of society except the rich. De Sica's powerful movie is an excellent example of the Italian Realist style of moviemaking. (See also *Rome, Open City*.) *Bicycle Thieves* won numerous awards in 1949 and 1950, including awards from the American Academy of Motion Picture Arts and Sciences, the Golden Globes, the National Board of Review, and the New York Film Critics for best foreign film. It also garnered recognition in other national film competitions and won six awards from the Italian film journalists' competition. *Bicycle Thieves* frequently appears on "ten best" lists compiled by movie critics.

When at last Antonio finds a real clue, it leads to people who are even poorer than he is. This circle of hopelessness creates a sense that there can be no solution, that the present system is broken and cannot be fixed. Desperate and defeated, Antonio takes matters into his own hands. Bruno, who has been his aide and his conscience, must now be his protector. The movie's grim ending does not offer much hope for their future happiness.

Suggested Discussion Questions

1. Based on images in the movie, how well is the Italian economy functioning? What kinds of work and workers does the movie show? What complaints do the workers express to the clerk at the employment agency who gives Antonio his job?

2. Describe the relationship between Antonio and Maria. Are they a happy couple? What is the effect of the scene when Maria pawns their sheets?

3. How old is Bruno? How old does he act? How does Antonio treat him? Is his treatment of Bruno consistent? Is it fair?

4. Describe the group that organized the theft of the bicycle. Try to identify the roles that various members perform during the theft. Was there anything Antonio could have done to prevent the theft of the bicycle? Analyze the bicycle market. Where have all those bicycles and bicycle parts come from?

5. How is religion depicted in the movie? Does it offer Antonio any assistance? If so, is it effective?

6. How does the movie present the wealthy?

7. Some of the people in the movie who are in positions of authority are presented as helpless or corrupt. Give examples and discuss why this might be the case. Do any of them offer Antonio any real help?

8. After Antonio catches the old man at the mission, he gets away. Explain the implication behind Bruno's comment, "Why did you let him go for the soup?" Why does Antonio hit Bruno?

9. During the meal they share at the restaurant, Antonio is cheerful and

then depressed. Should he have told Bruno that if they do not find the bicycle, they might starve? Why would he say this to his young son? How does Bruno react?

10. Describe the bicycle thief. Describe the response of the thief's neighbors and mother when Antonio shows up with a policeman to search for the bicycle. How does the thief's mother differ from Maria? Who is more desperate, Antonio or the thief?

11. How does Antonio change as the story goes on? Why? What does his change suggest about the future of Italy? After the war, other countries suffered the same kinds of economic problems that Italy suffered. How do these problems present a challenge to democracy? What kind of help did Antonio and, by extension, all the other poor throughout Europe need?

12. How did the many different factions within Italy during and after the war complicate relations with the United States? What was the likelihood that Italian Communists would be able to operate independently of the Soviet Union? Analyze how Communism and Italy's Catholic tradition would have coexisted.

13. What will Bruno's future be like and how will that affect the politics of Europe and relations with the United States?

14. Explain the Marshall Plan. Was it an unselfish act? Defend your answer.

The Third Man (1949)

(British, 104 minutes; American version, 93 minutes) *Director:* Carol Reed; *Stars:* Joseph Cotten, Alida Valli, Orson Welles, Trevor Howard, Bernard Lee, Wilfred Hyde-White.

In February 1945 the Yalta Conference brought the Big Three—Franklin Roosevelt, Winston Churchill, and Joseph Stalin—together for the last time. Roosevelt died two months later, and the British people voted Churchill out of office in July. But at Yalta the three leaders of the Allied powers were still very much in charge as they negotiated the fate of much of the world. *The Third Man,* Carol Reed's *film noir* vision of how their decisions affected millions of refugees, revolves around a charming opportunist whose crimes made the already-desperate circumstances faced by so many people in post-war Europe so much worse.

The Yalta agreements returned Germany to its traditional borders and stripped it of much of its wealth, partly to repay Russian demands for reparations. In addition, the Big Three agreed to establish boundaries for disputed territories, support democratically elected governments to replace Nazi-occupation governments, and return refugees to their homelands. Once the war ended, Germany would be divided temporarily into three zones of occupation overseen by Britain, the United States, and the Soviet Union. (France joined this arrangement by taking over territory carved out of the American zone.) Vienna and Berlin would also be divided into the same zones of occupation. The forces that jointly controlled these cities were to work together to keep the peace and sort out political and civilian issues.

On the surface, these aims seem reasonable, although challenging. But buried within them were the realities of life for millions of refugees who found themselves shunted around Europe to satisfy the demands of the Yalta agreements and later decisions made by the allies at the Potsdam Conference in July 1945.[98] Further complicating matters, the destruction of much of Europe's infrastructure and agricultural productivity made it difficult to house, feed, and provide medical aid to war-weary populations.

Other factors added to post-war Europe's despair and heartbreak. The dangers and strains of combat sometimes generated unacceptable behavior among troops who came into contact with civilian populations. In an effort to mitigate these abuses, the United States military instituted a policy of non-fraternization between American troops and civilians. (In 1942, General George S. Patton firmly reinforced this policy by warning soldiers heading to North Africa that he would shoot any American soldier who molested a Moroccan woman.)[99] These efforts to maintain appropriate relationships between soldiers and civilians paid off, and Americans were routinely welcomed as forces for civil order as they expanded their control throughout Europe.[100]

The Soviet military often did not abide by similar standards. In retaliation for the German invasion of Russia and the atrocities committed by German troops, Russian soldiers extracted a terrible revenge on the civilians they encountered. By the end of the war, Soviet troops had control of most of Eastern Europe, including Austria and Germany up to the Elbe River, which the Yalta agreements established as the western boundary of the Soviet army's advance. Available statistics suggest that 1,400,000 rapes occurred in the German territories of Pomerania, Silesia, and East Prussia alone.[101] These figures do not include other territories under Soviet military control. In addition, looting was rampant. The Soviets were determined to pillage the territories they occupied of any equipment or resources that would benefit their own industrial reconstruction.[102]

The post-war wreckage and chaos were disastrous for many, but they represented opportunity for some. Scarce goods could be had and sold if the profiteers were clever and careful to avoid the authorities. Because practically everything was scarce and the authorities were often preoccupied with more pressing problems such as feeding, relocating, and reorganizing the people in their charge, black markets emerged for many items.

British author Graham Greene distilled this grim sludge of depravity, despair, and opportunism into his screenplay for *The Third Man*. The movie presents a bleak vision of post-war Vienna where there are no real heroes, only an array of desperate characters confronting hard choices. Holly Martins (Joseph Cotten), an American writer of pulp Western novels, has traveled to Vienna at the invitation of his long-time friend Harry Lime (Orson Welles). Lime has promised him a business opportunity, but when Martins arrives he learns that Harry has been struck by a car and killed. He rushes off to his old friend's funeral, where he observes only a few mourners, among them a beautiful woman.

From a distance, British Major Calloway (Trevor Howard) also watches the funeral. When it is over, he strikes up a conversation with Martins and offers him a ride and a drink. At the bar Martins rambles on about what a good friend Harry Lime was. Once Calloway becomes convinced of Martins's ignorance and naïveté, he explains to him that Lime was one of the worst racketeers in Vienna, and that he is better off dead. Martins, by now thoroughly drunk, becomes angry at Calloway and defensive of Lime. After he takes a swing at Calloway and misses, the British officer strongly encourages him to leave on the next plane.

Instead, Martins stays and begins his own investigation into Lime's death. Martins tracks down Lime's girlfriend, Anna (Alida Valli), the beautiful woman at the funeral, and soon falls in love with her. Anna is a Czech citizen and should have been repatriated to the Soviet zone, but she has been able to remain in a part of Vienna outside of Soviet control because of the forged papers Lime had arranged for her. She is deeply depressed by his death. When Martins asks gently if she was in love with Lime, Anna replies, "I don't know. How can you know a thing like that afterwards? I don't know anything anymore except I want to be dead, too. Some more tea?"

Martins seeks out other witnesses and finds discrepancies in their stories. Two of Lime's friends say they discovered Lime at the accident scene and moved his body out of the road. They claim that, before he died, he spoke to them about Martins. But the porter in the building across the street from the accident insists that Lime could not have been alive when he was found and that a third man appeared at the scene to help move the body.

The end of World War II brought great joy followed by slowly but steadily growing anxiety over the direction of world events. Instead of a clear triumph of democracy over tyranny, it quickly became obvious that the Soviet Union, America's wartime ally, was determined to impose Communist governments on the territories under its control rather than allow the free elections agreed to at Yalta. There was a growing conviction that America had been deceived by the Russian Communists.[103] In 1946, these concerns were identified and given form by Winston Churchill in his historic speech at Fulton, Missouri. With typical rhetorical flourish, Churchill declared,

> From Stettin in the Baltic to Trieste in the Adriatic an "iron curtain" has descended across the Continent. Behind that line lie all the capitals of the ancient states of Central and Eastern Europe ... and all are subject ... not only to Soviet influence but to a very high and in some cases increasing measure of control from Moscow.[104]

Historical and political analyses from the period placed some of the blame on President Roosevelt for the naïve agreements he made at Yalta. One author titled a chapter devoted to the conference, "Yalta: Stalin's Greatest Victory."[105] Later analysts would treat Roosevelt more kindly and acknowledge there was little he could do, short of another war, to undo the Soviet army's occupation of so much territory in Eastern Europe.[106] But in the immediate post-war period, Roosevelt's confidence in his ability to secure Stalin's cooperation seemed misguided at best.

Straightforward heroes did not seem to fit these troubled and ambiguous times, although some movies still featured them. Neither did straightforward images like the camera shot of John Wayne emerging tall and commanding at the bend in the road in *Stagecoach*, or the scene in *The Best Years of Our Lives* when Harold Russell reverently stuffs a combat medal into his coat pocket. Instead, the times seemed to call for something less confident and more complicated. *Film noir*, a movie style that emerged in the late 1940s, seemed better suited to the complexities of the post-war era. It employed odd camera angles and shadowy lighting techniques, and its characters often had conflicted attitudes toward the law and conventional standards of behavior. The heroes in *film noir* often existed outside traditional law-enforcement organizations, if they enforced the law at all, and the women in them were not wholesome young girls or supportive wives or mothers (see *Kiss Me Deadly*). These movies "delved into the perverse side of human nature, exploring violence, greed, and existential loneliness."[107]

The Third Man, made in 1949, is an excellent example of the *film noir* style. Director Reed uses odd camera angles to throw off visual perspective, and the audience only gradually begins to understand what is going on. Many scenes play out in the shadows, and a key plot element is only revealed because someone inadvertently illuminates a darkened doorway. In another celebrated sequence, a chase takes place through the sewers of Vienna, where it is impossible to see clearly who is gaining on whom. The screenplay is filled with moments designed to confuse the audience. The porter makes a reference to the dead Lime and points up to hell and down to heaven. Characters frequently misstate one another's names: Callahan for Calloway, Harry for Holly. Martins is mistaken for a great writer, an error he uses to his advantage, and also for a

The Third Man (1949)

murderer, an error that almost gets him killed. Martins is often confused. When he finds a useful piece of evidence, he promptly shares it with suspicious characters. Misled by Calloway's indirect references to murder, Martins misunderstands Lime's crime, and, ultimately, he misunderstands Lime's death as well.

Calloway manipulates Martins into aiding his official investigation into Lime's murder. When he finally becomes convinced of the nature of Lime's criminal enterprise, Martins tries to use this information to help Anna. Anna refuses his efforts, and Martins, out of options, is finally forced to choose between good and evil, between his friend and the woman they both love.

Suggested Discussion Questions

1. As the movie opens and a narrator discusses black market professionals, an image of a corpse floating in an icy river appears on screen. What is the narrator's attitude toward the existence of the black market and of "amateurs" who attempt to profit from it?

2. How does the movie present Vienna through images of its citizens, its traditional architectural style, and the war's destruction? How does the city feel? Are there any beautiful images of the city?

3. Explain the goals of the Cultural Re-Education Section run by Mr. Crabbin. Explain the joke about "Hindu Dancers." Describe Mr. Crabbin. What image does he present of the ethics of the occupation forces?

4. Until Martins follows the cat into the street, how successful is he at figuring out what is going on?

5. In the scene on the Ferris wheel, how does Lime defend his actions? How does he respond to Anna's troubles with the Russians? Analyze the comparison Lime makes between the Renaissance and Switzerland. How valid is it?

6. Describe Calloway's view of Martins. Is Calloway's view accurate? Why, or why not?

7. Describe the relationship between Anna and Harry Lime. Why does Anna refuse to give up on Lime? What does she mean when she says, "There isn't enough for two laughs"?

8. Excluding Calloway, decide which one of the main characters exhibits the most ethical behavior. Defend your choice.

9. How does the sewer system affect the efforts of the four different powers to govern the city? The climactic chase scene takes place in the sewers. Analyze this scene as a visual metaphor.

10. Vienna is world renowned for its musical history. Major classical composers with ties to the city include Franz Schubert, Johannes Brahms, Johann

Strauss II, and Mozart. Rather than tap into this rich musical tradition, why would the director choose the zither, a rustic folk instrument, as the only musical accompaniment for the movie?

11. Based on the example of Vienna in *The Third Man*, what forces, attitudes, or circumstances were undermining economic recovery and the re-establishment of social order in post-war Europe?

12. Assume there are other people like the porter, Anna, and Harry Lime, whose behavior ranged from efforts to remain uninvolved to acceptance of criminality to the commission of criminal acts. When a country that was formerly under Nazi control finally establishes a functioning legal system, what should be done with all three kinds of people? Did any former Nazis from the lower ranks of the German bureaucracy become active in post-war German government at any level?

13. Unlike America, a relative newcomer to international politics, Britain had a long history of dealing with the complexities of international relationships. In Churchill's memoirs, he suggests that, after the war ended, America was not capable of navigating European and Soviet power politics successfully.[108] How do the behaviors and attitudes of Holly Martins and Major Calloway reflect this view? Based on the history of the period, was Churchill right and if so, why?

14. Soviet officials and their policies have important roles in the story. What has happened between 1945 and 1949 to cause America's former ally to be portrayed in such a negative fashion? In terms of national security and the threat of Communist subversion, were things significantly better or worse for the United States by 1949?

Godzilla, King of the Monsters (1956)

(80 minutes; original title: *Gojira;* Japanese, 1954, 98 minutes) *Directors:* Ishiro Honda, Terry Moore (English version); *Stars:* Takashi Shimura, Momoko Kochi, Akira Takarada, Akihiko Hirata, Raymond Burr (English version)

A movie poster for *Godzilla, King of the Monsters* hinted at the connection between the Japanese monster and the atomic bomb. "Belching fire that blasts mighty cities into oblivion," it read, "Diabolical Demon of Destruction ... Mightiest Monster of them all—Godzilla!"[109] The history behind the movie's storyline gave added resonance to Japan's efforts to vanquish an evil monster with a radioactive connection. The two atomic bombs that destroyed Hiroshima and Nagasaki in August 1945 killed more than 190,000 people and left lingering, deadly health problems and vast structural damage.[110]

Once the war ended, people focused the enormous ramifications of the discovery of the atomic bomb technology and the ethical questions surrounding the use of it. Reporter John Hersey traveled to Hiroshima in 1946 to interview survivors of the atomic bomb blast. He described the aftereffects of the bombing in a lengthy article that highlighted the stories of six survivors. The article was published in the August 31 issue of *The New Yorker,* one of the most influential magazines of the day. It was the only story featured in the issue and became a tremendous publishing success. The article was later reprinted as a book, titled simply *Hiroshima*. Like so many sad cities before and after it, the name alone had become a symbol for the tragedy of war.

Hersey presented a roughly chronological account of the experiences of each of his subjects. In many instances he used their own words to describe what they saw. He did not dramatize the human suffering or structural damage. The unadorned facts were enough to convey the staggering power and horrific effects of the bomb. The explosion was often described in terms of a blinding light. Even though there were many different kinds of injuries, Hersey paid particular attention to the types and severity of burn wounds because his subjects focused so strongly on them. Hersey tracked their attempts to find shelter and safety amid the incomprehensible chaos, and he also reported on their puzzlement over what kind of bomb could cause the strange health complications and unusual patterns of destruction they were seeing.

Even before nuclear destruction rained down on these two cities, however, the Japanese people had suffered greatly. From June 1944 on, American heavy bombers flying from Saipan were able to conduct sustained air attacks on the Japanese home islands. A large percentage of the houses in Tokyo were built of wood, and a single fire bomb raid on that city in March 1945 killed 83,000 people.[111] The raids drove millions of Japanese to seek safety in the interior, which added to the breakdown of social order. Also by 1945, the United States had surrounded Japan with an ever-tightening naval blockade, bringing the Japanese people close to starvation. But the government refused to allow any talk of defeat. War news was heavily censored, and the public only heard reports of military successes. The Kempei, Japanese military police who operated within Japan as well as in combat zones, strongly discouraged dissent. Although their efforts did not compare in extent to the work of the Gestapo, they were able to quash public criticism effectively.[112] Thus, the Japanese people soon came to distrust the government's official story.[113]

In 1954, Japanese director Ishiro Honda created *Gojira,* one of the classics of the monster movie genre. Two years later, American director Terry Moore re-edited the movie for American audiences, and released it with a new title, *Godzilla, King of the Monsters*. Moore's version included new scenes involving an American news reporter, Steve Martin (Raymond Burr), whose role evoked

Hersey's reporting in 1946. Throughout the movie, Martin comments on events or asks questions and reports back to his editor. Clever framing makes it appear that Martin was always part of the movie, and most of the remaining Japanese dialog was dubbed into English. However, the essentials of the original plot were unchanged. An ancient monster rises from the ocean near Japan and moves ever closer, killing, crushing, and destroying as it goes. The Japanese navy drops depth charges in an attempt to kill it, but the public celebration of success is premature. Godzilla emerges unscathed, wreaks more havoc, and inspires alarmed debate about what should be done.

Dr. Kyohei Yamane (Takashi Shimura), a respected paleontologist, leads the effort to research this deadly monster. He and his daughter, Emiko (Momoko Kochi), travel to Odo Island along with sailor Hideto Ogata (Akira Takarada) to investigate island legends that may shed some light on this terrifying threat from the deep. Yamane discovers that the monster is radioactive, and he believes that recent atomic testing has caused it to emerge from the ocean. When he returns and reports his findings to the government, there is a bitter debate over whether to share this news with the Japanese people.

The public becomes terrified when one after another of Japan's defensive efforts fails to stop Godzilla. Tokyo residents evacuate to the countryside, and the government sets up a ring of high-voltage electrical towers to protect the city. But Godzilla slashes through the power lines and rampages through Tokyo, setting the city on fire with his breath. He is impervious to any weapon Japan can throw at him. Fires erupt along his path, and people who remain in Tokyo are traumatized by his assault on the city. Afterward, as the gigantic monster strides away through Tokyo Bay, he generates a small tsunami, creating another threat that Japan must guard against. (In light of the earthquake, tsunami, and nuclear power catastrophe at Fukushima in 2011, this image seems disturbingly prescient.) The disaster and horror caused by Godzilla recall all the problems that afflicted the Japanese at the end of World War II—fire, devastation, dislocation, and death. The Japanese people are angry at the government for its failure to keep them informed, but unlike during the war, in the movie they publicly challenge officials to tell them the truth.

However, unknown to all but Emiko, Dr. Serizawa (Akihiko Hirata), a junior associate working with her father, has perfected a device that could defeat Godzilla. Emiko's engagement to Serizawa had been arranged when she was a child, and he has sworn her to secrecy about the device. But Emiko has fallen in love with Ogata, and the danger facing Japan finally compels her to describe Serizawa's "oxygen destroyer" to him. Together they approach Serizawa to ask him to use it against the monster. Serizawa refuses, and his response defines the central ethical issue that he and, by extension, other scientists face whenever technology advances in unexpected directions. There are no ethical guidelines for the use of his new weapon. It is so powerful that it poses a great danger to the planet, especially if it gets into the wrong hands. But nothing else is going to stop Godzilla. Does Serizawa unleash his creation to save his country or keep his secret and watch Godzilla destroy Japan? From a broader perspective, is science a means to save us or is it so dangerous it will ultimately destroy us?

No country had a more compelling interest than Japan in preventing another use of the atomic bomb. Serizawa's dilemma over the "oxygen destroyer," for which no antidote yet existed, paralleled the debate that Americans and others were having over the use of atomic weapons. Once the United States dropped the bomb, the American public was simultaneously awed and anxious. Mastering the complicated science necessary to develop this weapon was a tremendous accomplishment. But if America could create the bomb, then other countries could as well. Not surprisingly, the Soviets were able to begin testing their own atomic weapon by 1949.[114] The American government responded in part by arguing that atomic energy should be used for peace. In 1953, President Eisenhower proposed the International Atomic Energy Agency, which would explore peaceful uses for nuclear power. But the public remained uncertain about how secure atomic weapons had made America.[115]

Godzilla demonstrates that the United States, Great Britain, and the Soviet Union may have controlled the bomb technology, but they could not control people's views about it. Fictional monsters can display a variety of terrible powers. Significantly, the makers of this particular monster movie gave Gojira/Godzilla the power of fire and embellished it with radioactivity. The threat that atomic weapons posed to the entire world had become an international issue, and this movie represents Japan's cinematic contribution to the discussion.

The movie resolves the danger and the love triangle in a single heroic act. Japan triumphs because it has created a scientific device that is superior to the danger they face, a danger with its root cause in atomic science. At the time, the United States was the unidentified but most likely culprit. There is no reason the creature would confine its marauding only to Japan. Therefore, Serizawa's device and his resolution of the ethical dilemma it represents matters to the rest of the world as well.

Suggested Discussion Questions

1. Describe the relationship between members of the public and the people who were responsible for destroying Godzilla. Is it a harmonious or supportive relationship? Is there dissension, and if so, why? In a time of crisis, are the attitudes of either group unusual?

2. Compare the Japanese people's reactions to the scientists and politicians who are searching for answers about Godzilla to their reactions to government information about the country's progress during World War II. In a time of crisis, should people question their government's actions or remain unquestioning and united?

3. The creature's footprints on Odo Island contain traces of Strontium-90. What does the presence of this specific radioactive isotope indicate?

4. Why does Serizawa destroy his notes? What implications does this act have for other scientists who create dangerous technologies?

5. Japan was blamed for World War II in the Pacific. Instances of brutal behavior by the Japanese military resulted in war crimes trials and executions after the war. Analyze Steve Martin's relationship with the Japanese people. How does he respond to their plight? The movie was a success in the United States. What do Martin's attitudes and the movie's reception by American audiences suggest about attitudes toward Japan in the mid-1950s?

6. Does the movie portray science in a positive or negative light? Explain your answer. Describe some current scientific discoveries that conflict with ethical considerations or traditional views. How should these be resolved?

7. Emiko became engaged to Serizawa when she was a child. But she chooses an ordinary sailor over a scientist. Ogata could have been the one to save Tokyo. Why is Serizawa the one who gives up everything?

8. At one point, Dr. Yamane says that attempts by the military to destroy Godzilla are wrong. He should be "studied" instead. This plot element is similar to the debate between scientists and the military regarding the monster in *The Thing from Another World* (1951). A strong military response is the approach that both movies finally support. How does this approach reflect Cold War attitudes of the 1950s?

9. Godzilla and King Kong (1933 version) were iconic movie monsters who caused random death and destruction, but neither one seems to have been a hated figure. Based on subsequent movie versions and/or offspring, these monsters became very popular. Suggest some possible reasons why these dangerous creatures remained popular with audiences.

10. In 1947, during the American military occupation, the Japanese approved a new constitution. Article 9 requires that Japan reject the use of force to settle international disputes and not maintain an army, navy, or air force. (They could, however, maintain a small home defense force.) These provisions were designed to prevent any return to the extreme militarism that was widely believed to be the source of Japanese excesses during the war. Does the movie reflect this provision of the constitution in any way, and if so, how?

11. Because Japan could not maintain a significant military establishment, the United States and Japan signed successive mutual defense treaties that aug-

mented Article 9. By these treaties, the United States accepted responsibility for guaranteeing Japan's security against international threats. The United States continues to have a substantial military presence in Japan and on Okinawa. Discuss whether this arrangement was a good idea in the 1950s and whether it is still a good idea today.

12. Who succeeds in defending Japan from Godzilla, and who fails? How do images of the hero figure in the movie reflect post-war Japanese attitudes? Rewrite the ending of the movie to suggest some ways the same movie monster might have been defeated if the movie were made in 1942.

13. *Gojira*, the original version of this movie, was one of the most popular movies in post-war Japan.[116] Based on its plot, how did the Japanese people fit into the international anti-bomb movements that began to emerge in the 1950s?

14. At the time the movie was released, Japan's recent history was filled with failure. They had lost the war, much of the country had been devastated, they had been under the authority of an American army of occupation for seven years, and they had suffered the effects of the most destructive weapon ever created. To go forward with any sense of confidence and national self-respect, Japan needed a new vision of itself. Does this movie accomplish that, and if so, how?

PART III

Red Fears and Nuclear Anxieties, 1939–1966

Overview

The United States and the Soviet Union were engaged in a complicated and often hostile relationship throughout most of the twentieth century. Occasionally the two countries shared the same goals. Along with Great Britain they fought Nazi Germany during World War II. However, in the decades after the war, they were distrustful of one another, extremely competitive, and sometimes dangerously belligerent. Movies from that era reflect these Cold War realities as well as American attitudes about the Russians themselves. Although Americans were vigorously anti–Communist they were not necessarily antagonistic toward the Russian people.

Russia withdrew from the Great War in 1918 because it faced a great war at home. Tsar Nicholas II and his wife and children were assassinated by Russian revolutionaries in late 1917, ending the Romanov Dynasty that had ruled Russia for three centuries. As the Russian Revolution gathered momentum the country descended into chaos and could no longer defend itself against the German armies attacking from the west. Russian emissaries signed the Treaty of Brest-Litovsk in March 1918. The treaty ended Russia's role in the World War I and surrendered a huge swath of Russian territory to the Germans. When the revolution came to an end, Vladimir Lenin and the Communists attempted to establish control over Russia, but their initial efforts to replace the old tsarist regime resulted in an unstable government. Civil war and famine added to the chaos, and Lenin's death in 1924 threw the Communist Party leadership into turmoil.[1]

From the very beginning, the Soviets understood the potential of all types of propaganda, including motion pictures, to promote their cause. In 1925, Russian director Sergei Eisenstein created the brilliant—and officially sanctioned—*Battleship Potemkin*.[2] The movie dramatizes a mutiny by Russian sailors that occurred near the seaport town of Odessa in 1905, during the unsuccessful October Revolution. Eisenstein's cinematic version of the mutiny pits sailors against their officers in a way that mimics the conflict between peasants and nobility during the Russian Revolution. There is a startling immediacy to the camera work. The tragic massacre on the Odessa Steps is based loosely on an actual event, and it is an example of filmmaking that can still move an audience nearly a century later. The movie's triumphant last scene leaves no doubt that the tide is turning in Russia even if the revolution that will ultimately overthrow the Tsar is still a dozen years off.

The success of the Russian Communists generated a Red Scare in 1920s America. Many Americans feared that Communism would invade and overwhelm American democracy. But their worries died down as the Roaring Twenties barreled on, fueled by credit, consumer goods, and unchecked capitalism. At the end of the twenties, the Great Depression diverted the concerns of most Americans to domestic issues.

Soviet Communists—like American capitalists—also turned inward during this period, although for different reasons. The murder of the Tsar and his family was broadly condemned by other countries, and the Communists faced the task of consolidating political power in a world that was strongly critical of their brutal assault on an established government. Communist Party leaders spent most of their energies during their first two decades in power focused on internal affairs. Joseph Stalin proved to be the strongest consolidator among them. He rose through the ranks of the party to become the leader of the Soviet Union. He then waged a ruthless campaign against possible rivals. For example, Stalin purged the Soviet army of suspected traitors by arresting or killing 30,000 officers and soldiers for alleged treason.[3] Soviet policies during the 1930s such as industrialization and collectivization caused the deaths of millions more.[4]

Most of this internal turmoil was hidden from the outside world. Although many people in Europe and the United States were critical of the new Communist government, others either expected or hoped that Russia would emerge from its period of restructuring as a stable world power. This optimism found its way into in several Hollywood movies. A character in *Biography of a Bachelor Girl* (1935) jokes about how easily a beautiful American artist was able to enter Russia without a passport, and an American entrepreneur in *Dodsworth* (1936) speculates about getting permission from the Soviet government to open commercial air routes through Russia for an international airline.

The outside world was beginning to gain a better understanding of the turmoil in the Soviet Union by the late 1930s, and this realization altered the way Russia was portrayed in some movies. In *Knight Without Armour* (British,

1937) a British spy fluent in Russian infiltrates the growing Communist movement in pre-revolutionary Russia. But the revolution begins while he is there, trapping him in the country. Various plot twists lead him to a member of the nobility, Countess Vladinoff (Marlene Dietrich). There are too many coincidences for the plot to be convincing, and the love story and the political story keep getting in each other's way. However, the movie manages to capture the essence of Russia's civil strife in one vivid sequence. At the start of the revolution, the Countess awakens one morning and cannot find any servants to attend her. As she runs across her estate's vast lawns, searching in mounting fear and confusion for her servants, a crowd of peasants emerges from a hillside. They stand arrayed before her, a few bearing pitchforks. The image of the Countess alone in a diaphanous white dressing gown facing the crude, vengeful peasantry is emblematic of the disparity in Russian society that has brought it to this point—opulence and luxury for the few, and poverty and unrelenting labor for the many.

The Red Menace

From 1918 until the start of World War II, the Soviet Union appeared to be a nation trying to find its footing in the modern industrial world while struggling to overcome a recent peasant past and an all-consuming revolutionary upheaval, circumstances that did not lend themselves to aggressive efforts at international expansion. Although some viewed the Soviets as a possible military threat, others recalled the Russians as a former ally during World War I. Either out of optimism or naïveté, they failed to understand the existential threat presented by the Russian Communists who had cold-bloodedly assassinated their nation's royal family and purged millions as they went about totally restructuring the social, economic, and political life of a country that spanned one-sixth of the world's landmass. The movie *Ninotchka* (1939) illustrates the dismissive view some Americans had during this period of the actual danger Communist principles represented when they were confronted by the lure of freedom, the joys of true love, and the inviting, if decadent charms of capitalism. *Comrade X,* released a year later, revisits this same storyline, but it presents a much more cynical picture of Communism. For example, Stalin's purge trials and the resulting executions receive only a brief humorous mention in *Ninotchka,* but they are an important and grim plot element in *Comrade X.*

Some Americans were concerned that Communism might take root in the United States without overt Soviet aggression. They saw the Great Depression as fertile ground for the spread of an economic philosophy that encouraged the redistribution of wealth. Such fears were not based on fact. The number of Americans who claimed to be members of the Communist Party, never high to begin with, had risen to only 100,000 by 1939.[5] Even during hard times, the overwhelming majority of Americans did not seriously question capitalism. The freedom to own property and achieve personal wealth—the essence of capitalism—was deeply rooted in American society, and once Franklin D. Roosevelt was elected president in 1932, his New Deal offered hope to millions. The country slogged along through the thirties, not yet fully recovered from the Depression, but with reason for optimism.

While the United States slogged and the Soviet Union consolidated, Germany re-armed. Adolf Hitler rose to power in 1933 and led Germany as it reoccupied the Rhineland, rebuilt its navy, and expanded its military, all in direct violation of the Treaty of Versailles. These events were especially worrisome to France and Great Britain. The early focus of their concern was Poland, a country that had disappeared from maps of Europe in 1795 as a result of aggressive expansion by Prussia, Russia, and Austria. Germany was the successor state to Prussia, and, as part of Germany's post–World War I punishment, the Treaty of Versailles carved out a large chunk of German territory for the re-establishment of Poland in 1919. By the late 1930s, after Germany's non-military takeovers of Austria and Czechoslovakia, Britain and France saw Poland as the place where a resurgent Germany might be most likely to wage war. Attacking Poland allowed Hitler to say that the Germans were merely reclaiming territory that was rightfully theirs.

The British and the French, along with the rest of Europe, did place some hope in one significant force that stood in the way of German expansion. The Soviet Union bordered Poland, and any invasion by Germany would be all too reminiscent of German aggression in 1914 and would prompt the Soviets to declare war against Germany. After World War I, Britain and France had signed treaties guaranteeing Poland's sovereignty and they, too, would declare war against Germany. The result would present the Germans with a two-front war that would strain their ability to wage war while protecting the Fatherland.

The hope that these complex diplomatic alignments would deter German aggression evaporated on August 23, 1939, when Germany announced that it had signed a non-aggression pact with the Soviet Union. In effect, the pact granted Germany the right to attack Poland without the fear of a Soviet counterattack. Hitler was delighted with the agreement, and, in a part of the deal that was not made public, Stalin could expect to receive the eastern third of Poland in return for his forbearance.[6] Nine days later Germany invaded Poland. The Soviets attacked from the east on September 17, and Poland surrendered by the end of the month. The Great War became World War I, and World War II had begun. Between September 1939 and June 1941, Hitler waged a brilliant campaign. In the ten months after the invasion of Poland, Germany gained control of ten European nations and signed accords with Italy and Japan to come to each other's defense in the event that one of them was attacked by another nation. But in June 1941, Hitler overreached. He ordered more than three and a half million German troops assembled along a line from the Baltic to the Black Sea to attack the Soviet Union.[7] Hitler had betrayed Stalin, and the German army now had to fight a two-front war.

The Soviet Union needed help, and the United States and Great Britain did not want to see Germany swallow Russia whole and gain access to its production facilities and its food, mineral, and human resources. Both countries came to the Soviet Union's aid. Prime Minister Winston Churchill, a strong, consistent, and very vocal opponent of Communism, offered the British people this explanation for his support of a Communist nation: "If Hitler invaded Hell, I would make at least a favorable reference to the Devil in the House of Commons," and President Roosevelt told the press that America would "give all the aid we possibly can to Russia."[8] America suddenly found itself supporting Communists, with resources up until the attack on Pearl Harbor, with resources and military power after it. Not surprisingly and despite objections from some quarters, Hollywood made a few movies that showed the Soviet Union in a positive light, including *Mission to Moscow* (1943), *The North Star* (1943), *Song of Russia* (1944), and *Days of Glory* (1944).[9] The release dates tell the tale. There was only a narrow time frame during which American moviemakers were willing to say nice things about Communism.

After three years of desperate fighting, the Soviet Union had managed to drive the Germans back to the line they had started from in 1941, and in February 1945, 6.7 million Soviet soldiers marched westward into German territory.[10] By May they were in control of Berlin and all of Germany east of the Elbe River. In accordance with the agreement signed at Yalta that February, American and British armies had done their part against the Germans and were in control of all Germany west of the Elbe. The war in Europe was over, and the Soviets were in charge of those areas they had liberated.

All of the countries liberated by the Allies were to hold free elections to form new governments that would replace the puppet governments established by the Germans during the war years. But German armies had invaded Russian territory twice within 25 years, and Stalin wanted to be absolutely certain that it could not happen again. So he rigged elections or otherwise arranged that the countries of Eastern Europe liberated by Soviet armies would become Communist satellites, including the eastern half of Germany, which was then under Soviet control. The new governments established in these states created a buffer of Communist-controlled countries along Russia's western border.[11] Their citizens also added millions, willingly or otherwise, to the rolls of Communist Party members, a process that sets up the cruel civil crisis at the heart of the 1949 movie, *The Third Man*. The Allies—Great Britain, the United States, and the Soviet Union—were the victors of World War II, and Americans could not comprehend how this hard-earned triumph had led to a Communist colossus that straddled half of Europe, secure and powerful behind an Iron Curtain.

Developments in China contributed to the perception of a worldwide Communist takeover. During the thirties and forties China was threatened from within by independent warlords and Communist revolutionaries and from without by the Japanese. (The complications generated by these conflicts form the background for *The Inn of the Sixth Happiness,* a 1958 movie based on the life of British missionary, Gladys Aylward.) The crisis reached critical mass in 1949 when Mao Zedong and the Chinese Communists defeated Chiang Kai-shek and the Nationalist Chinese and drove them onto the small offshore island of Taiwan. Mao established a Communist government over mainland China, bringing another one-fifth of the world's population under Communist control.

After their valiant efforts to rid the world of totalitarianism, the American people were confused and frightened by the Communist victories in Russia and China. The escalating tensions between the United States and Soviet Union became known as the "Cold War." There were recriminations and investigations, suspicions of plots by spies or traitors, and eventually a limited war in Korea as Americans grew increasingly more concerned about the spread of Communism. The widely publicized trials of Alger Hiss and Julius and Ethel Rosenberg suggested that traitors within the United States may have contributed to the Communist successes abroad. Hiss was a Harvard-educated member of the State Department and part of the American delegation to Yalta. In 1951, he was convicted of being a Soviet spy. The Rosenbergs were convicted that same year for helping to pass atomic secrets to the Soviets. Fears that there might be traitors among us had suddenly turned into frightening reality.[12]

Even before the spy trials ended, the House Un-American Activities Committee (HUAC) intensified its investigations to determine whether Communists had infiltrated the country and its institutions. By the late 1940s the committee began to give special attention to the people who made movies. Members of the industry who were subpoenaed by HUAC often found themselves in a no-win situation. If they invoked the Fifth Amendment, the public often interpreted that as an admission of guilt. But answering the committee's questions could also be problematic.[13] Simply asserting their innocence was rarely successful. (Although when called upon to testify, Lucille Ball claimed that she had registered as a Communist in 1936 only because her grandfather asked her to. HUAC accepted her explanation, and she was able to continue in her hit series, *I Love Lucy*.)[14] People who admitted any Communist leanings at all had to atone for their actions by naming others they believed were party members or "fellow travelers," i.e., Communist sympathizers.[15]

The HUAC investigations went on for months. Many in the Hollywood community were tainted by the hearings and were then blacklisted, unable to get work because of suspected Communist sympathies. In a particularly well-publicized confrontation, the Hollywood Ten, a group of screenwriters who refused to testify when called by HUAC, were each given one-year prison sentences and fined $1,000 for contempt of Congress.[16] (In 1976, *The Front* focused on this period, and several writers and actors who were victims of the blacklist had roles in the movie.)

In 1952, Hollywood offered conflicting reactions to the HUAC investigations. In *High Noon*, the citizens of a town are threatened by outlaws, but they refuse to assist the town sheriff in their defense. The movie has been interpreted as a criticism of Hollywood's refusal to resist HUAC's investigations more strongly and support members of the industry who were forced to testify or be blacklisted.[17] *Big Jim McLain* and *My Son John*, also from 1952, were staunchly patriotic movies designed to reassure people that the United States government was working hard to protect them. HUAC even had a bit part in *Big Jim McLain*. At the movie's conclusion, Big Jim (John Wayne) sympathizes with the problems that HUAC faces when a character is able to avoid testifying by invoking his Fifth Amendment protections against self-incrimination.

For many Americans, Communism represented more than just a threat to private property and political dictatorship. It denied the existence of God, demanded adherence to the party line no matter what empirical evidence might prove, and subordinated individual rights to the needs of the masses. Concern that people would lose their individuality and become, in effect, passionless robots emerged as subtexts in movies such as *Invasion of the Body Snatchers* (1956) and *The Manchurian Candidate* (1962). The importance of using reason and evidence, not just following the dictates of the party or group think, were important themes in the courtroom drama, *12 Angry Men* (1957).

Intense patriotism was the order of the day for many Americans. If recognizing the dangers of Communism was one side of that coin, then celebrating American freedom and democracy was the other, and instilling these attitudes in the younger generation took on an urgency that drove many elements of 1950s popular culture. The phrase "under God" was added to the Pledge of Allegiance in 1953 to emphasize Americans' commitment to religion. *The Mickey Mouse Club*, Walt Disney's tremendously popular daytime television show for children, which ran from 1955 to 1959, presented frequent examples of the many wonderful opportunities that life in America offered young people.

A portion of the show was often given over to serialized stories that featured child actors and championed the triumph of American values and lifestyles (e.g., *The Adventures of Spin and Marty* and *Walt Disney Presents: Annette*).

Full-length Disney movies became significant entertainment events for early Baby Boomers, and they were also major promoters of patriotism. Children begged to attend them, and because they were quality productions aimed specifically at the youth market, parents could be confident that the content would be appropriate and the plots exciting. In 1955, Disney released *Davy Crockett, King of the Wild Frontier*, starring Fess Parker. The movie, edited from television episodes, celebrates the life of the legendary Tennessee Indian fighter and Congressional Representative. Parker brought an easygoing, common-man quality to his performance and also to a starring role the following year in Disney's *Westward Ho the Wagons!* (1956). A few of the young stars of *The Mickey Mouse Club* also appeared in this movie, and they were a big draw for its intended audience. In 1957, Disney offered a reasonably good adaptation of *Johnny Tremain*, Esther Forbes's novel about young people in the early days of the American Revolution. After seeing these movies, children left theaters with a glowing sense of the possibilities of American democracy, a greater understanding of the demands of responsible citizenship, and the lyrics to splendid theme songs dancing in their heads.

Interestingly, there are no significant movies from these years that depict an actual military attack against the United States by a Communist country. The military's technical capabilities and the nation's protective ocean barriers seemed to give Americans confidence in their physical security. But sinister plots and storylines about internal spies, which evoked Senator Joseph McCarthy's fears, became standard fare in movies as well as in people's perceptions. *Notorious* (1946), *I Was a Communist for the F. B. I.* (1951), *My Son John* (1952), *Invasion of the Body Snatchers*, and *The Manchurian Candidate* were just some of the movies that depict ominous threats rising Phoenix-like out of the destruction of World War II, or that exploit the fear of betrayal lurking just around the corner. Such movies, Richard A. Schwartz explains, portray "devious, emotionally detached communists [who] engage in illegal activities in order to weaken the United States and advance their own cause of world domination."[18]

Nuclear Anxieties

As the Cold War progressed and the arms race heated up, people began to question the sanity of nuclear warfare. What benefit would either side gain from a form of warfare that almost guaranteed mutual annihilation? International events in the 1950s and early 1960s, such as the Berlin Airlift, the Korean War, the Hungarian Revolution, and the building of the Berlin Wall, fueled these fears. The tense confrontation between the United States and the Soviet Union in 1962 over Soviet missiles in Cuba pointed to an ever-escalating threat and created real fear that nuclear war would erupt. Not surprisingly, movies were soon exploring the likelihood, morality, and logic of atomic warfare, including *On the Beach* (1959), *Dr. Strangelove or: How I Learned to Stop Worrying and Love the Bomb* (British, 1964), and *The Bedford Incident* (1965). In 1959, *The World, the Flesh, and the Devil* combined the horrors of atomic war with the theme of racial tolerance.

There were still movies that upheld the need for vigilance and aggressive action in the face of Communist threats. But, overall, the focus shifted away from fears about the spread of Communism to ways to prevent total nuclear war. The confused, unstable politics of Cold War Europe set the stage for several important movies. Alfred Hitchcock's 1956 version of *The Man Who Knew Too Much* was a witty, tense thriller about an American family that gets dragged into political maneuverings in Morocco and England. Cold War intrigue also powered the wildly popular James Bond series, even when the malevolent antagonists were not specifically Soviet Communists. The British secret agent's superior skills, technological capabilities, and charm, vividly on display in *From Russia with Love* (British, 1963), to cite only one example, guaranteed his success against the agents of doom in each new cinematic adventure.

As the sixties went on, Americans became less anxious about the threat of nuclear war. The tensions over Soviet missiles in Cuba had abated as a result of the combined effects of delicate diplomacy and America's muscular naval blockade. American and Soviet leaders began talking to one another. President John F. Kennedy proposed, and the Soviets accepted the Nuclear Test-Ban Treaty in early 1963. The two countries also established a "hotline" between their leaders in the hope of averting an accidental nuclear attack. When President Kennedy was assassinated, despite years of distrust and Lee Harvey Oswald's murky Communist connections, the American government did not officially accuse the Soviet Union of any role in the assassination. American fears of the Soviet Union eased for other reasons as well. The notion of a monolithic, worldwide Communist movement began to crumble as fissures appeared in the Chinese-Soviet alliance.[19] Ironically, even the escalation of the Vietnam War after 1964 helped reduce the tensions between the United States and the U.S.S.R. While Americans paid increasingly more attention to the guerrilla war in Vietnam, the Soviets were more than happy to see their rival bogged down in a land war in Asia.

Two extremely popular movies from the mid-sixties further demonstrate the shift in public attitudes toward the Soviet Union. *Doctor Zhivago,* by Nobel Prize-winning author Boris Pasternak, was made into a movie in 1965. The story follows the decades-long love affair between Zhivago (Omar Sharif) and Lara (Julie Christie) set amidst the chaos of the Russian Revolution. A grand epic in the cinematic tradition of *Gone With the Wind,* the sweeping tale chronicles Zhivago's complicated life story and includes some stunning scenes. Significantly, the storyline does not support Communism, but it does place the Communists' victory within a broader exploration of Russian history. Directed by David Lean, *Doctor Zhivago* received ten Academy Award nominations, including as Best Picture, and won in five categories. The acting and cinematography are excellent, and the portrayal of the Russian people is sympathetic to their recent tragic history. But the movie often plods along as it chronicles the chaotic, deeply divisive revolution and the early years of Communist control.

By 1966, the notion that the world would annihilate itself in a nuclear war was beginning to seem almost absurd and an absurd movie was made about it. *The Russians Are Coming, The Russians Are Coming* is a droll comedy that suggests there might be ordinary, bumbling human beings among all those threatening Russian Communists and that both sides are equally capable of foolishness and kindness. Therefore, the level of tension and threat that had prevailed for the previous 20 years could and should be reduced. The movie is set in and around a summer resort on a laid-back, sparsely populated island off the New England coast. The Soviet sailors who wash up on that American shore are reminiscent of the feckless, unsteady Communist jewelry salesmen who got sidetracked by the capitalist attractions of Paris in *Ninotchka*.

Cold War tensions, especially the fear of nuclear war, would flair up and recede throughout the second half of the twentieth century, and movies often reflected public concerns about these important issues. They helped Americans evaluate the threat they faced and sort out possible responses to the Cold War or to the possibility of nuclear warfare. In retrospect, these Cold War movies represent a barometer of attitudes and intensity, and they demonstrate how people assessed and responded to the complex, dangerous times.

Red Fears

Ninotchka (1939)

(110 minutes) *Director:* Ernst Lubitsch; *Stars:* Greta Garbo, Melvyn Douglas, Ina Claire, Bela Lugosi, Sig Ruman, Felix Bressart, Alexander Granach, Richard Carle.

Director Ernst Lubitsch's movies often exhibited a lighthearted "velvet" touch. *Ninotchka,* one of his best, manages to connect Paris, impoverished Russian royalty, wobbly Communists, and Greta Garbo in a romantic comedy that was advertised by the tagline, "Garbo laughs." So did 1939 audiences. It was nominated for a Best Picture Academy Award, and earned Garbo a nomination for Best Actress.

When the Communists took control of Russia, White Russians—members of the Russian nobility and others who supported the old regime—left the country if they could. Many settled in Paris. The more fortunate émigrés managed to smuggle out enough wealth to live on, often in the form of jewels because they were easily transportable. (Research in recently opened Soviet archives has revealed that when the tsar and his family were assassinated, the tsar's daughters proved difficult to kill because the assassins' bullets kept bouncing off their corsets. Jewels had been sewn into their undergarments, presumably to finance their escape.)[20] But many émigrés were left with little means to support themselves. Some took menial jobs. Others attempted to maintain their standard of living by attaching themselves to wealthy benefactors among other European nobility. These connections were often easy to establish because many of the royal families of Europe were related. In the late 1800s and early 1900s, for example, the crowned heads or their spouses of England, Germany, Greece, Norway, Romania, Spain, Sweden, and in Russia, the tsar's wife, Princess Alexandra, were all grandchildren of Queen Victoria, and were, therefore, first cousins.[21]

The Communists decreed that all property belonged to the state, and they confiscated whatever royal wealth the émigrés left behind. Because they were in need of ready cash, they soon began selling off the seized goods. However, many émigrés remained determined to recover what they believed was their rightful property.

Ninotchka is a love story that grows out of one of these attempted sales. The plot revolves around three slightly rumpled Communist delegates who have come to Paris to sell royal jewels to a French jeweler. The jewels had been the property of the Duchess Swana (Ina Claire), who is now living in Paris. She is appalled when she learns of the proposed sale, and her boyfriend, Count Leon (Melvyn Douglas), volunteers to try to get the jewels back. As Leon thwarts the sale he also befriends the delegation. Ninotchka (Greta Garbo), a smart, uncompromising Communist party loyalist, comes to Paris to rescue the sale, and, if possible, salvage the careers of the three wayward Soviet delegates. Count Leon is attracted to her and pursues her despite her rebuffs. The Duchess discovers Leon's interest in Ninotchka and tries to drive her away.

As the movie opens, a statement appears across the screen that reads:

"This picture takes place in Paris in the wonderful days when a siren was a brunette and not an alarm ... and if a Frenchman turned out the light it was not on account of an air raid!" This cavalier explanation of the setting implies that the movie will not be depressingly realistic, but it also reflects a real concern about the possibility of another war in Europe. During the late 1930s, Germany engaged in a series of actions in Austria and Czechoslovakia that were designed to acquire territory without waging war, but most thoughtful observers of European politics expected that another war of aggression would start soon. The movie's opening statement focuses on these concerns. It references both sirens and air raids, which will soon become commonplace throughout the continent.

For the most part, however, the movie takes a light-hearted approach. Leon is witty and handsome, the delegates are naïve and unthreatening, and most of the scenes have a sophisticated, carefree goofiness about them. Only Ninotchka is grim at first as she takes charge of issues related to the jewels' contested ownership, scolds the delegates for their failure to uphold Communist principles, and deals commandingly with French law and lawyers. Eventually, Leon's persistent pursuit wears her down. Her clothes, her manner, and her face soften and become giddy and girlish. Once the Duchess realizes what is going on, she takes immediate action. Her machinations, which include blackmail, send Ninotchka and the erstwhile jewelry salesmen hurrying back to the Soviet Union. With Ninotchka out of the way, Leon is free to come back to the Duchess.

Despite the image that existed at the time of ruthless, relentless Communist party loyalists, the three Soviet delegates in *Ninotchka* are not crude or threatening. They are wobbly party adherents at best. Leon is very charming as he tries to retrieve the jewels from the delegates, and they are easily seduced, first by the gorgeous gilded, almost palace-like hotel, and then by the cigarette girls. The delegates and Communist principles in general receive gentle and sometimes quite pointed criticism throughout the film. A good example is the exchange between Ninotchka and the train station porter who offers to help her with her bags. When she protests, he explains that it is his business to carry the bags.

Ninotchka: That's no business, that's social injustice.
Porter: That depends on the tip.

In another scene, Ninotchka informs her comrades that the recent mass trials of Russian citizens who are not considered sufficiently Communist have been a success and adds grimly, "There will be fewer but better Russians." This remark glosses over thousands of state-sanctioned killings of the politically suspect during the thirties.

The economic ramifications of applied Communism get their fair share of ribbing. When the French jeweler declines to buy the jewels, the delegates tell him that they can wait for a better deal. The jeweler calls their bluff by pointing out that there are other Soviet delegations right now trying to sell "fifteen Rembrandts in New York, and another in London mortgaging the oil fields in Baku." His remarks highlight the failure of the Communists to sustain their economy while operating on their poorly conceived economic principles. In another scene, Ninotchka reacts to Leon's first kiss with anthropological curiosity rather than passion. In order to win her over, Leon begins to explore Communism, but his valet (!) sets him straight on the impracticality of Communist economic theory.

The Russian people are represented as innocent victims, first of the tsar and later of the Communists. The film does take sides in the Communist-Tsarist controversy during a dinner conversation between Ninotchka and the Duchess Swana. They exchange comments about the Cossacks, and the Duchess has the final word. But in case the audience in unclear about the movie's view, Ninotchka is dressed in white, the Duchess in the traditional evil black. The entire excuse for the movie's plot demonstrates that Communism does not offer a viable economic model, and there are frequent reminders throughout the film of various forms of Communist oppression. The Russian people appear to bear these travails philosophically.

The movie has an interesting take on gender issues. The Duchess is not depicted as unintelligent, only self-absorbed and greedy. The movie also features generally accomplished Soviet women, all of whom are employed. Ninotchka is clearly very smart, hardworking, and loyal when she is not falling in love. One of her roommates is a cellist and an indifferent party member who easily succumbs to the attractions of capitalist underwear, albeit with some embarrassment. Her other roommate, however, is a silent barrel-shaped streetcar conductor who snores. This character is apparently intended to demonstrate what can happen when workers' rights go too far in the direction of gender equality.

The plot presents love as an undesirable emotion under Communism, in part because it can be complicated and ungovernable. The Soviet men in the film are portrayed as either incompetent backsliders abroad or robot-like bureaucrats at home. Americans can relax. How can the Communists be a serious threat if they fall off the party wagon every time they leave home?

Suggested Discussion Questions

1. What gender stereotypes are apparent in the movie's opening statement?
2. Explain the gender issues in the scene with the cigarette girls and in the

scene where Leon explains the potential problems a beautiful woman in front of a French jury can create if she "raises her skirt a little."

3. When the Duchess Swana and Ninotchka meet at the restaurant, they discuss the Cossacks, who were often employed as enforcers by the Tsarist government (see also *Battleship Potemkin*). How does their conversation illustrate the causes of the revolution?

4. Ninotchka tells Leon that the Tsar sold fifteen thousand serfs to pay for one piece of jewelry. Why does she accept the crown?

5. How does his valet explain the problem with Communist economic theory to Count Leon? What country currently controls the oil fields in Baku? Research the ownership of the fields. What companies and countries earn profits from them?

6. If the Soviet Union joined Great Britain and France in standing up to German expansion in the late 1930s, Hitler might be held in check. Most Americans hope a war can be avoided. (This movie was released after the German-Soviet Non-Aggression Pact was signed in August 1939.) How does the movie's presentation of Communism and Communist Party members fit into hopes for European peace? Based on the subsequent historical record, is this presentation accurate?

7. The story takes place in Paris, the fabled "City of Light," named after the ancient Greek who, by kidnapping Helen, caused the Trojan War. Why would this city have particular significance for the story?

8. The movie presents many comparisons of the economic differences represented by Communism and Capitalism: the Duchess's lifestyle, the hotel, the two French restaurants, Ninotchka's apartment and the omelet, and others. What do these examples show about life in France and in the Soviet Union, especially the lives of common people and royalty?

9. Does the movie offer any reasons America should consider Communists a serious threat, and if so, what are they?

10. Based on images from the movie, explain which government treated the Russian people better, the one led by the tsar or the one controlled by the Communists?

11. Construct an argument explaining why the United States should have supported (a) the tsar's government; (b) the Communists; or (c) neither, in 1917. How did the United States respond to the Russian Revolution?

12. How does love fit into Communist theory and practical application? How is Leon changed by love? How is Ninotchka changed by love? Who gives up more?

Notorious (1946)

(101 minutes) *Director:* Alfred Hitchcock; *Stars:* Cary Grant, Ingrid Bergman, Claude Rains, Leopoldine Konstantine, Louis Calhern, Reinhold Schunzel, Moroni Olsen.

Alfred Hitchcock's *Notorious* explores a real fear held by many people at the end of World War II—that the Nazis might be able to return to power. After the war there was chaos throughout much of Europe and Asia. Governments everywhere were unsettled. It was possible that Hitler was still alive, which raised concerns that he might somehow gather partisans, regroup, and return. (The Soviets knew Hitler was dead in 1945, but they did not reveal this information at the time.[22]) In the years immediately following the war there were numerous reports of Hitler sightings or new theories as to his whereabouts. Also, when Germany surrendered, the full extent of the Holocaust became apparent. Many Nazis fled to South America in order to avoid prosecution for their roles in the war and the Holocaust. Some people suspected that Hitler was hiding there among them. People were clearly exhausted by the war years, but all the jubilant celebrations that greeted returning soldiers could not hide the fact that the times were still threatening.

At war's end the world had been stunned by America's new weapon. The atomic bomb was like no other weapon in history. This new monster underscored science's dual potential for benefit or harm. Though proud of its scientific accomplishment, the United States did not want to release too many details about the new device. The dangerous atomic genie was best kept hidden inside an American-controlled bottle. So the bomb remained a mysterious unknown. However, German scientists had also been conducting atomic research for decades and some of them were now living in territories controlled by the Soviet Union. What had these scientists discovered? Where were they? Who might they be working for now?

In *Notorious*, Hirchcock blends anxieties over Hitler's whereabouts, unreconstructed Nazis, and secret science into a suspenseful love story that takes place shortly after the war ends. Alicia Huberman (Ingrid Bergman) and her father, a scientist, had emigrated from Europe to America before the war. Her father has sold American military secrets to the enemy during the war. He is caught and convicted of treason in the movie's opening few minutes. After the trial, Alicia puts on a tough front, but she hates her father for his crime and soon sinks into drunkenness and despair.

The United States government has plans for her, however, and T. R. Devlin (Cary Grant) is the man assigned to convince her to carry them out. The United States wants Alicia to use her beauty and her connections from abroad to infiltrate a group of German scientists living in Brazil. The government suspects that these men are trying to create a nefarious new weapon that will help them return to power. Alicia was introduced to the leader of the group, Alexander Sabastian (Claude Rains), when she was a young girl in Europe. The United States wants her to renew their acquaintanceship, even go so far as to convince him she is in love with him, in order to spy on his group.

Their plan is successful, but it becomes complicated by the fact that Devlin and Alicia have fallen in love. Alicia also runs into another unanticipated problem. Sabastian lives in a grand home with his mother (Loepoldine Konstantine), and even though he is in love with Alicia and believes that she shares his feelings, his mother is not convinced of Alicia's sincerity. She knows what could happen if her son is not careful. The story progresses in a series of moves and countermoves by these four characters as each tries to advance multiple, sometimes conflicting aims.

The other members of Sabastian's group are German, but their loyalties are never clearly stated, perhaps reflecting the confusion over who is or is not the enemy in the post-war world. Communism and Nazism are diametrically opposed political philosophies, but they were aligned once before, in 1939. Is there a chance that another marriage of convenience might emerge? What is clear is the uncompromising brutality these men display. When one of them seems to falter, he is summarily killed by another member of the group. This efficient, unemotional cruelty was a common trait among cinematic Nazis, and it will transfer over to a whole new crop of Communist antagonists as fears of Nazism abate and the Cold War gathers momentum. (See *My Son John* and *The Manchurian Candidate*.)

Both Alicia and Madame Sabastian are trying to promote the interests of the men they love, and gender stereotypes are clearly at work in the plot. Sabastian's mother is pushy, calculating, and domineering. Madame Sabastian wants her son to succeed for the cause and is very concerned when he marries Alicia. She feels threatened by the young and beautiful woman. Mothers have obvious responsibilities to their children, but she has distorted her role by becoming too actively involved in Sabastian's life. The implication here is that no son can mature successfully under the influence of such a woman. Alicia wants to get Devlin the information he needs because she supports his cause and also because she loves him. Once there is evidence that Alicia has betrayed Sabastian, his mother pushes him to deal harshly with her. But his mother's motives seem designed to protect herself as much as her son, and it is Madame Sabastian who inadvertently exposes her son to danger. Thus, both women fail to fully achieve their goals. By the film's conclusion it has become obvious that women can be counted on to help and be brave, but in the end it is the men who must finally confront and defeat one another. Women will eventually need to be rescued or will stand helplessly aside. Therefore, the real affairs of the world should be left to men.

During the war years, many women entered the work force in jobs previously held only by men, including defense plant work. It was an exhilarating experience that came to an abrupt end when the war was over. Millions of men returned home from the war to find plants either closing or shutting down to retool from war-related production work. Jobs were scarce, and women who had jobs were let go so that those jobs could go to men.[23] This movie makes the reasons for that reassignment of gender roles obvious: women cannot compete at the same level as men. Instead, it is Devlin's clever, brave, resourceful man-of-the-world who shows men just what they can accomplish even in the most dire circumstances. He is a less flamboyant prototype for a later spy hero, James Bond, who was known as much for escapades and romances as for his cleverness, savoir faire, and expertise in the use of fancy gadgets.

The director Alfred Hitchcock is referred to as "the master of suspense" so often that it has almost become attached to his name. The tribute is well earned. During a Hitchcock movie it is never a good idea to glance away from the screen. His movies feature taut structures and intricate plots. His heroes are men who may have some special talent that places them a cut or two above other men, such as doctor, government agent, or policeman, but for the most part they are not extraordinary. What sets each of his leading men apart from the pack is an intense devotion to the fight against the forces of one evil or another. Hitchcock's heroes stay alert to all possibilities and pursue each clue relentlessly. Their antagonists may be smarter or better armed, but Hitchcock's protagonists will not quit (see *The 39 Steps, Saboteur, North by Northwest, Vertigo, The Man Who Knew Too Much, To Catch a Thief,* and *Rear Window*). The women in Hitchcock movies were often complicated but still worthy matches for their male counterparts. However, even though his female characters may offer a strong assist, it is Hitchcock's men who ultimately triumph.

These elements are central to the structure of *Notorious*. Grant and Bergman were two of the most glamorous and admired stars of the era. Their characters compete with one another throughout the movie, hedging as they try to deal with the demands of the situation and their growing love for one another. Sabastian is a smarmy, middle-aged momma's boy, and he ultimately does not stand a chance, romantically or otherwise, against Devlin. The movie's tense conclusion reassures 1946 audiences that strong, determined Americans are on top of things. The "hot" war may be over, but if a "cold" war has begun, the United States government is still vigilant, clever, and capable of winning it, and handsome, daring, determined T. R. Devlin represents them at their best.

Suggested Discussion Questions

1. What threats still exist even though the war has ended? How does the movie's plot fit into fears generated by the war?

2. After she has spent time getting close to Sabastian, Alicia tells Devlin that Sabastian has become one of her "playmates." How does this statement reflect the Production Code?

3. Describe the relationship between Sabastian and his mother. How does Madame Sabastian fit into gender stereotypes of the era? How does she respond to her son's marriage to Alicia? Compare her relationship to Sabastian to post-war theories about proper mothering. Would she get a good grade from the psychologists of that time?

4. Wars, even "cold" ones, demand sacrifices. What sacrifices do all the characters in the film make? How are they rewarded?

5. When they face a threat from someone in their circle who is not strong enough to keep their secret, the members of Sabastian's group immediately kill him. Does the movie offer any reason to think that Devlin and the other American agents would behave differently if they encountered a weak link in their operations?

6. The action in this movie takes place mainly in South America. What role do the countries of South America play during World War II and in the years immediately following the war? Research Uruguay's role in the destruction of the *Admiral Graf Spee*. Was Uruguay's response to the damaged ship ethical, dangerous, smart, or deplorable?

7. Devlin is the hero of the film. How do Devlin and Sabastian's physical appearances support the success of one and failure of the other? What other traits does Devlin possess that indicate that he will succeed? Are these in any way particularly American traits?

8. Was the plot to urge Alicia to marry Sabastian ethical? Is unethical behavior ever acceptable? If the answer is yes, how do you decide when unethical behavior is acceptable?

9. The United States, with Great Britain's support, worked out the design of the atomic bomb. What were the chances in 1945 that the two nations would be able to maintain control of the knowledge of atomic bomb design? Was the attempt to control this knowledge a wise choice? Should it have been made available to the whole world or to some selected parts of the world?

10. Who is in the "atomic club" today and what are the ramifications of club membership for members and for non-members? Does this issue currently affect American foreign relations in any way, and if so, how?

My Son John (1952)

(122 minutes) *Director:* Leo McCarey; *Stars:* Helen Hayes, Robert Walker, Dean Jagger, Van Heflin, Frank McHugh, Richard Jaeckel.

McCarthyism was sweeping across the United States by the early 1950s. Many Americans became convinced that the Soviet threat they faced demanded eternal and ever-expanding vigilance. Leo McCarey's *My Son John*, a vigorously anti–Communist movie from 1952, warned viewers that the Soviets were so evil and so devious that they could infiltrate not just the American government—the American family was even at risk.

There was a frantic quality to American fears and actions by the early fifties. In the preceding few decades Americans had suffered through several crises that affected the country's sense of confidence and well-being. The Great Depression was a searing memory for most adults. Japan had surprised and shocked the United States at Pearl Harbor. Nazism had almost overrun Europe. America had won World War II, but in a cruel and inexplicable subversion of this accomplishment, Communism had overrun Russia, China, and Eastern Europe. In the late 1940s, the House Un-American Activities Committee investigated alleged Communist infiltration of the Hollywood movie industry and discovered a dangerous threat in one of America's most cherished pastimes: going to the movies. The Hiss and Rosenberg trials, both in 1951, pointed the finger at spies within the government. The Korean War, a multinational effort in a small conflicted country that bordered a large Communist one, was not rolling along smoothly to an easy triumph.

Victory in World War II should have made the world safer. Instead, by the early fifties, Americans were more worried than ever that Communists both at home and abroad were undermining American security, and the anxieties of the era developed a snowball-rolling-downhill momentum. Senator Joseph McCarthy (R-WI) made a name for himself when he inadvertently tapped into these anxieties. While giving a speech to a women's group in Wheeling, West Virginia, in February 1950, McCarthy insisted that he had a list of 205 Communists who were working at the State Department. A newspaper covering the event reported this figure, but there were no recordings of his speech. Over the next few weeks, McCarthy's list of Communists shifted and shrank to 57, then grew to 81.[24] The Senator's charges were so explosive that people ignored his uncertain numbers and focused instead on his frightening claims, giving rise to the movement that took his name. Congressional hearings were called, people were investigated, and careers were ruined as McCarthyism spread like wildfire across an already troubled nation.

McCarthy gained tremendous power as a result of this issue, and he wielded it like a bludgeon. By 1954, he had become bold enough to allege without any evidence that there were Communists in the United States Army. The Army refused to let this accusation remain unchallenged and conducted hearings to clear its reputation. When the Army-McCarthy hearings were televised, the American people had their first real opportunity to see McCarthy in action. He came across as an arrogant bully and vicious demagogue who intimidated witnesses with little or no evidence. The drama reached its climax on live national television when Joseph Welch, legal counsel for the Army, challenged McCarthy publicly. McCarthy had smeared a promising young lawyer with accusations of Communist sympathies, and Welch demanded of McCarthy, "Have you no sense of decency, sir, at long last? Have you no sense of decency?"[25] Some people continued to believe there was danger everywhere and retained a fierce combative patriotism, but soon after the hearings ended, McCarthyism imploded as a national movement.

The McCarthy Era is remembered as a truly divisive period in American history. The fearful political atmosphere seemed to require that everyone present a strong and unwavering devotion to everything American in order to avoid even the taint of Communism. Anything less patriotic was suspect. Although some people believed that they were, in a sense, "at war," others did not and were unwilling to maintain the unexamined patriotism the times demanded. They believed there were problems in the United States that the country should consider forthrightly and address.

My Son John was released into this tense political climate. It centers on the Jeffersons, a typical American family. The two younger twin boys played sports in school, have just joined the military, and are about to ship off to Korea. But the oldest son, John (Robert Walker), his mother's favorite, does not make it home from his job in Washington, D.C., in time for their farewell dinner. When he comes home a little later, it is clear that he does not share the family's enthusiastic patriotism. He treats his father with undisguised condescension and his mother with smarmy, insincere affection. Father and son spar over his lack of patriotic fervor. Mother and Father spar over John.

But even as she defends her son, Lucille Jefferson (Helen Hayes) is uneasy about his attitude toward his country and the exact nature of his vaguely defined job. Mrs. Jefferson goes to Washington to investigate the matter firsthand. Spurred on by a series of encounters with a man who turns out to be an FBI agent, she finally confronts John about his questionable political beliefs. She entreats him to admit and recant his Communist sympathies in a scene that includes a kind of cheerleader chant, "My son John, my son John," that calls to mind her other sons' athletic successes. It is as if by doing this she can bring John back into the fold, transform his indifference into patriotism, his intellectualism into athleticism, in essence, *fix* him. When he refuses, she must choose between her son and her country.

The plot carries special significance for the early fifties. After ten years of uncertain economic times and five years of war, people were looking to turn inward and focus on personal goals, a luxury that Americans had been denied for almost a generation. The American family came to represent personal fulfillment for many.[26] Following the war, men reclaimed jobs in the workplace, while women returned to the home as wives and mothers. Rates of weddings rose dramatically and children followed, the entirely predictable Baby Boom. As incomes rose, multifamily housing, which offered common living space to multiple generations or the option of rental income, gave way to small one-family homes that were affordable and available in the post-war era. The expanding economy also made automobiles more affordable, and they contributed to this social restructuring. People no longer had to live close to one another or along bus or train routes.[27] The march to the suburbs began, and the resulting single-family home and lifestyle were idealized.[28] *My Son John* was a manifestation of the fear that even this sacrosanct unit was no longer secure.

McCarey's movie hit on other concerns as well. During the 1930s, capitalism took a pounding from the daily realities of the Depression. Some people, especially intellectuals with ties to organized labor, began to consider the possible advantages that Communism offered. But over the next decade, the pact between Stalin and Hitler and the recovery of the American economy seriously undermined any enthusiasm for Communist theory. After the war, Soviet Premier Joseph Stalin's brutal enforcement of Communism across Eastern Europe further tarnished Communism's reputation. Stalin's ironfisted control and rigid ideology undermined the attractiveness of Communist economic theory. Many of those who had once contemplated the advantages of Communism backed away from the idea.[29] But just the notion that they had once considered such a system left them suspect in the eyes of many Americans. John's behavior and intellectualism put him squarely in this group.

In addition to reflecting anxieties about Communism, *My Son John* also mirrors the era's attitudes about religion and patriotism. Throughout the 1950s, Americans set records for church membership as Christians and Jews became increasingly concerned about the spread of Godless Communism, and Catholics in particular were troubled by Cold War developments.[30] Their anxiety may have been motivated, in part, by the denial of religious freedom in the predominantly Catholic countries of Eastern Europe that were controlled by Communists. In *My Son John*, the Jeffersons are a devoutly Catholic family, and a patriotic one. In addition, like many World War II veterans, John's father joined the American Legion post in his community. The American Legion and similar patriotic groups not only celebrated veterans' recent military service but provided a way for patriotic Americans to show their support for their government and for American values in the Cold War struggle against the Soviet Union.

By hitting on these topics, *My Son John* managed to cover practically all the significant issues of the Cold War. But it did not stop there. The film's credibility was reinforced by the respected actors who played John's parents. Helen Hayes was known as "the First Lady of the American Theater" and was one of the most revered actresses of her day. Hayes had come out of a near 20-year-retirement from movies to make this picture.[31] And in what may have been a subtle attempt to solidify the military credentials and unimpeachable patriotism of John's father, Dean Jagger was given the role of Dan Jefferson. Just two years earlier, Jagger had won an Academy Award as Best Supporting Actor in the successful World War II combat film, *Twelve O'Clock High*, where he looked commandingly military. Perhaps not coincidentally, he bore a striking resemblance to American war hero and soon-to-be-president Dwight D. Eisenhower. Using these two compelling actors suggests that the film was pulling out all the stops to warn Americans, especially young people, about the dangers of Communism.

At the film's end, John does recant. His final thoughts about Communism are read into the movie as a speech on tape in an effort to save other young people who might be foolish enough to be enticed by the false promises and premises of Communism. (Robert Walker died before filming on the movie was completed, a fact that partially dictated the structure of this scene.) In his review of the movie, Bosley Crowther, movie critic for *The New York Times*, complained, "[I]t seethes with the sort of emotionalism and illogic that is characteristic of so much thinking these days."[32] Crowther's assessment of the movie is exactly what was intended.

Suggested Discussion Questions

1. Describe Lucille Jefferson's relationship with her sons and husband at the start of the movie. In what ways does she exemplify the ideal wife and mother, and in what ways does she not fulfill this ideal?

2. Describe Dan Jefferson's relationship with his sons and wife at the start of the movie. In what ways does he exemplify the ideal father and husband, and in what ways does he not fulfill this ideal?

3. If both parents are "good" parents within reasonable limits (i.e., no more or less successful than average parents), why is Dan the one who understands John's true nature whereas Lucille is unable, at first, to accept the truth about her son?

Invasion of the Body Snatchers (1956)   131

4. In terms of raising and nurturing John, does the movie suggest who is to blame for his behavior? Why? How does this fit into attitudes toward the family and gender roles that were prevalent in the 1950s? What message does this movie send specifically to women in 1952?

5. Describe John's educational background. Is there any obvious connection between it and his adult beliefs and actions?

6. Describe instances in the film that directly employ religion or religious imagery. What messages do these send about religion and American life?

7. How are athleticism and intellectualism presented in the movie? What message does the movie send about the smart student in the class? Does that characterization still appear in popular-culture products of today, and if so, where and why?

8. Does the movie offer any clues as to why John would take positions and actions that seem so at odds with his upbringing?

9. The right to dissent is a cherished American principle. How does the movie support this principle? Is dissent dangerous, and if it is, when should it be suppressed?

10. Analyze the role of the FBI in the plot. How did you respond to their actions? Their suspicions about John are correct. What message does this movie send about American security in the early fifties?

11. Lucille Jefferson accepts the FBI's version of John's behavior. Was she acting like a good mother? Was she acting like a good citizen? Was there any other way she could have responded to her son's situation?

12. Based on its representation of the threats facing America, to what political response does the movie drive viewers? Are there any movies today that seem to send obvious political messages? If so, what are the messages, and how successful do you believe they are at changing audience attitudes?

Invasion of the Body Snatchers (1956)

(80 minutes) *Director:* Don Siegel; *Stars:* Kevin McCarthy, Dana Wynter, King Donovan, Larry Gates, Carolyn Jones, Virginia Christine.

Don Siegel's *Invasion of the Body Snatchers* is not just another 1950s monster movie. It is a classic of the genre and one of the best examples of the many horror and science-fiction movies that appeared during the decade. The plot operates on multiple levels. The central premise, an unknown alien invades small-town America, could just as easily be a metaphor for Communist subversion in the United States.

The tremendous popularity of movies about monsters and mutants in the years after World War II may have been partly the result of the anxieties and fears of the Cold War era. Concerns about atomic power, radiation, and nuclear holocaust, for example, could explain the proliferation of movies like *The Beast from 20,000 Fathoms* (1953), *Creature from the Black Lagoon* (1954), *Them!* (1954), *It Came from Beneath the Sea* (1955), *Creature with the Atom Brain* (1955), *It Conquered the World* (1956), *The Creature Walks Among Us* (1956), *The Monster That Challenged the World* (1957), *The Attack of the 50 Foot Woman* (1958), and *The Fly* (1958). The Japanese brought their own special insight to the genre with *Gojira* (1954). After it was transformed into English in 1956 and released in the United States as *Godzilla, King of the Monsters*, the movie went on to achieve cult status and turned into a production gold mine, generating multiple cinematic offspring.

The idea that Americans could be victimized by agents acting in secret was widely feared at the time and appeared as a subtext in many movies from the era. Movies about alien invasions, including classics such as *The Thing from Another World* (1951), *It Came from Outer Space* (1953), *It! The Terror from Beyond Space* (1958), and *The Blob* (1958) struck a responsive chord with American audiences who lived in daily fear of possible war with the Soviet Union. *Invasion of the Body Snatchers*, from 1956, offered an interesting take on the "unknown invader" scenario. In the opening scene, police pick up a seemingly deranged man, Dr. Miles Bennell (Kevin McCarthy), because of his bizarre behavior along a highway. They found him lurching through moving traffic trying to warn people of an alien threat. When they bring him to a hospital he frantically tries to convince a doctor that the country is under attack by something insidious and otherworldly.

The movie unfolds in a flashback. Bennell explains to the doctor that when he returned from a medical convention to his home in a remote California town, he encountered a slew of patients and friends all claiming that people well known to them were not themselves somehow. Initially, he is dismissive of these claims until he discovers a group of giant pods at a friend's house. The pods contain vaguely human forms. He realizes that the pods are turning into people when he discovers a nearly complete pod body waiting patiently to "snatch" the life of his friend, an exchange that can only occur when the victim is sleeping. Miles tries desperately to get help and to keep everyone awake, especially Becky Driscoll (Dana Wynter), a former girlfriend who has returned home after her divorce. But the pod people keep on coming. One by one, everybody he knows and trusts is transformed, and he and Becky are getting more and more tired. Eventually, despite Bennell's warnings, the fatigued Becky falls asleep and is transformed into an unfeeling alien pod person. When Bennell kisses her, he discovers the transformation and explains in a voiceover, "I never knew fear until I kissed Becky."

Cold war audiences familiar with McCarthyism could readily relate to the Bennell's warning about the coming of the pod people. The Cold War had settled into something that resembled a well-defended stalemate by the mid-1950s. Joseph Stalin, the Soviet dictator and architect of the Communist takeover of Eastern Europe, died in 1953. Times within the Soviet Union had changed enough that his successor, Nikita Khrushchev, was able to criticize Stalin's excesses and contemplate the possibility of "peaceful coexistence" with the West. However, Communism still remained a dangerous force in the world. Throughout the 1950s and early 1960s, the Soviet Union showed no signs of relinquishing its control over Eastern Europe, as evidenced by their swift, brutal military crackdown on Hungary when it tried to break away from Soviet control in 1956. Khrushchev also continued to push for the spread of Communism worldwide. His rhetoric see-sawed between "peaceful coexistence" with the West and warnings to the United States that "we will bury you," and the Soviet dictator practiced dangerous brinkmanship during the Berlin and Cuban Missile Crises.

America's Cold War culture of the 1950s and early 1960s demanded that people not let down their guard. Elementary schools practiced "duck and cover" drills that required students to duck under desks or crouch in interior hallways in the event of an atomic attack. People built bomb shelters in their basements or backyards where they could wait out the radioactivity that would linger after a nuclear bomb blast. (How long this wait should last was never explicitly stated.)[33] *Invasion of the Body Snatchers* reflected this view. Its dominant message is that people who appear normal may actually be threats to life as we know it. The alien subversives in the movie are capable of infecting others, but they can be detected by their lack of emotion. The pod people are bland, cold automatons (resembling Ninotchka before her transformation by love, a wild and disruptive emotion). For example, at one point in the movie Miles hears music and is convinced that whoever is playing it cannot have been taken over by the emotionless pods because the piece is too beautiful and moving. He concludes that wherever the sound is coming from must be safe, only to be dismayed a little while later when he discovers its true source.

In the decades since the release of *Invasion of the Body Snatchers,* various other interpretations of the movie have been offered. But the anti–Communist interpretation remains quite convincing. Much of the dialog and many plot elements appear to be obvious metaphors for American fears about the spread of Communism in the 1950s. For example, the pod people, like Communists, advocate a group mentality and display herd behavior. In addition, the alien threat, like the real Red Menace, is being waged by emotionless, soulless creatures who are intent on destroying the American way of life. Even the fact that the pod people infiltrate the town while innocent victims sleep reinforces a commonly held belief in Cold War America: the United States must always remain alert to defend against the spread of Communism.

No one at the hospital believes Miles's story until a highway accident involving a truck occurs. The ambulance personnel who bring in the injured driver report that the truck was carrying strange giant pods. Suddenly, Miles's claims are taken seriously, and the doctor who had previously dismissed him now demands to be connected to the FBI, "It's an emergency." Although the film ends here, the final scene leaves little doubt that now that the menace has been exposed, Americans, with the FBI in the lead, can take action and save themselves and their country.

Suggested Discussion Questions

1. Many characters in the movie appear as before-and-after versions of themselves. How do these versions differ?

2. During their first meeting, Becky and Miles use a metaphor about Reno, Nevada, to exchange information regarding the fact that they are both divorced. Why would they do this? Why would the plot use a divorced woman rather than one who had never married as Miles's love interest? Explain the nature of their relationship as the film progresses.

3. The people who have already been taken over by their "pod" replacements appear menacing. Besides their obvious lack of emotion, give examples of other negative traits. How do these traits reflect attitudes about Communists?

4. Miles and Becky are captured by the pod people. How do they escape? What characteristics or behavioral traits does Miles exhibit as he plots their escape?

5. During and after their capture, how does Becky respond to (a) the danger they are in; (b) the escape plan Miles proposes; and (c) carrying out the plan? Is she a help or a hindrance?

6. Describe Becky's clothes. What do they indicate about her lifestyle and character? How does Becky reflect gender attitudes of the 1950s?

7. As the movie goes on, Miles must ultimately save himself. Because he has no family, the danger comes from outside his personal life. In *My Son John*, the danger is to a traditional American family from one of their own. Evaluate the degree of the closeness of the threat in either or both movies. Where is the danger coming from and what does the source indicate about the Communist threat? What or whom should Americans fear?

8. The townspeople become a mob. Evaluate this plot device as a metaphor for the McCarthy Era. Does it seem applicable? Or does it seem to be unrelated to the attitudes of the McCarthy Era? Does the movie support mob violence or oppose it?

9. Ultimately, the entire town chases after Miles and Becky. Yet Miles continues to resist. How do the behaviors of the townspeople and Miles reflect American ideals?
10. Describe other moments in American history where mob behavior drove events, and evaluate their outcomes. What were the positive and negative results?
11. Miles is the only person who recognizes the threat. How far should he go to oppose it? Does he do enough?
12. The doctor calls the FBI when he realizes that there is a threat. What does his response show about attitudes toward the FBI? How is the audience likely to respond to his actions?
13. Compare and contrast Dr. Miles Bennell and Agent T.R. Devlin (Cary Grant's character in *Notorious*). Compare and contrast Becky Driscoll and Alicia Huberman (Ingrid Bergman's character in *Notorious*). How do they represent gender issues of the time?

The Manchurian Candidate (1962)

(126 minutes) *Director:* John Frankenheimer; *Stars:* Frank Sinatra, Laurence Harvey, Angela Lansbury, James Gregory, Janet Leigh, Henry Silva, John McGiver, Leslie Parrish, Khigh Dhiegh.

John Frankenheimer's complicated psychological thriller, *The Manchurian Candidate*, explores the anxieties of the Cold War era. The movie flashes backward, forward, and into the dream worlds of various characters who fought as a unit in Korea and who all come back believing that Sergeant Raymond Shaw, the man who saved their lives in a combat incident, is an American hero. The problem that nags at the captain of the unit is that despite this belief, he and his men truly hate Sergeant Shaw.

The Manchurian Candidate was released at a time when the Cold War was threatening to erupt into World War III. Americans elected John F. Kennedy to succeed Dwight D. Eisenhower as president in 1960. Kennedy represented a new generation of leadership for America. The youngest elected president in American history, he and his wife, Jacqueline, brought two small children with them to the White House. His vigorous approach to the presidency differed from Eisenhower's in style and attitude. Like his predecessor, however, Kennedy believed strongly in the policy of containment, and he specifically emphasized this in his Inaugural Address when he pledged that America would "pay any price, bear any burden" to prevent the spread of Communism.

But Kennedy was also open to non-military methods to win over Third World nations to America's side in the Cold War. His foreign policy featured humanitarian approaches such as the Alliance for Progress, which provided aid to Latin America, and the Peace Corps, which recruited idealistic Americans to work in Third World countries. The volunteers' mission was to help poor people in developing nations solve practical problems by, for example, digging wells, building schools, or improving irrigation systems. The larger intent was to improve people's lives and, in the process, limit the lure of Communism in a way that avoided conflict rather than invited it.[34]

Despite President Kennedy's innovative approach to the Third World, he was every bit as much a Cold Warrior as President Eisenhower. Just a few weeks after taking office, Kennedy gave his approval for an American-sponsored invasion of Cuba. The covert operation led by Cuban exiles was routed by Fidel Castro's forces at the Bay of Pigs. The debacle convinced the Soviet Union that the young, inexperienced American president could easily be pushed around.[35] When Soviet Premier Nikita Khrushchev met Kennedy for the first time at the Vienna Summit in 1961, the aggressive Soviet leader demanded that the United States pull its troops out of Berlin, but Kennedy adamantly refused. By the time the conference ended, the two superpowers were on the verge of World War III. A military confrontation was averted when Khrushchev ordered the building of the Berlin Wall in August 1961 to prevent East Germans from fleeing to freedom through West Berlin.[36] The world hardly had time to recover from these anxious moments before the Cuban Missile Crisis once again brought the United States and Soviet Union to the brink of nuclear war. For 13 days in October 1962, the world held its collective breath while the two superpowers played a high-stakes game of nuclear poker. Finally, the Soviets blinked and agreed to pull their missiles out of Cuba in return for America's agreement that it would not invade Cuba. Realizing how close the two countries had come to a nuclear exchange convinced both leaders to resume arms talks, which ultimately resulted in the Nuclear Test Ban Treaty of 1963.[37]

These Cold War tensions establish the context for *The Manchurian Candidate* from 1962. The movie unfolds in a series of flashbacks that occur as nightmares and are designed to be confusing and unsettling. The flashbacks take place during the Korean War. The North Koreans have captured a group of American soldiers, and they use brainwashing techniques to turn one of the POWs, Sergeant Raymond Shaw (Laurence Harvey), into an assassin who can be triggered to act by a handler. The choice of Shaw is not random. He is the stepson of Senator Johnny Iselin (James Gregory), a potential vice-presidential nominee. The Communists brainwash the other Americans to believe that Sergeant Shaw has saved all their lives in a combat incident. They are programmed to declare that Shaw is "the kindest, bravest, warmest, most wonderful human being I have ever known in my life." When the platoon is released back into the field, they report this false story of Shaw's heroics.

The Manchurian Candidate (1962) 137

Shaw is awarded the Congressional Medal of Honor for heroism on the battlefield, and he returns to the States somewhat befuddled by the all the attention he receives. Immediately upon his return, he is greeted by his conniving mother (played with reptilian menace by Angela Lansbury) and his obsequious stepfather. They bask in Raymond's reflected glory with embarrassing assertiveness because they have a bigger objective in mind. Their goal is to have Senator Iselin win the nomination for vice president. The story of Raymond's heroism has been planted by the Communists in order to help achieve this goal, and an American Communist "handler" will direct him as he assassinates various people to further that aim.

A flaw in the Communists' insidious assassination plan soon emerges. One member of Shaw's platoon, Captain Bennett Marco (Frank Sinatra), experiences relentless, deeply disturbing nightmares about strange events that occurred in Korea and involved Shaw. The troubling dreams affect Marco's health and job performance, and he seeks help from the military. At first, military psychologists are dismissive of his concerns, but they take action when another platoon member reluctantly reports the same nightmares. The movie's plot quickly becomes an unacknowledged competition between Marco and Shaw, who are trying to understand what is happening to them, and Raymond's mother, who is intent on using her son and her buffoonish husband to place her near the summit of American political power.

The Manchurian Candidate demonstrates that Americans of the early 1960s believed Communists would use any means to attack America. The movie picks up on the common wisdom that during the Korean War the Communists had brainwashed American POWs to obtain information and defections.[38] Brainwashing is an attack on the individual. It subverts the real person and replaces his or her intrinsic motivations with external manipulation. Raymond Shaw does not accept his role as an assassin, it is forced upon him. (The plot of *Invasion of the Body Snatchers* also suggests that infection from an external source is the only believable explanation for an American's acceptance of an alien ideology.) North Korean brainwashing and Shaw's intended subversion of the American political process reinforce the idea that the threat to America is real, but it is not likely to be by a military invasion.

Americans of the early 1960s were still quite anxious about Communism, but the movie also suggests that they would not tolerate another McCarthy-type demagogue. The movie holds the McCarthy Era up for reevaluation and ridicule by making Shaw's stepfather a pompous, unintelligent politician who uses false accusations and demagoguery in order to increase his own popularity and power, just as Senator Joseph McCarthy did back in the early 1950s. Like McCarthy, Senator Iselin tries to smear the Department of Defense, and he offers the press conflicting numbers for the people on his list of Communists who are working there. The movie takes it one step further when Raymond murders a man who opposes his father, opposition clearly intended to represent the rational, anti-demagogue position.

The sinister ease with which the movie's climactic assassination scene occurs is both deeply disturbing and a reaffirmation of America's ability to right itself no matter the threat. Marco is able to defeat the Communist plot to control America through his friendship with Shaw and his diligent pursuit of the truth. And, despite the psychological damage Shaw has suffered, he is able to thwart his mother and stepfather's ruthless ambition.

One year after its release, however, the movie took on a much darker and more frightening import when Lee Harvey Oswald, a loner with vague connections to the Soviet Union and Cuban leader Fidel Castro, assassinated President Kennedy using a high-powered rifle similar to the one used in the movie. The president's death rocked the nation. In the wake of this tragedy, *The Manchurian Candidate* looked less like fiction and more like a template for the crime. It was removed from circulation for many years. No official explanation was ever given for this action. It was re-released theatrically in 1987.

Suggested Discussion Questions

1. America celebrates well-rounded team players. Leaving aside behavior by Raymond Shaw that is the direct result of brainwashing, how does he fit this model?

2. Compare the three main female roles in the movie: Raymond's mother, Joclyn Jordan, and Rosie. What messages does the movie send about women and beauty? What message does the movie send about women and power?

3. The culture of the fifties celebrated mothers, motherhood, and the family. How does the character of Raymond's mother reflect this trend? Why would the movie include a scene where Raymond's mother kisses him on the lips? (Compare and contrast Raymond's mother, the mother in *Notorious*, and the mother in *My Son John*.)

4. The story takes place mainly in New York City and Washington, D.C. Civil rights was a major political and social concern during the 1960s. Discuss the African American characters in the movie. Do they represent the norm for African Americans throughout the country at the time? If not, why are they portrayed this way in the movie?

5. How does the movie portray Communists? Should Americans be concerned about the threat they pose? Why, or why not?

6. The Korean "doctor" who overseas Raymond's care in a New York hospital says at one point "I'm going to Macy's." What does his comment suggest

about the attitudes of some Communists to the availability and variety of goods in capitalist countries? (Compare his behavior to the reaction by the Soviet delegates to Paris in *Ninotchka.*)

7. Marco reports his nightmares to the military. Initially, they do not believe him. (Miles Bennell's claims are also dismissed in *Invasion of the Body Snatchers.*) Why would authorities not believe Marco (or Bennell)? How can authorities evaluate the validity of a person's claim of subversion or attack? Is this a problem now, and if so, how can we solve it?

8. Does Rosie represent a threat or security? Defend your answer. Give possible explanations for her remarks about Chinese labor and railroad construction.

9. In addition to Marco, the movie offers two other significant voices of reason, the New York editor who hires Raymond and Joclyn's father, Senator Jordan. How are these characters portrayed? Are their portrayals likely to win audience confidence and trust?

10. The movie has many offbeat moments that are based on visual images; for example, the death of Senator Jordan and the bottle of milk. Describe any other examples you found. There are many symbols of patriotism, particularly images of Abraham Lincoln, in the movie. Why would the director include these images and examples of visual humor?

11. Senator Johnny Iselin's remarks in a Senate meeting about Communists in the Department of Defense mimic those of Senator Joseph McCarthy about the State Department in 1952. What message is the movie sending about McCarthyism and about the threat of Communist subversion in America? Are these messages consistent or do they conflict? Explain your answer.

12. Continue the movie's storyline for a few more days. Describe how news stories might be written about the final scene at the rally and what happened to Raymond. How do you believe Americans would have reacted to an event like this?

13. Is the conclusion of the movie likely to make Americans in 1962 feel more or less secure? What will become of Rosie and Marco?

Nuclear Anxieties

Kiss Me Deadly (1955)

(105 minutes) *Director:* Robert Aldrich; *Stars:* Ralph Meeker, Albert Dekker, Maxine Cooper, Gaby Rodgers, Wesley Addy, Nick Dennis, Paul Stewart, Cloris Leachman, Jack Elam, Strother Martin, Jack Lambert.

Kiss Me Deadly, directed by Robert Aldrich and based on the novel by Mickey Spillane, features hero detective Mike Hammer in a *film noir* thriller about two mysterious women and a dangerous object of desire. Set in the early years of the Cold War, the hero's name bluntly describes his approach to confronting evil.

The Cold War dominated the nation's international outlook throughout the 1950s and generated in an aggressive patriotism. Americans who criticized their country were accused of giving psychological ammunition to the enemy. Constitutional protections for freedom of speech were ignored as those in power resorted to the Hollywood Blacklist, to loyalty oaths as a requirement for employment, and to FBI investigations of people involved in the civil rights movement.[39] Most Americans believed that the country should react forcefully to any Communist threat, external or internal. If necessary, Americans were even willing to go to war against the Soviet Union, which was also armed with atomic bombs. As a result, the threat of mutual nuclear destruction hung over every international incident, including the Korean War, the Suez Crisis, and the Hungarian Revolution. Only one question remained: what circumstances would warrant another use of an atomic bomb?

America's aggressive patriotism was personified by Senator Joseph McCarthy, who applied his ham-fisted tactics to anyone who opposed his belligerent anti–Communist rhetoric. Some historians have suggested that Mickey Spillane's detective Mike Hammer is the fictional counterpart of McCarthy. As a literary representation of the era's take-no-prisoners approach, Mike Hammer had a very large audience. Six out of the top ten best-selling works of fiction in the 1950s were written by Mickey Spillane, and Mike Hammer was featured in five of them.[40] A headline on a *LIFE* magazine cover from 1952 read: "Mickey Spillane: 13,000,000 Books of Sex and Slaughter."[41] Every time Hammer's character ran roughshod over people's constitutional rights or referred to "Commies" and "jerky Reds" it was as if the tensions between the Soviet Union and the United States were playing out in a fictional parallel universe.

The rise of international Communism was not the only source of anxiety in 1950s America. Social change involving gender roles, the rise of the Baby Boom, and the emergence of the consumer culture also triggered uneasiness on the part of the public. During the war the number of women in the workforce went from 14,600,000 in 1941 to 19,370,000 by 1944, and estimates suggest that 50 percent of all women worked at some time during the war years.[42] When men returned from the war to reclaim their jobs, many women felt a loss of independence as they returned to the traditional roles of mother and homemaker. A new focus on family and children added to the stress on both sexes, as did the demands of a new middle-class lifestyle that measured success through the consumption—sometimes pejoratively referred to as "conspicuous"—of consumer goods. Both men and women became anxious and uncertain about what their roles and goals should be in the new post-war world.

Philip Wylie's bestseller from 1942, *Generation of Vipers*, foreshadowed the gender conflicts that would become more prominent in the 1950s. Wylie viewed women as greedy and demanding, especially in their roles as wives and mothers. An example of his vituperative attitude can be found in Wylie's description of married women, which he supports with a crude sexual metaphor. He explains that when girls discover they are not "Cinderella," the only way they can get over the shock "is to institute momworship" and "teach their men that dowry went the other way ... that any male worthy of a Cinderella would have to work like a piston after getting one, so as to be worthy, also, of all the moms in the world."[43] The initial impact of the book was blunted as everyone geared up to support the war effort and women headed off to work. But once the troops came home and began looking for jobs and wives, Wylie's analysis seemed to explain some of the strains and dissatisfactions that emerged between the sexes and within marriage.

The cornucopia of anxieties swirling around issues involving changing gender roles, consumerism, Communists, and nuclear war gave moviemakers new concerns to address. *Kiss Me Deadly* deals with all these issues but relies on familiar gender stereotypes and plot devices. The movie follows the standard format for the detective story. It features brutal bad guys, a bizarre cast of suspicious characters, a couple of alluring women who might be victims or might be victimizers, and a mysterious object of desire. In Spillane's original story, published in 1951, the object was heroin. In the 1955 movie, it was radioactive material.[44] The change made box-office if not necessarily plot sense at a time when Americans were obsessed with fears of Communist spies and atomic threats.

The movie begins with a frantic woman running barefoot down a dark, lonely road, trying to hitch a ride. Desperate to stop someone, she steps in front of a car driven by private detective Mike Hammer (Ralph Meeker). He reluctantly lets her in. As Nat "King" Cole sings "I'd Rather Have the Blues" on the car radio, Christina (Cloris Leachman), dressed only in a trench coat, breaks down in gulping sobs and explains her predicament, which appears more paranoid than believable.

Hammer is brusque and unsympathetic. He subscribes to Wylie's misogynistic view of women and responds to them accordingly. But when his car is stopped at a roadblock and a policeman inquires about a woman who has just escaped from an insane asylum, Hammer covers for Christina by declaring that they are husband and wife. Shortly after they drive on, they are kidnapped by mysterious villains. Hammer is drugged, Christina is tortured, and they are left for dead in a faked car accident, which Hammer barely survives. When he recovers and learns of Christina's death he reconsiders her story. The plot that spins off this encounter is difficult to follow because most of it unfolds for the viewer as it does for Mike Hammer. He is confused by much of what he discovers, but he is determined to avenge himself and Christina, who left behind a cryptic note asking that he "remember me."

Kiss Me Deadly picks up on several common constructs of Cold War America. Hammer exhibits an aggressive take-no-prisoners response to any threat. Spies and criminals are able to operate seemingly unchecked as they undermine American security. The women in the movie have not accepted motherhood as their proper role in life, and they are therefore dangerous and untrustworthy. Men with intellectual professions or interests are caught up in the crime, but they are weak and ultimately not able to defend themselves.

Ralph Meeker is a stocky, broad-shouldered actor, and he plays Hammer as a competent thug who is reasonably good at connecting the dots but not inclined to reflect at length about the ethics of his methods. He attacks when he feels threatened. Stephen J. Whitfield described the Hammer character as "so preposterously hard-boiled that he was slightly cracked."[45] Hammer shows no respect for women and is comfortable using the seductive charms of his girlfriend, Velda (Maxine Cooper), to get information from unsuspecting sources, especially wayward husbands. Velda's behavior regarding his clients is never clearly defined, but audiences could infer from her comments that what she does is either prostitution or close to it. Almost every female in the movie is presented as dumb, drunk, sexually promiscuous, domineering, unstable, or criminal. Velda does manage to win some sympathy for her plight, her efforts to help Mike, and her love for him. But her role as his accomplice in shady investigations and the way she accepts his frankly dismissive attitude make her a problematic figure.

If *Kiss Me Deadly* perpetuates stereotypes about women and Communists, it challenges commonly held beliefs about race and ethnicity. Hammer frequents an African American bar where he treats the bartender and others with friendly respect. He also shows respect for an elderly Italian he encounters, respect that he does not extend to the Mafia-like criminals he meets during his investigation. Probably the most sympathetic character in the movie is a Greek immigrant named Nick, who is Hammer's mechanic and friend.

Significantly, whenever Mike Hammer encounters people who do fit his preconceptions, he responds with force and menace, as evidenced by the way he handles a Mafia leader and his associates, a scared and helpless science writer, an overweight art dealer so fearful he swallows sleeping pills rather than face whoever may be coming up his stairs, and a shrewish, domineering housewife.

"Tell her to shut up," Hammer tells her husband.

"Shut up," the husband willingly repeats.

Hammer's investigation of Christina's death eventually leads him to her roommate, Lily Carver (Gaby Rodgers), and to the box that contains the object everyone has been desperately seeking. Lily is as mysterious as Christina, but she has slightly better survival skills. Cleverly hiding her real motives up until the last scene, Lily becomes demanding, foolish, emasculating, and overeager to open the dangerous and mysterious box. The people who developed the atomic bomb technology and the people in this movie who conspire to steal it are overwhelmingly male. But Lily is Philip Wylie's "viper" personified, and, like a Pandora for the nuclear age, she is the one who ultimately brings about destruction.

Suggested Discussion Questions

1. As soon as he recovers from his injuries, Hammer is questioned by federal agents. He does not give them information, but pursues the case on his own. Why does he decide not to cooperate with the government in the investigation?

2. Which characters in the movie are likely to have the most formal education? How do they fare in the plot?

3. Hammer is friendly with police Lieutenant Pat Murphy (Wesley Addy). Analyze Murphy's physical appearance. Compare the physical appearances of Hammer and Murphy to Dr. Soberin, science writer Ray Diker, and the art dealer William Mist. Who among them appears most trustworthy? How do their appearances affect audience perceptions of them?

4. Define "vigilante justice." What is Lieutenant Murphy's view of it? Is it ever acceptable? How is vigilante justice different from revolution? How would vigilante justice affect the conduct of a democracy based on the rule of law?

5. Christina appears in the first scene and the movie immediately ties her to an insane asylum. How does this connection influence audience perceptions? Does the movie's ending do anything to redeem women?

6. Explain Soberin's references to Pandora, Lot's wife, and "feline perceptions" in the final scene. Compare Soberin's view of women with Hammer's.

7. Describe the movie's attitude toward the three female leads. Compare Velda, Lily, and Christina. Explain which one(s) would fit in best with the goals of the present-day Women's Movement, and why.

8. Hammer visits Eddie, an African-American fight promoter, and comments on his lack of ethics. Is this evidence of racial bias by Hammer? Defend your answer.

9. Try to determine Hammer's value system based on the characters he treats with disdain or violence and those he appears to favor. Do you agree with Christina's analysis of him as being only concerned with his own needs?

10. Hammer was a very popular literary hero in the 1950s, which suggests that readers supported his attitudes and actions. What can you infer from his popularity about audience attitudes toward women, minorities, and issues related to personal security and, by extension, national defense?

11. After viewing this movie would audiences in the fifties believe the government was capable of protecting the country? Would they be more or less likely to endorse criminal acts by individuals to ensure America's security? Would you have done so in the fifties? Would you now? Explain your answers.

12. Research Senator Joseph McCarthy. Compare McCarthy and Hammer. How are they similar? How are they different? Is either one, and by extension the methods he uses, the right way to respond to the tensions of the Cold War? Are they heroes or do they represent a danger to the country?

13. Should Hammer have let the government and the police handle this case? Why, or why not?

On the Beach (1959)

(133 minutes) *Director:* Stanley Kramer; *Stars:* Gregory Peck, Ava Gardner, Fred Astaire, Anthony Perkins, Donna Anderson, John Tate, Guy Doleman.

Billed on movie posters as "The Biggest Story of Our Time," *On the Beach* took direct aim at the era's ultimate fear: nuclear holocaust. Ever since the Soviet Union developed an atomic bomb in 1949, the two superpowers had teetered on the brink of mutual destruction. Anxieties about the danger of nuclear weapons began creeping into popular culture not long after the bombing of Hiroshima. In *The Thing from Another World* (1951), a scientist celebrates the triumph of pure science by declaring proudly, "We've split the atom," and another character gets a laugh when he responds, "Yes, and that sure made the world happy, didn't it?" Throughout the 1950s, the arms race between the United States and the Soviet Union involved the development and testing of nuclear weapons and missile-delivery systems. Technological accomplishment was the measure of victory as well as the means.

As the decade progressed, the issue took on greater urgency. Scientists like Linus Pauling predicted dire results from nuclear testing, including defects in children and increased cases of leukemia.[46] American pediatrician Dr. Benjamin Spock, author of the bestselling *Dr. Spock's Baby and Childcare* (its eighth edition appeared in 2004), worried about the effects of nuclear fears on children's emotional development.[47] People began to question whether just testing these weapons could cause overwhelming harm to the whole planet. Alison M. Scott and Christopher D. Geist describe the extent of these anxieties: "The specter of mushroom clouds rising over ravaged landscapes cast an inescapable shadow across all aspects of American life."[48]

The intense anti–Communist sentiment in America in the early 1950s may have been part of the reason that strong opposition to nuclear testing and warfare did not emerge sooner than it did. The Cold War generated such widespread public support for an aggressive foreign policy that people who were anti-war or anti-bomb were often suspected of being "Communist dupes." But, as McCarthyism ebbed in the mid–1950s, a significant anti-nuclear movement began to emerge. The American Friends Service Committee, a Quaker organization, led the effort to oppose hydrogen bomb testing. Other similar groups arose, including the Committee for Non-Violent Action (1957), the National Committee for a Sane Nuclear Policy (SANE, 1957), the Student Peace Union (1959), and Women Strike for Peace (1960).[49]

In an effort to counter these anxieties, the United States Office of Civil and Defense Mobilization took steps to assuage public concerns. In addition to promoting "duck and cover" drills, which sent school children scrambling under their desks to escape the dangers of atomic blasts, they advocated fallout shelters. This generic term was applied to sturdy public buildings, but it also referred to personal underground structures that families could stock with food, water, and other accommodations. Mom, Dad, and the kids could wait out the lingering effects of the radiation released during a nuclear attack in these backyard bunkers and emerge when the all-clear was declared. The government advertised the concept through films and pamphlets and even offered economical do-it-yourself building plans.[50]

On the Beach, Nevil Shute's best-selling 1957 novel about an atomic apocalypse, was one of the most effective literary representations of anti-nuclear and anti-war sentiment. The novel dramatized the era's anxieties in a story set in Australia in the aftermath of a nuclear war. It focuses on the characters' thoughts and actions as they await the arrival of an approaching cloud of deadly radiation let loose by the war. Between the book's publication in 1957 and the release of the movie in 1959, the Soviet Union stunned the world by launching *Sputnik*, the first man-made satellite, into space. *Sputnik* was an unexpected technological and public-relations victory by America's Communist enemy, and it raised nuclear anxieties to even greater heights. Not only had the Soviets trumped America's vaunted technology, but their accomplishment drove home the point that Russian missiles were powerful and accurate enough to hit American targets.

By 1959, the movie version of Shute's novel delivered a grim message that much of the country—and the world—was ready to hear. The opening scenes depict an American submarine, the *Sawfish,* commanded by a very starched and professional Dwight Towers (Gregory Peck), surfacing to a flat ominous ocean. It is bound for Australia, the only habitable place left on earth after the recent nuclear war. Who and what started the war is never explained. The next scenes offer a sharp contrast. They show Peter Holmes (Anthony Perkins), his wife, Mary (Donna Anderson), and their infant daughter waking up at home in Melbourne, Australia. It is a comfortable, almost cheery setting. But Mary is stressed and disconnected, and Peter is the one in charge of the home situation, which was a noticeable reversal of gender roles in the 1950s. As the baby cries, Peter quiets her with her bottle because Mary does not seem to be able to function effectively. Gloomy background music rises as the camera zooms in on a calendar showing the year—1964.

The plot covers a period of about five months between the end of the nuclear war, in which Australia has apparently had no part, and the expected arrival of a deadly cloud of radiation from the northern hemisphere. Peter is an officer in the Royal Australian Navy. When the *Sawfish* reaches Australia, Peter is assigned as liaison to it. The submarine will soon take off on a mission to measure radiation levels in various areas of the Pacific Ocean and try to determine where the radiation cloud will drift.

Peter and Mary host a party for Dwight after he arrives to help him settle in and perhaps distract him from his grief over the deaths of his wife and two children during the war. At the party Dwight spends time with Peter and Mary's very beautiful friend, Moira (Ava Gardner). She is charming and friendly when sober, but she is often drunk. Dwight never overtly expresses his grief, and at times he does not seem to accept that his wife and children are dead. He speaks of them glowingly in the present tense. Also at the party is Julian Osborne (Fred Astaire), a scientist who has trouble working through just how much guilt scientists should bear for creating the weapons that have brought the world to this point.

The movie follows these characters as they and the rest of Australia come to grips with the approaching end of the world. The Australian government has prepared suicide pills that it plans to distribute in the final days so its citizens will not have to suffer once radiation sickness sets in. Except for limited "petrol" supplies, however, people basically go about their daily lives. They acknowledge the approaching catastrophe in abstract or careful terms. Only Mary seems unable to handle the impending doom, but the other characters are affected by their collective fate in different ways. Moira has fallen in love with Dwight, and she attempts to curb her drinking. Julian becomes more and more fatalistic and reckless. Peter tries gently to help Mary cope with their situation. Eventually, Dwight begins to speak of his family as if he understands that they are dead.

The submarine, with Peter and Julian aboard, sets out to see whether there is any lessening of radiation near the Arctic Circle and also to investigate an erratic radio signal coming from California. Neither search produces good news, but the trip does provide opportunities for sad, stark shots of bleak, abandoned cities.

What the movie does not show, however, is civil disorder and death. The people in Australia are a bit grim, but they continue to go to work on bikes or on foot, go fishing, play billiards, attend a car race, and line up in an orderly fashion to get their allotment of suicide pills, all without any trace of end-times chaos. Author Nevil Shute was English, and the story he crafted pits the celebrated British emotional reserve against an approaching, unyielding apocalypse. Reserve won, and director Stanley Kramer filmed it that way. The lack of societal chaos and collapse may have been the sugar coating that both the book and movie needed in order to acquire an audience for so disturbing a story. (*Miracle Mile,* released in 1989, shows a much more primitive and brutal reaction to a similar situation. Unlike *On the Beach,* once nuclear war begins in *Miracle Mile* no one goes gently and lots of things blow up.)

An Australian folk song, "Waltzing Matilda," became the popular musical theme for *On the Beach* and served as a secondary form of publicity for it.[51] The song is played throughout the movie at various tempos using different instruments, but its haunting message remains the same. The lyrics describe a vagrant who steals to eat then defiantly commits suicide rather than be caught and hanged. As a theme for the movie, "Waltzing Matilda" offers a sad parallel to the impending fate of all Australians.

After Dwight returns from his mission and with time running out, he and Moira spend the night at an inn. During their dinner, a thunderstorm erupts and, in a nearby bar, a group of drunken men sing a raucous, off-key "Waltzing Matilda." The effect of the storm and the grating singing voices is almost painful to hear. But then one voice takes over and sings the song so beautifully that the meaning of the scene shifts, and what has been lost and what is about to be lost becomes piercingly clear.

As the deadly cloud drifts ever closer, people finally begin to unravel. Cases of radiation sickness develop, and people discuss openly how to get their suicide pills and when to take them. A religious revival, complete with band and banner, starts up and gathers participants. But aside from some added dependence on alcohol as a spine stiffener, there is still no breakdown of civil order. The last images of the town are scenes of emptiness. In the final shot, the camera closes in on the religious revival banner, which reads, "There is still time, brother."

Suggested Discussion Questions

1. In the opening scenes, most of the Australian characters display roughly the same approach to their situation. They accuse higher-ups of not knowing very much, but they are resolutely trying to get along in their current circumstances. No whining is permitted. Does this seem like the kind of behavior people would naturally exhibit at about five months before the expected end of the world? Why, or why not?

2. At the party, Julian and others debate who is to blame for what has happened. The principal suspects are scientists and politicians, although "mom" does get a mention. Who is the final winner in this conversation, or is it left unresolved? If you were at a party in 1964, who would you blame, and why?

3. Give examples from the movie of significant scientific and/or technological advances. How are they used and what are the results?

4. Analyze the significance of the subplot about the puzzling Morse code messages coming from San Diego. How does the setting and camera work for the trip to San Diego add to the movie's theme?

5. How are women portrayed in this movie? Among other examples, consider Mary's request for a lawn mower, Moira's drinking and sexuality, Dwight's explanation of why he cannot accept his family's deaths, and Nurse Hosgood's relationship to her superior.

6. Analyze the messages the movie sends about love, marriage, and sex. How are they connected to the movie's theme?

7. Instead of a story about the end of the world and aggressive scientific and military efforts to prevent or alter it, this movie presents a group of love stories with a submarine mission added on. Why use this plot structure for a movie about this subject?

8. During the 1950s there was a rise in church attendance and membership. How does the movie present religion? What role does it play in the principal characters' lives?

9. The movie never says why the war started or who started it. Why not give this information?

10. In the 1950s, the Soviet Union was a closed society. Few products, especially cultural products such as books, movies, and magazines, were allowed in. *On the Beach* premiered on October 17, 1959, in 17 cities worldwide, including Moscow.[52] Speculate about why the Soviets would allow this movie to be shown and what it might indicate about the status of the Cold War.

11. How effective is the movie as entertainment and also as propaganda? What political outcomes does it suggest to audiences? Is there any evidence that it achieved these goals? How did you respond to the movie's last image?

Dr. Strangelove or: How I Learned to Stop Worrying and Love the Bomb (1964)

(British, 93 minutes) *Director:* Stanley Kubrick; *Stars:* Peter Sellers (in three roles), George C. Scott, Sterling Hayden, Keenan Wynn, Slim Pickens, Peter Bull, James Earl Jones.

Dr. Strangelove or: How I Learned to Stop Worrying and Love the Bomb is one of the greatest movie satires of the twentieth century. It was a very successful movie and a very worrisome political statement. The movie's over-the-top depiction of the reactions of American and Soviet officials to an accidental launch of nuclear weapons seemed disturbingly possible.

Distinctive moments in American history when the country pivots from "before" to "after" are obvious and memorable, and the assassination of John F. Kennedy was one of the most profound of the post-war era. During the 1960 election campaign Kennedy had used Cold War fears to criticize his opponent. He claimed there was a "missile gap" and that the United States had fallen behind the Soviet Union in national defense, an accusation designed to undermine Richard Nixon's candidacy. But the Cuban Missile Crisis presented a real possibility of nuclear war and riveted the attention of the entire world. When it was over, both Kennedy and Soviet Premier Nikita Khrushchev seemed ready to rethink the strategies that had allowed such a near miss. By the time of his death, Kennedy was beginning to revise his approach to the Cold War,[53] which offered the tantalizing possibility of reduced world tensions in the early decades of the nuclear age. As a result, the response by Americans and others around the world to his assassination went beyond the standard sympathies that typically follow the deaths of national leaders. "Kennedy's sudden violent death seemed to deprive the country and the world of a better future," writes historian Robert Dallek. "When he urged nuclear arms limitations, he seemed to be not only a defender of the national interest but also a humanist arguing the case for a rational world struggling against the age-old blights of fear, hatred, and war."[54]

Popular culture suggests that the American public began rethinking attitudes and approaches to the Cold War even before the Cuban Missile Crisis. For example, *The Twilight Zone*, a science-fiction television series created by Rod Serling that ran from 1959 to 1965, often featured stories about the Cold War and nuclear anxieties. The main character in one famous 1959 episode, "Time Enough at Last" (played memorably by Burgess Meredith), is relentlessly interrupted by others as he tries to read. When he later discovers that he is the lone survivor of a nuclear apocalypse, the strange man is delighted because he can finally read his books without interference.[55] In "The Shelter," an episode from 1961, neighbors battle over access to one family's bomb shelter as they face a possible nuclear attack.[56] In a bizarre coincidence, during the Cuban Missile Crisis, *The Saturday Evening Post* serialized "Fail-Safe," a story about an accidental nuclear attack. It was later published as a book and went on to become a best seller and eventually a movie.[57]

The Cuban Missile Crisis had been a stunningly close call so it was not surprising that the debate in popular culture about the Cold War and atomic bombs picked up momentum after it was over. Shortly after the crisis, country singer Jimmy Dean earned a Top Forty hit on the pop charts with "Dear Ivan." The song delivered a populist message of friendship to an ordinary Russian. With "The Battle Hymn of the Republic" playing in the background, Dean tells his Russian counterpart that he would like to meet him and expresses the belief that even though their governments cannot resolve their differences, the two men might actually have much in common.[58] Peter, Paul, and Mary's 1962 hit "Where Have All the Flowers Gone?" and Bob Dylan's "A Hard Rain's Gonna Fall" and "Talkin' World War III Blues," both from 1963, were markedly less optimistic.

Whatever their beliefs, people had become involved. They were no longer willing to leave the fate of the world to chance or to politicians with little vision and, perhaps, big axes to grind. When President Kennedy was assassinated, the issue took on even greater urgency. People all over the world had looked to him as the leader who could steer world tensions toward less threatening solutions and where necessary to less than perfect accommodations. His death made the world that much less secure and the need to reduce tensions that much more pressing.

Stanley Kubrick's bleak, black comedy, *Dr. Strangelove or: How I Learned to Stop Worrying and Love the Bomb,* strode into this roiling mass of anxiety in 1964 with all its satiric guns blazing. The movie tells the story of General Jack D. Ripper (Sterling Hayden), the commander of an American Air Force base, who sends nuclear-armed B-52 bombers to attack sites in the Soviet Union because he believes the Soviets are using fluoridated water to sap America's "essence." He then orders his base completely shut down so that no one can call the bombers back. Group Captain Lionel Mandrake (Peter Sellers), a British officer assisting at the base, and others up the chain of command all the way to the president of the United States (Peter Sellers again) spend the rest of the movie trying to turn the bombers back. They do this not just out of fairness to the Soviets, who have not launched an actual military strike and are not guilty of undermining anyone's essence, but also out of necessity. The United States must save the Soviet Union because the Soviets have a terrible weapon at their disposal. If attacked, the Soviets will retaliate with their "Doomsday Machine," an irreversible nuclear response that will destroy the planet.

Dr. Strangelove (1964) 151

This diabolical plot device with a name that has all the earmarks of comic hyperbole was actually based on a legitimate 1960 study of defense planning in the nuclear age. Herman Kahn, a prominent military analyst, discussed the feasibility of a doomsday machine in his scholarly book, *On Thermonuclear War*. Kahn ultimately rejected the concept because he believed that it would be uncontrollable.[59] But the idea had been planted in the public discourse with all its staggering implications. The frenzy of Cold War fears had pushed people to the point where they were willing to consider destroying the planet rather than lose a war.

In *Dr. Strangelove*, Kubrick tackles this possibility and other fundamental arguments of the Cold War with all the intensity of a bewildered child shouting to the crowd, "But the emperor has no clothes." He is aided by an excellent ensemble cast. Peter Sellers was nominated for an Academy Award for three different roles (including the title character) where he gets the chance to exhibit muddled concern, ineffectual leadership, and grotesque parody. George C. Scott plays General "Buck" Turgidson, a hawkish and supremely confident Cold Warrior, who explains to the president of the United States that if the bombers cannot be called back, the result would be "no more than ten to twenty million killed, tops ... depending on the breaks."

To guarantee that the audience would not miss the intended satire, many characters' names turn on some form of pun or joke, many of which were sexual in nature. In addition to the title character, there are General Jack D. Ripper, Major "King" Kong, Colonel "Bat" Guano, General Turgidson, and Soviet Premier Dmitri Kissov. The fact that many of the characters seemed to be grounded in real-life figures of the Cold War era added a frightening element of realism to what might otherwise have been a totally absurd plot. The movie president bears a strong physical resemblance to Adlai Stevenson, the Democratic Party's candidate for president in 1952 and 1956. Dr. Strangelove appears to combine elements of Henry Kissinger and Edward Teller.[60] The character of General Jack D. Ripper shares traits and attitudes with Major Curtis LeMay, who commanded American aircrews during World War II.[61]

Many scenes focus on sex or make sly visual jokes about it. There is only one small female role so the movie's point of view is entirely male. The opening scene shows a bomber being refueled in midair through a long tube over the background music, "Try a Little Tenderness." When General Ripper experiences difficulties having sex, he suspects something sinister and blames the Soviets for stealing his "essence." As Major Kong reviews the survival kits for the airmen delivering a nuclear weapon, he finds condoms. At the movie's end, Dr. Strangelove proposes a secure shelter where he and other leading figures can wait out the radioactive fallout from the war. In order for civilization to survive, Strangelove calculates that the population ratio for this shelter should be ten sexually attractive women for every man.

The movie was nominated for four Academy Awards, including Best Picture, Director, and Actor (Sellers). Movie critics and historians also heaped praise on Kubrick's black comedy. Writer Stanley J. Solomon called it "the high point of the cinema of atomic cataclysm, and among the most dramatic antimilitary statements in the entire war genre."[62] Stephen J. Whitfield ranked it "among the most important achievements in the history of movies."[63] Further recognition came in 1989 when it was selected as part of the first group of movies entered into the Library of Congress's National Film Registry.

Dr. Strangelove was one of several movies about potential nuclear war from the mid–1960s, including *Fail-Safe* (1964), *Seven Days in May* (1964), and *The Bedford Incident* (1965). Studios invested heavily in these productions, which featured some of the era's biggest stars, including Martin Balsam, Kirk Douglas, Henry Fonda, Ava Gardner, Sterling Hayden, James Earl Jones, Burt Lancaster, Walter Matthau, Sidney Poitier, George C. Scott, Peter Sellers, and Richard Widmark. These projects represent an extraordinary assembly of Hollywood talent—there are six Academy Award winners among the stars listed above—and, more importantly, of money, all of it invested in movies that focus on the issue of nuclear war, and all of them dramatize the need to rethink the basic premises of the Cold War.

In *Dr. Strangelove*, none of the characters who try to stop the bombers succeeds. The president uses his direct phone line to Moscow to no effect (except comedy). The Soviets are helpless to reverse their Doomsday Machine. Dr. Strangelove becomes ever more unhinged in his declarations. And the inhabitants of the War Room, the setting for much of the movie, descend into petty bickering. As Vera Lynn sings the melancholy World War II hit, "We'll Meet Again," a string of nuclear explosions blossoms on the screen and blends into a graceful visual ballet of mushroom clouds representing technological success, advanced strategic thinking, careful planning, and the end of the world.

Suggested Discussion Questions

1. Does it seem plausible (even if unlikely) that some sort of accidental nuclear attack could occur? Were people right to be concerned with this possibility? Is there anything that could be done to prevent such an occurrence with 100 percent certainty?

2. Many of the male characters are hyper-masculine. Why would Kubrick take this approach? Is this a fair caricature of (a) the military; (b) men in leadership positions; and (c) men in general?

3. Many of the characters have issues related to sex. Why would Kubrick add this component to the story?

4. Analyze General Turgidson and Major Kong. How are they alike and how are they different? Do you have confidence in their ability to protect the United States? Do you have confidence in their ability to keep the world safe? Why, or why not?

5. Are protecting the United States and keeping the world safe mutually exclusive? Which is more important, and why?

6. Describe the design of the movie's war room set. How does it contribute to the movie's theme?

7. How does the movie portray the governments of America and the Soviet Union? Who is/are the hero(es) in the movie?

8. Discuss the difference between satire and farce. Which term best describes the movie? Why would Kubrick make Major Kong a cowboy, complete with hat?

9. Kubrick meant the movie to be an anti-war statement, but it is over-the-top in almost every sense. Discuss whether this approach reinforces his message or undercuts it.

10. There is only one female among the stars of the movies on this topic noted above. Is that likely to be the case in movies made today on this same topic? Why, or why not? If you believe that more women are currently involved in decisions about war and national defense, would you expect the outcome in a crisis to be different or the same? Defend your answer.

11. The United States military is under the command of the president, an elected civilian leader. Discuss what benefits and difficulties this relationship could generate between the government and the military. How does that relationship play out in this movie? Should this Constitutionally-defined relationship be redesigned, and if so, how?

From Russia with Love (1963)

(British, 118 minutes) *Director:* Terence Young; *Stars:* Sean Connery, Daniela Bianchi, Pedro Armendariz, Lotte Lenya, Robert Shaw, Bernard Lee, Lois Maxwell, Desmond Llewelyn.

From Russia with Love, based on Ian Fleming's novel of the same name, features spies, counter-spies, and double agents manipulating other double agents in a Cold War conflict that could erupt into World War III. World domination is the ultimate goal, and like all of Fleming's books, a beautiful woman is both the means and the reward in this version of the adventures of James Bond, British Super-Agent 007.

After World War II, the Communists did not limit their efforts to extend their political philosophy just to Western Europe. Throughout the 1950s, the

Russians made attempts to expand into Africa and Latin America. The Communist Chinese extended their influence into Indochina and the Korean peninsula, which put them within one hundred miles of Japan. The United States tried to contain the spread of Communism by defending Turkey and Greece with the Truman Doctrine and ensuring the sovereignty of the Nationalist Chinese in Taiwan with overt military muscle. Despite these tensions, during the Cold War no bombs dropped on Moscow, Washington, Beijing, or London. Instead "hot" flare-ups in these and other Third World countries often threatened to erupt into World War III.

By the early 1960s, the world appeared to be on the brink of nuclear destruction. The Cuban Missile Crisis of 1962 was particularly tense. Ultimately, the Soviets backed down and withdrew their missiles from Cuba. The two superpowers were well aware of how close they had come to war, and they took action to ratchet down Cold War tensions. By 1963, the United States and the Soviet Union had signed a partial Nuclear Test Ban Treaty and established a telephone "hotline" (a device that became a comic prop in *Dr. Strangelove*), which would permit direct communication between Moscow and Washington, D.C., and perhaps lessen the danger of war in the event of another crisis like Cuba.

Even if the Cold War was still on, other attitudes were changing. In 1960, the first Baby Boomers turned 14, a generation with no memory of World War II to frame its world view and the challenges of young love blossoming around them. Rock-and-roll song lyrics gave ample evidence of their passionate enthusiasm for romance, both the traditional monogamous version ("Bobby's Girl" by Marcie Blane, "I Will Follow Him" by Little Peggy March, "Angela Jones" by Johnny Ferguson) and the "playing the field" kind ("The Wanderer" by Dion, "Traveling Man" by Ricky Nelson, "Let's Have a Party" by Wanda Jackson). Also in 1960, the Food and Drug Administration gave its approval to the first drug designed for birth control.[64] It took almost no time at all for American youths to join their elders in taking advantage of the opportunity this drug offered to liberate sex from its traditional married boundaries and ethical responsibilities, and very often from its connection to love as well.

In an era obsessed with a handsome young president, fast cars, glitzy new technologies, and Baby Boomers reaching their teen years, Mickey Spillane's ham-fisted detective hero Mike Hammer soon seemed old-fashioned. The changing times required a different kind of hero. Ian Fleming transformed the old-style, local detective into suave, international superspy James Bond, who accomplishes his patriotic goals in spectacular fashion without resorting to Mike Hammer's crude behavior or primitive means. Unlike Hammer, Richard A. Schwartz writes, even though he may lack "compassion and his methods are sometimes brutal, Bond is never sadistic, and everything he does is ultimately 'for God and country.'"⁶⁵ The charismatic, science-friendly, sexually smooth agent of Her Majesty's Secret Service operates on a much bigger playing field with more evil and worldly competitors, more beautiful and happily compliant women, and much more interesting equipment than Hammer ever did. Most Bond girls were not angst-ridden "vipers" desperate to tie a man down. They were often eager rather than conflicted about sex, which reflected the era's changing sexual mores. The Bond girls' sexuality clearly violated the strictures of the movie industry's Production Code. When confronted with this challenge to the established order, Hollywood ignored the code.⁶⁶

The first Bond film, *Dr. No,* set the pattern for the series and also introduced the actors who would play continuing roles in later installments: Sean Connery as James Bond, Lois Maxwell as Miss Moneypenny, and Bernard Lee as "M." Desmond Llewelyn picked up the role of "Q" in the second movie, *From Russia with Love,* and continued with it for many years. The broad outlines of all of the plots set Agent 007 against representatives of an evil organization but usually not a nation state. Therefore, war, which is waged between countries, is not a suitable response. He is regularly aided by colorful locals who, on occasion, are double agents. Tough, vicious men try to defeat him, and beautiful women as well as less attractive types help him or hinder him. By the end of the movie, the world is often just minutes away from a catastrophe that only he can prevent. When his foes are defeated, Bond rewards himself with sex. The Bond formula also included fabulous cars and car chases, which expanded over time to include helicopters, planes, motorcycles, and boats; fantastic, deadly instruments that mirrored the high-tech weapons of war available during the Cold War era; and exotic locales, which allowed long beautiful shots of vast beautiful scenery.

In the 1963 installment, *From Russia with Love,* the Russians appear to be the evil organization, but they are actually being undercut by SPECTRE, a rogue criminal organization intent on world domination. The setting, Turkey, establishes its exotic credentials early on with scenes of mosques, belly dancers, and navigable sewers. The local help is supplied by Ali Kerim Bey (Pedro Armendariz) and his sons. The vicious opponents are Number 3, Rosa Klebb (played by celebrated German actress Lotte Lenya) and Red Grant (Robert Shaw). Grant is being trained by SPECTRE as part of a plan to lure Bond into a trap and destabilize the world order. Grant's mission is to steal the Lektor decoder, a Russian encryption device, but arrange for the British to get the blame. Tatiana Romanova (Daniela Bianchi) is the beautiful Bond girl.

Klebb, one of the masterminds of the plot, is a Communist official who has secretly defected to SPECTRE. She meets Grant while he is wrapped only in a towel and uses her brass knuckles to test the strength of his bare abdomen.

Later, Klebb recruits the lovely young Tatiana, a clerk in the Soviet consulate, to assist with the plan. Tatiana does not know that Klebb is now working for SPECTRE. Acting as her Communist superior, Klebb orders Tatiana to fake a defection to the British and offer them the decoder if Bond agrees to come get it and her. Klebb makes it clear that Tatiana may have to have sex with Bond in order to convince him that her defection is real. Klebb's meetings with Grant and Tatiana have obvious sexual overtones. She asserts a smarmy dominance over the barely dressed Grant and the earnest Tatiana.

Bond learns of his assignment while he is vacationing with a beautiful woman. He quickly returns to London for a briefing where he and "M" are puzzled by Tatiana's offer and suspect that it is a trap. But they cannot resist the possibility of acquiring the Lektor device, which is exactly what the SPECTRE plotters hoped. After some suggestive repartee with Moneypenny, Bond goes off to Turkey.

Upon his arrival, he is unsure whom to trust. Suspicious characters are everywhere. Turkey's proximity to Eastern Europe and the Soviet Union make it an easy target for spies and assorted villains who have arrived at a live-and-let-live arrangement. One of Kerim's sons, a Turk who works for the British, explains the ground rules to Bond, "They are Bulgarians working for the Russians. They follow us, we follow them. It's a sort of understanding we have." His point is clear—unlike America or Western Europe, countries on the frontiers of the Cold War, like Turkey, accept a certain degree of flexibility in their alliances when it comes to international spycraft.

Along with reflecting Cold War tensions, the movie mirrors the era's sexual tensions. Almost every scene includes some form of sexual subtext, or sex is the text. For example, a fight in a gypsy camp gives audiences the chance to watch two barely dressed women fight each other over an issue completely unrelated to the plot. A hunt for a Russian who is trying to kill Kerim ends in scene outside a building with an oversized billboard of the beautiful European actress Anita Ekberg painted on the wall. The Russian escapes from the building out a window that opens through Ekberg's mouth. Other scenes push the era's censorship limits by strongly suggesting that sex has occurred or is about to occur. When Bond arrives for a meeting, Kerim is fully dressed, as is the beautiful young lady who is making up the bed in the room. Later, Tatiana introduces herself to Bond by appearing naked in his bed (the audience sees only her bare shoulders above a sheet). The next scene takes place on the other side of a two-way mirror where Klebb and Grant watch and film the couple as they get acquainted.

From Russia with Love uses a complicated plot to stitch together scenes of implied sex, suspense, violence by people, and violence by unconventional technologies (exploding briefcases, crossbows, floating oil drums, a deadly

From Russia with Love (1963) 157

shoe). The actors are mostly lovely to look at, the scenery is attractive, and the outcome is in doubt up to the last.

Tatiana helps Bond steal the Lektor decoder, and together they board a train for the journey to England. Kerim and Grant are also on board and a game of cat and mouse begins. As they move from train to truck to boat, Bond remains one step ahead of their evil pursuers, always able to invent a means of defense or escape.

The James Bond franchise was enormously successful, churning out movies during the Cold War era and beyond that were eagerly awaited by faithful fans. For British and American audiences of the time there was so much to like. Men had a role model they could enjoy emulating and women had a man they could simply enjoy. Worldwide evildoers faced an enemy who would always defeat them, which sent moviegoers home feeling happy and safe. Bond was the perfect antidote to the scary political times and a helpful, handsome guide to the early years of the sexual revolution.

Suggested Discussion Questions

1. Describe James Bond's clothes, car, and overall style. How does he fit into the emerging post-war consumer culture? He likes his martinis "shaken, not stirred." Why would Fleming have given the character this preference?

2. Robert Shaw, the actor playing Red Grant, has a very blond Nordic appearance in the movie. Why did the character go with this look? Describe his attitude toward violence. In a desperate situation, would you want him to be on your team? *Should* you want him to be on your team?

3. Rosa Klebb must be tough to advance SPECTRE's interests. Her sexuality is not conventional. She demonstrates a sexual interest in Tatiana and capably threatens Bond in a physical confrontation. Are any of the men presented in a way that is inconsistent with traditional gender roles? Why would the movie define a major female character this way?

4. "Women are treated with respect in this movie." Agree or disagree with this statement and defend your answer.

5. The British and the United States are on the same side in battles such as this one. What are America's contributions to this particular fight? What does the contribution suggest about the movie's view of America's strengths? How does America fail to contribute?

6. Explain the Warsaw Pact. Consult a map and consider Cold War-era politics to determine the best course of action for Turkey in its relations with the Soviet Union and Bulgaria. Is the situation for Turkey different today, and if so, how?

7. Bond gets his orders from Her Majesty's Secret Service. He is not free-

lancing in this movie. How does this organizational structure reflect on Bond's ethics as an agent and on the British government's response to Cold War conflicts and espionage?

8. The Soviets also have an organizational structure for their espionage efforts, which they follow as much as circumstances allow. Explain why you believe state-run organizations are good or bad for maintaining world peace over the long term.

9. SPECTRE, the evil organization in the movie, does not have the resources to compete against superpower nation states. How does SPECTRE differ from a state-run operation? Explain why SPECTRE and other rogue organizations such as al Qaeda, drug cartels, or cyber criminals are a greater or a lesser threat to world peace than state-run organizations such as the CIA or KGB.

10. Explain how world powers such as the United States, Great Britain, Germany, India, Russia, and China currently deal safely with rogue threats, or propose some ways that they could. Is there any case in which you can imagine a rogue threat being a good thing?

11. Describe other movies in which a rogue, non-state actor or force threatens state power.

12. Is the world safer when there are only a few superpowers who determine the general course of world affairs and define the political battle lines, or is it better to have multiple players with multiple agendas? Which structure is more democratic?

The Bedford Incident (1965)

(102 minutes) *Director:* James B. Harris; *Stars:* Richard Widmark, Sidney Poitier, Martin Balsam, Eric Portman, James MacArthur, Wally Cox, Donald Sutherland.

Eric Finlander, captain of the USS *Bedford* and a true American patriot, puts his career on the line in James B. Harris's movie, *The Bedford Incident*. His years of military service and tested tactical vision come up against new views and methods in this Cold War thriller from 1965. A misstep in any direction could be catastrophic, perhaps even initiate nuclear war between the United States and the Soviet Union. But how does a veteran navy officer know when the winds of change are blowing in the right direction or when he should resist them with everything he's got?

Institutions—whether they are military or civilian—tend to stick with a position or point of view far longer than the public in general. Jackie Robinson made it to the big leagues, and Nat "King" Cole and Sarah Vaughn were recording stars long before Congress passed civil rights legislation. The slow pace of institutional change does not stem entirely from devotion to principle. Sometimes it is simply the result of conditioning or inertia. Institutional leaders often rise through the ranks of the institution. As a result they are introduced into a culture as young recruits and carry their initial views or attitudes with them as they move up through the ranks. After they achieve positions of responsibility, they often maintain those established views and attitudes, thereby slowing change or thwarting it altogether. The military promotes entirely from within and the practical effects of such an organizational dynamic are evident throughout military history. For example, during World War II, anachronistic cavalry leaders balked at using armored vehicles, and traditional army and navy officers repeatedly underestimated the importance of air power.[67]

Senior military officers who were in their 50s and 60s in the early 1960s had begun their careers during World War II. They faced powerful and tremendously disciplined armies in Europe and the Pacific. To confront these threats with the appropriate counter force and to ensure total victory, the Allies had launched vigorous military actions and demanded unconditional surrender from Germany and Japan. The subsequent Cold War did nothing to mitigate the prevailing belief that only the ruthless application of superior power could contain and defeat America's enemies. But the high stakes presented by the possibility of nuclear war led many experts in the 1960s to believe that more measured, less confrontational responses might be a better approach. By mid-decade, the buildup of nuclear weapons had begun to scare people around the world. They feared the weapons, as well as the process of developing and testing them. The attitudes of the early years of the Cold War were beginning to appear a bit overwrought, the Blacklist was starting to lose its grip on the movie industry, and "McCarthyism" was becoming a term of derision.

Any period of transition creates tension. If the pendulum of Cold War rhetoric and military preparation had swung too far in one direction, how far in the other direction should it go to adapt to new attitudes toward the enemy and toward the testing and use of nuclear weapons? Should there even be new attitudes? Were the fears of the early fifties entirely justified? Could America abandon them without seriously undermining her security? These concerns generated heated debate, a debate that would have its most divisive manifestation in America's involvement in Vietnam. The unwillingness of many young men of draft age to take part in that war presented a stark and painfully confusing contrast to the determination and enthusiasm exhibited by their fathers' generation during World War II.

The United States military found it particularly difficult to cope with the changing times after World War II. Unlike the civilian sectors of the federal government, which could change as often as every two- or four-year election cycle, the military establishment was more deeply entrenched. Throughout American history, military leaders have often bridled at strategies and policies developed by civilian leaders. The coming of nuclear arms and the Cold War only exacerbated the problem. If members of the armed services truly believed that reducing vigilance and curtailing the production of nuclear arms would threaten the country's safety, how could they in good conscience follow such policies? The other side of the coin was equally important; i.e., how could a civilian government maintain effective control over its military, especially in times of tension and uncertainty?

The Bedford Incident explores these issues by focusing on a potential confrontation between an American destroyer, the USS *Bedford*, and a Soviet submarine. The *Bedford* is pursuing the sub through the North Atlantic Ocean, one of the new frontlines in the Cold War, a war that by its nature is not fought with weapons. A helicopter drops a new medical officer, Lieutenant Commander Chester Potter (Martin Balsam), onto the *Bedford* along with Ben Munceford (Sidney Poitier), a reporter who is doing research for a story. Munceford is greeted brusquely by the ship captain, Eric Finlander (Richard Widmark), who stands up to the Soviets the best way he knows how, by harassing them and preventing them from gaining any advantage in the area under his command. The current focus of his suspicions is a submarine he believes is armed with nuclear-tipped torpedoes.

Also on board are Commodore Wolfgang Schrepke (Eric Portman) and Ensign Ralston (James MacArthur). Schrepke is now a member of the West German navy, but he was once at war with the United States when he was as a member of Hitler's navy. He is on the *Bedford* as an observer with NATO. He and Finlander have developed a military camaraderie based on the two warriors' mutual respect for one another's skills. Ensign Ralston is an eager seaman with a country boy's face who tries hard but never seems to measure up to Finlander's standards.

Potter and Finlander represent two different approaches to training and handling men. Finlander believes that to get the most from people they must be driven hard. He sets high goals, criticizes frequently, and rarely offers praise. Potter, a doctor, believes men who are pushed too hard can snap, act without thinking, or make irrational judgments. As they continue to track the movements of the Soviet submarine, Finlander drives his crew to the breaking point, Ralston in particular. Potter tries to get him to ease up. Finlander cuts him off and brings up some of Potter's past failings as a way to undermine his self-confidence. This exchange is a battle, which appears to be Finlander's preferred approach to any issue, and the outcome is no contest. Potter is simply outgunned.

The Bedford Incident (1965) 161

Munceford's article is supposed to focus on the ship, but he is really interested in why a commander as successful as Finlander has repeatedly been passed over for promotion. He suspects that warriors of Finlander's caliber are now a problem for the military. Times have changed and each side in the Cold War seems ready to ease up a bit. But Finlander and others like him in the field have not reduced their intensity or their distrust of the enemy. Munceford pushes Findlander for answers about whether the military should have more say in government defense policy, knowing that such a position would represent a shift in the Constitutionally-defined relationship between military and civilian authorities. Finlander asserts that he has never said that. But as their confrontation escalates, he finally declares, "I'd destroy any enemy if it meant saving my country. Now what the hell is wrong with that?"

As he pursues the Russian submarine through the ice floes, Finlander becomes more and more angry with the orders he receives that prevent him from taking aggressive actions. He believes the Soviets are taunting him, and he is not going to take it. A modern Ahab, he pushes the men on the *Bedford* to the limit of their endurance, and his intensity alarms Munceford, Potter, and finally even Schrepke. The German officer admires Finlander, but he views war professionally, in effect as a business, and he is not devoted to any ideal. He advises Finlander to ease up, telling him, "Give it up, Eric. You will find only trouble in this obsession."

As the debate swirls around him, Ensign Ralston sits in front of the controls for the destroyer's torpedoes. Subject to persistent criticism from Finlander, he is determined not to let his captain or his country down again. Calm heads do not prevail. The captain has driven his men to the edge. In the movie's last scene, even Finlander seems to understand what he has done. *The Bedford Incident* offers insights not only about the Cold War but also about how military officers, civilians, and institutions coped with social and political change in the 1960s.

Suggested Discussion Questions

1. Finlander and Potter represent two different approaches to handling men in the military. The movie demonstrates the flaws in Finlander's method but offers no evidence to support Potter's method. If you had to pick between the methods represented by these men in a time of great national danger, which one would you choose, and why?

2. Would an officer such as Commodore Schrepke be a better choice? Why, or why not? Who behaves in a more professional military manner, Findlander or Schrepke?

3. How would you characterize Finlander's treatment of Ralston? Is it a successful approach to handling subordinates?

4. Munceford, played by Sidney Poitier, does not conceal his critical attitude toward Finlander. Finlander, in turn, mostly tolerates Munceford's questions and opinions but does not budge from his own positions. Do you believe Poitier's race affects Finlander's reaction to him? If so, how? If not, what does casting an African American in a role that allows him to criticize a white man say about racial attitudes in 1965?

5. How do the sailors on the *Bedford* respond to Finlander's style of command and to the Soviets they are tracking?

6. Describe the physical characteristics of Finlander, Schrepke, Potter, and Munceford (in addition to his race). How could their appearances affect audience perceptions of their respective points of view?

7. The USS *Bedford* is patrolling in the North Atlantic. Soviet ships and submarines are nearby, and the two navies challenge each other. What would be the proper response from either side to displays of disrespect? Finlander believes that the Soviet navy is more than just disrespectful because he suspects that it is "setting up submarine missile firing positions." How should his suspicions affect his behavior and decisions?

8. The Constitution gives control of the military to elected civilian officials. The military cannot make policy decisions. Its job is to implement orders. Based on the events in this movie, does that seem like a good idea? Why, or why not?

9. If a military official believes that bad decisions have been made by those who are far from the frontline, what options does he or she have to challenge those decisions? As you consider the possible options, also consider their likely consequences. (Review General Douglas MacArthur, President Harry Truman, and the Korean conflict and General Stanley McCrystal, President Barack Obama, and Afghanistan.)

10. How do you imagine the Soviets will respond to the incident that ends the movie? How would you recommend the president respond? (Review the downing of Korean Airlines Flight 007, on September 1, 1983.)

11. Analyze Finlander's remark to Munceford, "I'm proud to be an old-fashioned patriot." What does Finlander mean? Is there any time when being an "old-fashioned patriot" is not a good thing? Defend your answer.

The Russians Are Coming, The Russians Are Coming (1966)

(126 minutes) *Director:* Norman Jewison; *Stars:* Carl Reiner, Alan Arkin, Eva Marie Saint, Brian Keith, Jonathan Winters, Paul Ford, Theodore Bikel, Tessie

The Russians Are Coming, The Russians Are Coming (1966) 163

O'Shea, John Phillip Law, Ben Blue, Andrea Dromm, Dick Schaal, Parker Fennelly, Doro Merande, Johnnie Whitaker, Michael J. Pollard.

The tensions of the Cold War were beginning to wear thin by the midsixties. Granted, many Americans were still convinced that danger lurked and they should not let down their guard. For them, the Russians *were* coming. But for others, that view, like permanent waves and wingtips, had acquired a stale 1950s stuffiness. It belonged to an era of rules, conventions, and proper appearances. In the 1966 comedy, *The Russians Are Coming, The Russians Are Coming*, the Soviet troops who show up in small town America offered another, mellower vision of the enemy. The movie encouraged people to rethink Cold War attitudes—just as soon as they stopped laughing.

In retrospect, Norman Jewison's Cold War comedy suggests that the irreverent social and cultural movement commonly known as "the sixties" had bloomed. After experiencing the traumas of the early 1960s involving Berlin, Cuba, and President Kennedy's assassination, many Americans were eager for new experiences and new attitudes, if not total escape from the world they used to know. Young people flocked to the new look and new sound associated with the Beatles, Rolling Stones, and other British rock-and-rollers. They also tuned in to the Motown Sound—billed as "The Sound of Young America"—which offered escape through polished songs, danceable beats, and glitzy, choreographed singers. Television audiences of all ages welcomed a provocative new program, *That Was the Week That Was*, which dazzled viewers with outrageous social and political satire. The program burned itself out in a blaze of glory with a run that began in January 1964 and ended just a year and a half later. But that was long enough for television audiences to get a taste for political comedy with a real edge to it, a taste that comics would continue to satisfy in other venues. On top of all these budding challenges to the established order, the advance guard of the Baby Boom was just entering college in 1964.

By the mid-1960s there was something about the earnestness of the 1950s that begged to be mocked, and comedians, in clubs and on television, rose to the challenge. The comics emerging at that time did not just lob one-liners about drunks, wives, mothers-in-law, and bad waiters or deal in the self-deprecating laments that were the stock in trade of Jimmy Durante, Abbott and Costello, Bob Hope, and Jack Benny, comedian-actors who began their careers during the twenties, thirties, and forties. Instead, they built on the satiric approach pioneered in the early 1950s by the brilliant comedy team of Sid Caesar and Imogene Coca on *Your Show of Shows* and delved into a broad range of social issues and behaviors, including political topics and figures.

New satirists poked fun at a variety of social and political concerns by the 1960s, including nuclear proliferation and militarism. Tom Lehrer's song, "Wernher von Braun," for example, lampooned the former Nazi rocket scientist. The United States had "liberated" von Braun out of Germany after the war, and he later became the director of NASA's Marshall Space Flight Center. Lehrer's song highlights his political flexibility and purely scientific approach. Von Braun's only goal was to get the rockets to go up. Once that was accomplished, "Who cares where they come down?" Comedians took on the establishment in other ways. Mort Sahl was inspired by the headlines of the day. Don Rickles used humor as a form of assault. Bob Newhart made sly fun of middle-class behaviors and neuroses. Lenny Bruce pushed standup comedy content further than any of them, frequently getting arrested for his unabashed enthusiasm for sex and drugs and for saying so onstage in terms considered obscene.[68] Bill Cosby did not go after social issues with the intensity of these white comics, but just being an African American who delivered standup comedy to white audiences in the 1960s was subversive enough to place the effect of his work in the same category.

Johnny Carson took over *The Tonight Show* in 1962 and turned it into part of the bedtime routine of millions of Americans for the next 30 years.[69] The show offered viewers content that was not always family appropriate, the perfect venue for comics with an edge. Regular guests included satirists such as Mort Sahl, Jackie Mason, and Bob Newhart, who broadened the public's appreciation for comedy aimed at social and political follies and the fools who promoted them. As the sixties progressed, this brand of humor would culminate in edgy TV variety shows such as Rowan and Martin's perpetually giddy *Laugh-In* and *The Smothers Brothers Comedy Hour*, which frequently ran into trouble with CBS censors.

By the mid-1960s, Hollywood was also exploring this dark and biting brand of humor in innovative comedies, as evidenced by Stanley Kubrick's bleak, controversial *Dr. Strangelove* (1964). Soon, even mainstream movies were taking comedic shots at the establishment. There was so much to lampoon by 1966, and in *The Russians Are Coming, The Russians Are Coming*, Hollywood stepped up and met the challenge in a movie that blended droll wit, political satire, and slapstick silliness into an Academy Award-nominated comedy.

The story takes place on a small sandy island populated by local provincials and summered on by sophisticates from nearby New York City. The breakfast routine of the vacationing Whittaker family is interrupted one morning by a hapless band of Soviet sailors, led by Lieutenant Rozanov (Alan Arkin, in an Academy Award-nominated role). Razonov and another sailor, Alexi Kolchin (John Phillip Law), can speak passable English, but the rest of their group cannot. They are searching as discreetly as a crew of Soviet sailors possibly can for a ship big enough to rescue their submarine, which has run aground on a sandbar near an unpopulated section of the island. This maritime disaster has not damaged the submarine, but if it becomes known to the Soviet

The Russians Are Coming, The Russians Are Coming (1966) 165

military it could cause serious damage to the careers of the captain (Theodore Bikel) and the rest of the crew. The Russian sub was not floating in American waters and risking World War III as part of any official military exercise. It was there merely because its curious captain could not resist the temptation to come in close, raise a periscope, and check out the enemy in its natural habitat. Of course, if the Russian visitors are discovered by the American military, the consequences could wreck more than careers, a fact that lends special urgency to the sailors' search.

The island population responds to the invaders with varying degrees of disbelief, terror, and resolve. Walt and Elspeth Whittaker (Carl Reiner and Eva Marie Saint) are torn between clumsy terror and an earnest effort to save America while not getting themselves, their two children, and Alison, the lovely young babysitter, killed. A motley assortment of locals catches on to what is happening and immediately believe that war has begun. Their collective response is a Paul Revere–like attempt to alert the island population by phone and on motorbike (with sidecar) to the danger at hand. There is even an effort to spread the alarm on the traditional horseback. Police Chief Link Mattocks (Brian Keith) is rumpled, bemused, and uncertain that there is anything to the hysterical reports he receives about enemy troop deployments. But his deputies are more easily convinced. Without any evidence or even minimal efforts to investigate, they quickly join other citizens who have banded together to defend the island. After a brief coup involving swords, Fendall Hawkins (Paul Ford) becomes the leader of this ragtag militia. Hawkins is a former military man, and he carries on with heroic valor as he leads the militia, some of whom are armed with weapons even older than he is.

Only Alan Arkin's portrayal of the Soviet lieutenant has a grim intensity to it. He is the one character who understands the danger inherent in their situation. He tries desperately and with mounting frustration to ward off the crazy locals, rescue the submarine, prevent his captain from blowing up anything American, and get out before nuclear war explodes around them.

As the plot unfolds, however, everyone becomes more and more unhinged and more likely to take drastic, irrevocable action. Misadventures, misunderstandings, and sight gags blossom. So, inevitably, does love. When the handsome Russian sailor, Kolchin, is left to guard the Whittakers, he botches the job and falls for the babysitter. She innocently returns his affections in a scene that includes his earnest declaration, "I wish not to hate anybody." More personal lament than political statement, his comment represents a fundamentally human response to the era's escalating fears of atomic catastrophe. Implicit in it is a sense of plaintive befuddlement. Why are we doing this? What is the point? If the world plunges into all-out war, how can any country really claim victory?

All of the players eventually confront one another at the town dock. Sailors, citizens, and local militia find themselves looking down the barrels of weapons of varying vintages, calibers, and accuracy. Even Chief Mattocks finally succumbs to the hysteria. Just at the point where earnest patriotism demands that everyone fire at everyone else, a crisis diverts their attention. In rapid succession the Russians come to the aid of their erstwhile enemies, American fighter jets arrive armed and ready to defend the country, and everyone scrambles to avert World War III for one more day.

Suggested Discussion Questions

1. Describe the submarine crew as they appear in the opening sequence. How menacing do they seem to be?

2. Describe your first impressions of the Whittaker family. How is Elspeth portrayed? Why is Pete such a determined anti–Communist and Walt more accommodating?

3. How does Lieutenant Rozanov treat the family? Why he would he behave this way toward them? Explain Rozanov's goals and methods.

4. As the Soviet sailors approach the town they hear church music, which they recognize. Why include this scene? How does this relate to the American view of "Godless Communism?" What does it suggest about internal Communist efforts to suppress religion?

5. Describe the townspeople's reactions to the possibility of an invasion by the Soviet Union. What actions do they take, and how effective are they?

6. How does Chief Mattocks respond to their actions, and how and why does his behavior change? What role does Walt Whittaker assume when he gets to the bar? How is he received?

7. How does Fendall Hawkins become the leader of the local militia? What role does he play in the town's response?

8. Among the townspeople and sailors, which characters most represent responsible adult behavior?

9. Compare and offer explanations for the reactions of Pete Whittaker and the babysitter, Alison, to the presence of the sailors. How do representations of gender and patriotism play out with other characters? The relationship between Allison and Alexei is a minor plot element. Why include it at all?

10. Once all the major players are together at the harbor, what prevents Lieutenant Rozanov and the Whittakers from just explaining the problem and arriving at a resolution that does not involve the use of force? How close are the townspeople and the sailors to firing their weapons and starting a chain reaction that will lead to war?

11. What prompts the sailors to help rescue the boy? How does the Soviet

captain react to his sailors' efforts? How do the townspeople react? Explain any possible significance in the circumstances of the boy's predicament.

12. Elspeth provides the solution to the submarine's fate. Why would the movie give this moment to a female character?

13. How might staunchly patriotic Americans react to the plot?

14. How does the Cold War perspective in this movie differ from those found in other Cold War movies such as *My Son John* (1952), *Invasion of the Body Snatchers* (1956), *On the Beach* (1964), or *The Bedford Incident* (1965)?

PART IV
Images of Women through Good Times and Bad, 1933–1969

Overview

Images of women in movies have evolved over time and represent a cinematic archive of changing social attitudes and behaviors. Movies from the thirties such as *The Public Enemy, Gold Diggers of 1933,* and *Petrified Forest* feature women whose lives reflect the economic conditions and social conventions of the Depression era. During the 1940s, women support the war effort and welcome the troops home in movies like *Four Jills in a Jeep, Watch on the Rhine, Since You Went Away,* and *The Best Years of Our Lives.* The Cold War and the Baby Boom seemed to occupy everyone's energies during the fifties, as evidenced by *Big Jim McLain, The Man Who Knew Too Much, Blackboard Jungle,* and *Gidget.* And new attitudes toward sex and gender in the sixties influenced women's relationships and behavior in *Sex and the Single Girl, Cat Ballou, Guess Who's Coming to Dinner,* and *Bob & Carol & Ted & Alice* just as they did other social groups. No social or cultural trend is independent of contemporary events, but long-term forces also influence attitudes and expectations. For example, the substantial increase in the number of women who earned high-school diplomas after 1900 is rarely highlighted in storylines, but it had a significant effect on how women behaved and how they were portrayed in movies.

The demand by women for more rights and more control over their lives has been one of the most important ongoing social movements of the last century and a half. The process has advanced in fits and starts, and by the end of the 1960s many forms of popular culture reflected substantial changes in how women were portrayed and a growing acceptance of new roles for them. But from about 1934 through the 1960s images of women leaned mostly toward traditional roles and standards of morality, images that, not coincidentally, met the demands of the Production Code. There were some counter-images that challenged tradition, for example, Ann Harding's Bohemian lifestyle in *Biography of a Bachelor Girl* from 1935 and the quirky marital relationships in *Too Many Husbands* from 1940. In general, however, changes in attitudes toward women were not widely endorsed by either sex during those decades.

In any given year, therefore, movies would feature women who stay within the margins of expected behaviors and express traditional attitudes. But they also might show women who embrace new attitudes, strike out on new paths, or demand more from life in general and from men in particular. Women in this latter group, however, could expect to suffer for their unorthodox behavior. Over the years, representations of loving, devoted mothers have been central to *Lady for a Day* (1933), *The Grapes of Wrath* (1940), *I Remember Mama* (1948), and *The Sound of Music* (1965). But other images of mothers, like those in *Min and Bill* (1930), *Stella Dallas* (1937), *Mildred Pierce* (1945), *Rebel Without a Cause* (1955), and *The Manchurian Candidate* (1962), defy easy categorization. Women's unconventional expectations propel the plots of *Politics* (1931), *His Girl Friday* (1940), *The Red Shoes* (1948), *Johnny Guitar* (1954), *Elmer Gantry* (1960), and *True Grit* (1969). And women criminals demonstrate that they are at least the equal of their male competitors—and occasional co-conspirators—in *Baby Face* (1933), *Destry Rides Again* (1939), *The Little Foxes* (1941), *The Killers* (1946), *Kiss Me Deadly* (1955), and *Bonnie and Clyde* (1967).

The overriding aim of the stories in most movies is to bring conflict to an end and restore the natural order, or, if that is not possible, to mourn its destruction.[1] Until the 1970s, the natural order for women usually meant capturing men's affections and approval or fulfilling their responsibilities as wives and mothers. If a woman succeeds beyond these parameters, very often her victory is aided or engineered by men. Movies such as *Imitation of Life* (1934), *Now, Voyager* (1942), *Westward the Women* (1951), *Inn of the Sixth Happiness* (1958), and *Charade* (1963) explore how women will acquire this male assistance and how they will use it. Several Katharine Hepburn movies offer good examples. Hepburn leads a varied and interesting group of women as they compete for theatrical success in *Stage Door* (1937), but the manipulations of powerful men and the ability of women to manipulate them in return are central to the outcome. Hepburn fails as an athlete in *Pat and Mike* (1952) until Spencer Tracy offers his help. In *Desk Set* (1957), she spends much of the movie trying to convince Tracy and other male executives that a corporation's female researchers are essential employees. Hepburn succeeds, and for her reward she gets to keep her support job and begin again with a new beau. Another notable

Hepburn, Audrey (in an Academy Award-nominated performance), is blind and amazing in *Wait Until Dark* (1967). But she is also married, and her skillful handling of a group of desperate criminals does not earn her husband's full approval until she walks into his arms at his order, a demand that creates a jarring pause in her moment of triumph.

However, if the female character is an older woman or a nun, like Mother Maria (Lilia Skala) in *Lilies of the Field* (1963), or if she is believed to be unavailable for marriage or sex, like the nearly blind Annie Sullivan (Anne Bancroft) in *The Miracle Worker* (1962), then success in a traditionally male endeavor is acceptable. Marie Dressler in *Politics*, Dame May Whitty in *The Lady Vanishes* (1938), and Lillian Gish in *The Night of the Hunter* (1955) are all older actresses, and they pull off unexpected successes in these movies. Whitty does need the assistance of Margaret Lockwood and Michael Redgrave, but in fairness, she is up against the coordinated efforts of a Nazi gang.

Pre-Code, the Production Code, and Very Determined Women

Many issues and concerns influenced how women were portrayed in movies over the years and how movie audiences responded. By 1930 movies were generating strong criticism for their portrayal of sex and their acceptance of ethically questionable behavior. A scandal in the early 1920s involving popular movie star Roscoe "Fatty" Arbuckle prompted the motion picture industry to set up a regulatory organization in 1922. Will H. Hays, a former postmaster general during the Harding administration, was appointed to head it.[2] In order to counter growing criticism later in the decade, Hays led motion picture producers to adopt a Production Code in 1930 (also referred to as the Hays Code) that specified what movies could and could not show and what could or could not be said. It prohibited "a vast range of human expression and experience— homosexuality ... interracial sex, abortion, incest, drugs, [and] most forms of profanity," and it also addressed how immoral behavior could be presented. The code demanded that if a bad act occurred, it "must be counteracted by punishment and retribution, or reform and regeneration, of the [sinner]."[3]

However, the Production Code was not rigorously enforced until 1934, and the years from 1930 to 1934 represent the pre-code era.[4] Before 1934, therefore, movies sometimes portrayed independent women who set their own agendas in relationships. The most notorious of these women characters were often played by Greta Garbo, Marlene Dietrich, Mae West, and Jean Harlow. Garbo played sexually uninhibited women in movies like *Mata Hari* (1931) and *Queen Christina* (1933). Marlene Dietrich achieved international stardom in *The Blue Angel* (1930; also released in German as *Der blaue Engel*), which featured her unforgettable portrayal of Lola Lola, the faithless, sexually assertive cabaret singer who seduces a stodgy schoolmaster. Lola Lola displays a taunting, sexual indifference similar to many of the characters played by Mae West, but while Dietrich sometimes seems only mildly or, at best, temporarily interested in her conquests, West manages to be both amusing and amused as she lures—rather than chases after—hers. West makes the sexual demands and determines whether or not men meet them in movies like *I'm No Angel* and *She Done Him Wrong*, both from 1933. Jean Harlow defined her sexuality, at least in part, by the clothes she wore. Many of her outfits look like lingerie and barely cover her body, highlighting Harlow's strikingly beautiful face and figure. But unlike the screen personas of West and Dietrich, Harlow's characters often seem to need men so much that they are willing to be dominated by them. Harlow is eager to submit to tough men in *The Public Enemy* (1931) and *Red Dust* (1932). Chester Morris slaps her hard in *Red-Headed Woman* (1932), and Harlow's response—"Do it again, I like it!"—still startles audiences.

Mainstream movies were generally more accepting of unconventional behavior and more willing to reward ethically challenged characters before 1934. During the pre-code era, strong women who lead morally questionable lives manage somehow to achieve happiness. In *The Divorcee*, from 1930, Jerry Martin (Norma Shearer, in an Academy Award-winning performance) discovers that her husband has had an affair. She still loves him but decides she must also have an affair to "balance [their] accounts." He expects to be forgiven for his illicit romance, but when he learns of hers, he leaves her. His insistence on the traditional double standard drives her into the arms of a series of men. Despite her promiscuity, he eventually takes her back. In *Night Nurse* (1931) Barbara Stanwyck thwarts the ambitions of a dangerous chauffeur. To do so, she needs help from another dangerous character with whom she becomes romantically involved. In *Trader Horn* (1931), a young woman (Edwina Booth) who has been held captive for many years by a cannibal tribe in Africa is rescued by white hunters. Although the movie implies that she has been sexually active, she still appears headed toward marriage to one of the hunters by the end of the movie. (The movie was shot mostly on location in Africa and includes scenes of partially nude African tribeswomen, which followed the cultural norms of the day. Nudity by non-whites was permissible, but Booth's breasts were covered.) In *Red Dust* (1932), another movie set in an exotic, steamy jungle locale, Jean Harlow plays a prostitute stranded at a rubber plantation. She overcomes the resistance of manager Dennis Carson (Clark Gable) and competition from his married upper-class lover, Barbara Willis (Mary Astor), to win his affections.

Pre-Code, the Production Code, and Very Determined Women 173

Ann Harding and Myrna Loy made a specialty out of playing sophisticated women with unconventional morals. In *The Animal Kingdom* (1932), Cecilia Tolliver (Loy) competes for her husband's affections with his former lover, free-spirited Daisy Sage (Harding). In the end, Daisy's forthright affection wins her lover's return. A year later, Harding and Loy teamed up again and reversed the roles in *When Ladies Meet*. Wife and girlfriend confront one another over Harding's husband, played by Frank Morgan, a debonair cad who is having an affair with Loy. The women end up liking one another and conclude that Morgan does not deserve either of them. In *Double Harness* (1933), Harding tricks her lover into marriage then admits her treachery. He is initially furious about this fraud, but he overcomes his anger and calls off their divorce.

The 1933 movie *Penthouse* also features a woman who succeeds despite a lack of morals. Myrna Loy stars as a call girl who has fallen in love with a lawyer (Warner Baxter). Throughout the movie, she pesters him cheerfully and sweetly for sex while he upholds conventional moral standards. Eventually, despite her disreputable lifestyle, he proposes marriage.

As movies became more risqué in the late 1920s and early 1930s, public criticism mounted.[5] In 1933, the New York Board of Censors refused to grant the state's theaters permission to show *Baby Face*, an action that could have cost Warner Bros., who financed the movie, a lot of money. In order to get past the censors, the studio removed objectionable lines and dubbed in others, thereby diluting the movie's message that women like Lily Powers (Barbara Stanwyck) should use their beauty and sexuality to achieve their goals. In the original version, a character encourages Lily to use her "power over men," to "use men, not let men use you." Warners removed some phrases and added, "Remember the price of the wrong way is too great" and, "Be clean, be strong, defiant." The movie's new message of repentance and reform earned it the censors' approval.[6]

In order to accommodate escalating public criticism and avoid further confrontations over movie content, studios began to enforce the Production Code. By 1934, immoral women would no longer go unpunished. Gone were the risqué dialog of actresses like West, Dietrich, and Harlow and the sexually scandalous roles played by Garbo, Shearer, Harding, and Loy. The Production Code not only clamped down on sexual license, but it delivered the message that women who triumph on their own will pay a steep price for their victories unless there were unusual extenuating circumstances. If a woman's ambitions were for self-aggrandizement or power, she would fail, but if they were for the benefit of others, she could succeed. Powerful women either accept true love or achieve professional success, but they do not do both in *Female* (1933), *Sister Kenny* (1946), *Bell, Book and Candle* (1958), *Kisses for My President* (1964), and *A Star is Born* (1937, 1954, 1976).

Other movies also made it clear that women had to follow traditional expectations or else face the consequences. In *Woman of the Year* (1942), Spencer Tracy puts celebrated female executive Katharine Hepburn in her place. In *Adam's Rib* (1949), Tracy's lawyer character nearly divorces wife Hepburn's when she beats him in a court case. But he outsmarts her and saves their marriage by appropriating some clever feminine wiles. (The movie's title gives the traditional hierarchy away.) Joan Crawford's Academy Award-winning portrayal of a businesswoman's success in *Mildred Pierce* (1945) leads only to heartbreak and betrayal. Audrey Hepburn, in an Academy Award-winning performance, plays a princess who falls in love in *Roman Holiday* (1953), but she reluctantly gives up her whirlwind romance with commoner Gregory Peck and returns to her royal responsibilities, alone. In *The Girl Can't Help It* (1956), Jayne Mansfield offers a different take on how women can succeed. She plays the "dumb blonde" role so shrewdly that she manages to outwit both of her male co-stars. Significantly, Mansfield uses her formidable beauty, talent, and cleverness in the successful pursuit of marriage and family. In the 1963 comedy, *The Thrill of It All,* Doris Day reprises the successful breadwinner role with less drama but the same sense of misguided effort that Joan Crawford's character experienced in *Mildred Pierce* some 18 years earlier. Fortunately for both, their forgiving husbands graciously take them back. Unfortunately for Mildred, her course correction comes only after great tragedy.

Jezebel (1938) and *Gone With the Wind* (1939) are two of the strongest condemnations of willful women in movies. The plot of *Jezebel* centers on Julie Marsden, a spoiled Southern belle played by Bette Davis with such fierce determination that she won an Academy Award for it. In the Bible, the notorious Jezebel was assassinated for promoting idol worship in the Hebrew kingdom of her husband, Ahab. No character in the movie is actually named Jezebel, so to be sure that audiences did not miss the point, the movie's trailer describes it as "the story of a woman who was loved when she should have been whipped."[7] Bette Davis's selfish character is punished for her behavior by the loss of love and perhaps even her life as she attempts to redeem herself through self-sacrifice. A year later another Southern belle won another Academy Award for the same stubborn willfulness. Vivien Leigh's Scarlet O'Hara in *Gone With the Wind* was just as self-serving as Davis's Julie Marsden, but Scarlet was also smart enough and tough enough to survive. Although she must accept compromises along the way, Scarlet is able to stay on her feet financially despite the devastation of the Civil War. What she is not able to do is earn the love of Ashley Wilkes or keep the love of husband Rhett Butler.

The actresses who played supporting roles in both of these movies were also nominated for Academy Awards. Fay Bainter in *Jezebel* and Hattie McDaniel and Olivia de Havilland in *Gone With the Wind* accept the parameters of the society in which they live and maneuver from within them to achieve their goals. Bainter and McDaniel won, and their awards were justly earned for outstanding performances. But perhaps as a counterpoint to Davis and Leigh's awards, this recognition may have also served to reinforce the value of women who follow tradition rather than upend it.

The Good, the Bad, and the Sidekick

Many movies between the 1930s and 1960s reflected changing gender roles in society and showcased very strong female characters, good or bad. Tough, resolute woman characters defend positive values and champion the fight against political corruption in *Manhattan Melodrama* (1934), *Johnny Come Lately* (1943), *The Farmer's Daughter* (1947), and *Born Yesterday* (1950), but, in keeping with gender expectations, they always receive strong support from men. Women characters hold families together by sheer determination. Academy Awards went to Marie Dressler in *Min and Bill* (1930) and Jane Darwell in *The Grapes of Wrath* (1940) for their roles as devoted, determined mothers, and Irene Dunne earned an Academy Award nomination for her outstanding performance in *I Remember Mama* (1948). Other strong female characters challenge social conventions and gender discrimination in *His Girl Friday* (1940), *Along Came Jones* (1945), *Auntie Mame* (1958), and *True Grit* (1969).

Some actresses played a variation of the "dangerous woman" character. Taking their cue from pre-code actresses Garbo, Dietrich, West, and Harlow, later actresses such as Mary Astor, Barbara Stanwyck, Joan Crawford, Lana Turner, Ava Gardner, Gloria Graham, Rita Hayworth, Lauren Bacall, Susan Hayward, and Elizabeth Taylor all created mesmerizing movie characters who were bad but beautiful. They were also big draws at the box office in *The Maltese Falcon* (Astor, 1941), *The Big Heat* (Graham, 1953), *I Want to Live* (Hayward, 1958), and *Cleopatra* (Taylor, 1963). Not surprisingly, as millions of men returned home from the war, the subject of women's virtue or lack thereof got plenty of movie coverage in 1946 in movies like *The Big Sleep* (Bacall), *Gilda* (Hayworth), *The Killers* (Gardner), and *The Postman Always Rings Twice* (Turner).

Strong women also served as helpful sidekicks, although this dynamic was often a setup for humor. William Powell and Myrna Loy delighted audiences in six pairings as Nick and Nora Charles in the *Thin Man* series of the 1930s and '40s. Loy kept Powell in line, provided a comic foil based on traditional wifely stereotypes, and was as game as he was when it came to solving the crime, but Powell was the one who figured things out. In *Penthouse* (1933),

Loy's witty call girl uses her underworld contacts to help Warner Baxter solve a murder. In many cases, the female sidekick, like Claudette Colbert's character in *It's a Wonderful World* (1939), helps unintentionally because she does not realize what she knows or what she should do. Madeleine Carroll is woefully unsupportive until she finally believes Robert Donat is on the level in *The 39 Steps* (1935). The sidekick often succeeds because she inadvertently discovers a clue or beans a villain. Occasionally she will bean her male partner (Jean Arthur does so twice in *The Ex-Mrs. Bradford,* 1936; Claudette Colbert above), providing amusing evidence of female ineptitude.

But sidekick roles often went beyond simply setting up sight gags and holding the hero's coat. Women made significant contributions to the Allied war effort during World War II, and movies reflected this fact through women characters who stand up to the Nazis so men can carry on the fight in *Man Hunt* (1941), *Joan of Paris* (1942), and *Five Graves to Cairo* (1943). Also supporting the war effort, Greer Garson holds her ground in the title role of *Mrs. Miniver,* and Joan Crawford pitches in with daring and determination in *Above Suspicion,* both from 1942. In the 1948 gangster movie *Key Largo,* Claire Trevor (in an Academy Award-winning performance) is abused once too often by Edward G. Robinson, and she gamely offers an assist to hero Humphrey Bogart. Grace Kelly must overcome deeply held religious principles in order to help husband Gary Cooper in *High Noon* (1952).

Director Alfred Hitchcock often used female sidekicks, and these characters made substantial contributions to the resolutions of the conflicts in many of his movies. Ingrid Bergman helps Cary Grant thwart an international conspiracy in *Notorious* (1946), and her search for an important clue forms one of Hitchcock's most suspenseful sequences. Grace Kelly faces grave danger in *Rear Window* (1954) as she helps James Stewart investigate a murder. In *To Catch a Thief* (1955), Kelly seduces and then rescues accused cat burglar Grant. In *The Man Who Knew Too Much* (1956), Doris Day plays a wife who eventually rises to the occasion to help thwart Cold War villains. Early in the movie husband James Stewart gives her a sedative because he knows she will not be able to handle really bad news. But by the movie's end, Day charms and distracts a distinguished crowd of partygoers to cover for Stewart as he hunts for their son's kidnappers. Similarly, Eva Marie Saint is a major player in the complex plot of Hitchcock's *North by Northwest* (1959).

Ungentlemanly Behavior, or: Violence Sells

Regardless of whether women characters in movies were strong or weak, they were still frequently abused by males, reflecting the social realities of the day. For example, Clark Gable throws Barbara Stanwyck against a wall in *Night Nurse*. In *Gone With the Wind,* Rhett's angry outburst terrifies Scarlett. Lee Marvin's vicious attack on Gloria Graham in *The Big Sleep* stunned audiences in 1953 but apparently not enough to drive that type of violence off the screen. Two decades later, another actress suffers a similar attack in *The Long Goodbye*. Robert Mitchum brutally assaults two women in *Cape Fear* (1962) and then sets his sights on Gregory Peck's teenage daughter. In 1971 Jane Fonda won an Academy Award for her portrayal of a prostitute who becomes the bait in a murder investigation in *Klute*. The expectation that she will suffer violence is the central element of tension in the movie. Some of these scenes of abuse have become iconic cinematic reference points. It is not absolutely clear if James Cagney's famous "grapefruit" scene in *The Public Enemy* (1931) and Rod Steiger's rape scene in *Doctor Zhivago* (1965) are notorious because they are offensive or because, according to the standards of the time, they were so brazen.

Presentations of casual violence against women are arguably even more problematic. When Uncle Oscar slaps Aunt Birdie in *The Little Foxes* (1941), the act itself is not as disturbing as the realization that his behavior is part of a pattern of abuse that she will accept without complaint. Humphrey Bogart's violent outbursts in *In a Lonely Place* (1950) create uncertainty about his possible role in a woman's murder. But the greater danger for Gloria Grahame is the way she meekly accepts his escalating dominance and violence. Wallace Beery threatens violence in the pre-code hit, *Dinner at Eight* (1933), but wife Jean Harlow forces him to back down. In *Born Yesterday* (1950), Broderick Crawford is not so easily put off. Casual violence toward women is a subtext in Sam Peckinpah's *Ride the High Country* (1962). Mariette Hartley escapes her stern, domineering father and runs away to marry a handsome prospector. Once she reaches him and his randy brothers at their remote mining camp, the threat of sexual assault hovers over the movie.

Although the violence toward women in movies released from the 1930s through the late 1960s is usually not graphic, it is nonetheless disturbing because it suggests that such behavior was acceptable, and physical abuse as an element of sexual desire drives some movie plots. In *Night Must Fall* (1937), Rosalind Russell suspects that the very charming Robert Montgomery is a psychotic killer, but that only appears to add to his allure. Jane Russell does not seem able to decide how to respond to sexual assault in *The Outlaw* (1943). Violence is fundamental to Marlon Brando's character in *A Streetcar Named Desire* (1951). His wife not only forgives this behavior, she is clearly drawn to it. Physical abuse is an important element in two movies that starred John Wayne and Maureen O'Hara, *The Quiet Man* (1952) and *McClintock* (1963). O'Hara and Wayne generate terrific on-screen chemistry, but the plots of these movies rest on the premise that the societies involved (rural Catholic Ireland in *The Quiet Man*, and the Old West in *McClintock*) find Wayne's abusive actions toward "his woman" squarely within the bounds of acceptable husband behavior. Citing the similarities both movies exhibit to Shakespeare's *Taming of the Shrew* does not add luster to the abuse. Rather, it suggests that there had not been any progress in attitudes toward the abuse of women in more than 350 years.

Love, Marriage, and Liberation

Before the late sixties, marriage was one area in which a woman could establish a goal and achieve it, and society would approve as long as she conducted her pursuit honorably. This theme was (and still is) a frame for many movie plots, but Hollywood certainly did not invent the storyline. One popular prototype is Jane Austen's novel, *Pride and Prejudice,* which was published in 1813. The book details the marital ambitions of the Bennett daughters, and versions of it have been re-appearing on movie and television screens for decades. Greer Garson starred in a 1940 version, and in 2004, Bollywood, the Mumbai-based Indian equivalent of Hollywood, ignored centuries of unwanted British rule (or perhaps celebrated them?) with a boisterous musical interpretation, *Bride and Prejudice.* The Bollywood version highlights the timelessness of the topic and the cross-cultural empathy different portrayals of the Bennett girls can still generate as the husband hunt drags on through the cruel twists and turns of fate.

Separating the right mate from all the wrong ones is an ancient and universal challenge that allows a woman to configure her own future, provided the right man is willing. Sometimes he is not, and getting him to the altar takes serious effort from the dedicated women in *Double Harness* (1933), *The Best Years of Our Lives* (1946), *The Searchers* (1956), and *Charade* (1963). The effort takes on elements of a military campaign in *Every Girl Should Be Married* (1948). Sometimes he never gets there, as in *Now, Voyager* (1942), *The Heiress* (1949), or *Splendor in the Grass* (1961). Many movies across the decades have featured women who must resist the attentions of an imperfect suitor or the demands of her parents or social circle in order to find true happiness with the right guy. Examples include *It Happened One Night* (1934), *The Philadelphia Story* (1940), *The Little Foxes* (1941), *Pat and Mike* (1952), and *The Graduate* (1967). Of course, sometimes even the most determined women fail in this effort, as evidenced by *Kitty Foyle,* a 1940 Academy Award winner for Ginger Rogers, and also by the numerous film productions of Shakespeare's *Romeo and Juliet* (1908, 1916 [two versions], 1936, 1954, 1968, 1996).

Studios usually knew better than to anger female audiences by forcing women into loveless marriages. In movies in which that did happen, the woman either endured it for some overriding benefit or noble sacrifice, as in *Wuthering Heights* (1939), *Brief Encounter* (1945), and *Notorious* (1946), or she suffered and despaired and possibly bailed or wriggled her way out. Scarlett O'Hara is set free twice by widowhood in *Gone With the Wind*. Sometimes drastic measures seem like the only solution. Marital misery and an attraction to another man drive a wife to murder her husband in *The Letter* (1940), *Double Indemnity* (1944), and *The Postman Always Rings Twice* (1946). She gets away with it in the short story by William Somerset Maugham, on which *The Letter* was based.[8] However, in all three of these post-code movies, the characters played by Bette Davis, Barbara Stanwyck, and Lana Turner, respectively, pay for their crimes.

Divorce offers a way out for women and men in unhappy marriages, as demonstrated by *In Name Only* (1939). But it is an inherently unpleasant subject, and divorced women in particular suffered considerable social disapproval up through the 1950s. Movies about divorce often use it as a setup for marital reunions, as in *The Divorcee* (1930) and *The Women* (1939). (*The Women* was remade as *The Opposite Sex* in 1956, and again as *The Women* in 2008.) Between 1937 and 1940, Cary Grant manages to reunite with three former wives in three great movies, *The Awful Truth*, *The Philadelphia Story*, and *His Girl Friday*. Separated couples find reasons to get back together in *Lady Be Good* (1941), *Bedtime Story* (1941), two couples in *Adam's Rib* (1949, and despite the fact that one of the wives shoots her husband), *Rio Grande* (1950), *Let's Make It Legal* (1951), and *Divorce American Style* (1967). Lee and Lyn Wilde starred in the 1945 movie *Twice Blessed* as separated twin sisters who trade places and connive to reunite their parents. Walt Disney produced it as *The Parent Trap* in 1961 with Hayley Mills playing both roles. The movie was so successful that Disney remade the same title in 1998 with Lindsay Lohan in the dual role, again to great success.

Divorce rates dropped during the 1950s then began to rise again in the 1960s.[9] The increasing number of movies that featured couples that did not reunite reflected this trend. Among the movies that began to portray divorced women sympathetically were *A Summer Place* (1959), *The Misfits* (1961), and *Funny Girl* (1968). However, divorce also continued to be a setup for reunions, as evidenced by *Blume in Love* (1973), *Die Hard* (1988), *Independence Day* (1996), and *Ocean's Eleven* (2001). The only catch was that there still had to be genuine love between the husband and wife, and in almost every case, it is the wife who agrees to take the husband back.

Funny Girl and *The Way We Were* (1972), two of Barbra Streisand's biggest hits, offer evidence of the shift in attitudes toward women and divorce that developed as the sixties came to a close. *Funny Girl* is based on the life of *Ziegfeld Follies* comedienne Fanny Brice. At the end of the movie, Fanny (Streisand) and husband Nick Arnstein (Omar Sharif) separate, and a heartbroken Fanny describes her anguish over their split in the memorable closing number, "My Man." Five years later, Barbra Streisand and Robert Redford played Katie Morosky and Hubbell Gardiner in *The Way We Were*. At the time they were two of Hollywood's most popular stars, and audiences would have left theaters happy if they were able to overcome their differences and reunite, especially because they have a daughter, as did Fanny and Nick. But this movie's final scene offers a different vision of life after divorce for women. When they part, Katie steps right back into the new life she has built for herself, saddened but not crushed. In contrast to Fanny's disconsolate rendition of "My Man," this movie concludes with the title song, "The Way We Were," a wistful celebration of the couple's time together. Unlike her character's response in *Funny Girl*, Katy's reaction in 1973 demonstrates that a woman can survive and succeed after divorce.

Rumblings and Discontents

Movies that portrayed divorced women sympathetically were part of a larger trend toward women's rights that gained momentum in the 1960s and early 1970s. The modern woman's liberation movement often traces its "click" moment to writer Betty Friedan's clarion call, *The Feminine Mystique* (1963). Friedan's bestseller was a direct assault on the common wisdom of the day, which insisted that a woman's place was in the home as wife and mother. Friedan, notes historian Elaine Tyler May, urged women "to break away from their domestic confines, go back to school, pursue careers, and revive the vision of female independence that had been alive before World War II."[10]

Significantly, popular culture offers ample evidence that even before Friedan came onto the scene, women were already beginning to question the era's ideal of female domesticity. Many movies from the 1950s feature strong, independent women who take the initiative and press their own agendas. In *The African Queen* (1951), Katharine Hepburn decides they are going to support the war effort by sinking the *Louisa*, and she pushes hard to get a reluctant Humphrey Bogart to agree. Joan Crawford runs a bar, meets a payroll, and stands up to a town in *Johnny Guitar* (1954). Rosalind Russell is a force of nature in *Auntie Mame* (1958). Ingrid Bergman outmaneuvers Chinese officialdom, the Japanese military, and wandering bandits while leading a small army of children through war torn China in the *Inn of the Sixth Happiness*

(1958). Arlene Dahl agrees to give James Mason the mountaineering equipment he needs but only if he includes her in his *Journey to the Center of the Earth* (1959). All these movies were very successful at the box office, and all except *Johnny Guitar* were Academy Award nominees or winners. Even though the women in them depend upon men to aid their efforts, they are the ones who set up those efforts and determine what challenges they will face.

Given the gender stereotypes of the 1950s, what is significant is that among the actresses listed above all except Dahl were over 40 when they starred in these movies. These characters and the women who played them are adults and expect to be treated like adults. Young actresses such as Marilyn Monroe, Audrey Hepburn, and Debbie Reynolds were getting romantic roles during this decade, as had always been the case. However, mature women in movies were beginning to demand more out of their lives than just romance or the responsibilities of wifehood, a trend that parallels the shift among women who had worked during the war years then returned to home and hearth to care for the Baby Boom. When these women began re-entering the workforce in the late 1950s, they wanted to be taken seriously.

Following the publication of Betty Friedan's *The Feminine Mystique*, the movement for women's rights began picking up momentum. In the summer of 1963, Congress passed the Equal Pay Act. The following year Title VII of the Civil Rights Act prohibited discrimination in employment based on race and sex. The National Organization for Women (NOW) was established in 1966 and began promoting women's rights through lobbying and protests. In 1967, President Lyndon B. Johnson issued an executive order that expanded affirmative action to include gender. In 1971, Gloria Steinem launched *Ms.*, a magazine that quickly became a resource guide and rallying point for the rising women's liberation movement.

Hollywood jumped on the women's liberation bandwagon with numerous movies featuring strong, independent female characters. In *From Russia with Love* (1963), tough, dangerous Rosa Klebb is a serious threat to James Bond, who is rescued by the beautiful and impressive Soviet agent, Tatiana Romanova. In *The Russians Are Coming, The Russians Are Coming* (1966), Eva Marie Saint's character solves the final crisis after all of the men get bogged down in screwball bungling and high-pitched hysteria. Audrey Hepburn's character is blind in *Wait Until Dark* (1967) and is set up by criminals to thwart a police investigation, but she discovers the plot, outfoxes the bad guys, and becomes the hero. Even though Kim Darby is rescued by John Wayne and Glen Campbell in *True Grit* (1969), she is the galvanizing force in the movie, and John Wayne works for her. By 1971 audiences could watch an older but still very stylish Rosalind Russell take charge of a C.I.A. operation and engineer a sly triumph in *Mrs. Pollifax—Spy*.

Strong women characters had major opportunities to shine in big-budget musicals in the 1960s. Four popular Broadway musical productions that made it to the silver screen were lavish star vehicles for their female leads. Their storylines anticipate by several years the rise of a women's rights movement in America. *Mary Poppins, The Unsinkable Molly Brown,* and *My Fair Lady,* all from 1964, and *The Sound of Music* from 1965 feature strong female characters who begin to stretch but never completely break the rules for women. Julie Andrews plays a nanny in *Mary Poppins,* a job traditionally filled by women. Her Academy Award-winning performance, however, is anything but traditional. She blends fantasy with reality in magical cartoon Technicolor to help her stodgy employer rethink his values and connect with his children. Quintessential tomboy Molly Brown (Debbie Reynolds, Andrews's competition for the Academy Award that year) rides roughshod over the conventions of society and the confines of her marriage, but she repents and gallantly redeems herself on a freezing *Titanic* lifeboat. *My Fair Lady* stars Audrey Hepburn as Eliza Doolittle, a working-class flower girl who seeks assistance from Professor Henry Higgins (Rex Harrison) in order to better herself through education. Initially she has no interest in men. At the end of G. B. Shaw's play *Pygmalion,* on which *My Fair Lady* was based, Eliza asserts her independence and leaves her grumpy, demanding mentor, but in the immensely popular musical version, she returns to Professor Higgins. In *The Sound of Music,* Novice Maria (Julie Andrews) is torn between her commitment to her religious vows and Baron Georg von Trapp (Christopher Plummer) and his children. Although her decision is not easy, she eventually chooses love and a very large family over the religious life. En route to self-discovery, romance, and marriage, Maria guides the children and their father to a happier relationship in the most successful movie since *Gone With the Wind.*

The portrayal of independent women in many dramas released in the 1960s offered alternatives to traditional images and storylines. Sometimes they became the focus of stories that, while not celebrating immorality, acknowledged the fact that women did not always live up to the wholesome, virtuous images ordained by the Production Code. For example, the unmarried women portrayed sympathetically in *The Apartment* (1960), *Splendor in the Grass* (1961), *The Americanization of Emily* (1964), *Any Wednesday* (1966), and *Two for the Road* (1967) are sexually active and do not wholeheartedly repent. Yet each of them still achieves a measure of happiness. Undermined by these broad cultural shifts within the United States, the Production Code was scrapped in 1968 and replaced by a rating system that permitted greater freedom in movie content but restricted theater attendance based on age.[11]

Two movies—one made in 1946 and the other in 1967—demonstrate how much movie images of women changed in the decades following World

War II. In *The Killers,* a 1946 crime drama, an insurance investigator and a former policeman pursue a gang they suspect committed a payroll theft and murder. The story unfolds in a series of flashbacks. The murder victim, Swede Anderson (Burt Lancaster), and the criminal mastermind, Big Jim Colfax (Albert Dekker) are both in love with Kitty Collins (Ava Gardner). Kitty has a few memorable scenes, but she is overshadowed by the male characters. The plot focuses on the hunt for the Swede's killers. Ultimately, the audience discovers that Kitty was a major player in the gang's crimes, but despite her substantial criminal activity, the story concentrates primarily on the actions and ambitions, romantic and otherwise, of Colfax, Anderson, and their pursuers. By contrast, in *Bonnie and Clyde* from 1967, Bonnie Parker (Faye Dunaway) actively participates in the couple's crimes and looks like the kind of woman who could handle the demands of the business on her own if she had to. Bonnie receives roughly the same weaponry and screen time as Clyde Barrow (Warren Beatty) and is the more sexually aggressive of the two. She shares equally in her partner's bizarre pride in their lifestyle and also in the violent end of their joint venture. Even the title offers evidence of a change in women's status in movies.

As women gained entry into a broader range of employment opportunities, the ego problems of the husband who is out-earned by his wife were a rich source of comedy. *The Thrill of It All* (1963) and *Kisses for My President* (1964) highlight men's obvious dilemma. The husbands in these movies are made slightly irrational (i.e., feminine) by their wives' successes. In the former, he seeks psychological counseling. In the latter, the First Husband briefly winds up wandering the halls of the White House in a frilly dressing gown. Doris Day, the new wage earner in *The Thrill of It All,* eventually gives up her high-paying job for marriage and family and promptly becomes pregnant. Polly Bergen, the first female president of the United States, gives up her job because she is pregnant. By reaffirming male dominance through pregnancy, their husbands are able to resolve their concerns privately and in a very public way as well. These issues had been explored before in movies from the 1940s like *Adam's Rib* and *Bedtime Story,* but following the family-focused social conventions of the fifties, changes in the sixties gave the topic renewed relevance.

Movies of the 1960s reflected the growing number of women in the workplace by focusing on the contrast between women who worked outside of the home and women who married. Businesswoman Doris Day's main concern in *That Touch of Mink* (1962) is virginity and whether or not to keep it. By 1964, Natalie Wood is still struggling with the same issue in *Sex and the Single Girl.* Lest audiences leave theaters feeling unfulfilled, Doris Day resolves the issue by getting married. Two years later, Natalie Wood's solution, although monogamous, is more ambiguous. In *Man's Favorite Sport?* (1964), sports gear salesman Roger Willoughby (Rock Hudson) knows nothing about fishing, but he pretends to be a fishing expert to boost his store's sales. When someone enters him in a national fishing competition, Abigail Page (Paula Prentiss), a competent, athletic, witty public-relations professional, must rescue Roger from a potentially humiliating public failure. She takes command of his situation while wearing stylish ensembles and sports clothes with equal ease. For women seeking professional respect, she is a heroine to cheer for—right up until she realizes she is in love with Roger. At that point, Abigail becomes helpless and weepy and starts wearing girlish-looking knee socks, clear evidence of a woman's tendency to unravel into juvenile incoherence when her emotions get the better of her.

Movies were not the only form of popular culture in the 1960s that reflected changing attitudes toward gender. Rock-and-roll hits that featured submissive and dependent young women like Marcie Blane's "(I Want to Be) Bobby's Girl" (1962) or Little Peggy March's "I Will Follow Him" (1963) soon gave way to the more independent women found on Gail Garnett's "We'll Sing in the Sunshine" (1964) and "Different Drum" (1965) by Linda Ronstadt and the Stone Poneys. By 1972, the year after Gloria Steinem launched *Ms.*, Helen Reddy's hit record, "I Am Woman (Hear Me Roar)," had become an anthem for the women's movement and a *Billboard* Top Ten hit for eight weeks.[12] On television, Eve Arden's anxious hunt for a man in *Our Miss Brooks* (1952–56), and the dutiful wives and mothers featured in long-running hits like *The Adventures of Ozzie and Harriet* (1952–66), *Father Knows Best* (1954–60), and *Leave It to Beaver* (1957–63) were supplanted by shows that featured more independent women. For example, the capable, competent, take-charge witch Samantha (Elizabeth Montgomery) came to her husband's rescue on a weekly basis in *Bewitched*, which ran for eight years starting in the mid-sixties, and career women like Mary Richards in *The Mary Tyler Moore Show* and Sgt. Pepper Anderson (Angie Dickenson) in *Police Woman* glorified working women professionals in the seventies.

Two tennis matches in the summer of 1973 serve as a collective exclamation point to the evolution in women's attitudes and aspirations. Bobby Riggs, a tennis champion from the 1940s, challenged Margaret Court to a match as a celebrity stunt designed to reinforce male superiority. Court was the top women's tennis player that year, but Riggs upstaged and outplayed her. Billie Jean King was determined not to let that stand. She had already won five women's singles titles at Wimbledon, and she challenged Riggs to another match. King captured international headlines when she won the match resoundingly, 6–4, 6–3, 6–3.[13]

"You've Come a Long Way, Baby"

Phillip Morris introduced Virginia Slims cigarettes in 1968, and they marketed their new brand to young women with a sexist slogan that quickly became iconic: "You've Come a Long Way, Baby." The same could be said for images of women in movies. From the 1930s through the late 1960s, women characters on screen gradually became more independent and sophisticated in keeping with the changes in real women's aspirations and opportunities. The dramatic cultural and social changes of the late 1960s pushed that change even further. After 1970, portrayals of women went beyond images of helpless females, dangerous harlots, devoted mothers, conflicted professional women, and miserable, abandoned wives. Although old stereotypes did not disappear completely, they received serious competition from new images of women.

Movies began to depict women who achieve their goals without men's love or help (*Julia*, 1977; *Alien*, 1979). They demonstrate that violence against women by men will beget violence against men *by* women (*The Legend of Billie Jean*, 1985; *Blue Steel*, 1989; *Thelma and Louise*, 1991). Professional cooperation between men and women does not have to lead to romance (*Norma Rae*, 1979; *The Silence of the Lambs*, 1991; *Erin Brockovich*, 2000), and groups of women can bond and succeed (*Nine to Five*, 1980; *The Color Purple*, 1985; *Fried Green Tomatoes*, 1991; *Sister Act* and *A League of Their Own*, 1992) or fail (*Thelma and Louise*). Movies begin to feature men as the sidekicks while women lead the quest to solve mysteries or defeat bad guys (*Desperately Seeking Susan*, 1985; *Buffy the Vampire Slayer*, 1992; *The Net*, 1995; *Fargo*, 1996; and *Miss Congeniality*, 2000).

Gone were the days when beautiful divorced couples were certain to reunite. By 1978, Hollywood's vision of an abandoned wife in *An Unmarried Women* is not just sympathetic to her newly single state, it endorses it as a liberating and empowering experience. Other movies like *Private Benjamin* (1980), *Cross Creek* (1983), and *Murphy's Romance* (1985) continued to expand on the idea that leaving a man can result in a positive outcome rather than define a failure. Divorce as combat gets an overheated treatment in the black comedy *The War of the Roses* (1989) wherein everybody loses. All these plotlines appear to converge in the 1996 hit, *First Wives Club*, a giddy over-the-top celebration of women, divorce, and revenge that gives three popular actresses—Goldie Hawn, Diane Keaton, and Bette Midler, with multiple Academy Award nominations and wins among them—the opportunity to triumph. They are ably assisted by Sarah Jessica Parker's deliciously vapid trophy wife.

Even the traditional princess or princess-like characters who must be rescued, Candice Bergen in *The Wind and the Lion* (1975) and Carrie Fisher in

Star Wars (1977), for example, have acquired a new assertiveness. By 1998, Drew Barrymore could portray Danielle, the Cinderella at the center of *Ever After*, as one smart, tough cookie and still get her prince. Expanding on this trend, Walt Disney Studios, which had capitalized so prodigiously on the princess-rescued-by-her-prince theme throughout the twentieth century, turned the dynamic on its head in 2007 when Amy Adams as a determined Giselle picked up a sword and defended her prince from the evil witch in *Enchanted*. Audiences responded favorably to this reversal of the traditional storyline. After only four weeks in theaters, the movie had earned $92.3 million at the box office.[14] Post–1970 movies demonstrated—and continue to demonstrate—that women have indeed come a long way.

Representative Movies

Dinner at Eight (1933)

(113 minutes) *Director:* George Cukor; *Stars:* Marie Dressler, Lionel Barrymore, Wallace Beery, Jean Harlow, John Barrymore, Billie Burke, Lee Tracy, Edmund Lowe, Madge Evans, Jean Hersholt, Karen Morley, Phillips Holmes, May Robson.

The Great Depression had an obvious impact on poor and middle class people, but the rich suffered as well, often to their great surprise. George Cukor's 1933 hit, *Dinner at Eight*, explores how husbands, wives, and lovers from the upper class cope with the complications of the Depression as well as the complexities of love and finance in the midst of changing times. Although their survival mechanisms may be a bit rusty, the rich—like the poor—must eventually come to grips with the new economic reality.

Dinner at Eight is just one of many 1930s movies that feature plots driven by the Great Depression, and upper-class women in particular often found themselves navigating unfamiliar territory in those troubled times. During the Roaring Twenties, self-absorbed flappers had embraced the optimistic hedonism of the era, a character type brilliantly explored and eviscerated by F. Scott Fitzgerald in *The Great Gatsby*.[15] But once the Depression hit, the carefree flapper image quickly became outmoded as many women were forced to find work outside the home. Movies kept pace with the times and portrayed women who suffer and struggle alongside men or on their own, and some of their options were not always socially acceptable or even legal. Before the Production Code was fully enforced in 1934, movies could portray ethically challenged women who still find success and romance, which is the whole point of Mae West's career. Jean Harlow in *Red-Headed Woman* (1932) and Barbara Stanwyck in *Baby Face* (1933) use sex to manipulate men in order to finance comfortable lives for themselves. Harlow is counting on a husband to support her. Stanwyck is more enterprising and sleeps her way to the top of a large banking firm.

When women joined the workforce during the Depression, movies often treated their employment as just a way station on the road to matrimony, which meant that men were still portrayed as the significant breadwinners. Even resourceful, career-oriented women who were uninterested in getting married were rescued by love by the end of the movie. In the pre-code movie, *Female* (1933), Ruth Chatterton is an aggressive, ambitious, successful executive who uses men for casual sex, an arrangement they are happy to accept. When she finally does fall in love with a man, she must abandon her professional life to win him. If a woman is determined to hang on to her independence and her job, the movie will underscore the error of her ways, as the title and plot of *Imitation of Life* (1934) demonstrate. Claudette Colbert plays a widow with a successful business who ignores her personal life and focuses instead on work. As an apparent punishment for her ambitions, when she finally meets a man she is interested in, circumstances force her to give him up. The bluntly titled *Wife vs. Secretary* (1936) suggests that even ambitious women who aim for a career rather than a husband will wind up falling in love with the boss. Depression-era movies that are set in other historical eras still reflect 1930s gender attitudes. The stories from *Stagecoach, Gone With the Wind,* and *Drums Along the Mohawk,* all made in 1939, are set in the past, but they feature women who struggle to survive financial difficulties that would have been painfully familiar to Depression-era audiences.

The expectation that men would be the providers was a fixed mark in the traditional views of most men and women, and it could not be abandoned abruptly in the early years of the Depression. Therefore, what will happen when men can no longer provide and how women who are unprepared to work outside the home will respond are the main issues that frame the plot of *Dinner at Eight*. Millicent Jordan (Billie Burke) is the silly, shallow wife of a New York businessman. She has achieved a society coup by getting British nobility to come to her dinner party, but she has trouble setting up the rest of the guest list to her high standards. Her husband, Oliver (Lionel Barrymore), does not care about social considerations and suggests people he likes to fill in Millicent's table, including Carlotta Vance (Marie Dressler), an older actress well past her prime.

However, Oliver's shipping company is on the verge of collapse, and he is trying to lure investor Dan Packard (Wallace Beery) into a deal that will save it. The company has been in the family for 60 years, and Oliver believes that inviting Dan and his social climbing wife, Kitty (Jean Harlow), to this dinner will help him get Dan's support. Millicent is unaware of Oliver's financial concerns or the health problems he is keeping from her. She considers Carlotta and Kitty beneath her, but she agrees to invite them. Others on her guest list include daughter Paula (Madge Evans), who is having a secret affair with a famous but much older actor, Larry Renault (John Barrymore); Paula's fiancé, Ernest (Phillips Holmes); Doctor Talbot (Edmund Lowe), who is having an affair with Kitty; and his wife, Lucy (Karen Morley), who knows all about his affair and all of his other affairs as well.

The characters offer an upper-class view of the era's financial crisis. They all must face the escalating financial effects of the Depression. Except for Carlotta, however, the women in this movie operate on the assumption that whatever options they have depend upon men to succeed, and they appear oblivious to the connections between the country's economic situation and their own. Only Carlotta evaluates her options based on a realistic assessment of economic factors, perhaps because the aging actress realizes that she can no longer attract a man for financial support. During her successful acting career Carlotta accepted many expensive "gifts" from her admirers. But now that she is older and less attractive to men, she understands that she needs a new plan to ensure her future financial security. Although she seeks guidance from Oliver, Carlotta takes stock of her circumstances and ultimately acts on her own initiative.

The women play their characters very broadly in keeping with the era's expectations. Millicent accepts the social standards of the day. In the movie's opening line of dialog, she announces delightedly, "Darlings, I've got Lord and Lady Ferncliff!" But she loves Oliver, and when she becomes aware of the true state of his health and finances, she is determined to rise to the occasion. Carlotta is an exaggerated, almost cruel version of the aging theatrical beauty. Her makeup and furs border on grotesque, and her efforts at playing the helpless coquette are ludicrous. To her credit, even she knows it, and she abandons the pose abruptly whenever it appears to be failing her. Paula is young and foolishly in love with the alcoholic Renault. Kitty uses sex to control men but is perfectly comfortable resorting to blackmail when sex will not work. Lucy is the humiliated wife who accepts her husband's behavior because she loves him. But her husband is a doctor with wealthy clients, which ensures that the couple's income is relatively secure from the effects of the Depression. Therefore, Lucy does not have to struggle financially as she copes with her husband's infidelities.

The men in the movie, on the other hand, do look for ways to deal with the negative and positive opportunities that the Depression presents. They and their audience expect them to take action to try to survive. Oliver attempts to salvage the shipping line by encouraging Dan to invest in it, but Dan knows that the line is in financial trouble and he is hoping to get it at a steal. Renault tries desperately to find stage work, even considering a theatrical role that he believes is beneath his star stature. The men must also take women's responses into account as they plan for the future. Oliver is suffering from a serious heart condition, and he tries gently to convey this to his wife in order to avoid the stresses of the dinner she has planned. Millicent has invited the Packards to her dinner for Oliver's sake, and Kitty is eager to attend this socially advantageous event. When she finds out about Dan's efforts to capitalize on Oliver's misfortune, she threatens to expose her husband's underhanded dealings unless he takes her to the dinner and helps Oliver. Paula wants to break off her engagement to her wealthy fiancé and devote herself to her lover, but Renault pushes her away in a gallant effort to spare her the humiliation of his depleted finances and rapidly collapsing career.

The characters in this movie are all engaged in various kinds of fraud or are oblivious to reality. The inexorable effects of the Depression grind on no matter how they envision their individual circumstances, and they must eventually acknowledge the truth about their lives. All of their personal and financial complications come to a head as they prepare for Millicent's "dinner at eight."

Suggested Discussion Questions

1. Why is Oliver's shipping company failing? How does this reflect the broader economic effects of the Depression? How do Oliver's financial problems compare to situations that can arise in the board game Monopoly?

2. Research where and what Antibes is. Explain the connections between Antibes and the guests at Millicent's dinner party.

3. How has Carlotta supported herself in the past? Describe her current finances. How did they get to this point? When she mentions guests like "Noel, Winston, and occasionally Wales" what does her remark say about the life she has led?

4. Describe Carlotta's relationship to the Jordan family. She reminds Oliver that when he was 21 and she was "30-ish" he proposed marriage, and she adds, "They didn't often ask me to marry them." What does this say about the men in her life? Does she seem remorseful over how she has lived her life?

5. Stock in Oliver's shipping line is privately held by a handful of investors, including Carlotta. Explain the connection between the stock's price and the financial plans of Oliver, Carlotta, and Dan Packard. Who are the potential winners and losers among them?

6. Describe Kitty's relationship with Dan. Describe her relationship with Dr. Talbot. Based on her behavior, explain her value system. What problem does she face with Tina and how does she resolve it? Have Kitty's actions put her in any danger?

7. What professional and personal problems is Larry Renault facing? How does he treat Paula? How is he treated by the hotel management? Are Renault's problems related to the Depression or are there other causes?

8. How does Carlotta react when she finds out about Paula and Larry? How does Paula react to Larry's death? Was it a good decision? Paula is not in love with her fiancé. Assume that her father's shipping line goes bankrupt. Instead of marriage, what were some other reasonable options for her in 1933?

9. When Millicent learns the truth about Oliver's health, she is determined to economize and help him. Based on her previous behavior, does it seem likely that she will be able to help? How would she do it?

10. At the dinner how does Dan offer to help Oliver? How does Oliver respond when Dan explains his plans to him? Consider the national and international history of the 1930s. If Dan pumps money into the shipping line in 1933, either in the form of a loan or by buying stock (some of which he already secretly owns), could it survive and prosper? Why, or why not?

11. Is the movie supportive, mocking, or dismissive toward women? Toward men? Describe any admirable qualities the main characters exhibit. Which character(s) would you like for a friend?

12. The movie's final bit of dialog between Carlotta and Kitty has become iconic. Kitty describes a book's claim that "machinery will take the place of every profession." Carlotta says, "Oh, my dear, that's something you need never worry about." What does this line mean, and why would the director give it to Carlotta?

His Girl Friday (1940)

(92 minutes) *Director:* Howard Hawks; *Stars:* Cary Grant, Rosalind Russell, Ralph Bellamy, Gene Lockhart, Helen Mack, Ernest Truex, Clarence Kolb, Porter Hall, Roscoe Karns, Abner Biberman, Cliff Edwards, John Qualen, Frank Jenks, Billy Gilbert.

His Girl Friday highlights the challenges women faced when they stepped into male-dominated professional careers. Both sexes experienced culture shock, but when love complicated the picture, things could get ugly. If, however, Cary Grant and Rosalind Russell were the couple at the heart of the movie, then things were more likely to descend—or soar, depending on your point of view—into screwball comedy.

In the early years of the twentieth century women had limited opportunities to work outside the home, but they found plenty of work inside the home caring for children, laundering, cleaning, cooking, gardening, canning foods, and creating clothing and home décor through basic craft skills.[16] Few women who worked outside the home had jobs in heavy industry or in professional positions. Women's jobs outside the home were typically limited to teaching, nursing, and clerical or service work. Women were accepted and, to a degree, confined in these labor categories.

As more and more women began entering professional fields by the 1930s, they often found themselves in inhospitable work environments. Their presence challenged traditional workplace conventions, which set the stage for many movie comedies. Fitting women into the workplace in movie plots usually meant putting them in support positions. Jean Arthur plays tough, cynical workingwomen who offer their support to Gary Cooper in *Mr. Deeds Goes to Town* (1936), Cary Grant in *Only Angels Have Wings* (1939), and James Stewart in *Mr. Smith Goes to Washington* (1939), which ultimately allows these men to triumph in their endeavors. (The plot of *High Road to China* shares some similarities with *Only Angles Have Wings* and features Tom Selleck as an accomplished pilot. But it came out in 1983, well after the start of the Women's Movement, and the last heroic flight is made by Bess Armstrong, the *other* accomplished pilot in the movie.) Jean Harlow fulfills a similar support role opposite Clark Gable in *Wife vs. Secretary,* while Ruth Hussey helps James Stewart get his scoop in *The Philadelphia Story* (1940). Barbara Stanwyck pushes the construct up a notch in *Breakfast for Two* (1937) when she meets her match in Herbert Marshall and bests him by buying his company right out from under him. The two entrepreneurs are wearing nearly identical pinstripe suits when Marshall discovers this treachery and explodes at her breach of gender-appropriate behavior. "You're the type of woman who wants to wear the pants," he shouts at her. "All right, mister, wear them, trip over them, and break your neck."

The men in these movies interact with women through business relationships rather than romantic ones. At the same time, marriage is the usual outcome for these couples, and no matter how lovingly she may enter into it, the union usually removes the woman from the professional workplace. The overriding message is clear: a woman can only find happiness if she accepts a role that is subordinate to a man. A major question at the core of this dynamic is whether a woman can be an accomplished professional without losing her femininity. Since most professions were reserved for men in the 1930s and '40s, how could women perform successfully in a male-dominated workplace?

Howard Hawks's 1940 screwball comedy, *His Girl Friday,* explores this issue and other concerns of the era in a plot that manages to skewer gender roles, politicians, the media, the insurance business, and Albany, New York, with lightning fast dialog, zany plot developments, and equal zest. It even includes a dose of real drama. The basis for the movie was the Ben Hecht-Charles MacArthur play, *The Front Page,* which originally featured two male leads and had already been made into a movie in 1931. But in his remake, Hawks changed one of the male leads to a woman, which resulted in an entirely different professional relationship.[17]

Hildy Johnson (Rosalind Russell) is a tough, dedicated, wisecracking news reporter who gives as good as she gets from the male reporters on her beat. She has just returned to her newspaper office after a four-month vacation during which she got a divorce and quickly became engaged to Bruce Baldwin (Ralph Bellamy), a humble, earnest, honest insurance salesman from Albany, New York. Marriage to Bruce offers her an escape from the aggravations of the news business and from Walter Burns (Cary Grant), her lying, conniving, witty, and annoying ex-husband—and boss! The title of the movie neatly sums up Hildy's problems with Walter. The first scene in *His Girl Friday* shows her striding confidently back into the office to see him, a slightly bewildered Bruce in tow. She wants to deliver the news of her upcoming marriage personally and just a bit vengefully. She is greeted with affection by everyone. When the help columnist mentions that her cat has had kittens, Hildy's response—"It's her own fault"—sets the tone for her interactions with Walter.

Walter is delighted she has returned because a major story is just breaking. Earl Williams (John Qualen), an unemployed bookkeeper, is about to be executed for accidently shooting and killing an African-American policeman. The mayor is up for re-election, and his cynical political calculation is that Earl's execution will help him with an important bloc of voters. The newspaper has championed a reprieve for Earl, but so far the governor has refused to grant one. Walter is not completely surprised that Hildy has returned because he knows how much she loves her work, and he wants her to write this story as only she can. Walter proceeds rather ungallantly to taunt her over the fact that she has come back, confident that he holds the upper hand. When she finally manages to tell him she is getting married, he is truly (but only momentarily) stunned.

Walter is suspicious of her determination to marry and leave her work behind, so he invites Hildy and her fiancé to lunch in order to check Bruce out. It soon becomes obvious that in terms of personality Walter is a just-opened bottle of champagne whereas Bruce is a warm glass of milk. Throughout lunch, jokes and sarcasm sail over Bruce's head. But even though Hildy and Walter are feuding, they still communicate in the intimate glare-and-glance way of couples who are truly in synch. Meanwhile, Bruce remains oblivious.

Once Walter realizes Bruce's limitations, he immediately dives in with

His Girl Friday (1940)   193

multiple agendas, and he manages to keep them all moving forward with one crooked deal after the other. Walter uses each solution to solve as many problems as possible. He finally entices Hildy to spend just a few minutes covering the Earl Williams story before she heads for Albany and a new home with Bruce and his mother. Hildy greets other reporters at the jail and tells them that after this one last story she plans to leave the business and get married. Cynicism raises its ugly head and bets are made. The clever Hildy soon lands an interview with Earl, and she crafts a story that undercuts the image of Earl as a ruthless criminal, which is how the mayor keeps defining him to the press. Meanwhile, Walter connives with a local small-time crook to have Bruce arrested so Hildy's departure will be delayed. Complicated plot developments follow in rapid succession. Everyone is playing an angle while Earl Williams's life hangs in the balance.

The only characters who seem on the level are Bruce, Earl, and Earl's friend, Molly (Helen Mack). The others all understand that they are playing various angles and also playing to their audiences—even the movie itself does—and they increase the volume of their rhetoric accordingly. In one scene, as a reporter goes through a list of injured policemen, he describes each one's relationship to the sheriff, thereby highlighting the rampant nepotism in the sheriff's office. But the reporters are hardly sterling examples of integrity. They watch the police capture Earl after an escape attempt and immediately phone in their stories. Each reporter delivers a different, very dramatic, and completely false report. During one phone call, a reporter makes a gratuitous joke using a racially offensive term, "pickaninny," which suggests that audiences in the 1940s would have been quite familiar with that insult to African Americans. The plot is based on the mayor's willingness to hang a man simply to win the support of African American voters. While the mayor and sheriff engage in multiple frauds to keep Earl's execution on track, Walter responds with multiple frauds of his own so that he can keep Hildy working on Earl's story. Throughout the ordeal, Walter and Hildy's relationship ricochets from anger to jealousy to mutual manipulation to their shared disdain for Bruce's naïveté.

The cynical political calculations of the mayor and the sheriff finally catch up with them. They try to spin the situation to their advantage, but even in handcuffs, Walter and Hildy are more than a match for the forces of corruption. In fact, Walter's special expertise in this area proves decisive.

Suggested Discussion Questions

1. In the first few scenes, how does Hildy react to Bruce's flattery and gentlemanly attentions? When and why does she lie to Bruce about her true feelings?

2. How does Walter treat Hildy in the movie's first scene? Why did Hildy divorce Walter? Are there any obvious red flags about Hildy's plans to marry Bruce? How does Hildy's attitude toward Bruce change as the movie progresses? Give specific examples to support your answer.

3. Define the public relations term, "spin." What went on between Molly and Earl? How have the reporters treated Molly in their stories? How do they react to her accusations at first? How do they react after Molly leaves the room? What does Hildy mean when she says, "Gentlemen of the press"?

4. How do references to "Reds" (Communists) figure in Earl's escape? Why would the sheriff use this tactic?

5. Explain Diamond Louis's role in Walter's schemes. When Hildy figures out how he and a very platinum-blonde woman named Evangeline have set Bruce up, Hildy refers to her as Louis's "albino." Louis responds that she was born in this country. Explain the joke.

6. How and why has Earl Williams's crime become such an important political issue? How do the mayor, sheriff, and governor react to Earl's impending execution?

7. Describe any crimes or criminals who have an effect on current political affairs. How have various politicians or others of importance, such as news commentators, business leaders, or celebrities, responded? Do their reactions seem authentic or are there possible ulterior motives for their responses?

8. There are three main female characters in this movie: Hildy, Molly, and Bruce's mother. How are they treated by the men in the movie and by each other? Sum up each woman's motivation for her actions in a brief phrase. Do any of them accomplish their goals? How?

9. In what ways are men presented as stereotypes? Cite specific examples. How do the other reporters view Hildy?

10. Why does Hildy send Bruce home and return to Walter? Should she have married Bruce? Does Walter really love Hildy? How does Walter view women, work, and marriage? Will Hildy be happy with her decision to return to Walter? Is there going to be honeymoon?

11. The movie explores issues regarding marriage and gender relations, race, the ethics of the news business, and the behavior of politicians. Are these issues relevant today, and if so, how? Cite specific contemporary examples to support your answer.

12. How have new technologies or forms of social media affected the way people can learn about and influence major events that they previously would only have known about through traditional media? Cite specific examples and analyze whether or not this influence has been a good thing.

Christmas in Connecticut (1945)

(101 minutes) *Director:* Peter Godfrey; *Stars:* Barbara Stanwyck, Dennis Morgan, Sydney Greenstreet, Reginald Gardiner, S.Z. Sakall, Robert Shayne, Una O'Connor.

Christmas in Connecticut (1945) reflects the conflicted feelings Americans had about the many women who went to work outside of the home during World War II. Throughout the 1940s, the war, the expanding economy, and post-war employment and production issues created a social and economic paradox. Spending for the war finally brought the Depression to an end, and people went back to work. The total national income was at $70.8 billion in 1939. By 1945, it had risen to $161 billion.[18] But the war also took men out of the employment picture, roughly 15.5 million of them, and sent them off to war. While the war was on, therefore, women went to work in record numbers and in all kinds of jobs, although when women were hired for work that had been done primarily by men, employers emphasized that it would only be "for the duration."[19]

The economic and social effects reversed themselves when the war ended. The economy contracted for a while as plants retooled and shifted to peacetime production. In order to find jobs for all the returning veterans, industry and government encouraged women to leave the labor force and return to traditional roles as wives and homemakers. However, by the end of the war, two-thirds or more of the women who had gone to work wanted to stay at work.[20] Returning veterans had a different vision. They were eager to return to the way things used to be, not as they were in the thirties, but before the Depression.[21] They wanted jobs and they wanted women back in the home where they belonged. Data on rates of marriage, employment for women, and the Baby Boom suggest that men prevailed. After the war, for example, women's rates of employment in the auto industry went from 25 percent down to 7.5 percent, and in the durable-goods industries they fell by 50 percent nationwide. In place of jobs in the workforce, women were encouraged to welcome men home with support and "submissiveness."[22]

But not all women were convinced. After all, work outside the home did have its benefits, and one of the most compelling for women was the ability to earn money and do with it whatever they pleased. As the war wound down, therefore, millions of men who thought they were coming home to the girls they left behind were about to confront independent women with money of their own to spend and no one to tell them how to spend it. Could the transition to the "good old days" possibly go smoothly?

The movies of the late 1940s did their part to champion a return to tradition. They broadly supported the notion that the best way to welcome the troops back was by pretending that nothing had changed during the four years they were at war.[23] Movies from the mid- to late 1940s like *Meet Me in St. Louis* (1944), *It's a Wonderful Life* (1946), *Life with Father* (1947), and *I Remember Mama* (1948) celebrate the joys of traditional family life, and even if they do it with a wink and a nod, they put fathers in charge. Not coincidentally, three of these movies are set in earlier eras when men were expected to be the heads of their households. The women in these films succeed only with the support or consent of men, and the basic patriarchal structure remains the standard. For example, the daughters in *Meet Me in St. Louis* succeed because they convince their father to change his plans. Mama really runs the operation in *I Remember Mama,* but she is careful to observe proper respect for her husband, and the movie's main power player is the indomitable Uncle Chris. Movies about career women like *Mildred Pierce* (1945), *The Red Shoes* (1948), and *Sunset Blvd.* (1950) demonstrate that work will not lead to happiness, and each one includes an unnecessary death to drive the point home. In *The Harvey Girls* (1946), *The Bachelor and the Bobby Soxer* (1947), and *Miracle on 34th Street* (1947), a relationship with a man is presented as the superior outcome, even for those women who enjoy their work.

There were a few counter images. Even though Judy Garland's character is determined to find a husband out West in *The Harvey Girls,* the movie portrays work as a great adventure. In *The Farmer's Daughter* (1947), Loretta Young (in an Academy Award-winning performance) runs for Congress and wins, an unusual outcome at the time. Perhaps to ensure that audiences would not be put off by this subversive achievement, however, the movie ends as her fiancé carries her over the threshold of the House of Representatives. Apparently, having Young walk into Congress under her own steam would have pushed the point too far. (In *The Ballad of Josie,* from 1967, Doris Day achieves similar success in a male-dominated industry. Twenty years after Young's victory, this movie also finds it necessary to conclude with Day being carried off in a man's arms.) Annie Oakley (Betty Hutton) keeps her job and her man in *Annie Get Your Gun* (1950), but this movie suffers the disadvantage of being based on fact.

Christmas in Connecticut (1945) is far more typical of the gender attitudes found in movies released after World War II. Directed by Peter Godfrey, the story focuses on writer Elizabeth Lane (Barbara Stanwyck), who has established a very successful career as a columnist for a major women's magazine. She combines cooking tips from her Uncle Felix (S. Z. Sakall), descriptions of a gracious country home, and her own somewhat cynical imagination to produce a magazine column about her cooking successes, interior-decorating abilities, and stellar housekeeping skills. Elizabeth has developed a huge national readership, which makes the magazine's demanding, competitive owner, Alexander Yardley (Sydney Greenstreet), very happy. The column is so influential that a nurse at a military hospital becomes convinced a visit with happy housewife Elizabeth will finally get her boyfriend to set a wedding date. The nurse writes to Yardley in the hope that the columnist will extend a Christmas invitation to her war-hero boyfriend, Jefferson Jones (Dennis Morgan). Yardley sees a promising public relations opportunity and demands that Elizabeth welcome Jeff to her home for Christmas. The movie blends these elements into a silly, sweet holiday comedy complete with mistaken identities, narrow escapes, and romantic longings as traditional as those in any romance novel.

Yardley's plan to have Elizabeth and her family entertain Jeff at the country house about which she writes with such pride generates multiple problems. Elizabeth has no husband, she has no country house, and even though a chronicle of her recent pregnancy drove the magazine's circulation numbers up substantially, she has no child. The fact that she cannot cook is just the icing on the cake. Yardley knows nothing of her many frauds, and when he finds himself at loose ends for Christmas, he decides he will visit as well. Jeff has somehow become engaged to the nurse, partly because he wants to get better treatment at the facility where he is recuperating. He is stalling about a wedding date because he is not really interested in the nurse.

Elizabeth does have an admirer, however, and he comes to her rescue— with one big string attached. Wealthy architect John Sloan (Reginald Gardiner), whose house she writes about in her columns, has repeatedly asked Elizabeth to marry him, but she has always declined, citing the demands of her career as her excuse. The real reason, however, is because she does not love him. Sensing an opportunity in her dilemma, Sloan asks her once again and assures her that whatever her feelings may be, love will grow. He seems eager to land a wife the way some people are eager to get the right lamps to go with the end tables. To sweeten the deal, he offers to let her use his house for Jeff's upcoming visit. With her career about to collapse, she no longer has any reason to refuse him. She believes that if Yardley, who is a stickler for honesty, finds out that she is a fraud, she will be fired. Under great pressure and after telling him she does not love him, Elizabeth agrees to marry Sloan. They head to his country home for a quick wedding with a justice of the peace so they will be able to welcome their guests as husband and wife.

Uncle Felix comes along to do the holiday cooking, and Sloan's housekeeper (Una O'Connor) babysits at the house for a woman who works at a local defense plant. Although not exactly seamless, Elizabeth's fake family is essentially complete. All everyone has to do is keep the charade going until war hero Jeff and publisher Yardley leave. The plan, however, soon begins to unravel. Jeff arrives just as the wedding is about to start. Elizabeth promptly falls for the handsome young sailor and all bets are off, as is the wedding—temporarily. Jeff, too, is smitten, but as far as either one of them knows, she is married and he is engaged.

Christmas in Connecticut explores the era's concepts of gender, love, family, and fraud, and it uses some set pieces to emphasize these themes. Jeff is a good-looking Everyman who has fought for his country and is now hoping to enjoy life again. In keeping with the common wisdom of the day, the way to his heart is through food. He also personifies the notion of the perfect father because, unlike career woman Elizabeth, he is perfectly comfortable dealing with the baby. Sloan, on the other hand, typifies the businessman who is more concerned about profits than family. He is strongly focused on his work, and although he wants to marry Elizabeth, he cannot stop himself from over thinking everything. Sloan is not concerned about Elizabeth's lack of love for him, but he becomes extremely focused when Yardley suggests that he write a column about architecture for the magazine. Elizabeth soon realizes that the real reason she does not want to marry Sloan is because he is simply not the right man. Meeting Jeff changes everything. At long last, Elizabeth has found a man who makes it worthwhile for her to give up her career for hearth and home.

Uncle Felix does not care about her job, and he does not approve of her impending marriage to Sloan. All he cares about is Elizabeth. When he decides that Jeff is a perfect match for her, he focuses all his efforts and his idiosyncratic English language skills on getting them together and keeping her and Sloan apart. With the unintentional assistance of some local farm animals and mislaid babies, everything turns out "hunky dunky."

Suggested Discussion Questions

1. How much control does Elizabeth have over her life as an employee of Alexander Yardley? Would this relationship be different if she were a male employee? Defend your answer.

2. What is Uncle Felix worried about when he discovers the mink coat? Why is the coat so important to Elizabeth?

3. Why would audiences find the server's explanation of the meaning of "catastrophe" amusing? Explain whether this joke makes the movie racist or ahead of its time.

4. Food is an important plot element. How do the main characters relate to food and cooking? Which stereotypes are supported and which ones are challenged when it comes to food?

5. The first view of Sloan's house could have come right out of a print by Currier and Ives. There are horses, sleds, sleigh bells, deep drifts of snow, and a dog. The house is decorated in traditional New England style. The Christmas

tree is huge. Imagine the life experiences of members of the audience who are over ten years old in 1945. How would they probably respond to these images?

6. How does Sloan view Elizabeth? How does he treat her? Why does he want to marry her? Define his value system based on specific incidents in the movie.

7. Elizabeth believes that Yardley is a man of integrity and always insists on the truth from his employees. Why does Yardley ask Elizabeth to have another child? Does his request support the image of his integrity? How well would Yardley succeed in today's media world? Explain whether you believe his promotional methods would work today or are too old-fashioned to work now.

8. Felix functions as a kind of parent for Elizabeth. Cite specific examples of his role in getting her and Jeff together. What message does this send about how capable women are at finding husbands on their own? Should women or men look to their parents for help or approval before marrying?

9. Explain the significance of the rocking chairs. What do they say about Elizabeth's effect on her readers? What do they say about her readers?

10. At the end of the movie Elizabeth turns down Yardley's job offer. She gives a speech about how tired she is of a long list of things and ends with, "In short, I'm tired." What is the point of a speech like this in 1945? Does this movie support women's work outside the home, and if so, how? Did Elizabeth's declaration of tiredness surprise you? Why, or why not?

11. What kind of man is Jeff, and what does he represent to women who do not want to quit working when the war ends?

12. Are Americans still concerned about the issues of women, work, and family? Cite specific contemporary examples that support your answer.

13. The plot contrasts a fraudulent version of love, home, and family life with the real thing. The movie was a big success. What does this say about attitudes in 1945? It is still a success and appears on television regularly every holiday season. Why?

Born Yesterday (1950)

(103 minutes) *Director:* George Cukor; *Stars:* Judy Holliday, William Holden, Broderick Crawford, Howard St. John.

George Cukor's *Born Yesterday* (1950) reflects the desired status and function of women in early Cold War America. By general consensus, they should be beautiful, blonde, and not too bright.

Many international issues contributed to the strains that beset Americans in the immediate post-war era. Victory in World War II brought the country great jubilation and relief. But it soon became obvious that the Communists had also won. By war's end, the Soviet Union had expanded its control to all of Eastern Europe and half of Germany. In 1949, after a long and bitter civil war, Chiang Kai-shek led the Nationalist Chinese to the tiny offshore island of Taiwan and left the mainland to Mao Zedong and the Communists. Political issues in Korea were complicated, and they eventually spun out of control. In terms of Communist expansion, the Middle East and Africa were also in play. Adding to the fears and anxieties of the Cold War, the dangers of Communism were amplified in the early 1950s by the strident demagoguery of Senator Joseph R. McCarthy.

None of these developments was enough to send America to war against the Soviet Union, but they did draw the country into a belligerent, hyper-vigilant, hyper-patriotic posture that vilified Communism and vigorously celebrated America's democratic virtues. In the face of all of these tensions, Americans wanted someplace secure that would serve as a psychological harbor and offer refuge from the forces that rose up again and again to batter them. The home became that harbor.[24] Perhaps as a way to give women a valuable alternative to the loss of their wartime jobs, the role of wife and mother became the celebrated centerpiece of that domain.[25]

However, if women were central to the sanctuary that home and family represented, then their intelligent pursuit of their own interests threatened men, family life, and, by extension, the nation as well. In order to keep women in their place everybody piled on. In *Modern Woman, The Lost Sex* (1947), Ferdinand Lundberg and Marynia F. Farnham, M. D., insisted that women could only find validation in the traditional roles of wife and mother.[26] *LIFE Magazine* declared that having babies was the greatest accomplishment of American women. *Dr. Spock's Baby and Child Care,* which extolled the value of good mothering, became a best seller. Many people strongly believed that fulfilling her anatomical destiny through childbearing was central to a woman's psychological health. This belief inspired a Montana state senator to declare that children were better off with high school graduates as teachers rather than college-educated spinsters.[27] Walt Disney, a dominant cultural force for young people in movies and on television during the 1950s, consistently reinforced the idea that women were here to serve by featuring heroines who suffer willingly, sing through their unending chores, and ultimately are rewarded for their self-sacrifice—by marriage to men.[28]

Even fashion played a part in redefining women's purpose in life. During the war, designers had trimmed the standard outlines of women's and men's clothing in order to conserve fabric. Women wanted something different once the war ended. They found it in the New Look, which featured an exaggerated figure and emphasized large busts, small waists, and wide swirling skirts that consumed yards of fabric. The ultra-feminine silhouette was criticized by some feminists as a return to a less independent lifestyle.[29] In order to achieve the requisite look, many women needed painful figure-altering undergarments that added or compressed where necessary.[30]

Whatever it meant and whatever it took, women bought it. If they were unsure how to pull it off, a how-to guide from 1959, *Wife Dressing: The Fine Art of Being a Well Dressed Wife,* offered advice on what to wear, and when. The title identifies women not as independent consumers but in terms of their function as wives who hope to impress their husbands with their sense of style. It encourages them to conform in order to receive the approval of men. A line at the bottom of the book's cover reinforces the point: "With provocative notes for the patient husband who pays the bills."[31] The New Look originated with Christian Dior and other male European designers. Therefore, one of the most popular fashion trends of the 1950s was dictated by men who not only redefined women's standard silhouette, but told women what clothes to buy and confidently assured them that men would pay the bills.

Billie Dawn (Judy Holliday), the gum-chewing, brassy-voiced "dumb blonde" at the center of *Born Yesterday*, and Harry Brock (Broderick Crawford) distill gender relations into their most basic form. Harry is a scrap metal tycoon, and Billie is his girlfriend/fiancée/business partner. Billie first sashays onto the screen draped in jewelry and trailing extravagant furs, and she appears in other scenes also wearing glamorous, expensive outfits. At one point, Billie cavalierly explains that she can get whatever she wants, all she has to do is ask. If Harry does not "act friendly," then she does not "act friendly." Their relationship is a form of structured prostitution, a caricature of marriages where wives can expect an allowance when things go well and some kind of punishment when things do not go according to plan—the plan formulated by the man of the house.

Reporter Paul Verrall (William Holden) is there to greet them when Harry and Billie arrive in Washington, D. C. Paul wants to do a story on Harry's business background and ambitions, and he establishes his journalistic credentials by wearing thick glasses and speaking in a consciously sophisticated manner. He is a fervent patriot with an inclination toward the underdog and an aversion toward bullies, no matter how large or mean.

Harry is large and mean, but he is also charming in a bulky, threatening kind of way. He quickly goes to work to win over a Congressman to his scheme, but when he introduces Billie to the man and his wife, the visit does not go well. Beneath Billie's aloof, insulting behavior is a self-conscious woman smart enough to recognize that she is in over her head. Harry is blithely unaware of the fact that he, too, is completely out of his depth. Instead, he worries that Billie's lack of education and crude manners may undermine his efforts to bribe the Congressman. Harry comes up with a way to solve his "problem" with Billie. He was impressed by the studious reporter with glasses, and he offers Paul the job of tutoring Billie in history, politics, and social graces. Harry's lawyer, Jim Devery (Howard St. John), is a jaded alcoholic, but he sizes up Paul and immediately sees trouble coming. Harry is oblivious to any potential problems with his idea and refuses to marry Billie, even though he admits he is "nuts about her." Jim keeps explaining to Harry that the reason he should marry her is that a woman cannot testify against her husband. Harry continues to refuse, and Jim continues to drink.

Paul is reluctant to tutor Billie. But after he witnesses her humiliation during a moment of real cruelty by Harry, he agrees to take the job. Billie is unsure exactly what to make of this arrangement and tries with limited enthusiasm to seduce Paul. He politely declines, and by doing so he begins her education with an important lesson—there are men who treat women with respect.

Judy Holliday was the perfect choice to play the guileless Billie. She had initiated the role in the play on Broadway, and she won an Academy Award for her performance in the movie version. Holliday was a delightful comedic actress whose roles often exhibited some of the stereotypical characteristics of the dumb blonde. This ditzy image has a long history, but it was particularly popular in the 1950s. The criteria for the type went beyond blonde hair and a lack of intellectual depth. Other standard elements included an hour-glass figure and a vocabulary that represented a lower-class background. If such blondes drew double-takes from men, they were coolly received by women who understood that their good looks, fabulous figures, sunny dispositions, and even sunnier hair all too often landed them all the good things in life, including men, money, and adulation.

Marilyn Monroe's career was just beginning in the early fifties, and she is the preeminent example from that era. The characters she frequently played exhibited a sweet, earnest vulnerability that made them seem sympathetic and sexually available. In the public's mind, these roles were not all that different from the real Marilyn. As a result, she inspired a protective instinct in audiences.[32] This vulnerability reinforced men's sense of superiority, a desired effect in the broader fight against the threatening forces that defined the Cold War.

The image of the dumb blonde became the stock in trade for numerous other 1950s actresses and was so overused that it inspired parody. Jean Hagen received an Academy Award nomination as Best Supporting Actress for her portrayal of the vacuous blonde egomaniac Lina Lamont in *Singin' in the Rain* (1952). But the stereotype played out in different ways. Sometimes the blonde really is dumb and is happy to depend upon her looks to succeed. Other times she wants to be valued for more than her appearance. Occasionally, the beautiful blonde actually *is* intelligent (see *The Girl Can't Help It,* 1956). But the very fact that the intelligence of a woman was important to the plot reinforces the idea that smart women were viewed as some kind of problem or aberration in the 1950s.

Paul falls in love with Billie, but although he has a clear understanding of her relationship with Harry, he does not address the issue directly. Instead, he instructs her about American history and the workings of democracy. In 1950s America, patriotism and civic duty were potent forces, and Paul uses them to frame his message. He takes her on a tour the nation's capital to educate her about the fundamentals of American government and the responsibilities of citizenship. He is patient, sometimes professorial, and always respectful. Billie is a quick, eager learner, but she believes that she is tied to Harry. Billie must decide whether to break free of a man who is her sole means of financial support.

However, the real challenge in the movie is more subtle. It is to educate Billie only up to the point where she is smart enough to leave Harry, but not so smart that she is willing to strike out on her own, independent of any man. This goal meshed perfectly with the views of even the most liberal thinkers in the early 1950s. Adlai Stevenson, the Democratic presidential nominee in 1952 and 1956 and a leading figure among American liberals, summed up the prevailing view of women and intelligence in a 1955 Commencement Address at Smith College, one of the nation's leading women's colleges. Stevenson extolled the ways in which their educations could ennoble and enrich the lives he expected Smith graduates to lead. He believed marriage and motherhood would not lead women "away from the great issues of the day, [they bring] you back to their very center.... [W]hat you have learned [fits] you for the primary task of making ... whole human beings in whom the rational values of freedom ... and free inquiry can take root."[33]

Shorter version: education will make you a better wife and mother *and* save the Republic!

Eventually her education and growing self-confidence clarify for Billie what her life has become. She and Paul figure out how to thwart Harry's efforts to bribe the Congressman. Harry does not give up without a fight, but this time neither does Billie.

Suggested Discussion Questions

1. Why does Billie stay with Harry? Are Billie and Harry equally matched intellectually? Why does the director include the scene of the card game?

2. Describe Billie's clothes in various scenes. How does her appearance change as the movie goes on? Why does her appearance change and what do the changes represent?

3. How and why does her father become a reference point for Billie?

4. What is the main point of the article Paul wrote? What criticism does Billie make about his writing? Is her criticism fair?

5. Why has Jim Devery put Harry's businesses in Billie's name? What does Billie discover about the business arrangement that makes her a "multiple corporate officer"?

6. Jim Devery is an alcoholic. How does he view Harry? Why does he work for him? At one point, Billie decides that Jim's behavior is even worse than Harry's. Explain why she believes this.

7. It is clear from various comments that Harry has hit Billie before. How does she react to the beating he gives her this time? How does education affect the relationship between abuser and abused?

8. Explain Paul's view of Harry? How does he relate Harry's behavior to the functioning of a democracy? How does Paul define fascism? Explain Paul's political philosophy.

9. Explain the Thomas Jefferson quote. How does this statement relate to Billie's situation? How has Billie's education created problems for her? How does Paul believe the life of a democracy is affected by the education of its citizens? Does America face any contentious educational issues today, and if so, what are they? What positions would Paul, Billie, and Harry take on these issues?

10. As he tries to explain his efforts to influence the Congressman, Harry refers to "government between friends." What does Harry mean by this? Do people with a lot of money influence the direction of government today? Cite specific examples. Is there any current phrase that describes a deal like this? How does Jim view elected officials? Why does Jim drink?

11. How does Billie connect the principles of democracy and representative government to Harry's business practices and his treatment of her and Congressman Hedges? How does the movie fit into the political attitudes of the time? How does Harry react to Billie's rebellion? Is Harry a sympathetic character, and if so, why?

12. By the end of the movie, Billie has learned a great deal and has married Paul. As a woman is she better off? As a person is she better off? Explain your answers. Are women and/or women's issues a prominent concern in politics today? Give specific examples.

Picnic (1955)

(115 minutes) *Director:* Joshua Logan; *Stars:* William Holden, Kim Novak, Rosalind Russell, Betty Field, Arthur O'Connell, Cliff Robertson, Verna Felton, Susan Strasberg, Nick Adams, Phyllis Newman, Elizabeth W. Wilson.

The setting for Joshua Logan's *Picnic* seems like small-town America at its very best, with community get-togethers, smiling neighbors, and traditional

Picnic (1955) 205

values galore. Yet, like other elements of American society in the 1950s, not everything is what it appears to be. Just as conflicts involving race, youth culture, and politics bubbled beneath the decade's façade of conformity and consensus behavior, tensions over gender, social class, and sex also smoldered below the surface. Despite the movie's innocent-sounding title, *Picnic* explores powerful emotions and provides fascinating glimpses of daily life in 1950s America. It offers valuable insights about gender relationships, changing sexual attitudes, and popular notions regarding conformity and community.

As the Cold War took root in the early 1950s, Americans commonly showed their patriotism by adhering to the tried and true values that had made the nation great. Many people looked to old neighborhoods, strong family ties, and traditional gender relationships to set boundaries and establish social order. But asserting these old values was not always easy. The Great Depression and World War II had played havoc with old neighborhoods, strong family ties, and traditional gender relationships. In the previous two decades, people had moved all over the country for all kinds of reasons, including lost jobs, the Dust Bowl, the demands of military enlistments, the African-American migration out of the South, and the expanded industrial and agricultural production generated by the war. In addition, World War II offered new work opportunities for women and minorities, which allowed them to gain a modicum of independence. All of these forces contributed to changing expectations, especially regarding gender relationships.

Demobilization at the end of World War II brought millions of men home all at once, adding to the social upheaval. Returning veterans established families with such determination that the resulting birth cohort acquired its own label—the Baby Boom. The soaring marriage and birth rates sent ripple effects throughout American society, influencing the economy, the rise of suburbs, the growing popularity of single-family homes, and a newfound focus on nuclear families. Gender roles reflected a new domesticity that relegated mothers to hearth and home. By the 1950s, the perfect housewife was expected to care for her husband and children, cook nutritious meals, keep a clean and orderly home, and also get involved in volunteer and civic work, activities made possible by new household appliances that gave housewives more free time.[34]

These new activities were deemed important because they offered women a non-career track outside of the home that contributed support service to the community. Seen from another perspective, such activities allowed women to contribute to America's Cold War struggle against Communism. In effect, they could help their families, neighborhoods, and country by becoming leaders in the social lives of the new suburban communities in institutions such as churches, schools, libraries, and park systems. They joined groups like the

PTA and the YWCA as an extension of their roles as organizers and facilitators of the family's daily life.[35]

Part of the role of women, wherever they were, was to champion the rules, and the rules of post-war America were simple. Men were the breadwinners. Women were the nurturers. The family was the sacred institution that would keep America strong and raise up a new generation to protect the country from the ever-more threatening dangers that seemed to surround it. Conformity became evidence of right thinking and good behavior. Alongside assumptions about the benefits of conformity ran a parallel concern that sex unfettered from marriage would destabilize the family. Therefore, the push for conformity during this decade included a focus on women's sexuality by those who sought to contain it within the bounds of matrimony. If it were not contained it could undermine the benefits that sound marriages were expected to generate for society and thereby weaken the nation.[36] Men's sexuality did not generate these same concerns.

Not surprisingly, the images of women in movies released in the years right after World War II reinforced the traditional domestic roles of women. In accordance with the demands of the Production Code, which was effectively enforced from 1934 on, women who pursue sex outside of marriage in movies are punished fairly consistently. The theme of containing female sexuality reached an apex of sorts in *Anatomy of a Murder* (1959) when lawyer James Stewart tells the randy Lee Remick to dress more conservatively when she testifies in court for his client and adds emphatically, "Wear a girdle." At the same time, attitudes that ran counter to this traditional view began to creep into movie plots in the 1950s. Storylines in major movies such as *Summertime* (1955), *An Affair to Remember* (1957), and *South Pacific* (1958) address the question of whether women who engage in sex outside marriage are beyond redemption. Women characters in these movies are portrayed as guilty of love rather than bad behavior, and the resolutions of their plots suggest that the punishments women like these had suffered in the past in movies, and by extension in real life as well, were not entirely deserved.

If movies from the post-war years suggested that ideas about gender behaviors were changing, Alfred Kinsey's pioneering works on human sexuality offered empirical evidence of the shift in attitudes regarding women and sex. The Kinsey Reports on sexual behavior, published in 1948 (about men) and 1953 (about women), revealed that what Americans wanted to believe about sex and the reality of sex were quite different. The data showed that 68 to 90 percent of men and nearly 50 percent of women were having premarital sex. Kinsey also shed light on other forms of sexual expression, including findings on masturbation and homosexuality. Soon an angry reaction by various conservative groups set in. They disagreed with his data, and they believed that by publishing it Kinsey made these sexual activities permissible.[37] Whatever the causes, by the mid-1950s sex had become a danger, a puzzle, and an obsession all at the same time.

But despite changing attitudes toward sex, society continued to champion marriage as a woman's ultimate goal. Women were taught how to attract and hold onto men. It was not enough to look and act natural. Manipulations and façades were required. Women in search of husbands were told to concentrate on men's interests and satisfy—up to a point—their needs. By general agreement, "catching" or "snaring" a man was the way to proceed.[38] In *Gentlemen Prefer Blondes* and *How to Marry a Millionaire*, both from 1953, Marilyn Monroe cheerfully illustrated the process for those in need of instruction.

In the immediate post-war world, marriage was supposed to represent a joyous return to the business of living as defined by its most basic social unit. But by the 1950s, it had become a Procrustean bed that constricted and confined some of the couples who rushed to marry after the war. As a result, even though divorce rates remained artificially low throughout most of the fifties,[39] the image of the happy home life began to unravel. Dysfunctional marriages became the focus of movies such as *From Here to Eternity* (1953), *Rebel Without a Cause* (1955), *A Summer Place* (1959), and *Cat on a Hot Tin Roof* (1958). Each explores the disconnect between how Americans wanted families to be and how they really were, how appearances did not reflect reality. Even though the male perspective dominates these stories, they are set in the context of the interests, attitudes, and behaviors of both sexes. They demonstrate how men and women sometimes fail to match the gender expectations of the times, and the chaos and occasional tragedy that can result.

Joshua Logan's *Picnic* (1955) offers one of the best movie explorations of 1950s gender expectations and sexual attitudes. Based on the 1953 Pulitzer Prize-winning play by William Inge, it delves beneath the public appearances residents of a small Midwestern town maintain to expose their real needs and desires. All of the storylines revolve around Madge Owens (Kim Novak), a beautiful but moody young woman, and most of the action takes place at the town's annual Labor Day picnic. The picnic is a big local event and attracts strong community support. A queen of the picnic will be crowned that evening, and Madge is expected to win. Madge's date for the picnic is her boyfriend, Alan Benson (Cliff Robertson), the son of a wealthy businessman. Madge's mother, Flo (Betty Field), is anxious for Madge to begin pushing Alan toward marriage. The financial security Alan could offer Madge is very important to Flo, as is getting her daughter married to the "right" man from the wealthy part of town. Flo points out all the monetary and social benefits that will result from marriage to Alan and tells her 19-year-old daughter that she needs to act quickly before she becomes old and unattractive.

Madge lives in a world of women. Flo is a single parent. Her husband abandoned her many years before, soon after a second daughter, Millie (Susan Strasberg), was born. Millie is a smart, awkward adolescent who chafes at the fact that everyone views Madge as "the pretty one." Flo rents a room to Rosemary (Rosalind Russell), an unmarried school teacher who flaunts her independence with a grimness that belies her dismissive attitude toward men. Their next-door neighbor, Mrs. Potts (Verna Felton), is an older single woman who takes care of her elderly mother. Other women teachers drop by to visit Rosemary during the day as they prepare for the picnic and the start of the school year. These women's lives are filled with end-of-summer traditions so familiar and well established that many of the characters appear to be just going through the motions.

Everything about their lives changes when an old college friend of Alan's hops off a freight train on Labor Day morning. Hal (William Holden) has come to renew his friendship with Alan and also to ask him for a job in his father's business, something "cushy." Alan points out that he has had to start at the bottom and Hal will, too. Alan invites Hal to join them at the annual community picnic partly because he wants to show off his beautiful girlfriend. He suggests Hal as a big brother-like escort for Millie, who has no date. Hal is good natured about it, and Millie is delighted to have the handsome Hal for her date, but the reactions of the other women are mixed. Flo is suspicious of all men. Madge is curious but reserved. Mrs. Potts has no problem admitting she finds Hal attractive. Rosemary watches from a distance, but she eventually must come to terms with Hal's earthy masculinity and her own terrifying spinsterhood.

In keeping with 1950s conformity, all the characters are concerned with appearances. Alan tells Hal that if Madge wins the competition that evening it will mean a great deal to his father who does not approve of Madge but is easily impressed by winners. Millie lies about smoking and is resentful over the attention everyone pays Madge because of her looks. Flo fusses over a dress she is sewing for Madge, how it fits and where she should wear it, thereby emphasizing the significance of rules for dresses. Although Madge protests that she does not want to be thought of only as pretty, she is clearly aware of the effect of her looks and seems unable to break free of the value others place on appearances. Hal worries that he will not know how to act at a picnic. When Alan lends him a sport jacket to wear, Hal complains (or boasts?) that it does not fit comfortably because he is too "beefy."

But Rosemary exhibits the greatest concern for appearances. She shows off a new dress and mentions the cost of a matching hat. She is appalled when her longtime boyfriend, the amiable but uncommitted Howard (Arthur O'Connell, in an Academy Award-nominated performance), keeps coming up with socially subversive ideas, such as drinking liquor at the picnic and not wearing his suit coat over his shirt and tie. Rosemary is not upset because his actions are inappropriate but because she fears someone might see them and worries about the effect it could have on her job. She is intrigued by Hal and keeps sidling up to and away from him until finally, in a moment of lust disguised as rage, she physically attacks him.

Madge and Hal are the only characters who seem willing to act on how they really feel. At the picnic, Hal can no longer pretend he has no interest in Madge, even though he realizes it will ruin his friendship with Alan. Madge does not seem to understand her own desires, but at the end of the evening she surrenders to the music and shimmies her way into Hal's arms for a dance. She is the object of desire for all the male characters, but this is her first deliberately sensual behavior in the movie. Her sensuality ultimately inspires even Rosemary to abandon appearances, with humiliating results.

Later after halfheartedly protesting to Hal, "The others ... we gotta get back to the picnic," Madge stays with him and abandons the secure, confining rituals of the community. Appearances no longer matter to her and neither does Alan. Rosemary confronts Howard and forces him to imagine the life they could have together. When Howard protests using "what would people say" for an excuse, Rosemary explodes. For both of these women, at least for the moment, the tyranny of appearances is over.

Suggested Discussion Questions

1. What does Madge's mother want for her, and what does Alan's father want for him? How do Madge and Alan respond to their parents expectations? Does Alan love Madge?

2. How does Millie feel about her family life and her town? Is she being fair to her mother and her community? How does she envision her future?

3. The movie repeatedly shows children and pets behaving badly at the picnic. Why include these scenes? Analyze the contests at the picnic. How do they reflect gender stereotypes? Are there any games like these now?

4. The movie includes obvious instances of conformity, such as when the picnic crowd sings "Juanita," the way people salute Madge's float, and the strong community participation in the picnic. Are these acts of conformity good for the community? Are they good for the country? Are they good for the individual?

5. Describe any contemporary social rituals or political, professional, or school-related examples of conformity. Are these actions good for the specific group, and if so, why? Are they good for the individual?

6. Explain the reactions of Flo, Mrs. Potts, Millie, and Rosemary to Hal

and Madge's dance to "Moonglow." Why does the dance become the pivotal moment in the movie?

7. How does Howard view Rosemary? How does he view Madge? Why does he help Hal? When Rosemary asks Howard why he cannot dance like Hal, Howard says, "Golly, honey, I'm a businessman." What does he mean?

8. Presentations of sex in movies in the 1950s were still limited by the Production Code. Couples Hal and Madge and Howard and Rosemary disappear for part of the evening. How likely is it that either couple has had sex? Cite specific evidence to support your answer.

9. Explain Howard's reaction immediately after Rosemary begs him to marry her. How does he react when Rosemary misunderstands his morning visit? Why does he show up at all? Will this marriage last?

10. Mrs. Potts and the women teachers comment on events as a kind of local Greek chorus. Give examples of their support for social rules or their willingness to ignore the rules. Why are the rules so important to them? How are they likely to respond when they find out that Madge has gone to Tulsa? If you believe that their responses will differ, explain why.

11. How does the movie, not the characters, view rules, conformity, and the individual? How does this view fit into general attitudes of the 1950s? How does it fit into general attitudes that will emerge in the 1960s? When does the era of rebellion against conformity begin?

12. Why does Millie have to encourage Madge to get her to go to Tulsa? What does Madge want? Will the relationship between Hal and Madge succeed?

Tammy and the Bachelor (1957)

(89 minutes) *Director:* Joseph Pevney; *Stars:* Debbie Reynolds, Leslie Nielsen, Walter Brennan, Mala Powers, Mildred Natwick, Fay Wray, Sidney Blackmer, Louise Beavers.

Gidget (1959)

(95 minutes) *Director:* Paul Wendkos; *Stars:* Sandra Dee, James Darren, Cliff Robertson, Arthur O'Connell, Mary LaRoche, Joby Baker, Yvonne Craig, Doug McClure, Tom Laughlin.

The two lead characters in *Tammy and the Bachelor* and *Gidget* were clearly in the right place at the right time. An airplane accident and a near drowning lead to happily ever-afters for both of them. However, even though these movie plots were aimed directly at the youth audience, they still reflected the traditional social standards and values of 1950s America. Their collective message to teenage girls—whether they were the traditional type like Tammy or super trendy like Gidget—was to rely on their parents to guide them into adulthood, at least until a deserving young man comes along to take over the job.

The timing of the two movies was equally fortuitous. *Tammy and the Bachelor* and *Gidget* appeared in theaters across the country just as teenagers were overwhelming the American cultural landscape. Rock-and-roll had recently arrived on the scene, with Elvis Presley leading the charge in 1956. Dick Clark's *American Bandstand* debuted in 1957, spotlighting the new sound and teen dances and fashions. Bandstand regulars like Kenny Rossi, Arlene Sullivan, Bob Clayton, and Justine Carelli became celebrities in their own right, pulling in thousands of fan letters each week.[40]

Tammy and the Bachelor and *Gidget* not only reflected the rise of youth culture in the years after World War II, they also mirrored other changes going on in 1950s America. Matters involving sex had become an important social issue for a variety of reasons. Some people thought that changes in sexual standards and roles for women were a threat to the family. The data in Alfred Kinsey's reports on male and female sexuality infuriated those who believed in the moral steadfastness of Americans.[41] Either Kinsey was wrong to suggest that so many people were having sex outside of marriage, or society was at risk of crumbling under the weight of its immorality. Many adults feared that the culture was becoming much too open about sex. They condemned mail-order sales of alleged pornographic books, like D. H. Lawrence's *Lady Chatterley's Lover*. They were appalled when explicit films such as *...And God Created Woman* (1956), *Peyton Place* (1957), and *Butterfield 8* (1960) disregarded the sexual boundaries established by the Production Code. And they were shocked by rock-and-roll, which they saw as a threat to innocent young teenagers. Many adults were concerned that teenage girls were coming under the influence of sexy rock-and-rollers who sang suggestive songs. Elvis Presley's "Love Me Tender," Fabian's "Turn Me Loose," and Jerry Lee Lewis's "Whole Lotta Shakin' Goin' On" seemed to be sending coded messages about sex to young girls. Clerics and commentators weighed in, insisting that sex needed to be brought under control. However, with the double standard still firmly in place, it was women's sexuality that seemed most worrisome.[42]

The Baby Boom cohort was coming of age by the late 1950s, and early hints of what sex might mean to them began making their way into the public consciousness on the broad shoulders of handsome new movie stars and singers. A new breed of matinee idol hit the silver screen in the 1950s. The characters played by earlier male stars such as Clark Gable, Kirk Douglas, or Gregory Peck accepted social responsibility and ultimately conformed to society's needs. But young newcomers like Montgomery Clift in *A Place in the Sun* (1951), Marlon Brando in *The Wild One* (1954), and James Dean in *Rebel Without a Cause* (1955) played surly, rebellious loners who brought sex appeal to the fine art of introspection or, when necessary, just led with their fists. Their style unsettled some but their acting drew strong critical praise.

On the other hand, in music, there was Elvis. If some adults were made uneasy by the rebellious characters played by Brando, Clift, and Dean, they were scandalized by the uninhibited performance style of Elvis Presley. Critics ridiculed him as "Elvis the Pelvis" or condemned him for being "obscene," a "Sexhibitionalist," or a "whirling dervish of sex."[43] Many cultural historians, however, view Presley's arrival on the American popular music scene as a watershed moment.[44] John Lennon, an admirer with some experience in the profession, once said, "Before Elvis there was nothing."[45]

Actually, before Elvis there was Frank Sinatra. Although not an exact parallel, Sinatra offers interesting points of comparison. Like Elvis, he wowed women. Female admirers screamed and swooned at his early performances, but their devotion eventually ebbed. Once his female fan support settled down to a more modest level, Sinatra got on with the business of becoming a major singing and movie star.[46] (He won an Academy Award in 1954 for his supporting role in the 1953 drama *From Here to Eternity*.) Sinatra's sensational early singing performances, however, occurred before television. Although people were aware of his strong emotional effect on women, there was less opportunity to observe and comment on it.

Elvis appeared on television before large nationwide audiences beginning in 1956. His thrusts, swivels, shimmies, and struts were something totally new. During some of his appearances, the camera showed him only from the waist up, which naturally led younger viewers to become inordinately curious about what was going on below the picture frame. In addition, the camera showed female audience members screaming wildly, grinning, giggling, and clearly enjoying themselves. What adults saw as a cringe-worthy moment of unmasked, over-the-top libido obviously delighted many young women.[47] In addition, whatever Sinatra's other attractions, he recorded songs by some of the greatest composers of the era, including Cole Porter, Irving Berlin, Johnny Mercer, and Hoagy Carmichael. Elvis sang low-class rock-and-roll, and many adults saw a rebellion against middle-class values in the new musical form, which combined elements of black rhythm and blues, white hillbilly music, and traditional pop.

Elvis's appearance on *The Milton Berle Show* in 1956 was an early effort to capitalize on his sexy image. Berle kidded Elvis about his effect on women. Elvis demurred. He said he preferred quiet girls like Debra Paget, his co-star in a soon-to-be released movie, *Love Me Tender*. Berle told him he had no chance with the classy Paget, and he called her onstage to prove it. When she saw Elvis she gripped him in a passionate kiss.[48] The scene was played for laughs, but the essence of the joke was that nice girls did not behave this way. Adults took note. Young women were getting way too far ahead of themselves with their interest in sex. Something had to be done.

Some people viewed Pat Boone as a far safer rock-and-roll alternative, and the image he projected offered a counterweight to the Elvis phenomenon. Along with being a nice, young married fellow, Boone was also the second-biggest selling record artist (after Elvis) of the decade.[49] He willingly did interviews to promote his hit records and fledgling movie career, and he even authored an advice book for teenagers entitled *'Twixt Twelve and Twenty*. A good Christian who did not smoke, drink, or swear, Boone advocated a traditional approach to family, faith, and lifestyle choices. His chapter on marriage, titled "The Happy Home Corporation," describes his family-management philosophy. Although he believed that marriage should be an equal partnership, a corporation needs a "president" (i.e., the husband) who will have the final say in matters. He explained that his wife, Shirley, likes this arrangement "because she is a normal female."[50] He and Elvis sent teenagers diametrically opposed messages about sex, which gave young people options in their preferred role models and reflected the conflicting attitudes about sexual behavior that were prevalent at the time.

But something new involving young women and sex was percolating through society and into the movies. Earlier movies like *The Miracle of Morgan's Creek* from 1944 may have focused on the pregnancy of an unmarried 17-year-old, but it takes an affectionate view of Betty Hutton's character. She is not seductive or immoral; she is just naïve and briefly unsupervised. Although everyone thinks Shirley Temple's crush on Cary Grant in *The Bachelor and the Bobby Soxer* (1947) is cute, all the adults, including Grant, agree it has to end. Traditional attitudes toward young girls and romance continued in movies from the 1950s, such as *Friendly Persuasion* (1956) and *The Reluctant Debutant* (1958). But the decade also saw movies ratchet up the sexuality and lower the age of the alluring girl-women who starred in them. Relatively tame conventional romances that feature older men who successfully pursue younger women appeared. Romantic relationships involving older men and younger women were nothing new, but what was new in 1950s movies were relationships that start when the women are very young. The movies make a point of acknowledging that they are too young for romance. However, the girls all receive educations that are designed to turn them into objects of desire, after which the men involved re-evaluate and accept them as romantic partners. Maurice Chevalier neatly sums up this process in "Thank Heaven for Little Girls," which he performed in *Gigi* when he was 70 years old.

Four movies from the mid-fifties exemplify this trend toward romantic involvements with very young girls. Mature established actors Humphrey Bogart, William Holden, Fred Astaire, and Louis Jourdan become romantically involved with much younger actresses Audrey Hepburn in *Sabrina* (1954) and *Funny Face* (1957), and Leslie Caron in *Daddy Long Legs* (1955) and *Gigi* (1958). In each movie, the female lead starts out as a young girl and is then "educated." However, instead of emphasizing general knowledge or business skills, their educations emphasize skills and attitudes that will make these young women more attractive to men. In a triumph of image over substance, and in keeping with the materialism of 1950s consumer culture, expensive clothes are an important feature of all the plots. Once the young women become more sophisticated and are outfitted in glamorous grown-up clothes, their romantic involvements with older men become acceptable. All of these movies were major studio productions and received multiple Academy Award nominations. *Gigi* won a record-breaking nine awards, including Best Picture.

The aging of the first cohort of Hollywood stars to come through the studio system may have played a part in these May-December romances. From the 1930s until around the 1960s, many stars were under contract to major studios, and the studios needed to keep them working in order to make those contracts profitable. By the 1950s, stars who had begun their careers in the 1930s were all approaching their fifties and sixties. Most women in this group had already retired or given up romantic roles, but many of the men were still interested in playing romantic leads or, at least, their studios ordered them to. The actresses available as their co-stars were getting younger as a result of simple demographics. Clark Gable publicly declared his disinterest in these kinds of roles, saying in an interview that he should "start acting his age."[51] When Cary Grant and Audrey Hepburn were cast as the romantic leads in *Charade* (1963), Grant was so concerned about their 25-year age difference that he asked the studio to rework the script to make Hepburn the pursuer.[52]

But the trajectory for films about young girls and sex was set. In addition to semi-sedate romantic storylines, movies in the 1950s also featured teenage girls in situations that explicitly implied sex unrelated to marriage. A lascivious neighbor pursues a teenage tease in *Baby Doll* (1956); John Wayne hunts for the kidnappers and rapists of his young nieces in *The Searchers* (1956); and a malevolent daughter defends a disturbing relationship with her father in *Bonjour Tristesse* (1958).

By the 1960s, sexual activity by young women, including instances of rape, began occurring in movies even more frequently. In *Sergeant Rutledge* (1960), a youthful-looking teenage girl with long blonde braids is found raped and murdered, setting the stage for the movie's tense courtroom drama. Rape is a subplot in another teen-oriented hit, *Where the Boys Are,* also from 1960.

Holly Golightly (Audrey Hepburn), the free-spirited, sexually available adult waif at the heart of the 1961 hit *Breakfast at Tiffany's,* is married at age 14. Although the marriage had been annulled, the much older Doc Golightly (Buddy Ebsen) seems to be a loving and confused ex-husband when he comes to New York to retrieve his young wife. Holly views him affectionately and has difficulty sending him away brokenhearted. Also in 1961, Sophia Loren won a Best Actress Academy Award for her performance as a devoted mother who fails to protect her young daughter from the horrors of war in *Two Women.* The title is intentionally ironic. By 1962 the public's apparent acceptance of the sexuality of young teenage girls made it a prominent feature in several major productions, including *Cape Fear,* which focuses on, but does not show, the rape of a teenager; *Gypsy,* a musical about the complicated family life and budding career of the youthful star stripper, Gypsy Rose Lee; and *Lolita,* which spotlights the love affairs of a supremely self-confident 14-year-old seductress.

In the 1950s, however, most movies about teenage girls still remained true to the traditional gender expectations of the post-war period and promoted these expectations as the right way for young girls to enter into romantic relationships. *Tammy and the Bachelor* (1957) and *Gidget* (1959) are two of the best examples. These movies offer a simple solution to young girls' romantic difficulties. Fathers, or in Tammy's case, a grandfather, should choose for them. Although the settings and styles of each movie are different, they exhibit remarkable similarities, including the fact that both movies specifically set 17 as the lower age limit for serious romantic involvement by teenage girls.

Tammy (Debbie Reynolds) and her grandfather (Walter Brennan) rescue Peter Brent (Leslie Nielsen), a wandering botanist, after his small plane crashes near their houseboat on a Mississippi bayou. A temporary bout of amnesia requires him to stay with them and recover under Tammy's care. Tammy is the quintessential backwoods country girl. She whips up homemade meals in a cast-iron kettle, makes frequent Biblical references, prays often, and falls in love with Peter, who appears to be the first marriageable man she has ever met. Peter finds the unsophisticated, forthright girl charming but too young. Soon after Peter recovers and leaves for home, Grandpa is arrested for making corn liquor. Peter spoke about repaying their kindness and told Grandpa that if anything ever happened to him, Tammy should come to live with Peter and his family. Grandpa insists that Tammy go to Peter's home, Brentwood Hall, while he serves his jail time. When she arrives she finds that although they maintain appearances out of a sense of community responsibility, Peter's mother (Fay Wray), father (Sidney Blackmer), and Aunt Renie (Mildred Natwick) are disconnected from any real ties to their family's substantial local history. Tammy's homespun goodness, common sense, and down-home cooking skills brighten their lives, and her genuine enthusiasm for everything about Brentwood eventually changes their attitudes.

Peter hopes to get Brentwood back on solid financial footing by creating a new kind of tomato plant that is hardier and more productive than other varieties. Tammy offers energetic support for his project. But Peter is engaged to a woman who is closer to his own age, and she encourages him to abandon his plan so he can accept a job in her father's business. Peter's fiancée believes that his tomato plants are a distraction keeping him from her, letting him avoid financial seriousness, and postponing their marriage. Tammy has no social skills or pretensions, which is charming in a naïve kind of way, but it also means that she is unable to figure out how to use conventional feminine strategies to attract Peter, and her natural interest in kissing leaves her unprepared to deal with Peter's friend Ernie, who is looking for a very casual romance.

Gidget (Sandra Dee) is really 17-year-old Francie Lawrence. She is not interested in boys just yet, although she worries that she should be. So do her parents, and her father keeps trying to get her to accept a date he has arranged with the son of a business associate, an idea she adamantly rejects. When she and some friends go to the beach, the other girls do their best to attract boys while Francie goes swimming on her own in order to avoid the boy issue. She gets tangled in kelp, and surfer Moondoggie (James Darren) comes to her rescue. As he takes her back to the beach on his surfboard, Francie is transformed. She becomes passionately interested in surfing and also in Moondoggie. Which passion came first is not entirely clear. She cobbles together enough money to buy a surfboard and convinces her worried parents that she will ride responsibly with the gang.

What Mom (Mary LaRoche) and Dad (Arthur O'Connell) do not understand, and Francie does not make clear, is that the members of the gang are all older boys. Francie asks them to teach her to surf, an activity that does not interest other girls and establishes her as a tomboy rather than date material. At first they are unsure how to behave toward such a young girl, but when the Big Kahuna (Cliff Robertson), their older mentor and drop-out role model, gives the idea his blessing, the gang comes on board. They delight in nicknames, and because Francie is a girl and short, they combine girl and midget to make Gidget. She soon learns to surf under Moondoggie's instruction. He initially dismisses her as a kid, but as he gradually becomes attracted to her, the dating rituals of the 1950s complicate their relationship.

The settings for the movies differ substantially. *Tammy and the Bachelor* is set in rural Louisiana and has a heavy emphasis on Biblical references and rustic country living. Tammy begins the movie barefoot, with her hair in braids, wearing jeans and a red plaid shirt. She uses archaic speech patterns, and whenever she is confronted with a serious problem, she resorts to Scripture for guidance or converses earnestly with her pet goat, Nan. *Gidget* is set in Los Angeles and presents a much more forward-thinking approach to teen angst. Gidget uses the latest slang and follows the newest trend—surfing. She is authentically enthusiastic about both. Surf culture was just beginning to attract the attention of young Americans, and this movie served as its exuberant introduction to a wide audience, even though the surfing scenes were clearly filmed in the studio rather than on location.

But beyond these obvious differences, the movies have much in common. Both Tammy and Gidget are outsiders in the teenage-girl culture of the late 1950s, and they must compete with women—clearly identifiable as women because they wear clothes that define and enhance their figures—who have an edge socially and physically in the pursuit of men. Both girls benefit from parental figures who love and worry about them but treat them indulgently. The girls venture into new social groups where they are initially dismissed because they are so young. But they acquire older champions who help them navigate unfamiliar rules and terrain. Aunt Renie and the Big Kahuna may be willing to help because they, too, do not fit comfortably within their social groups. An important element of each girl's story is that she must pursue her true nature, being spiritual, kind, and genuine, or learning to surf and being genuine, in order to succeed. The examples they set inspire their mentors, Aunt Renie and Kahuna, to change course and reconnect with their own interests.

Tammy and Gidget are interested in physical affection, so sex becomes a significant concern in both movies. Even though other characters are less scrupulous about how they attract the attention of the opposite sex, the two young women instinctively endorse physical affection based on real feelings rather than as a negotiating device in a relationship. Tammy is a child of nature who lives in a houseboat on a river. She acts on what she feels. Her straightforward enthusiasm for kissing is a manifestation of her willingness to trust her feelings rather than a way to manipulate Peter. In terms of sex, her honesty implies that a woman should enjoy physical affection within the limits of the relationship she has established with a particular man, but sexual intercourse should not figure into her plans until after marriage.

Gidget reacts in similar ways. Although she initially finds boys unappealing, she, too, becomes interested in being kissed once she meets the right guy. While Tammy is oblivious to the prevailing dating codes of Peter's social circle, Gidget is all too aware of the complicated gender rules set by members of her peer group who are willing to use sexual attraction to manipulate others. Unlike Tammy, who remains true to her values and goes home to the houseboat when Peter does not return her affections, Gidget finally succumbs to social pressure and decides to use a date with someone else to make Moondoggie jealous. Furthermore, in an effort to appear sophisticated, Gidget decides to deal straightforwardly with sex. She sets off to do so, but her misguided date plan unravels in spectacular fashion. Gidget misunderstands Kahuna, misjudges Moondoggie, and winds up in jail. The movies' messages are obvious: true feelings, not social norms, should guide physical affection, and young girls should not be the ones to initiate sex.

The male characters in both movies have to determine who these girls really are and whether they are ready for romantic relationships. Initially, both Peter and Moondoggie do not believe the girls are mature enough. Other men are less discriminating, however, and Tammy and Gidget's naïveté leaves them vulnerable and in need of male champions to defend their honor. Peter comes to Tammy's rescue when his lascivious friend Ernie invites her on a date. Moondoggie takes over Gidget's surfing lessons from another member of the gang who clearly intends to take advantage of her, and, later on he believes he has to defend her from Kahuna as well.

Both movies were aimed squarely at the teenage audience. Not only do the movies highlight young love, but they capitalized on the youth culture's growing obsession with rock-and-roll. Debbie Reynolds's recording of the movies' theme song, "Tammy," became a huge hit, and stayed at number one on the music charts for five weeks.[53] James Darren sings "Gidget" and "The Next Best Thing to Love," songs that seem designed to establish him as a new teen idol. Although Darren was not as successful as Elvis or even Reynolds, his songs reflected the era's musical interests and fed into female audience members' infatuation with handsome male singers.[54]

Tammy and the Bachelor and *Gidget* were not the first fifties movies aimed at the era's growing youth culture, but they were among the most successful. Not surprisingly, the two box-office hits inspired numerous other movies aimed at youth culture. *Tammy and the Bachelor* was soon followed by three more Tammy movies, although Debbie Reynolds was replaced as the lead. In addition to more *Gidget* movies and a television series, *Gidget* touched off a whole new movie genre. The idea of putting attractive young people in bathing suits for much of their screen time caught on in a big way as did the surf craze and the use of rock-and-roll singers and songs in movies. Among the most popular were Annette Funicello and Frankie Avalon's beach party movies, including *Beach Party* (1963) and *Beach Blanket Bingo* (1965). Numerous other beach movies also tried to catch the wave, including Fabian and Shelley Fabares's *Ride the Wild Surf* (1964) and Noreen Corcoran and the Beach Boys' *The Girls on the Beach* (1965). Even Elvis tried to cash in on the craze with *Blue Hawaii* (1961).

However, the emphasis that *Tammy and the Bachelor* and *Gidget* place on the love and wisdom of father figures did not persist in most of the later movies aimed at the teen market. Young people on the leading edge of the Baby Boom were reaching their mid- to late-teen years by the early 1960s. They were beginning to make decisions on their own, and movies from the early sixties reflect this in storylines that feature teenagers who manage to elude parental control or that do not include any significant parent figures.

At the conclusion of both *Tammy and the Bachelor* and *Gidget*, it is clear that the popular 1950s television show, *Father Knows Best*, got it right. Grandpa understands intuitively that Peter will protect and care for Tammy, and he helps her cause when he sends her to Brentwood Hall. Although Grandpa cannot make the couple's relationship work, he does make it possible for his resourceful granddaughter to do that on her own. *Gidget* follows a similar formula. After her luau date debacle lands her in jail, Gidget's father can demand a certain level of cooperation from his daughter. He uses that leverage to get her to go out with the boy he has been suggesting all summer. Gidget is surprised, embarrassed, and ultimately pleased by his choice.

Suggested Discussion Questions

1. Describe Tammy or Gidget's self-image. How does she compare herself to other women? How do other girls or women relate to her? How is her behavior nontraditional?

2. Describe Tammy or Gidget's relationship with her parents/grandparent. How do they view her? What concerns do they have about her? How do they try to help her? Are they too indulgent or too strict?

3. Describe Tammy or Gidget's behavior. How does Tammy's religiosity fit into Cold War attitudes of the 1950s? Why include scenes about the Brent family history? How do Gidget's use of slang and her desire for more independence fit into social attitudes of the times?

4. How does the movie view other young women who represent traditional girl behaviors and attitudes toward men?

5. Tammy is presented as a child of nature who responds honestly to people or events. Gidget's mother says she is "genuine." Why do these traits become a problem for either girl? What does that indicate about other girls? About boys?

6. Both movies suggest that naturalness (and by extension, innocence and honesty) is a good thing. But they also imply that it can be dangerous. How can someone respond naturally to a person or situation and have a successful outcome if others are acting unnaturally or dishonestly? In situations like this, what is the best approach?

7. Explain the relationship between Tammy and Aunt Renie, or Gidget

and Kahuna. Why does either one offer help? How does Tammy or Gidget help in return?

8. How do Peter and his family view Osia (Louise Beavers)? How does Osia view them? How do she and Tammy get along? What does Osia's comment about her "slave-time bandanna" suggest about racial attitudes in 1957?

9. Describe Tammy's attitude toward kissing. How does Peter respond to her behavior and to Ernie's interest in her? What role does Aunt Renie play in their relationship?

10. Describe the relationship between Gidget's parents. How does it compare to the description that Pat Boone gives of a "happy home corporation?" How does her mother react to her father's worries about Gidget? When and why does her father take charge?

11. Describe Gidget's attitude toward sex. How does her mother respond when Gidget brings up the topic? Why would her mother take this approach? How do Moondoggie and Kahuna respond to Gidget's intention to engage in sex? Explain the term "paternalism."

12. How is Peter or Moondoggie different from other men? When does he realize that Tammy or Gidget is old enough to be of romantic interest? How does he react to this realization?

13. Both movies feature girls who are in some ways nontraditional. Describe instances of traditional female behavior by either girl. Does either movie support gender equality?

14. In what way does Tammy or Gidget become educated about or initiated into the lifestyle and interests of Peter or Moondoggie? Is there any reciprocal education or initiation for the man? What message does this dynamic send to young women about how to relate to men?

15. Research the success of the hit song "Tammy" or the emergence of surf culture in America. What effect does either movie have on audience behaviors? (For historical comparisons, consider how *It Happened One Night* affected the men's T-shirt market, *Davy Crockett: King of the Wild Frontier* and the coonskin cap craze, or the effect *E.T.* had on the popularity of Reese's Pieces.) Cite current examples of movie products or character attitudes or actions that affect audience behavior. Or research product placement deals (i.e., conspicuous images of products like cars, designer clothes, or electronics that appear in movies by commercial agreement). How do advertisers believe movies affect audience behaviors and attitudes? Does it follow logically that violence in movies will cause viewers to behave violently or that liberal or conservative viewpoints represented in movies will alter audience attitudes? Defend your answer.

16. Assume that Tammy marries Peter or Gidget marries Moondoggie within the year. How will their marriages compare with Pat Boone's recommendations in "The Happy Home Corporation"? The women's movement

will begin in earnest in 1970. What is the likelihood that it will affect either marriage, and if so, how?

The Thrill of It All (1963)

(108 minutes) *Director:* Norman Jewison: *Stars:* Doris Day, James Garner, Arlene Francis, Edward Andrews, ZaSu Pitts, Reginald Owen, Elliott Reid.

Doris Day's comedic talents are on full display in *The Thrill of It All*. Her happily married character must come to terms with the ramifications of a trend that picked up momentum in the early sixties—women working outside the home. Her new job generates marital misery and delightful comedy.

At the height of her acting career, Doris Day was the female embodiment of sunshine. She was a very capable, beautiful, bright-eyed, blonde actress with a lovely singing voice and the ability to pull off physical comedy almost as well as Lucille Ball. Day was tremendously popular with audiences. She could be sexy, tough, grumpy, or funny while still holding on to their affections. In an annual poll of theater owners, she was named the top female star for eight consecutive years, from 1957 to 1964.[55] She starred in a string of romantic comedies opposite some equally funny leading men, including Cary Grant, David Niven, two movies with James Garner, and three with Rock Hudson. Unlike some of the sexy blonde actresses from the 1950s who patterned themselves, intentionally or not, after Marilyn Monroe, Day did not seem to threaten other women. Even when she was dressed in the most glamorous outfits, she managed to come across as the cute kid next door rather than as a threatening female competitor.

Historians Douglas T. Miller and Marion Nowak suggest that Day's public image and many of the roles she chose reflected changing sexual attitudes after World War II. "In Victorian times, woman was either sexless saintly wife or sensual dirty whore," they point out. In the 1950s, Americans still applied these two traits to *un*married women, but they found both types acceptable in married women. The result was a new model for sexual expression by women. Miller and Nowak add, "A wife could enjoy sex, as long as she obediently catered to her man. Doris Day's sexy propriety was the perfect mirror of this belief."[56] Her character's conflict over whether or not to have sex before she marries was either stated or implied in movies such as *Pillow Talk, That Touch of Mink,* and *Lover Come Back*. It reflected the fact that moviemakers were still guided by the Production Code, although the code's influence was rapidly being undercut by cultural products from Europe (*Smiles of a Summer Night,* 1955; *...And God Created Woman,* 1956; *La Dolce Vita,* 1960) as well as changing social attitudes in the United States.

Women's sex lives and their work outside the home were a growing concern for many women and men by the 1960s, reflecting trends that began after World War II. Among Americans of "marriageable age," an astonishing 97 percent had married by 1957. Yet, by 1960, the number of women entering the workforce was growing four times as fast as the number of men.[57] There is an obvious tension built into this data. Women spent the first decade and a half after the war hearing about the joys and significance of family life, proper mothering, and carefully mastered homemaking skills (see *Christmas in Connecticut*). Then, in the next ten years, they began hearing about the benefits of working outside the home.

Women in the 1960s faced a complicated set of social expectations and personal demands. They were being tugged at by many constituencies. Husbands wanted the perfect wife, mother, and girlfriend. The focus on giving the children of the Baby Boom the best possible upbringing expanded to include a whole range of child-centered activities, most of which were managed by women (room mothers, den mothers and Girl Scout leaders, chauffeuring to lessons and sporting events). Home decorating and cleaning became a measure of accomplishment and status. A growing number of women, however, wanted more than to be other people's wives and mothers. They had personal goals, hopes, and dreams, and they welcomed the sexual freedom that resulted from the introduction of the birth control pill in 1960. In addition, the cumulative effects of post-war technological advances in housework allowed women wider choices in leisure and employment. The clothes dryer and permanent press fabrics, for example, brought a sea change to the routines of laundry day.

Society of the 1950s and early 1960s, however, did not take women's personal desires into consideration. Instead, women were relegated to the home front, where they were encouraged to focus on husbands, babies, and domesticity. After the initial exuberance of the post-war Baby Boom tapered off, this domestic ideal was not enough for some women. Betty Friedan's seminal work, *The Feminine Mystique,* published in 1963, explored the discontent that many women experienced as they found their lives almost exclusively confined to the demands of home and family. "I'm desperate," confided one young housewife to Friedan, "I begin to feel I have no personality. I'm a server of food and a putter-on of pants and a bed maker, somebody who can be called upon when you want something. But who am I?"[58]

Comedian and screenwriter Carl Reiner ruminated on this same issue in his screenplay for *The Thrill of It All,* also from 1963. At the center of Reiner's comedy are typical suburban couple Beverly Boyer (Doris Day) and her husband, Gerald (James Garner). They live in a typical suburban house with two typical suburban children, a boy and a girl, the boy having been born first. They employ a slightly addled housekeeper, Olivia (ZaSu Pitts), who helps

Beverly keep things running smoothly on the home front. Smoothly, that is, until Beverly stumbles into a job she never went looking for. But while Friedan's prescription for what ailed women was to expand their options and return to work or engage in other productive endeavors, Reiner concluded that more, not less, family was the solution to women's discontent.

Reiner tips his hand early. Gerald is an obstetrician, and the movie's opening scene is a glorious celebration of pregnancy. One of his patients, a deliriously happy Mrs. Fraleigh (Arlene Francis), suffers a fit of giggles as she heads to her husband's office at a Manhattan advertising firm to tell him that she is pregnant. She and her husband, Gardiner (Edward Andrews), the son of the firm's owner, Old Tom Fraleigh (Reginald Owen), are an older couple, and they are absolutely giddy over the much-hoped-for news. They phone Gerald and invite him and Beverly to dinner that evening at Tom Fraliegh's house to celebrate. Gerald tries to decline, but they insist, so he calls Beverly to report the change of plans.

Once the scene shifts to the home front, Beverly takes over. She is a frazzled mother trying to wash her daughter's hair while her son misinterprets Gerald's phone call. The standard babysitter complications arise, but Gerald and Beverly finally make it to the dinner. When they arrive they find their hosts watching a new, sadly uninspired soap commercial that Fraliegh's firm has just produced. Without any prompting, Beverly delivers a spontaneous and sincere endorsement of the soap product based on her earlier experience with her daughter. Tom decides that *she* is the perfect person to sell that soap, and he offers her a job on the spot. Beverly is incredulous at the offer and declines, and Gerald is smugly confident that she would never want to work outside of the home. Then Tom mentions the ridiculously large sum of money she will make for one day's work. Beverly jumps at the commercial, and despite her fumbling delivery, she is a believable spokesperson for the product. Her sincere but awkward performance endears her to the audience and to the advertising firm. She, however, is humiliated by her television appearance and stunned when the firm signs her up to do more. A career is born, and a marriage is in trouble.

Gerald struggles through a variety of responses to her newfound career that begin with hesitant support, morph into annoyed tolerance, escalate to extreme irritation, and explode into jealousy. Ultimately, he moves out of the house and seeks professional help. Beverly starts out as an insecure and willing neophyte, becomes a committed professional trying to balance the demands of all the people who have their hooks into her, and winds up furious but guilt ridden when her entire catalog of responsibilities overwhelms her.

Based on the huge salary she is earning, she could have hired help in addition to Olivia to fulfill some of her duties, but two factors work against that solution. Although it appears that the Boyers are not in any financial trouble, she has taken the job because she wants to increase the family's income. Hiring help would subtract from that goal, thereby making her job less of a net benefit. Also, even though the job grows to require a bigger time commitment than it did at first, she has sold Gerald on the growing demands on her time by promising to maintain their home and family situation just as it was when she was a full-time wife and mother. Beverly never says that she should continue to work because the work itself is fulfilling. That would imply that there are activities beyond mothering and housework that have value for women, an idea so subversive the movie simply does not force the audience to consider it. The movie does address the idea that women need interests outside the home, but they are presented as brief respites from the routine, such as hobbies or volunteer work, that require limited commitments. The whole point of the movie is what can happen when a serious career competes with her family for a woman's attention and energy. Demanding work lives can interfere with the claims of family and home life. Chaos will surely result. Therefore, Beverly must still be the mom and the wife because if she does not perform her domestic duties, she will have failed to live up to society's expectations for the ideal woman, which at the time did not place any value on women's work outside the home.

The dilemma faced by Doris Day's character epitomizes the women's problem described in *The Feminine Mystique*. For many women of the 1960s, domestic roles were not enough. Friedan does not focus on women who work out of necessity.[59] Instead, she takes aim at educated women who can afford to be stay-at-home moms and who might even have the aid of a housekeeper and babysitter. Friedan's research showed that women in this demographic were unhappy and, in many cases, could not clearly articulate why.[60]

Do-it-yourself trends from the era suggest that some women overcompensated for their lack of fulfillment as housewives by taking the role to extremes. Crafts became crazes. Women learned to bake their own bread or sew clothes or items such as slipcovers or curtains for personalized home décor. They took up macramé and découpage. Needlepoint became enormously popular, and it is an apt metaphor for the entire trend. To complete a 12 × 12-inch needlepoint pillow took thousands of stitches. It was a time-consuming effort that resulted in a small, attractive but relatively useless object. Overachieving 1960s housewives could showcase these crafts as proof that they were not just run-of-the-mill homebodies who washed dishes, made beds, cooked, and cleaned house. Instead, they had "creative" interests. Beverly receives a job offer from a Madison Avenue advertising firm surrounded by bushels of tomatoes she will use to make homemade ketchup, a creative but unnecessary exercise that fits this model.

Carl Reiner's movie explores the dilemma of underemployed women. Beverly could be earning a lot of money instead of washing her children's hair and bottling her own ketchup. But that begs the question of who will take care of the needs of her children and husband if she works outside the home. At no point does the movie consider daycare, dinner out for the whole family, or any increase in Gerald's household responsibilities. In one scene he expresses extreme irritation that the demands of her job make it hard for him to fulfill the demands of his, and asks sarcastically, "Is it all right if I take time out from my household duties to deliver a baby?" In 1963, there was also a concern about whether or not a woman could do a job outside the home in a professional manner, which the movie emphasizes by highlighting Beverly's initial inept commercial.

Beyond just the Boyer marriage, Reiner's script takes aim at society's foibles as if they were ducks in a shooting gallery. The original soap commercial represents advertising strategies that are designed to sell a product but offer no real information to consumers. An untrained housewife who believes in the product does a better job selling it than a nearly nude glamor girl in a bubble bath. Reiner also skewers television melodramas that recycle old ideas and stock players, and he does the hammy acting in them himself to be sure he makes his point. Junior executives who offer their advice as soon as they know what the boss wants to hear have their own scene, complete with pandering so blatant even the boss in question finds it difficult to accept. The script makes the point that demanding careers keep fathers from spending time with their children and suggests that it will be no different for mothers if they go to work. Reiner also blasts television for being formulaic and sending homogeneous messages to audiences. At one point, he has the owner of the soap company comment about an idea for a new television show: "Give me one of them damn shows where everyone is smarter than the father."

The lingering demands of the Production Code create some odd moments in the movie. Beverly and Gerald are very physically affectionate, and the movie includes a scene where he arrives at their bedroom door clearly expecting sex. Yet, in accordance with the requirements of the code, their bedroom prominently features twin beds, a sleep choice that hardly reflected married reality. Also, the code prohibited scenes of childbirth, so when Mrs. Fraleigh has her baby under less than ideal circumstances, Gerald emerges from the experience with no trace of blood on his clothes. Such unrealistic scenes were becoming harder for sophisticated audiences to accept in the 1960s, and they created stresses that movies were hard pressed to finesse under the parameters of the Production Code. Something had to give and, in 1968, it was the code.

As the feminist movement gained momentum throughout the decade,

Doris Day's characters became more liberated. In the 1967 movie, *The Ballad of Josie*, for example, she plays an independent and determined Wyoming widow who nearly starts a range war because she insists on raising sheep. Day strides through the movie wearing men's jeans as she defies the local cattle ranchers. Once all the conflicts are resolved the movie softens its message of feminist success by having Day burn her jeans and leap into a man's arms in the last scene. Still, as far as liberated women go, Josie is quite a few steps ahead of Beverly, which suggests how far women characters had traveled in the four years between *The Thrill of It All* and *The Ballad of Josie*. By 1967, Doris Day and, more importantly, the Hollywood executives who financed her movies believed there was an audience for a female character who steps outside her role as wife and mother and gets what she wants.

In 1963, Beverly's attempt to step beyond the traditional role of wife and mother results in a separation that pains her and Gerald, but neither one will relent and reach out. They battle over whose job matters more and how to divide the money. Their crisis coincides with the birth of the Fraleigh baby, complete with traffic jam and gallant doctor-knight coming to the rescue. Gerald's heroic professionalism re-establishes his superiority in the workplace and in the marriage, and prompts Beverly to rethink her career ambitions.

Suggested Discussion Questions

1. Describe the people Mrs. Fraleigh encounters on the elevator, at the advertising firm, and at the hospital. How are women represented?

2. Describe ways in which the movie talks about sex without talking about sex. Review the Production Code.[61] How did the demands of the code create problems for movies made in 1963? Explain the term "sexy propriety."

3. Part of the reason Beverly offers such a good endorsement of the soap is that her support of the product is authentic. How is authenticity reflected in other behaviors and attitudes in the movie? Cite specific examples. How does authenticity figure in the attitudes of young people in the 1960s?

4. After her success with the soap, Old Tom decides to use Beverly in commercials to sell other products as well. How does this idea reflect his view of consumers? Is Beverly likely to be effective as a salesperson for other products? Compare advertising today with Beverly and the model in the bubble bath. Has anything changed, and if so, how?

5. Gerald has written an article that encourages women to pursue the "planned cultivation of outside interests and hobbies." How does Beverly's new job match up with his advice?

6. Make a list of television shows where "everyone in the family is smarter than the father" and another list where everyone is smarter than the mother.

Compare the lists based on (a) when the shows first appeared; and (b) the number of shows on each list. What trends can you discover, and how do you explain them?

7. Explain why Gerald believes that the money he earns is theirs but the money she earns is hers. Should spouses who work have separate checking accounts?

8. Beverly and Mike have a conversation in which both refer to her as a "career girl." Are men ever called "career boys?" Why, or why not? Early in the women's movement, women made an issue out of how they were addressed. Substituting Ms. for Miss or Mrs. is one example; changing chairman to chairperson is another. Were these changes really significant? Are they still?

9. Describe the behavior of the Boyer children. Mrs. Fraleigh's pregnancy and delivery frame the movie's plot, and she looks very elegant throughout the movie. What messages do these representations send about children, pregnancy, and birth? Do the messages reflect reality?

10. Why did the movie use the horse gimmick?

11. How does Beverly respond to Gerald after he delivers the baby? How does she compare his work to her own? How and why do her goals change by the end of the movie? Will this marriage last?

True Grit (1969)

(128 minutes) *Director:* Henry Hathaway; *Stars:* John Wayne, Kim Darby, Glen Campbell, Jeremy Slate, Robert Duvall, Jeff Corey, Strother Martin, Dennis Hopper.

The Western is one of the most successful and, in many ways, the most American of movie genres. Beginning with Edwin S. Porter's 1903 classic, *The Great Train Robbery*, Westerns typically evoked two of the country's most significant achievements: national expansion and the settlement of the frontier. As a result, the tension in Western movies often stems from a confrontation over how the rules of civilization will be established on the frontier, which, by definition, is beyond the influence of those rules. By the early 1930s, John Wayne's career had become inextricably entwined with the genre. The rules were changing by the late 1960s, making Henry Hathaway's *True Grit* at once a traditional Western starring John Wayne, and a modern feminist tale featuring newcomer Kim Darby.

Many of the female characters in Western movies are forces for order and civilization, and they often face a conflict between maintaining society's rules and conventions and dealing realistically with the situations they encounter in unsettled territory. This conflict is the driving force in *True Grit*, but it can be found in the earliest representations of the American West in popular culture. Owen Wister's *The Virginian*, published in 1902, is often considered the prototype for Western novels, and, by extension, Western movies as well. Wister employs almost every convention associated with Westerns in his story, including cowboys, Indians, cattle rustling, a climactic shoot-out in the streets between good guy and bad guy, and a woman who represents order and civilization. *The Virginian*'s main female character, Molly Stark Wood, brings her books along with her when she accepts a teaching job in Wyoming, a position that essentially requires her to assert a civilizing influence on the frontier. To reinforce this point, many of her books are well-known literary classics. But she becomes more than just a champion of academics and traditional standards. Molly falls in love with the Virginian, and at one point she must rescue him from near death, a feat she pulls off with ingenuity and determination. She argues with, out thinks, and out maneuvers one of the strongest and most independent heroes in American literature.

Molly's situation demonstrates that the challenges women face as they navigate the often-rowdy Western storylines also represent opportunities. Women characters in Westerns tackle farm chores, deal with Indians and outlaws, and take over or establish businesses either because they can or because they must. Strong, independent women who wear pants just like men do, can be found in numerous Western movies, including Jean Arthur in *Shane* (1953), Vera Miles in *The Searchers* (1956), Mariette Hartley in *Ride the High Country* (1962), and Barbara Stanwyck in *Cattle Queen of Montana* (1954) and the numerous other Westerns she made during her long Hollywood career. (From the 1930s through the 1950s, Stanwyck was celebrated for doing her own stunts in Westerns and repeatedly expressed her enthusiasm for the genre.)[62]

Fending off bad guys also gives women a chance to load guns and/or fire them in such Western movie classics as *Annie Oakley* (1935), *Stagecoach* (1939), *Along Came Jones* (1945), *High Noon* (1952), *The Guns of Fort Petticoat* (1957), *The Unforgiven* (1960), and *Firecreek* (1968). Frontier women must take charge and pick up the pieces whenever men disappear for long periods of time or die, as is the case in *Cimarron* (1931, 1960), *Hondo* (1953), *Johnny Guitar* (1954), *Cat Ballou* (1965), *The Ballad of Josie* (1967), *Once Upon a Time in the West* (1968), and *The Shootist* (1976). Some female characters do not need a man's absence in order to motivate their entrepreneurial ambitions, as evidenced by Katy Jurado in *High Noon* (1952), Barbara Stanwyck in *The Maverick Queen* (1956), Annelle Hayes in *Two Rode Together* (1961) and Julie Christie in *McCabe and Mrs. Miller* (1971). Joanne Woodward pushes things a step further when she overcomes poker protocol, a stalwart cast of Western movie regulars, and a strong dose of gender bias in *A Big Hand for the Little Lady* (1966).

Regardless of how women were portrayed in Western movies, the responsibilities of guiding the civilizing process were never far away. Unless some sense of security could be assured, the frontier would never become a welcoming home for anyone but the hard-bitten and dangerous. Many movies feature male characters who champion this process, but women have a central role in civilizing the American West, as is apparent in movie titles like *Angel and the Badman* (1947) and *Mail Order Bride* (1964), and it is the primary motivation for the plot of *Westward the Women* (1951). Sometimes, women's demands for social order are denigrated, at least at first. In *Stagecoach* (1939), the leader of The Ladies Law and Order League is depicted as mean and self-righteous. She is also married to a crook, a plot element designed to humiliate her and, by extension, the other very proper league ladies as well. In *Seven Brides for Seven Brothers* (1954), Howard Keel's brothers do not immediately appreciate the benefits his new wife's housekeeping plans represent, but Jane Powell ultimately establishes a civilized regimen in her new home. *The Harvey Girls* (1946) plays off women's civilizing effect. Led by Susan Bradley (Judy Garland), a crew of proper young ladies working in Harvey House Restaurants in the dirty, dusty towns along the "Atchison, Topeka and the Santa Fe" offer Western travelers an oasis of good food, clean tablecloths, and cheerful waitresses in starched white aprons.

Images of women found in the many Westerns directed by John Ford reflect changing gender attitudes during the early and middle decades of the twentieth century. The female characters in *Stagecoach* (1939) are based on traditional stereotypes of devoted, dependent wives or hookers with hearts of gold. But following World War II, Ford's female characters become more subtle and far more involved in the resolution of conflicts. Ford's experiences as a government filmmaker during the war may have affected his views of conflict as well as his perceptions of the civilizing role that women could play on the frontier. In his first post-war Western, *My Darling Clementine* (1946), Ford seems to recognize that the West, and perhaps the rest of the world as well, was in need of serious civilizing. When Wyatt Earp and Doc Holiday go after the Clanton gang, the climatic shootout at the OK Corral feels more like a sad, empty victory than a triumph. The movie's last scene between Wyatt Earp (Henry Fonda) and Clementine Carter (Cathy Downs) hints that the right woman could bring order and stability to the bleak, wild frontier.

In his later movies, Ford began to emphasize women and family more directly. "In [Ford's] domesticated West, with its often feminized heroes, its threatened families, and emerging Americas, women are celebrated as an indispensable force," explains film historian Jim Kitses. Women become "major players in an unsung history that his work clearly addresses and corrects."[63] For example, women and family issues were major themes in *Red River* and

Fort Apache, two Ford Westerns released in 1948. In *3 Godfathers,* the meaning of family is the movie's principal theme. *Fort Apache* is part of Ford's Cavalry Trilogy, which also included *She Wore a Yellow Ribbon* (1949) and *Rio Grande* (1950), and the plots of all three movies include a prominent focus on soldiers and their families on the frontier.

Significantly, the women characters in the cavalry pictures are not there just for window dressing and plot crises. They contribute to the social order by fulfilling their roles as wives and homemakers, which Ford highlights in a number of scenes. In *Fort Apache,* the women of the fort help the new commander, played by Henry Fonda, and his daughter, played by Shirley Temple, set up their home. The presence of families at the fort implies a safe environment, and the women reinforce this with their support for proper military etiquette. An early scene highlights the protocol for presenting calling cards, and the movie ends with a scene featuring a married Shirley Temple and her own young family, which suggests that civilization has not only maintained its foothold but is flourishing. In *She Wore a Yellow Ribbon,* Mildred Natwick must step in to assist in military and medical matters, and she does so in a manner at least as commanding as any of the officers in the movie. Victor McLaglen, a large Englishman who battled onscreen with some of Hollywood's largest leading men (including a memorable fight with John Wayne in *The Quiet Man*), is helpless before her. In *Rio Grande,* Maureen O'Hara returns to estranged husband John Wayne and asserts her influence on a cavalry outfit that is improved by her presence, as is Wayne himself.

By the time Ford made *The Searchers* in 1956, his expanded vision of the role of women in the West resulted in strong female characters such as the accomplished frontierswoman, Mrs. Jorgensen (Olive Carey), her determined daughter, Laurie (Vera Miles), and their brave young neighbor, Debbie (Natalie Wood). At one point, Mrs. Jorgensen solemnly extols the contributions she and her husband and other early settlers have made that will pave the way for new arrivals. Her task is made harder by the sacrifices she must endure, but she is buoyed by the affection and respect of the entire frontier community, which has benefitted from her undiscriminating hospitality. Her proud husband repeatedly reminds visitors, "She was a school teacher, you know," as if to certify the value of her influence. Ford expanded on the important role of women in bringing justice and fairness to the West in the 1960 movie, *Sergeant Rutledge,* which reflected the concerns of the era's expanding civil rights movement. Jeffrey Hunter plays a military lawyer who is dedicated to ensuring a fair trial for a black soldier accused of the rape and murder of a white girl. Without the testimony and resolute support of Constance Towers, Hunter and his client, played by Woody Strode, would have no case.

As the women's movement gathered momentum in the 1960s, the Western genre proved particularly well suited to plots that offered women the chance to expand their roles and influence outcomes. One classic example is the quest for justice by 14-year-old Mattie Ross (Kim Darby). When she learns that her father has been murdered, and that his killer, Tom Chaney (Jeff Corey), has skipped town, Mattie sets out to hire someone with true grit to help her track down the murderer and bring him to justice. Some 40 years after he began his career in the movies, John Wayne as Rooster Cogburn more than fit the bill.

However, Mattie's hunt for her father's killer almost does not get off the ground, in part because Rooster, a cynical, slobbering drunk, initially refuses to be hired by a young girl. In addition, Texas Ranger La Boeuf (Glen Campbell) arrives in town, intent on bringing Chaney to justice in Texas and collecting the reward money the state has offered for Chaney's part in a different murder. Mattie will not be put off. Determined to avenge her father's death, she out hustles a shady, dismissive horse trader (Strother Martin), deals disdainfully with the smug, overbearing La Boeuf, and catches up to Rooster and La Boeuf despite their best efforts to leave her behind.

Mattie shapes the movie's central quest. Although Tom Chaney is the object of her hunt, she is motivated by a basic desire to see justice done. There is an innocent purity at the heart of Mattie's goal. A wrong has been committed and must be righted. She badgers, battles, or outfoxes anyone who stands in her way. She makes significant sacrifices and accepts the dangers of the journey. She evades bad guys, goes hungry, and sleeps out in the cold as they search for Chaney and the outlaw gang he has joined. These difficulties are just part of the cost of avenging her father's death. Rooster and La Boeuf's motives for participating are much less pure. Rooster is being paid for his efforts, while the smooth-talking Le Boeuf is only after Chaney for the money and glory it will earn him back in Texas. But Mattie's single-minded determination, intelligence, and her own true grit earn their respect and support.

True Grit was released at the end of one of the most tumultuous periods in American history. The 1960s were complicated for America. In many respects it was a terrible decade. The divisive politics of the times polarized public opinion and deepened the fault lines between races, generations, and political viewpoints. The era's civil rights struggles led to widespread rioting and deaths. The anger many Americans had toward the war in Vietnam spilled over into confrontations, some of which were public and violent, such as those at the 1968 Democratic Convention. Others were more personal, as fathers who fought proudly in World War II watched their sons refuse to fight in this conflict. Political assassinations occurred with alarming frequency. In addition to President John F. Kennedy, his brother Robert, and Martin Luther King, Jr., Medgar Evers, George Lincoln Rockwell, and Malcolm X were all assassinated in the 1960s.

Young people in particular had a hard time making sense of these disturbing events. Something seemed to have gone terribly wrong with the American Dream, and the much discussed, coddled, and courted Baby Boom generation became the catalyst for the anger that mushroomed as the decade progressed. Evidence of the young generation's anguish can be found in the era's popular folk music. Songs like "We Shall Overcome," "Blowin' in the Wind," "Eve of Destruction," "The Great Mandela," "For What It's Worth," and "Give Peace a Chance" challenged the status quo and often generated outrage among older Americans.

John Wayne represented the other end of the political spectrum, and his conservative views were well known at the time. His characters, especially in Westerns, were tough, no-nonsense fighters. Wayne's role in *Big Jim McLain* (1952) emphasized the importance of the work done by the House Un-American Activities Committee. He believed that Carl Foreman's script for the much-acclaimed *High Noon,* released in 1952, was un-American, and Wayne and director Howard Hawks responded to Foreman's vision in 1959 with their own take on responsible behavior by civil authorities in *Rio Bravo.* (Foreman was later blacklisted for his alleged Communist sympathies.) Wayne produced, directed, and starred in the 1968 pro-Vietnam war movie, *The Green Berets.* Critics panned the movie, but it went on to become the tenth biggest box-office success of the year.[64]

True Grit, therefore, contrasts the entrenched conservatism of an older generation in the person of one of its most publicly recognizable representatives with the determined innocence of youth. And not just any youth—Mattie is tough, smart, and relentless. She has no illusions and refuses to allow others that luxury. Kim Darby's straightforward approach to the character ensures that Mattie more than holds her own in her scenes with Rooster. When challenged by his excessive brutality, she hangs on and keeps up. When Rooster behaves stupidly, she tells him so, not with the type of drama often associated with critical female characters but plainly and bluntly. The matter-of-fact quality of her criticisms makes it impossible to dismiss them as the emotional disapproval of an overly prim and proper young lady. A 14-year-old girl treats Rooster Cogburn as an equal. Eventually, the most widely recognized and popular interpreter of the Western hero in American movies returns the compliment.

The tension and conflict between Mattie and Rooster paralleled the generational divide that seemed so insurmountable in the 1960s. The movie's conclusion demonstrates that whatever differences we may have, our American values unite us. As one of the most tumultuous and tortured decades in American history came to an end, audiences could watch an old man—the jaded alcoholic Rooster Cogburn played by the very public patriot, John Wayne—accept the gauntlet thrown down by a teenager and prove to her and to himself that honor and justice transcend genders and generations. After four decades of playing some of the most compelling characters in movies, cowboy or otherwise, John Wayne finally earned a Best Actor Academy Award for his performance.

True Grit became one of the year's most critically acclaimed and commercially successful movies partly because it struck a responsive chord with viewers. It spoke directly to gender and generational issues of the 1960s, and it assured viewers that despite the difficult times, Americans shared common values and a common faith in liberty and justice for all. Like the other movies discussed in this book, it is an excellent example of how movies can serve as primary sources about the times in which they are made, and it clearly demonstrates the value of "movies as history."

Mattie, Rooster, and La Boeuf eventually catch up to Chaney, and the resulting complicated plot developments make it doubtful who will succeed or even survive. But if the "walkdown" in *The Virginian* helped establish a fundamental element of the American Western, the climactic "ridedown" in *True Grit* carried it to its logical, triumphant conclusion.

Suggested Discussion Questions

1. Mattie is supposed to be 14 years old. In what ways does Kim Darby's portrayal fit that age? How do Mattie's clothes and appearance reflect her character and affect the way audiences will respond to her?

2. How does Mattie treat her mother? Why? Describe Mattie's relationship with her father. How does he treat her? Why?

3. How does the woman who runs the boarding house respond to La Boeuf? Describe how Mattie initially responds to La Boeuf, and explain her attitude toward him.

4. How does Mattie respond to the hanging? Explain the judge's reason for watching. How does the community respond to the hanging? Is their interest ghoulish or are there other possible explanations for their participation? What responsibilities does a community have in relation to the decisions of the justice system?

5. Analyze the actions of all three characters in the scene where La Boeuf spanks Mattie. Why does he do it and why does Rooster make him stop? How does the movie resolve concerns about a young woman traveling with two men?

6. One of the consistent elements of male-female interaction in movies up to this point is that women of marriageable age generally do not triumph over men. How well does Mattie Ross fit into this construct?

7. Mattie keeps threatening people with her lawyer. Does her gender explain why she wants to resort to a lawyer or are there other reasons for her actions?

Describe Mattie's homestead. How can she and her family ensure their safety at home? Will having a lawyer help?

8. Evaluate the actions of Rooster, Mattie, and La Boeuf toward the various criminals they encounter. Were their actions always just? How would Rooster and La Boeuf fare in a modern professional police force?

9. Tom Chaney and the outlaw gang he joins travel to Indian country, outside the reach of local law enforcement. How can civilized society defend itself against criminals if they move beyond a society's legal jurisdiction? How does Rooster's role as a federal official affect his ability to track Tom Chaney and Ned Pepper's gang?

10. Does the issue of legal jurisdiction have any applications for national or international criminals today? Explain your answer and offer a solution to any problems you have described that depend upon issues of jurisdiction.

11. When Mattie swims across the river on her horse, Rooster says, "By God, she reminds me of me." Analyze this remark in terms of the conflicts Rooster and Mattie experience in the movie, the gender issues of the 1960s, and the generational conflicts that were going on in American society in 1969. Describe any recent movies in which female characters take on male roles or responsibilities. How are they treated and how well do they succeed?

12. Would you be more likely to vote for Mattie Ross or Rooster Cogburn for president of the United States? Explain your choice.

13. *Stagecoach* made John Wayne a star. Why would an actor so closely associated with the Western hero portray a character as unsavory and cynical as Rooster Cogburn?

14. In his first scene in *Stagecoach,* Wayne twirls his rifle. In the climactic shootout at the end of *True Grit,* he also twirls his rifle. How does this action reflect John Wayne's interpretation of the hero in the American West?

Appendix

Information on copyright law and the fair use of movies in the classroom can be found in the United States Code at http://www.copyright.gov/title17/92chap1.html#110.

Under "Limitations on Exclusive Rights: Exemption of certain performances or displays" the code permits

(1) performance or display of a work by instructors or pupils in the course of face-to-face teaching activities of a nonprofit educational institution, in a classroom or similar place devoted to instruction, unless, in the case of a motion picture or other audiovisual work, the performance, or the display of individual images, is given by means of a copy that was not lawfully made under this title, and that the person responsible for the performance knew or had reason to believe was not lawfully made ... if (A) the performance or display is made by, at the direction of, or under the actual supervision of an instructor as an integral part of a class session offered as a regular part of the systematic mediated instructional activities of a governmental body or an accredited nonprofit educational institution; (B) the performance or display is directly related and of material assistance to the teaching content of the transmission; (C) the transmission is made solely for, and, to the extent technologically feasible, the reception of such transmission is limited to—(i) students officially enrolled in the course for which the transmission is made.

Refer to the complete code for further up-to-date information on the appropriate use of copyrighted works for instructional purposes.

Notes

Introduction

1. James J. Lorence, *Screening America: United States History Through Film Since 1900* (New York: Pearson Longman, 2006), 5.
2. Kay Sloan, "Film," in *Encyclopedia of American Social History*, vol. 3, eds. Mary Kupiec Cayton, Elliott J. Gorn, and Peter W. Williams (New York: Charles Scribner's Sons, 1993), 1820a-21b.
3. Steven Mintz and Randy Roberts, *Hollywood's America: United States History Through Its Films* (St. James, NY: Brandywine Press, 1993), 11.
4. Lorence, *Screening America*, 2; Mintz and Roberts, *Hollywood's America*, 27.
5. Mintz and Roberts, *Hollywood's America*, 145.
6. Stanley J. Solomon, *Beyond Formula: American Film Genres* (New York: Harcourt, Brace, Jovanovich, 1976), 12–17.
7. Richard W. Etulain and Glenda Riley, eds., *The Hollywood West: Lives of Film Legends Who Shaped It* (Golden, CO: Fulcrum, 2001), viii.
8. Sloan, "Film," 1829a.

Part I

1. David M. Kennedy, *Freedom from Fear* (New York: Oxford University Press, 1999), 13.
2. Stanley Coben, "The First Years of Modern America 1918–1933," in *The Unfinished Century: America Since 1900*, ed. William E. Leuchtenburg (Boston: Little, Brown, 1973), 258.
3. Christopher H. Sterling and John M. Kittross, *Stay Tuned: A Concise History of American Broadcasting*, 2d ed. (Belmont, CA: Wadsworth, 1978), 60.
4. Peter Jennings and Todd Brewster, *The Century* (New York: Doubleday, 1998), 131.
5. Coben, "First Years," 326.
6. Jay Lovinger, *LIFE Celebrates 1945: The Old Order Dies, a New America Is Born* (New York: Time, 1995), 135.
7. Kennedy, *Freedom from Fear*, 10–11.
8. Ibid., 9.
9. Richard J. Evans, *The Coming of the Third Reich* (New York: Penguin, 2005), 66.
10. Kennedy, *Freedom from Fear*, 162–65.
11. Sara M. Evans, *Born for Liberty* (New York: Free Press, 1989), 198.
12. Gerald D. Nash, *The Great Depression and World War II* (New York: St. Martin's, 1979), 7.
13. Sara M. Evans, *Born for Liberty*, 176.
14. Ibid., 197.
15. *Joel Whitburn's Pop Memories 1890–1954* (Menomonee Falls, WI: Record Research, 1986), 427; and Ibid., 104.
16. Edmund H. Harvey, Jr., *Our Glorious Century* (Pleasantville, NY: Reader's Digest Association, 1994), 160.
17. Daniel Eagan, *America's Film Legacy* (New York: Continuum, 2010), 222.
18. Ibid., 199.
19. Richard J. Evans, *The Third Reich in Power* (New York: Penguin, 2005), 627.
20. Ibid., 671.
21. Yale Divinity Law School Library, "The Nanking Massacre Project," http://www.library.yale.edu/div/Nanking/Magee.html (accessed January 31, 2012). In 2007, HBO Documentary Films produced the award-winning documentary, *Nanking*. It traces the attack on the city through voice actors, primary documents, interviews with survivors, and contemporary photographs

and film footage, including the film smuggled out by John Magee.
22. Eagan, *America's Film Legacy*, x.
23. Ibid., xvii.
24. Melinda Corey and George Ochoa, eds., *The American Film Institute Desk Reference* (New York: Dorling Kindersley, 2002), 92.
25. Diane Ravitch, "History's Struggle to Survive in the Schools," *OAH Magazine of History* 21, no. 2 (April 2007), 29.
26. Sara M. Evans, *Born for Liberty*, 147.
27. Paul S. Boyer et al., *The Enduring Vision: A History of the American People*, 7th ed. (Boston: Wadsworth Cengage Learning, 2011), 577.
28. Arthur Mann, "From Immigration to Acculturation," in *Making America: The Society and Culture of the United States*, ed. Luther Luedtke (Chapel Hill: University of North Carolina Press, 1992), 75.
29. Richard M. Abrams, "Reform and Uncertainty: America Enters the Twentieth Century, 1900–1918," in *The Unfinished Century: America Since 1900*, ed. William E. Leuchtenburg (Boston: Little, Brown, 1973), 55.
30. Morris Dickstein, *Dancing in the Dark: A Cultural History of the Depression* (New York: Norton, 2009), 229–30.
31. G. D. Lillibridge, *Images of American Society: A History of the United States*, vol. 2 (Boston: Houghton Mifflin, 1976), 117.
32. Robert M. Levine, *Insights Into American History: Photographs as Documents* (Upper Saddle River, NJ: Pearson Education, 2004), 55.
33. Eagan, *America's Film Legacy*, 199.
34. Nash, *Great Depression*, 7.
35. Frank Freidel, *Franklin D. Roosevelt* (Boston: Little, Brown, 1990), 75.
36. Nash, *Great Depression*, 10–11.
37. Ibid., 27.
38. *Leonard Maltin's 2007 Movie Guide* (New York: Plume, 2006), 729.
39. Bruce Murphy, ed., *Benét's Reader's Encyclopedia*, 4th ed. (New York: HarperCollins, 1996), 897.
40. Franklin D. Roosevelt, "First Inaugural Address," *The Yale Avalon Project*, March 4, 1933, http://avalon.law.yale.edu/20th_century/froos1.asp (accessed October 10, 2012).

41. Kennedy, *Freedom from Fear*, 132.
42. Joan Didion, "John Wayne: A Love Song," in *Slouching Towards Bethlehem* (New York: Simon & Schuster, 1968), 30–31.

Part II

1. Hew Strachan, *The First World War* (New York: Penguin, 2005), 188.
2. John Keegan, *The First World War* (New York: Vintage, 2000), 176–77.
3. Joseph E. Persico, Eleventh Month, Eleventh Day, *Eleventh Hour: Armistice Day, 1918, World War I and Its Violent Climax* (New York: Random House, 2005), 373.
4. Richard J. Evans, *The Third Reich in Power* (New York: Penguin, 2005), 627.
5. *History*, "September 30—This Day in History," http://www.history.co.uk/this-day-in-history/September-30.html;jsessionid=AC259CA04C2B5C162457026148600DD0 (accessed April 17, 2013).
6. Robert H. Ferrell, "The Price of Isolation: American Diplomacy, 1921–1945," in *The Unfinished Century: America Since 1900*, ed. William E. Leuchtenburg (Boston: Little, Brown, 1973), 486.
7. Daniel Eagan, *America's Film Legacy* (New York: Continuum, 2010), 169.
8. Richard J. Evans, *Third Reich in Power*, 125.
9. Blanche Wiesen Cook, *Eleanor Roosevelt: The Defining Years 1933–1938*, vol. 2 (New York: Penguin, 1999), 332–33.
10. Keegan, *First World War*, 422.
11. Persico, *Eleventh Month*, 381.
12. "The Lost Battalion," *IMDb*, http://www.imdb.com/title/ tt0010386/ (accessed October 9, 2012).
13. Eagan, *America's Film Legacy*, 106.
14. Andrew L. Yarrow, "Exhibition on Film Makers Who Fled Nazi Germany," *The New York Times*, April 21,1989, http://www.nytimes.com/1989/04/21/movies/exhibition-on-film-makers-who-fled-nazi-germany.html (accessed April 19, 2013).
15. Killian Jordan, ed., *LIFE, Our Finest Hour: The Triumphant Spirit of America's World War II Generation* (New York: Time, 2001), 111.

16. Eagan, *America's Film Legacy*, 320.
17. Richard Lingeman, *Don't You Know There's a War On? The American Home Front 1941–1945* (New York: Thunder's Mouth Press/Nation Books, 2003), 171–72.
18. Eagan, *America's Film Legacy*, 350.
19. Gerald D. Nash, *The Great Depression and World War II* (New York: St. Martin's, 1979), 118.
20. Allan M. Winkler, *Home Front U.S.A.: America During World War II* (Wheeling, IL: Harlan Davidson, 2000), 47.
21. Lingeman, *Don't You Know*, 173.
22. Ray White, "The Good Guys Wore White Hats: The B-Western in American Culture," in *Wanted Dead or Alive*, ed. Richard Aquila (Urbana: University of Illinois Press, 1996), 153–54.
23. Lingeman, *Don't You Know*, 182–84.
24. John W. Jeffries, *Wartime America: The World War II Home Front* (Chicago: Ivan R. Dee, 1996), 180.
25. Melinda Corey and George Ochoa, eds., *The American Film Institute Desk Reference* (New York: Dorling Kindersley, 2002), 64.
26. Lingeman, *Don't You Know*, 183.
27. Ben Cosgrove, ed., "Behind the Picture: The Liberation of Buchenwald," *Life*, http://life.time.com/history/buchenwald-photos-from-the-liberation-of-the-camp-april-1945/#1 (accessed October 9, 2012).
28. Eagan, *America's Film Legacy*, 813.
29. Norman Stone, *World War I: A Short History* (New York: Basic Books, 2009), 131–36.
30. Richard J. Evans, *The Third Reich at War* (New York: Penguin, 2010), 147.
31. Winston S. Churchill, *Memoirs of the Second World War* (Boston: Houghton Mifflin, 1959), 25.
32. Norman Angell, *The Great Illusion*, at *Open Library*, http://archive.org/stream/cu31924007365467#page/n0/mode/2up (accessed April 22, 2013), x.
33. Ibid., ii.
34. Barbara Tuchman, *The Guns of August* (New York: Ballantine, 1994), 10.
35. Keegan, *First World War*, 279.
36. Strachan, *First World War*, 188.
37. Richard J. Evans, *Third Reich in Power*, 606–09.
38. Barbara Tuchman, *The Proud Tower: A Portrait of the World Before the War, 1890–1914* (New York: Ballantine, 1962), 224–26.
39. David M. Kennedy, *Freedom from Fear* (New York: Oxford University Press, 1999), 381.
40. Erik Larson, *In the Garden of Beasts: Love, Terror, and an American Family in Hitler's Berlin* (New York: Crown, 2011), 153.
41. Richard J. Evans, *Third Reich at War*, 9.
42. H. W. Janson and Dora Jane Janson, *History of Art: A Survey of the Major Visual Arts from the Dawn of History to the Present Day* (Englewood Cliffs, NJ: Prentice-Hall and New York: Harry N. Abrams, 1970), 529.
43. Frank Freidel, *Franklin D. Roosevelt* (Boston: Little, Brown, 1990) 295.
44. Cook, Eleanor Roosevelt, 500.
45. Ibid., 502.
46. "The Lady Vanishes," *IMDb*, http://www.imdb.com/title/tt0030341/?ref_=fn_al_tt_2 (accessed April 17, 2013).
47. "Sergeant York," *IMDb*, http://www.imdb.com/title/tt0034167/?ref_=sr_1 (accessed March 12, 2013).
48. Kennedy, *Freedom from Fear*, 402–03.
49. Ibid., 444.
50. David Brinkley, *Washington Goes to War* (New York: Ballantine, 1988) 43.
51. William L. O'Neill, *A Democracy at War: America's Fight at Home and Abroad in World War II* (Cambridge: Harvard University Press, 1995), 44.
52. Freidel, *Franklin D. Roosevelt*, 323.
53. Brinkley, *Washington Goes to War*, 25–27.
54. Doris Kearns Goodwin, *No Ordinary Time: Franklin and Eleanor Roosevelt: The Home Front in World War II* (New York: Simon & Schuster, 1994), 145.
55. Keegan, *First World War*, 351–52.
56. Sam K. Cowen, *Sergeant York and His People* (New York: Grossett & Dunlap, 1922) 7–16.
57. Persico, *Eleventh Month*, 293.
58. Eagan, *America's Film Legacy*, 334.
59. Brinkley, *Washington Goes to War*, 63.

60. Alistair Cooke, *The American Home Front, 1941–1942* (New York: Atlantic Monthly Press, 2004), 191.
61. Nash, *Great Depression*, 135.
62. O'Neill, *A Democracy at War*, 248.
63. Winkler, *Home Front*, 42.
64. Max Hastings, *Inferno: The World at War, 1939–1945* (New York: Alfred A. Knopf, 2011), 427.
65. Ibid., 68.
66. *Joel Whitburn's Pop Memories 1890–1954* (Menomonee Falls, WI: Record Research, 1986), 428.
67. Eagan, *America's Film Legacy*, 358.
68. Rick Atkinson, *An Army at Dawn: The War in North Africa, 1942–1943* (New York: Henry Holt, 2003), 101.
69. Goodwin, *No Ordinary Time*, 415.
70. Sara M. Evans, *Born for Liberty* (New York: Free Press, 1989), 221–22.
71. Goodwin, *No Ordinary Time*, 369.
72. Cooke, *American Home Front*, 79.
73. Brinkley, *Washington Goes to War*, 105.
74. Jordan, *LIFE, Our Finest Hour*, 31.
75. Lingeman, *Don't You Know*, 102–04.
76. Richard J. Evans, *Third Reich at War*, 471.
77. Churchill, *Memoirs*, 795–97.
78. Antony Beevor, *The Second World War* (New York: Little, Brown, 2012) 529–30; Hastings, *Inferno*, 445.
79. I.C.B. Dear, ed., *The Oxford Guide to World War II* (Oxford: Oxford University Press, 1995), 472.
80. D. G. Williamson, *The Third Reich*, 3d ed. (London: Pearson Education, 2002), 122–23.
81. Richard J. Evans, *Third Reich at War*, 24.
82. M. Burleigh, *The Third Reich: A New History* (London: Macmillan, 2000) 707, quoted in D. G. Williamson, *Third Reich*, 5.
83. Churchill, *Memoirs*, 727.
84. Selective Service System, "History and Records," http://www.sss.gov/induct.htm (accessed January 31, 2012).
85. Studs Terkel, *The Good War: An Oral History of World War II* (New York: New Press, 1984), 110–112; Sara M. Evans, *Born for Liberty*, 225.
86. Winkler, *Home Front*, 63.
87. David Halberstam, *The Fifties* (New York: Villard, 1993), 669.
88. O'Neill, *Democracy at War*, 4.
89. Ibid., 269.
90. Lingeman, *Don't You Know*, 93.
91. The movie's title had been translated as *The Bicycle Thief*, but *Bicycle Thieves* is the correct translation.
92. David McCullough, *Truman* (New York: Simon & Schuster, 1992), 508.
93. Dear, *Oxford Guide*, 702.
94. John Patrick Diggins, *The Proud Decades: America in War and Peace, 1941–1960* (New York: W. W. Norton, 1988), 76.
95. David F. Trask, "The Imperial Republic: America in World Politics, 1945 to the Present," in *The Unfinished Century: America Since 1900*, ed. William E. Leuchtenburg (Boston: Little, Brown, 1973), 597.
96. McCullough, *Truman*, 547–48.
97. Diggins, *Proud Decades*, 80.
98. Bernard Wasserstein, *BBC History*, "European Refugee Movements after World War II," http://www.bbc.co.uk/history/worldwars/wwtwo/refugees_01.shtml *(accessed April 17, 2013)*; Dear, *Oxford Guide*, 702.
99. Atkinson, *Army at Dawn*, 37.
100. Stephen E. Ambrose, *Band of Brothers: E Company, 506th Regiment, 101st Airborne from Normandy to Hitler's Eagle's Nest* (New York: Simon & Schuster, 2001), 250–51.
101. Richard J. Evans, *Third Reich at War*, 710–11.
102. Antony Beevor, *The Fall of Berlin 1945* (New York: Viking, 2002), 406.
103. Ferrell, "Price of Isolation," 557.
104. McCullough, *Truman*, 489.
105. Robert Leckie, *Delivered from Evil: The Saga of World War II* (New York: Perennial Library, 1988), 841.
106. Richard M. Abrams, "Reform and Uncertainty: America Enters the Twentieth Century, 1900–1918," in *The Unfinished Century: America Since 1900*, ed. William E. Leuchtenburg, 1–111 (Boston: Little, Brown, 1973), 557; O'Neill, *Democracy at War*, 193.
107. Kay Sloan, "Film," in *Encyclopedia of American Social History*, vol. 3, eds. Mary

Kupiec Cayton, Elliott Gorn, and Peter W. Williams (New York: Charles Scribner's Sons, 1993), 1828b-29a.

108. Churchill, *Memoirs*, 937-38.

109. *Godzilla* poster, http://www.imp awards.com/1956/godzilla_king_of_the_ monsters_xlg.html (accessed March 24, 2013).

110. Dear, *Oxford Guide*, 419; Ibid., 603.

111. Norman Polmar and Thomas B. Allen, *World War II: The Encyclopedia of the War Years 1941-1945* (New York: Random House, 1996), 430-31.

112. Dear, *Oxford Guide*, 480-82.

113. David Horner, *Essential Histories: The Second World War (I), The Pacific* (Oxford: Osprey, 2002), 81.

114. McCullough, *Truman*, 747.

115. Helen Schwartz, "Tales Told by Godzilla and Rodan," in *The Writing on the Cloud: American Culture Confronts the Atomic Bomb*, eds. Allison M. Scott and Christopher D. Geist (New York: University Press of America, 1997), 144-45.

116. Richard A. Schwartz, *Cold War Culture: Media and the Arts, 1945-1990* (New York: Checkmark Books, 2000), 129.

Part III

1. Robert Leckie, *Delivered from Evil: The Saga of World War II* (New York: Perennial Library, 1988), 85-86.

2. Melinda Corey and George Ochoa, eds., *The American Film Institute Desk Reference* (New York: Dorling Kindersley, 2002), 37.

3. Antony Beevor, *The Second World War* (New York: Little, Brown, 2012), 11.

4. Max Hastings, *Inferno: The World at War, 1939-1945* (New York: Knopf, 2011), 140.

5. Paul S. Boyer, ed., *The Oxford Guide to United States History* (New York: Oxford University Press, 2001), 149.

6. Beevor, *Second World War*, 17.

7. Hastings, *Inferno*, 141.

8. Doris Kearns Goodwin, *No Ordinary Time: Franklin and Eleanor Roosevelt: The Home Front in World War II* (New York: Simon & Schuster, 1994), 255-56.

9. John Patrick Diggins, *The Proud Decades: America in War and Peace, 1941-1960* (New York: Norton, 1988), 161.

10. Antony Beevor, *The Fall of Berlin 1945* (New York: Viking, 2002), 11.

11. Leckie, *Delivered from Evil*, 844-49.

12. Douglas T. Miller and Marion Nowak, *The Fifties: The Way We Really Were* (Garden City, NY: Doubleday, 1977), 27-28.

13. Diggins, *Proud Decades*, 162.

14. Richard A. Schwartz, *Cold War Culture: Media and the Arts, 1945-1990* (New York: Checkmark Books, 2000), 25.

15. Gerald Mast, *A Short History of the Movies*, 3d ed. (Indianapolis: Bobbs-Merrill Educational, 1981), 262.

16. Corey and Ochoa, *American Film Institute*, 69.

17. Stephen J. Whitfield, *The Culture of the Cold War* (Baltimore: Johns Hopkins University Press, 1991), 146-47.

18. Schwartz, *Cold War Culture*, 100.

19. Diggins, *Proud Decades*, 309.

20. Robert K. Massey, *The Romanovs: The Final Chapter* (New York: Ballantine, 1995), 8.

21. Christopher Hibbert, *Queen Victoria: A Personal History* (New York: Da Capo Press, 2001), xvi-xvii.

22. Beevor, *Fall of Berlin*, 399.

23. Allan M. Winkler, *Home Front U.S.A.: America during World War II* (Wheeling, IL: Harlan Davidson, 2000), 63.

24. Miller and Nowak, *The Fifties*, 29-30.

25. Diggins, *Proud Decades*, 151.

26. Elaine Tyler May, *Homeward Bound: American Families in the Cold War Era* (New York: Basic, 1988), 162.

27. Milller and Nowak, *The Fifties*, 134-36.

28. Diggins, *Proud Decades*, 181-82.

29. Norman F. Cantor, *The American Century: Varieties of Culture in Modern Times* (New York: HarperCollins, 1997), 263.

30. James T. Patterson, *Grand Expectations: The United States, 1945-1974* (New York: Oxford University Press, 1996), 328; Ibid., 180.

31. Whitfield, *Cold War*, 137.

32. Douglas Brode, *The Films of the Fifties* (New York: Carol, 1992), 64.

33. Miller and Nowak, *The Fifties*, 51.
34. Patterson, *Grand Expectations*, 487.
35. Robert Dallek, *An Unfinished Life: John F. Kennedy, 1917–1963* (New York: Little, Brown, 2003), 407.
36. Ibid., 425–26.
37. Whitfield, *Culture of the Cold War*, 211.
38. H. H. Wubben, "American Prisoners of War in Korea: A Second Look at the 'Something New in History' Theme," in *American Experiences: Readings in American History, Volume II—Since 1865*, 7th ed., eds. Randy Roberts and James Olson (New York: Pearson Longman, 2008), 229.
39. Whitfield, *Culture of the Cold War*, 21.
40. David Halberstam, *The Fifties* (New York: Villard, 1993), 61; Schwartz, *Cold War Culture*, 294.
41. *Time*, http://life.time.com/culture/when-cover-lines-collide-mixed-messages-from-life-magazine/#6 (accessed March 12, 2012).
42. Winkler, *Home Front U.S.A.*, 56.
43. Angela G. Dorenkamp, et al., *Images of Women in American Popular Culture* (New York: Harcourt Brace Jovanovich, 1985), 240.
44. Schwartz, *Cold War Culture*, 160.
45. Whitfield, *Culture of the Cold War*, 197.
46. Daniel Belgrad, "SANE and Beyond Sane: Poets and the H-Bomb, 1958–1960," in *The Writing on the Cloud*, eds. Alison M. Scott and Christopher D. Geist (Lanham, MD: University Press of America, 1997), 81.
47. Daniel Gomes, "Bert the Turtle Meets Doctor Spock: Parenting in Atomic Age America," in *The Writing on the Cloud*, eds. Alison M. Scott and Christopher D. Geist (Lanham, MD: University Press of America, 1997), 14.
48. Alison M. Scott and Christopher D. Geist, eds., *The Writing on the Cloud* (Lanham, MD: University Press of America, 1997), v.
49. Eugene E. Leach, "Peace Movements," in *Encyclopedia of American Social History*, vol. III, eds. Mary Kupiec Cayton, Elliott Gorn, and Peter W. Williams (New York: Charles Scribner's Sons, 1993), 2195–96.

50. John Gregory Stocke, "'Suicide on the Installment Plan': Cold-War-Era Civil Defense and Consumerism in the United States," in *The Writing on the Cloud*, eds. Alison M. Scott and Christopher D. Geist (Lanham, MD: University Press of America, 1997), 49.
51. *Joel Whitburn's Pop Singles Annual 1955–1990* (Menomonee Falls, WI: Record Research 1991), 85.
52. Patrick Robertson, *Film Facts* (New York: Billboard, 2001), 234.
53. Patterson, *Grand Expectations*, 508.
54. Dallek, *An Unfinished Life*, 694–95.
55. Tim Brooks and Earle Marsh, *The Complete Directory to Prime Time Network and Cable TV Shows*, 8th ed. (New York: Ballantine, 2003), 1242.
56. *The Twilight Zone*: "The Shelter," IMDb, http://www.imdb.com/title/tt0734676/ (accessed November 5, 2012).
57. Whitfield, *Culture of the Cold War*, 224.
58. Whitburn, *Pop Singles Annual*, 117.
59. Steven Mintz and Randy Roberts, *Hollywood's America: United States History Through Its Films* (St. James, NY: Brandywine Press, 1993), 260.
60. Ibid.
61. Beevor, *Second World War*, 447.
62. Stanley J. Solomon, *Beyond Formula: American Film Genres* (New York: Harcourt Brace Jovanovich, 1976), 254.
63. Whitfield, *Culture of the Cold War*, 220.
64. Halberstam, *The Fifties*, 605.
65. Schwartz, *Cold War Culture*, 41.
66. Mast, *History of the Movies*, 268–69.
67. Goodwin, *No Ordinary Time*, 51–52; I. C. B. Dear, ed., *The Oxford Guide to World War II* (Oxford: Oxford University Press, 1995), 11.
68. Schwartz, *Cold War Culture*, 46.
69. Brooks and Marsh, *Complete Directory*, 1214.

Part IV

1. Dominic Strinati, *An Introduction to Studying Popular Culture* (New York: Routledge, 2000), 121.

2. Ronald L. Davis, *The Glamour Factory: Inside Hollywood's Big Studio System* (Dallas: Southern Methodist University Press, 1993), 177.

3. Robert Sklar, *Movie-Made America: A Cultural History of American Movies* (New York: Vantage, 1975), 174.

4. Morris Dickstein, Dancing in the Dark: A Cultural History of the Great Depression (New York: W. W. Norton, 2009), 358.

5. Gerald Mast, *A Short History of the Movies*, 3d ed. (Indianapolis: Bobbs-Merrill Educational, 1981), 219.

6. Scott Simon, "Revealing the Racy Original Cut of 'Babyface,'" *NPR Weekend Edition,* Jan. 29, 2005, http://www.npr.org/templates/story/story.php?storyId= 4470843 (accessed January 1, 2012).

7. "Jezebel" Movie Trailer, *IMDb, http:// www.imdb.com/video/screenplay/ vi3652124 953/* (accessed November 6, 2012).

8. Barbara Leaming, *Bette Davis, A Biography* (New York: Simon & Schuster, 1992), 180.

9. Sara M. Evans, *Born for Liberty* (New York: Free Press, 1989), 267.

10. Elaine Tyler May, *Homeward Bound: American Families in the Cold War Era* (New York: Basic Books, 1988), 209.

11. Melinda Corey and George Ochoa, eds., *The American Film Institute Desk Reference* (New York: Dorling Kindersley, 2002), 214.

12. *Joel Whitburn's Pop Singles Annual 1955–1990* (Menomonee Falls, WI: Record Research, 1991), 297.

13. Neil Amdur, "Mrs. King Defeats Riggs, 6–4, 6–3, 6–3, Amid a Circus Atmosphere," in *The New York Times,* September 20, 1973, https://www.nytimes.com/learning/ general/onthisday/big/0920.html#article (accessed April 9, 2012).

14. Pamela McClintock, "'Legend' Lands Legendary Opening," in *Variety,* Dec. 16, 2007, http://www.variety.com/article/VR 1117977800 (accessed August 10, 2013).

15. Evans, *Born for Liberty*, 176.

16. Robert A. Caro's chapter, "The Sad Irons," in *The Years of Lyndon Johnson: The Path to Power,* is particularly vivid in its description of the burdens of household labor.

17. Daniel Eagan, *America's Film Legacy* (New York: Continuum, 2010), 306.

18. Gerald D. Nash, *The Great Depression and World War II* (New York: St. Martin's Press, 1979), 135.

19. Evans, *Born for Liberty*, 229.

20. John W. Jeffries, *Wartime America: The World War II Home Front* (Chicago: Ivan R. Dee, 1996), 102.

21. Allan M. Winkler, *Home Front U.S.A.: America During World War II* (Wheeling, IL: Harlan Davidson, 2000), 109.

22. Evans, *Born for Liberty*, 230–31.

23. Richard Lingeman, *Don't You Know There's a War On? The American Home Front, 1941–1945* (New York: Thunder's Mouth Press/Nation Books, 2003), 150–51.

24. May, *Homeward Bound*, 107–08

25. David Halberstam, *The Fifties* (New York: Villard, 1993), 590–92.

26. Angela G. Dorenkamp, et al., *Images of Women in American Popular Culture* (New York: Harcourt Brace Jovanovich, 1985), 230.

27. Douglas T. Miller and Marion Nowak, *The Fifties: The Way We Really Were* (Garden City, NY: Doubleday, 1977), 154.

28. Susan J. Douglas, *Where the Girls Are: Growing Up Female with the Mass Media* (New York: Three Rivers Press, 1994), 29.

29. Richard Maltby, Passing Parade: A History of Popular Culture in the Twentieth Century (New York: Oxford University Press, 1989), 126.

30. May, *Homeward Bound*, 112.

31. Anne Fogerty, *Wife Dressing: The Fine Art of Being a Well-Dressed Wife,* at *AbeBooks Reading Copy, http://www.abe books.com/blog/index.php /2012/04/03/wife- dressing-the-fine-art-of-being-a-well-dressed- wife* (accessed April 17, 2012).

32. Halberstam, *The Fifties*, 565.

33. Dorenkamp, *Images of Women*, 116–17.

34. John Patrick Diggins, *The Proud Decades: America in War and Peace, 1941– 1960* (New York: Norton, 1988), 212.

35. May, *Homeward Bound*, 183–85.

36. Evans, *Born for Liberty*, 245.

37. James T. Patterson, *Grand Expecta-*

tions: The United States, 1945–1974 (New York: Oxford University Press, 1996), 356.

38. May, *Homeward Bound*, 119.

39. Diggins, *Proud Decades*, 207.

40. John A. Jackson, *American Bandstand: Dick Clark and the Making of a Rock 'n' Roll Empire* (New York: Oxford University Press, 1997), 70–71.

41. Halberstam, *The Fifties*, 278.

42. Patterson, *Grand Expectations*, 355.

43. Linda Martin and Kerry Segrave, *Anti-Rock: The Opposition to Rock 'n' Roll* (New York: Da Capo Press, 1993), 59–63.

44. Alanna Nash, *The Colonel: The Extraordinary Story of Colonel Tom Parker and Elvis Presley* (Chicago: Chicago Review Press, 2003), 119; Peter Guralnick, *The Last Train to Memphis: The Rise of Elvis Presley* (Boston: Little, Brown, 1994), 259–60; Diggins, *Proud Decades*, 194; Patterson, *Grand Expectations*, 372–73.

45. Halberstam, *The Fifties*, 457.

46. Diggins, *Proud Decades*, 194.

47. Ibid., 195.

48. Guralnick, *Last Train*, 283.

49. *Joel Whitburn's Pop Singles Annual*, data compiled from pages 4, 14, 30, 46, 62.

50. Pat Boone, *'Twixt Twelve and Twenty* (New York: Dell, 1960), 87.

51. Warren G. Harris, *Clark Gable, A Biography* (New York: Three Rivers, 2002), 361.

52. Donald Spoto, *Enchantment: The Life of Audrey Hepburn* (New York: Three Rivers Press, 2007), 225.

53. *Joel Whitburn's Top Pop Singles 1955–1990* (Menomonee Falls, WI: Record Research, 1991), 481.

54. Ibid., 146.

55. Paul Brogan, *The Films of Doris Day*, http://www.dorisday.net/Film_List/Doris_Day/ doris_day. html (accessed June 30, 2012).

56. Miller and Nowak, *The Fifties*, 157.

57. Diggins, *Proud Decades*, 212–13.

58. Betty Friedan, *The Feminine Mystique* (New York: Norton, 2001), 21.

59. Ibid., 26.

60. Ibid., 30–31.

61. Steven Mintz and Randy Roberts, *Hollywood's America: United States History Through Its Films* (St. James, NY: Brandywine Press, 1993), 142–52.

62. Glenda Riley, "Barbara Stanwyck: Feminizing the Western Film," in *The Hollywood West: Lives of Film Legends Who Shaped It*, eds. Richard Etulain and Glenda Riley (Golden, CO: Fulcrum, 2001), 140.

63. Jim Kitses, *Horizons West: Directing the Western from John Ford to Clint Eastwood* (London: Palgrave Macmillan, 2009), 133.

64. Richard A. Schwartz, *Cold War Culture: Media and the Arts, 1945–1990* (New York: Checkmark, 2000), 132; Julian Brown, ed., *The Chronicle of the Movies: A Year-by-Year History from* The Jazz Singer *to* Today (New York: Crescent, 1991), 283.

Bibliography

Print Sources

Abrams, Richard M. "Reform and Uncertainty: America Enters the Twentieth Century, 1900–1918." In *The Unfinished Century: America Since 1900*, edited by William E. Leuchtenburg, 1–111. Boston: Little, Brown, 1973.

Ambrose, Stephen E. *Band of Brothers: E Company, 506th Regiment, 101st Airborne from Normandy to Hitler's Eagle's Nest.* New York: Simon & Schuster, 2001.

Aquila, Richard, ed. *Wanted Dead or Alive: The American West in Popular Culture.* Urbana: University of Illinois Press, 1996.

Atkinson, Rick. *An Army at Dawn: The War in North Africa, 1942–1943.* New York: Owl Books, 2003.

Barson, Michael, and Steven Heller. *Red Scared! The Commie Menace in Propaganda and Popular Culture.* San Francisco: Chronicle, 2001.

Beevor, Antony. *The Fall of Berlin, 1945.* New York: Viking, 2002.

———. *The Second World War.* New York: Little, Brown, 2012.

Belgrade, Daniel. "SANE and Beyond Sane: Poets and the H-Bomb, 1958–1960." In *The Writing on the Cloud,* edited by Alison M. Scott and Christopher D. Geist, 80–94. Lanham, MD: University Press of America, 1997.

Boone, Pat. *'Twixt Twelve and Twenty.* New York: Dell, 1960.

Boyer, Paul S., Clifford E. Clark, Jr., Karen Halttunen, Joseph. F. Kett, Neal Salisbury, Harvard Sitkoff, and Nancy Woloch. *The Enduring Vision: A History of the American People,* 7th ed. Boston: Wadsworth Cengage Learning, 2011.

Boyer, Paul S., ed. *The Oxford Guide to United States History.* New York: Oxford University Press, 2001.

Brode, Douglas. *The Films of the Fifties.* New York: Carol, 1992.

Brooks, Tim, and Earle Marsh. *The Complete Directory to Prime Time Network and Cable TV Shows,* 8th ed. New York: Ballantine, 2003.

Brinkley, David. *Washington Goes to War.* New York: Ballantine, 1988.

Brown, Julian, ed. *The Chronicle of the Movies: A Year-by-Year History from* The Jazz Singer *to Today.* New York: Crescent Books, 1991.

Burleigh, M. *The Third Reich: A New History.* London: Macmillan, 2000.

Cahill, Thomas. *Desire of the Everlasting Hills.* New York: Nan A. Telase/Anchor Books, 2001.

Cantor, Norman F. *The American Century: Varieties of Culture in Modern Times.* New York: HarperCollins, 1997.

Caro, Robert A. *The Path to Power: The Years of Lyndon Johnson,* vol. 1. New York: Knopf, 1990.

Cayton, Mary Kupiec, Elliott J. Gorn, and Peter W. Williams. *Encyclopedia of American Social History,* vol. 3. New York: Charles Scribner's Sons, 1993.

Chafe, William H. *The Unfinished Journey: America Since World War II.* New York: Oxford University Press, 1986.

Churchill, Winston S. *Memoires of the Second World War.* Boston: Houghton Mifflin, 1959.

Coben, Stanley. "The First Years of Modern America 1918–1933." In *The Unfinished Century: America Since 1900,* edited by William E. Leuchtenburg, 255–356. Boston: Little, Brown, 1973.

Cook, Blanche Wiesen. *Eleanor Roosevelt,*

Volume 2: The Defining Years 1933–1938. New York: Penguin, 1999.

Cooke, Alistair. *The American Home Front, 1941–1942*. New York: Atlantic Monthly Press, 2004.

Corey, Melinda, and George Ochoa, eds. *The American Film Institute Desk Reference*. New York: Dorling Kindersley, 2002.

Cowen, Sam K. *Sergeant York and His People*. New York: Grossett & Dunlap, 1922.

Dallek, Robert. *An Unfinished Life: John F. Kennedy, 1917–1963*. New York: Little, Brown, 2003.

Davis, Bette. *The Lonely Life: An Autobiography*. New York: G. P. Putnam's Sons, 1962.

Davis, Ronald L. *The Glamour Factory: Inside Hollywood's Big Studio System*. Dallas: Southern Methodist University Press, 1993.

Dear, I.C.B., ed. *The Oxford Guide to World War II*. Oxford: Oxford University Press, 1995.

Dickstein, Morris. *Dancing in the Dark: A Cultural History of the Depression*. New York: Norton, 2009.

Didion, Joan. "John Wayne: A Love Song." In *Slouching Towards Bethlehem*. New York: Simon & Schuster, 1968.

Diggins, John Patrick. *The Proud Decades: America in War and Peace, 1941–1960*. New York: W. W. Norton, 1988.

Dorenkamp, Angela G., et al. *Images of Women in American Popular Culture*. New York: Harcourt Brace Jovanovich, 1985.

Doughboy Center, Great War Society, wfa-usa.org. Quoted in Joseph E. Persico, *Eleventh Month, Eleventh Day, Eleventh Hour: Armistice Day, 1918, World War I and Its Violent Climax*. New York: Random House, 2005.

Douglas, Susan J. *Where the Girls Are: Growing Up Female with the Mass Media*. New York: Three Rivers Press, 1994.

Eagan, Daniel. *America's Film Legacy*. New York: Continuum, 2010.

Egan, Timothy. *The Worst Hard Time*. New York: Mariner Books, 2006.

Esposito, Brigadier General Vincent J., ed. *The West Point Atlas of War: World War I*. New York: Tess Press, 1995.

———. *The West Point Atlas of War: World War II: European Theater*. New York: Tess Press, 1995.

Etulain, Richard, and Glenda Riley, eds. *The Hollywood West: Lives of Film Legends Who Shaped It*. Golden, CO: Fulcrum, 2001.

Evans, Richard J. *The Coming of the Third Reich*. New York: Penguin, 2003.

———. *The Third Reich at War*. New York: Penguin, 2010.

———. *The Third Reich in Power*. New York: Penguin, 2005.

Evans, Sara M. *Born for Liberty*. New York: Free Press, 1989.

Ferrell, Robert H. "The Price of Isolation." In *The Unfinished Century: America Since 1900*, edited by William E. Leuchtenburg, 463–571. Boston: Little, Brown, 1973.

Friedan, Betty. *The Feminine Mystique*. New York: W. W. Norton, 2001.

Freidel, Frank. *Franklin D. Roosevelt*. Boston: Little, Brown, 1990.

Gabler, Neal. *An Empire of Their Own: How the Jews Invented Hollywood*. New York: Crown, 1988.

Gomery, Douglas. *The Hollywood Studio System: A History*. London: British Film Institute, 2005.

Gomes, Daniel. "Bert the Turtle Meets Dr. Spock." In *The Writing on the Cloud*, edited by Alison M. Scott and Christopher D. Geist, 11–23. Lanham, MD: University Press of America, 1997.

Goodwin, Doris Kearns. *No Ordinary Time: Franklin and Eleanor Roosevelt: The Home Front in World War II*. New York: Simon & Schuster, 1994.

Graham, Jr., Otis L. "Years of Crisis: America in Depression and War, 1933–1945." In *The Unfinished Century: America Since 1900*, edited by William E. Leuchtenburg, 357–462. Boston: Little, Brown, 1973.

Guralnick, Peter. *The Last Train to Memphis: The Rise of Elvis Presley*. Boston: Little Brown, 1994.

Halberstam, David. *The Fifties*. New York: Villard, 1993.

Harris, Warren G. *Clark Gable, A Biography*. New York: True Rivers Press, 2002.

Harvey, Jr., Edmund H. *Our Glorious Century*. Pleasantville, NY: Reader's Digest Association, 1994.

Hastings, Max. *Inferno: The World at War, 1939–1945*. New York: Alfred A. Knopf, 2011.

Hersey, John. *Hiroshima*. New York: Alfred A. Knopf, 1946.

Hibbert, Christopher. *Queen Victoria: A Personal History*. New York: Da Capo Press, 2001.

Hodgson, Godfrey. *America in Our Time: From World War II to Nixon, What Happened and Why*. New York: Vintage, 1978.

Horner, David. *Essential Histories: The Second World War (I) The Pacific*. Oxford: Osprey, 2002.

Jackson, John A. *American Bandstand: Dick Clark and the Making of a Rock 'n' Roll Empire*. New York: Oxford University Press, 1997.

Janson, H. W., and Dora Jane Janson. *History of Art: A Survey of the Major Visual Arts from the Dawn of History to the Present Day*. Englewood Cliffs, NJ: Prentice-Hall and New York: Harry N. Abrams, 1970.

Jeffries, John W. *Wartime America: The World War II Home Front*. Chicago: Ivan R. Dee, 1996.

Jennings, Peter, and Todd Brewster. *The Century*. New York: Doubleday, 1998.

Jones, Landon Y. *Great Expectations: America and the Baby Boom Generation*. New York: Ballantine, 1980.

Jordan, Killian, ed. *LIFE: Our Finest Hour: The Triumphant Spirit of America's World War II Generation*. New York: Time, 2001.

Keegan, John. *The First World War*. New York: Vintage, 2000.

Kennedy, David. M. *Freedom from Fear*. New York: Oxford University Press, 1999.

Kitses, Jim. *Horizons West: Directing the Western from John Ford to Clint Eastwood*. London: Palgrave Macmillan, 2009.

Kleinfelder, Rita Lang. *When We Were Young: A Baby Boomer Yearbook*. New York: Prentice Hall, 1993.

Larson, Erik. *In the Garden of Beasts: Love, Terror, and an American Family in Hitler's Berlin*. New York: Crown, 2011.

Leach, Eugene E. "Peace Movements." In *Encyclopedia of American Social History*, vol. III, edited by Mary Kupiec Cayton, Elliott Gorn, and Peter W. Williams, 2189–99. New York: Charles Scribner's Sons, 1993.

Leaming, Barbara. *Bette Davis, A Biography*. New York, New York: Simon & Schuster, 1992.

Leckie, Robert. *Delivered from Evil: The Saga of World War II*. New York: Perennial Library, 1988.

Lenihan, John H. "John Wayne: An American Icon." In *The Hollywood West: Lives of Film Legends Who Shaped It*, edited by Richard W. Etulain and Glenda Riley, 82–99. Golden, CO: Fulcrum, 2001.

Leuchtenburg, William E., ed. *The Unfinished Century: America Since 1900*. Boston: Little, Brown, 1973.

Levine, Robert M. *Insights into American History: Photographs as Documents*. Upper Saddle River, NJ: Pearson Education, 2004.

Lillibridge, G. D. *Images of American Society: A History of the United States*, vol. 2. Boston: Houghton Mifflin, 1976.

Lingeman, Richard. *Don't You Know There's a War On? The American Home Front, 1941–1945*. New York: Thunder's Mouth Press/Nation Books, 2003.

Lorence, James J. *Screening America: United States History Through Film Since 1900*. New York: Pearson Longman, 2006.

Lovinger, Jay. *LIFE Celebrates 1945: The Old Order Dies, A New America is Born*. New York: Time, 1995.

Luedtke, Luther, ed. *Making America: The Society & Culture of the United States*. Chapel Hill: University of North Carolina Press, 1992.

Maltby, Richard. *Passing Parade: A History of Popular Culture in the Twentieth Century*. New York: Oxford University Press, 1989.

Maltin, Leonard, ed. *Leonard Maltin's Movie and Video Guide 1992*. New York: Plume, 1991.

———, ed. *Leonard Maltin's 2007 Movie Guide*. New York: Plume, 2006.

Mann, Arthur. "From Immigration to Acculturation." In *Making America: The So-*

ciety and Culture of the United States, edited by Luther Luedtke, 68–82. Chapel Hill: University of North Carolina Press, 1992.

Martin, Linda, and Kerry Segrave. *Anti-Rock: The Opposition to Rock 'n' Roll*. New York: Da Capo Press, 1993.

Massey, Robert K. *The Romanovs: The Final Chapter*. New York: Ballantine, 1995.

Mast, Gerald. *A Short History of the Movies*, 3d ed. Indianapolis: Bobbs-Merrill Educational, 1981.

May, Elaine Tyler. *Homeward Bound: American Families in the Cold War Era*. New York: Basic Books, 1988.

McCullough, David. *Truman*. New York: Simon & Schuster, 1992.

McDonald, Paul. *The Star System: Hollywood's Production of Popular Identities*. London: Wallflower, 2000.

McLean, Adrienne L. *Glamour in a Golden Age: Movie Stars of the 1930s*. Piscataway, NJ: Rutgers University Press, 2011.

Miller, Douglas T., and Marion Nowak. *The Fifties: The Way We Really Were*. Garden City, NY: Doubleday, 1977.

Mintz, Steven, and Randy Roberts. *Hollywood's America: United States History Through Its Films*. St. James, NY; Brandywine Press, 1993.

Murphy, Bruce, ed. *Benét's Reader's Encyclopedia*, 4th ed. New York: HarperCollins, 1996.

Nash, Alanna. *The Colonel: The Extraordinary Story of Colonel Tom Parker and Elvis Presley*. Chicago: Chicago Review Press, 2003.

Nash, Gerald D. *The Great Depression and World War II*. New York: St. Martin's, 1979.

O'Neill, William L. *A Democracy at War: America's Fight at Home and Abroad in World War II*. Cambridge: Harvard University Press, 1995.

Patterson, James T. *Grand Expectations: The United States, 1945–1974*. New York: Oxford University Press, 1996.

Persico, Joseph E. *Eleventh Month, Eleventh Day, Eleventh Hour: Armistice Day, 1918, World War I and Its Violent Climax*. New York: Random House, 2005.

Polmar, Norman, and Thomas B. Allen. *World War II: The Encyclopedia of the War Years 1941–1945*. New York: Random House, 1996.

Ravitch, Diane. "History's Struggle to Survive in the Schools." *OAH Magazine of History* 21, no. 2 (April 2007): 28–32.

Riley, Glenda. "Barbara Stanwyck: Feminizing the Western Film." In *The Hollywood West: Lives of Film Legends Who Shaped It*, edited by Richard W. Etulain and Glenda Riley, 121–40. Golden, CO: Fulcrum, 2001.

Robertson, Patrick. *Film Facts*. New York: Billboard, 2001.

Schwartz, Helen. "Tales Told by Godzilla and Rodan." In *The Writing on the Cloud: American Culture Confronts the Atomic Bomb*, edited by Alison M. Scott and Christopher D. Geist, 139–50. New York: University Press of America, 1997.

Schwartz, Richard A. *Cold War Culture: Media and the Arts, 1945–1990*. New York: Checkmark Books, 2000.

Scott, Alison M., and Christopher D. Geist, eds. *The Writing on the Cloud*. Lanham, MD: University Press of America, 1997.

Sklar, Robert. *Movie-Made America: A Cultural History of American Movies*. New York: Vantage, 1975.

Sloan, Kay. "Film." In *Encyclopedia of American Social History*, vol. 3, edited by Mary Kupiec Cayton, Elliott J. Gorn, and Peter W. Williams, 1819–34. New York: Charles Scribner's Sons, 1993.

Smith, Kathleen E. R. *God Bless America, Tin Pan Alley Goes to War*. Lexington: University Press of Kentucky, 2003.

Solomon, Stanley J. *Beyond Formula: American Film Genres*. New York: Harcourt Brace Jovanovich, 1976.

Spillane, Mickey. *Kiss Me Deadly*. New York: E. P. Dutton, 1952.

Spoto, Donald. *Enchantment: The Life of Audrey Hepburn*. New York: Three Rivers Press, 2007.

Sterling, Christopher H., and John M. Kittross. *Stay Tuned: A Concise History of American Broadcasting*, 2d ed. Belmont, CA: Wadsworth, 1978.

Stocke, John Gregory. "'Suicide on the Installment Plan': Cold-War-Era Civil Defense and Consumerism in the United States (1945–1962)." In *The Writing on*

the Cloud, edited by Alison M. Scott and Christopher D. Geist, 45–60. Lanham, MD: University Press of America, 1997.
Stone, Norman. *World War I: A Short History.* New York: Basic Books, 2009.
Strachan, Hew. *The First World War.* New York: Penguin, 2005.
Strinati, Dominic. *An Introduction to Studying Popular Culture.* New York: Routledge, 2000.
Sulzberger, C. L. *The American Heritage Picture History of World War II.* New York: Bonanza Books, 1996.
Terkel, Studs. *"The Good War": An Oral History of World War II.* New York: New Press, 1984.
Tobin, James. *Ernie Pyle's War: America's Eyewitness to World War II.* Lawrence: University Press of Kansas, 1997.
Toplin, Robert Brent. *History by Hollywood: The Use and Abuse of the American Past.* Urbana: University of Illinois Press, 1996.
Trask, David F. "The Imperial Republic: America in World Politics, 1945 to the Present." In *The Unfinished Century: America Since 1900,* edited by William E. Leuchtenburg, 575–671. Boston: Little, Brown, 1973.
Tuchman, Barbara. *The Guns of August.* New York: Ballantine, 1962.
———. *The Proud Tower: A Portrait of the World before the War 1890—1914.* New York: Ballantine, 1962.
Whitburn, Joel. *Joel Whitburn's Pop Memories 1890-1954.* Menomonee Falls, WI: Record Research, 1986.
———. *Joel Whitburn's Pop Singles Annual 1955-1990.* Menomonee Falls, WI: Record Research, 1991.
———. *Joel Whitburn's Top Pop Singles 1955-1990.* Menomonee Falls, WI: Record Research, 1991.
White, Ray. "The Good Guys Wore White Hats: The B Western in American Culture." In *Wanted Dead or Alive: The American West in Popular Culture,* edited by Richard Aquila, 135–59. Urbana: University of Illinois Press, 1996.
Whitfield, Stephen J. *The Culture of the Cold War.* Baltimore: Johns Hopkins, 1991.
Willaimson, D. G., *The Third Reich,* 3d ed. London: Pearson Education, 2002

Winkler, Allan M. *Home Front U.S.A.: America During World War II.* Wheeling, IL: Harlan Davidson, 2000.
Wubben, H. H. "American Prisoners of War in Korea: A Second Look at the 'Something New in History' Theme." In *American Experiences: Readings in American History, Volume II—Since 1865,* 7th ed., edited by Randy Roberts and James Olson, 228–39. New York: Pearson Longman, 2008.

Electronic Sources

Amdur, Neil. "Mrs. King Defeats Riggs, 6–4, 6–3, 6–3, Amid a Circus Atmosphere." *New York Times,* September 20, 1973. http://www.nytimes.com/learning/general/onthisday/big/0920.html#article
Angell, Norman. *The Great Illusion.* 1913. April 22, 2013. http://archive.org/stream/cu31924007365467#page/n0/mode/2up.
Brogan, Paul. "The Films of Doris Day." http://www.dorisday.net/Film_List/Doris_Day/doris_day.html.
Cohen, George M. "Over There." 1919. *Vintage Audio*—Over There. http://www.firstworldwar.com/audio/overthere.htm.
Cosgrove, Ben. "LIFE Behind the Picture: The Liberation of Buchenwald." *LIFE Magazine,* May 7, 1945. http://life.time.com/history/liberation-of-buchenwald-the-story-behind-an-iconic-life-photo-1945/#1.
Fogerty, Anne. *Wife Dressing: The Fine Art of Being a Well-Dressed Wife,* 1959. Available at AbeBooks.com. http://www.abebooks.com/blog/index.php/2012/04/03/wife-dressing-the-fine-art-of-being-a-well-dressed-wife/.
Godzilla movie poster, http://www.impawards.com/1956/godzilla_king_of_the_monsters.html.
History. "30 September 1938: Chamberlain declares 'peace in our time.'" This Day in History. http://www.history.co.uk/this-day-in-history/September-30.html; jsessionid= AC259CA04C2B5C16245 7026148600DD0.
Hitchcock, Alfred. "The Lady Vanishes," IMDb. http://www.imdb.com/title/tt0030341/ ?ref_=fn_al_tt_2.

"Jezebel" Movie Trailer. IMDb. http://www.imdb.com/video/screenplay/vi3652124953/.

"The Lost Battalion." IMDb. http://www.imdb.com/title/tt0010386/.

McClintock, Pamela. "'Legend' Lands Legendary Opening," *Variety*, Dec. 16, 2007. http://www.variety.com/article/VR1117977800.

Roosevelt, Franklin D. "First Inaugural Address." *The Yale Avalon Project,* March 4, 1933. http://avalon.law.yale.edu/20th_century/froos1.asp.

Selective Service System. "History and Records," May 28, 2003. http://www.sss.gov/induct.htm.

"Sergeant York." IMDb. http://www.imdb.com/title/tt0034167/?ref_=sr_1.

Serling, Rod. *The Twilight Zone*: "The Shelter." IMDb. http://www.imdb.com/title/tt0734676/.

Simon, Scott. "Revealing the Racy Original Cut of 'Baby Face.'" *Weekend Edition Saturday,* January 29, 2005. http://www.npr.org/templates/story/story.php?storyId=4470843.

Stamberg, Susan. "A Depression-Era Anthem for Our Times." *Weekend Edition Saturday,* November 15, 2008. http://www.npr.org/2008/11/15/96654742/a-depression-era-anthem-for-our-times.

Time. http://life.time.com/culture/when-cover-lines-collide-mixed-messages-from-life-magazine/#6.

Wasserstein, Bernard. "European Refugee Movements After World War Two." BBC History, last updated January 2, 2011. http://www.bbc.co.uk/history/world wars/wwtwo/ refugees_01.shtml.

Yale Divinity Law School Library. "The Nanking Massacre Project." http://www.library.yale.edu/div/Nanking/Magee.html.

Yarrow, Andrew. "Exhibition on Film Makers Who Fled Nazi Germany." *New York Times,* April 21, 1989. http://www.nytimes.com/1989/04/21/movies/exhibition-on-film-makers-who-fled-nazi-germany.html.

Index

Abbott, Bud 5, 163
Above Suspicion 176
abuse 176–78, 204
Adams, Nick 204
Adam's Rib 174, 179, 183
Addy, Wesley 139, 143
The Adventures of Ozzie and Harriet 184
The Adventures of Spin and Marty 116
An Affair to Remember 10, 206
Africa 154, 172, 200
African American 6, 29, 37, 48, 79, 138, 142–43, 162, 164, 192–93, 205; *see also* Civil Rights; racism
The African Queen 180
El Alamein 76
alcohol 18, 23–24, 26, 40–41, 72–73, 147, 188, 202, 204
Aldrich, Robert 139–40
Alien 185
All Quiet on the Western Front 47, 50; novel 47
Alliance for Progress 136
allotment checks 90–91
Along Came Jones 175, 228
Al Qaeda 158
America First Committee 47, 71
American Friends Service Committee 145
American Legion 129
The Americanization of Emily 182
Anatomy of a Murder 206
... And God Created Woman 211, 221
Anderson, Donna 144, 146
Anderson, Eddie 34
Andrews, Dana 88, 90
Andrews, Edward 221, 223
Andrews, Julie 182
Angel and the Badman 229
Angell, Norman 62, 69; *see also The Great Illusion*
Angels with Dirty Faces 20
Animal Crackers 19
The Animal Kingdom 173
Annichiarico, Vito 84, 85
Annie Get Your Gun 196
Annie Oakley 228
Anschluss 21, 49, 66
anti–Semitism 50, 62–64, 66
Antonucci, Vittorio 93
Any Wednesday 182

The Apartment 10, 182
Arbuckle, Roscoe "Fatty" 171
archetype 11, 21
Arden, Eve 184
Arkin, Alan 162, 164–65
Armendariz, Pedro 153, 155
Armstrong, Bess 191
Army-McCarthy hearings 128
Arnold, Edward 34, 35
Arthur, Jean 34, 35, 79, 82, 176, 191, 228
"As Time Goes By" 78–79
Astaire, Fred 18, 144, 146, 214
Astor, Mary 172, 175
atomic bomb 58–59, 90, 102–5, 114, 117, 123, 126, 132–33, 140–45, 150, 152, 165
Auntie Mame 175, 180
Auschwitz 60
Australia 147–48
Austria 21, 49, 65–66, 98, 112
Austria-Hungary 16
Avalon, Frankie 218
The Awful Truth 19, 179

B-Westerns 53–54
Baby Doll 214
Baby Face 18, 19, 170, 173, 187
Bacall, Lauren 175
The Bachelor and the Bobby Soxer 196, 213
Badoglio, Pietro 86
Bainter, Fay 56, 174–75
Baker, Joby 210
Ball, Lucille 114, 221
The Ballad of Josie 196, 226, 228
Bancroft, Anne 171
Bancroft, George 38, 39
Bank Holiday 30
Barrymore, Drew 186
Barrymore, John 186, 188
Barrymore, Lionel 34, 35, 186–87
Battleship Potemkin 109–10, 122
Baxter, Warner 173, 176
Bay of Pigs 136
Beach Blanket Bingo 218
Beach Boys 218
Beach Party 218
Beatty, Warren 183
Beavers, Louise 210, 220
The Bedford Incident 6, 10, 117, 152, 158–62, 167

251

Bedtime Story 179, 183
Beery, Noah, Jr. 70
Beery, Wallace 177, 186, 187
Belgium 45–46, 61, 71
Bell, Book, and Candle 173
Bellamy, Ralph 190, 192
Bennett, Bruce 79
Benny, Jack 52, 163
Bergen, Candice 185
Bergen, Polly 183
Berkeley, Busby 18
Berlin 45, 98, 113, 117; Airlift 117; Olympics 47–48; Wall 117, 133, 136, 163
The Best Years of Our Lives 61, 88–93, 100, 169, 178
Bewitched 184
Bianchi, Daniela 153, 155
Biberman, Abner 190
Bicycle Thieves (Ladri di Biciclette) 58, 93–97
A Big Hand for the Little Lady 228
The Big Heat 175
Big Jim McLain 115, 169, 232
The Big Parade 50
The Big Sleep 175, 177
Bikel, Theodore 162, 165
Biography of a Bachelor Girl 19, 110, 170
birth control 15, 154, 222
birth rate 17, 205
black market 58, 77, 98, 101
Blackboard Jungle 6, 169
Blacklist 115, 140, 159, 232
Blackmer, Sidney 210, 215
Blaine, Marcie 154, 184
Blondell, Joan 22, 25
Blue, Ben 163
The Blue Angel 172
Blue Hawaii 218
Blue Steel 185
Blume in Love 179
Bob & Carol & Ted & Alice 169
Bogart, Humphrey 51–53, 75–77, 176, 177, 180, 214
Bois, Curt 75
Bollywood 178
bomb shelter 133, 150
Bond, James 11, 117, 153–58, 181
Bond, Ward 70
Bonjour Tristesse 214
Bonnie and Clyde 170, 183
Bonus Army 28
Boone, Pat 213, 220
Booth, Edwina 172
Born for Liberty 17
Born Yesterday 175, 177, 199–204
Boys Town 10, 20
Bracken, Eddie 53
brainwashing 136–38
Brando, Marlon 177, 212
Breakfast at Tiffany's 215
Breen, Joseph I. 9
Brennan, Walter 70, 72, 73, 210, 215

Bressart, Felix 118
Brice, Fanny 180
Bride and Prejudice 178
Brief Encounter 179
Bringing Up Baby 19
British Expeditionary Force (BEF) 71
British Navy 54
Broadway 16, 32, 35, 78, 182, 202
"Brother, Can You Spare a Dime?" 17–18
Bruce, Lenny 164
Buchenwald 59
Buck Privates 53
Buffy the Vampire Slayer 185
Bulgaria 79, 156, 157
Bull, Peter 149
Bureau of Motion Pictures (BMP) 54
Burke, Billie 186, 187
Burns, Robert E. 27–28
Burr, Raymond 102, 103
business 30, 35–38, 43, 99, 120, 161, 174, 183, 187, 191, 192–94, 198, 201, 204, 207–8, 210, 214, 216, 228
Butterfield 8 211
Byington, Spring 34, 35

Caesar, Sid 163
Cagney, James 22, 24, 25, 177
Calhern, Louis 123
Campbell, Glen 181, 227, 231
Canada 54
Canutt, Yakima 40
Cape Fear 177, 215
Capra, Frank 30, 34, 35
Carell, Lianella 93, 95
Carey, Olive 230
Carle, Richard 118
Carmichael, Hoagy 88, 92
Caron, Leslie 214
Carradine, John 38, 39
Carroll, Madeleine 176
cars 15, 23, 129, 154–55, 195
Carson, Johnny 164
Casablanca 52, 53, 55, 63, 75–79
Castro, Fidel 136
Cat Ballou 169, 228
Cat on a Hot Tin Roof 207
Catholics 23, 86–88, 97, 129, 178
Cattle Queen of Montana 228
chain gangs 27
Chamberlain, Neville 46, 66, 68
Chaplin, Charles 51
Charade 170, 178, 197, 214
Chatterton, Ruth 187
Chevalier, Maurice 213
Chiang Kai-shek 114
children 19, 47, 49, 56, 60, 80, 86–89, 95–97, 115–16, 124, 129, 140, 144–46, 180, 182, 191, 197, 199–200, 205, 209, 217, 222, 225, 227; child labor 17, 22
China 16, 21, 38, 58, 66, 114, 117, 127, 139, 154, 180, 191, 200

Index

Christie, Julie 118, 228
Christine, Virginia 131
Christmas in Connecticut 60, 195–99, 222
Churchill, Berton 29, 38, 40
Churchill, Winston 66, 97, 100, 102, 113
Cimarron 228
Citizen Kane 11
City Lights 18
Civil Rights 6, 138, 140, 159, 181, 230, 231; see also African American; racism
Civil War 21, 22, 50, 174; Chinese 58, 199; Russian 16, 109; Spanish 66
Claire, Ina 118, 119
Cleopatra 175
Clift, Montgomery 212
Coburn, Charles 79, 81
Coca, Imogene 163
Colbert, Claudette 176, 187
Cold War 1, 3, 6, 10, 106, 109–67, 176, 200–2, 205, 219
Cole, Nat "King" 141, 158
Committee for Non-Violent Action 145
Comrade X 111
concentration camp 51–52, 59, 60, 77
Confessions of a Nazi Spy 50
Connery, Sean 153, 155
Connolly, Walter 30
consumer culture 91, 140, 157, 214
Cook, Donald 24
Cooper, Maxine 139, 142
Cooper, Gary 11, 70, 72, 176, 191
Corcoran, Noreen 218
Corey, Jeff 227, 231
Cosby, Bill 164
Costello, Lou 53, 163
Cotten, Joseph 97, 99
Coughlin, Charles E. 71
Court, Margaret 184
Cox, Wally 158
Craig, Yvonne 210
Crawford, Broderick 177, 199, 201
Crawford, Joan 6, 60, 174–76, 180
Crosby, Bing 17
Cross Creek 185
Crowther, Bosley 130
Cuba 117, 133, 136, 138, 149–50, 154, 163
Cukor, George 186, 199, 201
Curtiz, Michael 75
Czechoslovakia 21, 46, 66, 68, 112, 120

Dachau 51
Daddy Long Legs 214
Dahl, Arlene 181
Dalio, Marcel 61, 63, 75
Dallek, Robert 149
Dantine, Helmut 75
Darby, Kim 6, 181, 227, 232–33
Dark Journey 49
Darren, James 210, 216, 218
Darwell, Jane 21, 175
Davenport, Harry 34

Davis, Bette 52, 55, 174, 175, 179
Davy Crockett, King of Wild Frontier 116, 220
Day, Doris 174, 183, 196, 221–22, 224, 226
A Day at the Races 19
Days of Glory 113
Dean, James 212
Dean, Jimmy 150
"Dear Ivan" 150
Dee, Sandra 210, 216
The Defiant Ones 6
de Havilland, Olivia 174
Dekker, Albert 139, 183
Dennis, Nick 139
De Sica, Vittorio 93, 96
Desk Set 170
Desperately Seeking Susan 185
Destry Rides Again 50–51, 170
Devine, Andy 38–40
Dhiegh, Khigh 135
The Diary of Anne Frank 59
Dickenson, Angie 184
Didion, Joan 40–41
Die Hard 179
Dietrich, Marlene 50–51, 111, 171–73, 175
Dinner at Eight 18, 177, 186–90
Dion 154
Dior, Christian 201
Dirty Harry 11
Disney, Walt 3, 19, 115–16, 179, 186, 200
divorce 132, 134, 172–74, 179–80, 185, 192, 194, 207
The Divorcee 19, 172, 179
Dr. No 155
Dr. Spock's Baby and Child Care 144, 200
Dr. Strangelove or: How I learned to Stop Worrying and Love the Bomb 10, 117, 149–54, 164
Doctor Zhivago 118, 177
Dodsworth 18, 110
La Dolce Vita 221
Doleman, Guy 144
Donovan, King 131
"Doomsday Machine" 150–52
Doran, Ann 79
Double Harness 19, 173, 178
Double Indemnity 179
Douglas, Kirk 152, 211
Douglas, Melvyn 118, 19
Downs, Cathy 229
Drake, Betsy 60
Dressler, Marie 171, 175, 186, 187, 190
Dreyfus Affair 63–63
Dromm, Andrea 163, 165
Drums Along the Mohawk 18, 39, 187
Duck Soup 19
Duel at Diablo 6
Dunaway, Faye 183
Dunkirk 55, 71
Dunne, Irene 18, 175
Durante, Jimmy 163
Dust Bowl 21, 205

Duvall, Robert 227
Dylan, Bob 150

Eastern Europe 23, 57, 98, 100, 113, 129, 133, 156, 199
Ebsen, Buddy 215
Edison, Thomas 5
education 1, 11, 22, 24, 101, 131, 143, 182, 201–4, 213–14, 220
Edwards, Cliff 190
18th Amendment (Volstead Act) 24
Eisenhower, Dwight D. 105, 130, 135, 136
Eisenstein, Sergei 109–10
Elam, Jack 139
Elbe River 98, 113
Ellis, Edward 27
Elmer Gantry 170
Emergency Banking Act 30
Enabling Act 66
Enchanted 186
England *see* Grat Britain
Equal Pay Act 181
Erin Brockovich 185
E.T. 220
ethnicity 6, 7, 24–26, 42, 48, 142
Evans, Madge 186, 188
Evans, Richard J. 47
Evans, Sara M. 17
Ever After 186
Every Girl Should Be Married 60, 178
The Ex-Mrs. Bradford 176
Exodus 59

Fabares, Shelley 218
Fabian 211, 218
Fabrizi, Aldo 84–85
Fail-Safe 152; story 150
fallout shelters 133, 145
Fantasia 10
A Farewell to Arms 50
Fargo 185
The Farmer's Daughter 175, 196
Farnham, Marynia F. 200
Farrell, Glenda 18, 27, 30, 32
Father Knows Best 184, 219
Federal Bureau of Investigation (FBI) 128, 131, 134–135, 140
Feist, Henry 84, 87
Felton, Verna 204, 208
Female 173, 187
The Feminine Mystique 180–81, 222, 224
Fennelly, Parker 163
Fenton, Leslie 22, 25
Ferguson, Johnny 154
Field, Betty 204, 207
Fifth Amendment 114, 115
The Fighting 69th 50
film noir 9–10, 60, 97, 100, 140
"final solution" 59
Firecreek 228
The First Wives Club 185

Fisher, Carrie 185
Fitzgerald, F. Scott 186
Five Graves to Cairo 10, 176
Flapper 17, 26, 186
Fleming, Ian 153–54, 157
Fonda, Henry 152, 229, 230
Fonda, Jane 177
Ford, John 21, 38–40, 42, 229–30
Ford, Paul 162, 165
Foreign Correspondent 49
Foreman, Carl 232
Fort Apache 230
49th Parallel 54
42nd Street 18
The Four Horsemen of the Apocalypse 50
Four Jills in a Jeep 169
Francis, Arlene 221, 223
Franco, Francisco 66
Frankenheimer, John 135
Fresnay, Pierre 61, 62
Fried Green Tomatoes 185
Friedan, Betty 180–81, 222–24
Friendly Persuasion 213
From Here to Eternity 207
From Russia with Love 117, 153–58, 181
The Front Page 192
Fukushima 104
Funny Face 214
Funny Girl 179–80

Gabin, Jean 61, 62
Gable, Clark 50, 172, 177, 191, 211, 214
Gaines, Richard 79, 82
Garbo, Greta 118, 119
Gardiner, Reginald 195, 197
Gardner, Ava 142, 146, 152, 175, 183
Garland, Judy 57, 196, 229
Garner, James 221, 222
Garnett, Gail 184
Garson, Greer 54–55, 176, 178
Gates, Larry 131
Geist, Christopher D. 145
Generation of Vipers 141, 143, 155
genre 9, 19, 59, 103–31, 132, 152, 218, 227–28, 231
Gentleman Prefer Blondes 297
Germany 16, 21, 38, 45–59, 61–80, 84–88, 94, 97–98, 102, 109, 112–13, 119–20, 122–24, 136, 155, 158–61, 164, 172, 199; *see also* Hitler, Adolf; Nazism; Third Reich
Gestapo 103
Gettysburg, Battle of 45
G.I. Bill 93
Gibson Girl 17
Gidget 169, 210–20
Gigi 213–14
Gilbert, Billy 190
Gilda 175
The Girls on the Beach 218
Gish, Lillian 171
Glass-Steagall Act 38

Index 255

Godfrey, Peter 195, 196
Godzilla, King of Monsters 59, 102–7, 132
Gojira 59, 102–7, 132
Gold Diggers of 1933 18–20, 169
Gone With the Wind 2, 19, 21–22, 39, 54, 118, 174, 177, 179, 187
The Good Fairy 18
Goodbye, Mr. Chips 55
Government Girl 53
The Graduate 178
Graham, Gloria 175, 177
Granach, Alexander 118
Grand Illusion (La Grand Illusion) 49, 61–65, 86
Grandjacquet, Francesco 84, 85
Grant, Cary 52, 69, 91, 123–26, 176, 179, 190–94, 213–14, 221
The Grapes of Wrath 10, 170, 175; novel 21
Great Britain 3, 12, 17, 46, 49, 51–62, 65–71, 75, 80, 84–85, 88, 94, 97–102, 110–14, 117, 119, 147, 149–53, 155–58, 163, 178, 187
Great Depression 1, 16–23, 26–30, 32, 34, 36, 38–39, 42–43, 73, 89, 92, 110–12, 127, 129, 169, 186–90, 195, 199, 205
The Great Dictator 51
The Great Gatsby 186
The Great Illusion 62, 69
The Great Train Robbery 6, 227
Greece 56, 94, 119, 154
The Green Berets 232
Greene, Graham 99
Greenstreet, Sydney 75, 79, 195, 197
Gregory, James 135, 136
Guadalcanal 80
Guess Who's Coming to Dinner 169
Gunga Din 21
The Guns of Fort Petticoat 228
A Guy Named Joe 55
Gypsy 215

Hagen, Jean 11, 202
Hail the Conquering Hero 53
Hall, Michael 88, 90
Hall, Porter 190
Hamilton, Margaret 11
Hammer, Mike 11, 140–44, 154–55
"A Hard Rain's Gonna Fall" 150
Harding, Ann 119, 170, 173
Harding, Warren G. 171
Harlow, Jean 22, 25, 171–73, 175, 177, 186–88, 191
Harris, James B. 158
Harrison, Rex 182
Hartley, Mariette 177, 228
Harvey, Laurence 135, 136
Harvey Girls 196, 229
Hathaway, Henry 227
Hawks, Howard 70, 190–92, 232
Hawn, Goldie 185
Hayden, Sterling 149–50, 152
Hayes, Annelle 228

Hayes, Helen 127, 128, 130
Hays, Will H. 9, 171
Hays Code 9; *see also* Production Code
Hayward, Susan 175
Hayworth, Rita 175
Hearst, William Randolph 71
Heflin, Van 127
The Heiress 178
Hell's Angels 50
Henreid, Paul 50, 75, 77
Hepburn, Audrey 171, 174, 181–82, 214–15
Hepburn, Katharine 170, 174, 180
Hersey, John 103–4
Hersholt, Jean 186
Hide-Out 19
The Hiding Place 60
High Noon 115, 176, 228, 232
High Road to China 191
Hinds, Samuel S. 34
Hine, Lewis W. 22
Hirata, Akihiko 102, 104
Hiroshima 58, 102, 103, 144; book 103
His Girl Friday 10, 170, 175, 179, 190–94
Hiss, Alger 114, 127
Hitchcock, Alfred 49, 65, 67–68, 70, 117, 123, 125, 176
Hitler, Adolf 16, 38, 47–48, 51, 54, 58, 61–62, 66–69, 84, 86, 112–13, 122–23, 129, 160; *see also* Germany; Nazism; Third Reich
Hobbes, Halliwell 34
Holden, William 12, 199, 201, 204, 208, 214
Holland 52, 71
Holliday, Judy 199, 201–2
Hollywood 5, 9, 11, 15, 21, 50–52, 54, 74, 76, 88, 110, 115, 140, 152, 155, 164, 178, 180, 181, 185, 214, 226, 228, 230
Hollywood Ten 115
Holmes, Phillips 186
Holocaust 50, 58–60, 123; *see also* "final solution"
homosexuality 85, 171, 206
Honda, Ishiro 10, 103
Hondo 228
Hoover, Herbert 16–18, 27–30
Hoovervilles 31
Hope, Bob 163
Hopper, Dennis 227
Hotline 117, 154
House Un-American Activities Committee (HUAC) 114, 127, 232
How to Marry a Millionaire 207
Howard, Leslie 54
Howard, Trevor 97, 99
Hudson, Rock 184, 221
The Human Comedy 55–56
Hungarian Revolution 117, 140
Hungary 16, 133
Hunter, Jeffrey 230
Hussey, Ruth 191
Hutton, Betty 196, 213
Hyde-White, Wilfred 97

Index

I Accuse 49
I Am a Fugitive from a Chain Gang 20, 29–30, 40, 43
I Am a Fugitive from a Georgia Chain Gang 27
"I Am Woman (Hear Me Roar)" 184
I Remember Mama 170, 175, 196
I Want to Live 175
I Was a Communist for the F.B.I. 116
Idiot's Delight 50
I'm No Angel 172
Imitation of Life 170, 187
Immigration 6, 23, 25–26, 142
Immigration Act of 1924 23, 25
In a Lonely Place 177
In Name Only 179
In the Heat of the Night 7
In the Navy 53
In Which We Serve 55
Independence Day 179
Indians 38, 39, 228
Inge, William 207
The Inn of the Sixth Happiness 114, 170, 180
Internal Revenue Service 35–36
International Atomic Energy Agency 105
Interventionism 47, 50, 51, 67, 70–71
Invasion of the Body Snatchers 3, 115–16, 131–35, 137, 139, 167
Irish 23, 24–25, 50
Iron Curtain 100, 114
Isolationism 46, 66, 70, 72, 75
It Happened One Night 10, 19, 178, 220
Italian realist film style 96
Italians 23, 68–69, 142
Italy 2, 46, 55, 58, 60–61, 66, 72, 76, 80, 84–88, 93–97, 113

Jackson, Wanda 154
Jaeckel, Richard 127
Jagger, Dean 127, 133
Japan 3, 21, 38, 46–47, 58–59, 62, 66, 72–76, 90, 102–27, 113, 127, 154, 159
Japanese military 16, 21, 76, 114, 180
The Jazz Singer 15
Jenkins, Allen 27
Jenks, Frank 190
Jewison, Norman 162–63, 221
Jews 23, 25, 48, 50, 58–59, 62–66, 118, 129
Jezebel 74–75
Joan of Paris 176
Johnny Come Lately 175
Johnny Guitar 6, 170, 180–81, 228
Johnny in the Clouds 55
Johnny Tremain 116
Johnson, Lyndon B. 181
Johnson, Van 56
Jolson, Al 16
Jones, Carolyn 131
Jones, James Earl 149, 152
Jourdan, Louis 214
Journey to the Center of the Earth 181
Judgment at Nuremburg 59

Julia 185
Jurado, Katy 228

Kahn, Herman 151
Karns, Roscoe 190
KDKA radio 15
Keaton, Diane 185
Keel, Howard 229
Keith, Brian 162, 165
Kellogg-Briand Pact 46
Kelly, Gene 11
Kelly, Grace 176
Kempei 103
Kennan, George F. 94
Kennedy, David 65–66
Kennedy, John F. 117, 135–36, 138, 149–50, 163, 231
Kennedy, Joseph P. 70
Key Largo 176
KGB 158
Khrushchev, Nikita 133, 136, 149
Kibbee, Guy 30, 32
The Killers 170, 175, 183
King, Billie Jean 184
King Kong 20
Kinnell, Murray 22, 24
Kinsey Reports 206–7, 211
Kiss Me Deadly 100, 139–44, 170
Kisses for My President 173, 183
Kissinger, Henry 151
Kitses, Jim 229
Kitty Foyle 178
Klute 177
Knight Without Armour 111
Kochi, Momoko 102, 104
Kolb, Clarence 190
Konstantine, Leopoldine 123, 124
Korea 114, 117, 127–28, 135 -38, 140, 154, 162, 200
Korean Airlines Flight 007 162
Kramer, Stanley 144, 147
Ku Klux Klan 23
Kubrick, Stanley 149–53, 164
Kurosawa, Akira 58–59
Kursk 80

Lacey, Catherine 65
Lady Be Good 77
Lady Chatterley's Lover 211
Lady for a Day 2, 18, 30–34, 170
The Lady Vanishes 49, 65–70, 171
Lamarr, Hedy 50
Lambert, Jack 139
Lancaster, Burt 152, 183
Lane, Charles 34
Lang, Fritz 50
Lansbury, Angela 57, 135, 137
LaRoche, Mary 210, 216
Lasky, Jesse L. 74
Lassie Come Home 56–57
The Last Days 60

Index

"The Last Time I Saw Paris" 77–78
Laugh-In 164
Laughlin, Tom 210
Law, John Phillip 163–63
Leachman, Cloris 139, 141
League of Nations 46
A League of Their Own 185
Lean, David 118
Leave It to Beaver 184
Lee, Bernard 97, 153, 155
Lee, Gypsy Rose 215
The Legend of Billie Jean 185
Lehrer, Tom 163
Leigh, Janet 135
Leigh, Vivien 174, 175
LeMay, Curtis 151
Lenin, Vladimir 109
Lennon, John 212
Lenya, Lotte 153, 155
LeRoy, Mervyn 27
Leslie, Howard 54
Leslie, Joan 70, 73
Let's Make It Legal 179
The Letter 179
Lewis, Jerry Lee 211
Life Is Beautiful (La Vita e Bella) 60
Life with Father 196
Lilies of the Field 6
Lindbergh, Charles 15, 71
The Little Foxes 10, 170, 177, 178
Little Lord Fauntleroy 18
Llewelyn, Desmond 155
Lockhart, Gene 190
Lockhart, June 70
Lockwood, Margaret 65, 67, 171
Logan, Joshua 204, 207
Lohan, Lindsey 179
Lolita 215
Lombard, Carole 52
The Long Goodbye 177
Loren, Sophia 215
Lorre, Peter 50, 75, 77
The Lost Battalion 50
Love Me Tender 212; song 211
Lover Come Back 221
Lowe, Edmund 186, 188
Loy, Myrna 88, 90–91, 173, 175–76
Lubitsch, Ernst 52, 118–19
Ludlow Amendment 70
Lugosi, Bela 118
Lukas, Paul 52, 65, 67
Lundberg, Ferdinand 200
Lynn, Vera 152

MacArthur, Douglas 162
MacArthur, James 158, 160
Mack, Helen 190, 193
"Madame La Gimp" 32
Magee, John 21, 237n21
Maggiorani, Lamberto 93, 95
Maginot Line 46, 71

Magnani, Anna 84, 85
Mail Order Bride 229
The Maltese Falcon 175
Man Hunt 51, 56, 176
The Man Who Knew Too Much (1956) 49, 117, 125, 169, 176
The Manchurian Candidate 115–16, 124, 135–39, 170
Manhattan Melodrama 20, 175
Man's Favorite Sport? 184
Mansfield, Jayne 174
March, Fredric 88, 91
March, Little Peggy 154, 184
marriage 17, 19, 32, 42, 52, 55, 60, 83, 91–92, 194–95, 198, 200–3, 205–7, 210–21, 222, 225–27, 233; *see also* women
"La Marseillaise" 63, 79
Marshall, Herbert 191
Marshall Plan 97
Martin, Strother 139, 227, 231
Marvin, Lee 177
Marx Brothers 19, 52
Mary Poppins 182
The Mary Tyler Moore Show 184
Mason, James 181
Mata Hari 171
Matthau, Walter 152
The Maverick Queen 228
Maxwell, Lois 153, 155
May, Elaine Tyler 180
McCabe and Mrs. Miller 228
McCambridge, Mercedes 6
McCarey, Leo 127, 129
McCarthy, Joseph 116, 127–28, 137, 139, 140, 144, 200; McCarthyism 127, 132, 134, 145, 159
McCarthy, Kevin 131, 132
McClintock 177–78
McClure, Doug 210
McCrea, Joel 79, 81
McCrystal, Stanley 162
McDaniel, Hattie 22, 174–75
McDowell, Roddy 56
McGiver, John 135
McHugh, Frank 127
Medal of Honor 2, 11, 50, 72, 137
Meek, Donald 34, 35, 38, 39
Meeker, Ralph 139, 141–42
Meet Me in St. Louis 57, 196
Merande, Doro 163
Meredith, Burgess 149
Merrily We Live 19
MGM 57
Michi, Maria 84, 85
The Mickey Mouse Club 115–16
Middle East 16, 45, 58, 200
Midler, Bette 185
Midway 57
Mildred Pierce 60, 170, 174, 196
Miles, Vera 228, 230
militarism 62, 65, 67, 68, 106, 163

Miller, Ann 34, 35
Miller, Douglas T. 221
Mills, Hayley 179
The Milton Berle Show 212–13
Min and Bill 170, 175
Minnelli, Vincent 57
minorities 42, 52, 94, 144, 205
Miracle Mile 8, 147
The Miracle of Morgan's Creek 53, 213
Miracle on 34th Street 196
The Miracle Worker 171
The Misfits 179
Miss Congeniality 185
Mission to Moscow 113
Mr. Deeds Goes to Town 10, 18, 191
Mr. Smith Goes to Washington 10, 39, 191
Mr. Winkle Goes to War 53
Mitchell, Thomas 38, 40
Mitchell, Margaret 21
Modern Women: The Lost Sex 200
Monroe, Marilyn 181, 202, 207, 221
monster movies 59, 102–7, 131–32
Monte Cassino 86
Montgomery, Elizabeth 184
Montgomery, Robert 19, 177
Moore, Terry 102, 103
The More the Merrier 53, 55, 79–83
Morgan, Dennis 195, 197
Morgan, Frank 51, 173
Morley, Karen 186, 188
Morocco 76–78, 117
Morris, Chester 172
The Mortal Storm 51–52
Moscow 100, 148, 152, 154
motherhood 12, 21, 23, 31, 33, 36, 56–57, 59–60, 72–74, 90, 97, 100, 124, 128–31, 137–38, 140–42, 145, 148, 163, 170–75, 180, 184,-85, 193–94, 200, 203, 205, 207–9, 215–16, 219–20, 222–26, 233; *see also* women; Women's Movement
Motown 63
Mrs. Polifax—Spy 181
Ms. 227; *Ms.* 181, 184
Muni, Paul 27
Munich Conference 46, 49, 68
Murphy's Romance 185
Mussolini, Benito 51, 61, 84–86
My Darling Clementine 229
My Fair Lady 182
"My Man" 180
My Son John 115–16, 124, 127–31, 134, 138, 167
myths 7, 10

Nagasaki 58, 102
Nanking (Nanjing) 21, 237*n*21
National Committee for a Sane Nuclear Policy 145
National Film Registry 21
National Organization for Women 181
National Velvet 57
Nationalist Chinese 114, 154, 200

Natwick, Mildred 210, 215, 230
Nazism 47–52, 54, 59, 62, 66–67, 71, 85–87, 94, 97, 102, 109, 123–24, 127, 163, 171, 176
Nelson, Ricky 154
The Net 185
Neutrality Acts 38, 46
New Deal 2, 20, 33, 39, 112
New Look 200–1
New York Board of Censors 173
New York City 18, 31–31, 50, 51, 57, 121, 138–39, 164, 187, 215
Newhart, Bob 164
Newman, Phyllis 204
Nicolson, Harold 66–67
Nielsen, Leslie 210, 215
A Night at the Opera 19
Night Must Fall 177
Night Nurse 172, 177
Night of the Hunter 171
Night Riders 53
Night Train to Munich 49
19th Amendment 17
Ninotchka 21, 22, 111, 118–22, 133, 139
Niven, David 221
Nixon, Richard 149
North by Northwest 125, 176
The North Star 113
Norway 71, 119
Notorious 49, 51, 58–59, 116, 123–26, 135, 138, 176, 179
Novak, Kim 12, 204, 207
Now, Voyager 170, 178
Nowak, Marion 221
Nuclear Test Ban Treaty of 1963 117, 136, 154
Nuremberg 47; Nuremberg Laws 66; *see also Triumph of the Will*
Nye, Gerald P. 51, 76

Obama, Barak 162
O'Brien, Margaret 57
Ocean's Eleven 179
O'Connell, Arthur 204, 208, 210, 216
O'Connor, Robert Emmett 22, 24
O'Connor, Una 195, 197
October Revolution 110; *see also* Sergei Eisenstein
O'Donnell, Cathy 88
Office of Civil Defense and Mobilization 145
Office of War Information (OPI) 54
O'Hara, Maureen 177, 230
Olsen, Moroni 123
Olympia 47–48
On the Beach 8, 117, 144–48, 167; book 145
On Thermonuclear War 151
Once Upon a Honeymoon 52
Once Upon a Time in the West 228
Only Angels Have Wings 191
The Opposite Sex 179
O'Shea, Tessie 163
O'Sullivan, Maureen 19
Oswald, Lee Harvey 117, 138

Index

Our Miss Brooks 184
The Outlaw 177
Owen, Reginald 221, 223
Owens, Jesse 48

Page, Joy 75
Paget, Debra 212–13
Pagliero, Marcello 84, 85
Palance, Jack 11
The Parent Trap 179
Parker, Cecil 65
Parker, Fess 116
Parker, Jean 30, 31
Parker, Sarah Jessica 185
Parlo, Dita 61
Parrish, Leslie 135
Pat and Mike 170, 178
Patton, General George S. 98
Pauling, Linus 144
The Pawnbroker 59
Peace Corps 136
Pearl Harbor 47, 52–54, 72, 75–76, 113
Peck, Gregory 144, 146, 174, 177, 211
Pecora Commission 36, 43
Pendleton, Nat 30, 32
Penthouse 173, 175
Perkins, Anthony 144, 146
Pershing, John J. 45
Personal Property 19
Pétain, Henri-Philippe 76, 78
Peter, Paul, and Mary 150
The Petrified Forest 10, 169
Pevney, Joseph 210
Peyton Place 211
The Philadelphia Story 10, 178, 179, 191
Picasso, Pablo 66
Pickens, Slim 149
Picnic 10, 12, 204–10
Pidgeon, Walter 51, 55, 56
Pillow Talk 221
Pitts, ZaSu 221, 222
A Place in the Sun 212
Platt, Louise 38, 39
Pledge of Allegiance 115
Plummer, Christopher 182
Poitier, Sidney 6–7, 22, 152, 158, 160, 162
Poland 38, 51, 52, 66, 70, 94, 112–13
Police Woman 184
Porter, Edwin S. 6
Portman, Eric 158, 160
The Postman Always Rings Twice 175, 179
Potsdam Conference 98
Powell, Jane 229
Powell, William 175
Powers, Mala 210
Prentiss, Paula 184
Presley, Elvis 211–12
Pride and Prejudice 178
prisoner of war (POW) 49, 63, 86, 136–37
Private Benjamin 185
Production Code 1–2, 9, 19, 34, 43, 126, 155,
170, 171–75, 177, 179, 182, 186–87, 206, 210, 211, 221, 225–26; pre-code 171,-75, 177, 187
Progressive Era 17, 22, 28
Prohibition 15, 22–26, 28; 18th Amendment 24
propaganda 47, 51, 54, 58, 68, 76, 79, 109–10, 148
prostitution 20, 142, 201
The Public Enemy 20, 22–26, 169, 172, 177

Qing Dynasty 16
Qualen, John 190, 192
Queen Christina 172
Queen Victoria 17; Victorian 119, 221
The Quiet Man 177–78, 230

racism 1, 2, 7, 16, 142, 162, 181, 194, 205, 231; *see also* African American; Civil Rights
radio 15, 23, 71, 147
Rains, Claude 75, 77, 123, 124
A Raisin in the Sun 6
The Rake's Progress 59
Random Harvest 55
Rashomon 59
Rear Window 125, 176
Rebel Without a Cause 170, 207, 212
Red Dust 172
Red-Headed Woman 172, 187
Red Scare 110
The Red Shoes 170, 196
Reddy, Helen 184
Redford, Robert 180
Redgrave, Michael 65, 67, 171
Reed, Carol 97, 100
refugees 52–53, 58, 97–98
Reid, Elliott 221
Reiner, Carl 162, 165, 222–23, 225
religion 23, 73, 86, 96, 115, 129, 131, 148, 166
The Reluctant Debutant 213
The Remains of the Day 67
Remarque, Erich Maria 47
Remick, Lee 206
Renoir, Jean 49, 61–65
Revere, Anne 57
Reynolds, Debbie 11, 181, 182, 210, 215, 218
The Richest Girl in the World 19
Rickles, Don 164
Ride the High Country 9, 177, 228
Ride the Wild Surf 218
Ridges, Stanley 70
Riefenstahl, Leni 47–48
Riggs, Bobby 184
Rio Bravo 232
Rio Grande 179, 230
Roaring Twenties 15–18, 22–23, 28, 34–35, 38, 46–47, 110, 163, 171, 173, 186
Roberta 18
Robertson, Cliff 204, 207, 210, 216
Robinson, Edward G. 53, 176
Robinson, Jackie 158
Robson, May 18, 30, 31, 186

Index

rock-and-roll 154, 163, 184, 211–213, 218
Rodgers, Gaby 139, 143
Rogers, Ginger 18, 20, 52, 178
Roman Holiday 174
Romania 94, 119
Romanov Dynasty 109–10, 119, 121–22
Rome, Open City (Roma Citta Aperta) 55, 56, 84–88, 96
Romeo and Juliet 8, 178
Ronstadt, Linda 184
Rooney, Mickey 20, 56, 57
Roosevelt, Franklin D. 2, 18, 20–21, 25, 26, 30–31, 33, 34–39, 43, 58, 66, 70–71, 97, 100, 112–13
Rosenberg, Ethel 114, 127
Rosenberg, Julius 114, 127
Rosie the Riveter 80
Rossellini, Roberto 84, 88
Ruman, Sig 118
Runyon, Damon 32
Russell, Harold 88, 90–92, 100
Russell, Jane 177
Russell, Rosalind 177, 180, 181, 190, 192, 204, 208
Russia 16–18, 22–23, 45, 57–58, 61–62, 65, 69, 75, 80, 93–94, 97–102, 105, 109–67, 181, 199, 200
Russian Revolution 109–10, 118, 122
The Russians Are Coming, the Russians Are Coming 118, 162–67, 181

Sabrina 49
Sahl, Mort 164
Saint, Eva Marie 162, 165, 176, 181
St. John, Howard 199, 202
Sakall, S.Z. 75, 195, 196
Saltamerenda, Gino 93, 95
Saroyan, William 55
Savage, Ann 79
Schaal, Dick 163
Schindler's List 60
Schunzel, Reinhold 123
Schwartz, Richard A. 116, 154
Scott, Alison M. 145
Scott, George C. 149, 151, 152
screwball comedy 19, 81, 181, 190–91
The Search 59
The Searchers 6, 178, 214, 228, 230
Selective Service 2, 71–74, 88, 159
Selleck, Tom 191
Sellers, Peter 149–52
Sergeant Rutledge 6, 214, 230
Sergeant York 2, 11, 50, 70–74
Serling, Rod 149–50
Seven Brides for Seven Brothers 229
Seven Days in May 152
The Seventh Cross 52
sex 2, 9, 83, 140–42, 144, 148, 151–52, 154, 155–57, 164, 169–86, 187–88, 200, 202, 205–7, 210–20, 221–22, 225–26
Sex and the Single Girl 169, 183

Shane 9, 11, 228
Sharif, Omar 118, 180
Shaw, Robert 153, 155, 157
Shayne, Robert 195
She Done Him Wrong 172
She Wore a Yellow Ribbon 230
Shearer, Norma 50, 172–3
Shimura, Takashi 102, 104
The Shootist 228
Shute, Nevil 145, 147
Siegel, Don 131
The Silence of the Lambs 185
Silva, Henry 135
Sinatra, Frank 135, 137, 212
Since You Went Away 55–56, 169
Singin' in the Rain 11, 202
Sister Act 185
Sister Kenny 173
Skala, Lilia 171
Slate, Jeremy 227
Smiles of a Summer Night 221
The Smothers Brothers Comedy Hour 164
Snow White and the Seven Dwarfs 19
Solomon, Stanley J. 152
Song of Russia 113
Sophie's Choice 60
The Sound of Music 10, 22, 49, 170, 182
South Pacific 206
Soviet Union 22, 57–58, 69, 75, 93–94, 97–99, 105, 109–167, 199, 200; see also Russia; Stalin, Joseph
Spanish Civil War 66
Sparks, Ned 30, 34
Spillane, Mickey 140–41, 154
The Spirit of St. Louis 15
Splendor in the Grass 178, 182
Spock, Benjamin 144, 200; see also Dr. Spock's Baby and Child Care
Sputnik 145
Stage Door 170
Stagecoach 9, 10, 21, 38–43, 100, 187, 228–29, 234
Staiola, Enzo 93, 95
Stalin, Joseph 97, 106, 110–13, 129, 133; see also Russia; Soviet Union
Stalingrad 76, 80
Stanwyck, Barbara 18, 19, 172, 173, 175, 177, 179, 187, 191, 195, 196, 228
A Star Is Born 173
"Star System" 5
Star Wars 186
State Department 114, 127, 139
Steiger, Rod 177
Steinbeck, John 21
Steinem, Gloria 181, 184
Stella Dallas 170
Stevens, George 79–80
Stevenson, Adlai 151, 203
Stewart, James 15, 34, 35, 51, 176, 191, 206
Stewart, Paul 139
stock market 16

Stone Poneys 184
The Stranger 59
Strasberg, Susan 204, 208
A Streetcar Named Desire 177
Streisand, Barbra 179–80
Strode, Woody 6, 150, 230
Student Peace Union 145
Sturges, Preston 53
suburbs 129, 205
Sudetenland 49, 68
Suez Crisis 140
Sullavan, Margaret 51
Sully, Frank 79
A Summer Place 179, 207
Summertime 206
Sunrise at Campobello 11
Sunset Blvd. 196
surfing 216–18
Sutherland, Donald 158
Sutton, Grady 79

Taiwan 114, 154, 200
Takarada, Akira 102, 104
"Talkin' World War III Blues" 150
The Taming of the Shrew 178
"Tammy" 218, 220
Tammy and the Bachelor 210–21
Tarzan the Ape Man 19
Tate, John 144
Taylor, Dub 34, 35
Taylor, Elizabeth 56–57, 175
television 9, 57, 115, 116, 128, 149, 163, 178, 184, 199, 200, 212, 218–19, 223, 225–26
Teller, Edward 151
Temple, Shirley 19, 20, 213, 230
That Touch of Mink 183, 221
Thelma and Louise 185
Theme 1, 6–12, 18, 49, 56, 63, 67, 115, 117, 148, 178, 186, 198, 206, 229–30
There Goes My Heart 19
The Thin Man 11, 175
The Thing from Another World 106, 144
The Third Man 58, 97–102, 114
Third Reich 38, 47–50, 87; *see also* Hitler, Adolf; Nazism
39 Steps 49, 125, 176
3 Godfathers 229–30
The Thrill of It All 174, 183, 221–27
To Be or Not to Be 52
To Kill a Mockingbird 10
Tobias, George 70
Tokyo 81, 103–4, 106
Toland, Gregg 92
Too Many Husbands 17
Towers, Constance 230
Tracy, Lee 186
Tracy, Spencer 20, 170, 174
Trader Horn 172
Travers, Linden 65
Treaty of Versailles 16, 21, 62, 66, 1112
trench warfare 45, 49, 71, 73

Trevor, Claire 38, 39, 176
Triumph of Will 47–48
True Grit (1969) 6, 170, 175, 181, 227–34
Truex, Ernest 190
Truman, Harry 162; administration 94; Doctrine 94, 154
Tsar Nicholas II 109–10, 119, 122
Turkey 94, 154, 155–57
Turner, Lana 175, 179
12 Angry Men 10, 115
Twelve O'Clock High 130
Twice Blessed 179
Twilight Zone 149–50
'Twixt Twelve and Twenty 213
Two for the Road 182
Two Rode Together 228
Two Women 215

The Unforgiven 228
United Nations Relief and Rehabilitation Administration 59
United States Army 15, 28, 46, 50, 58–59, 71–74, 78, 90–91, 98, 106–7, 128, 136, 159, 230
United States cavalry 38–42, 159, 230
United States Congress 20, 21, 24, 28, 38, 71, 115, 116, 127, 137, 152, 159, 181, 196, 201–4
An Unmarried Woman 185
The Unsinkable Molly Brown 182

Vallee, Rudy 17
Valli, Alida 97
van Hulzen, Joop 84, 86
Vatican 85
Vaughn, Sarah 158
Veidt, Conrad 75, 77
Verdun, Battle of 45–46, 63
Vertigo 125
veterans 28–29, 60, 89, 91, 129–30, 195, 205
Vichy, France 76–77
Victor Emmanuel III 84
Victorian Era *see* Queen Victoria
Vienna 98–102; Summit 136
Vietnam 117, 159, 231, 232
Vinson, Helen 27
Virginia Slims 185
The Virginian 228, 233
von Falkenhayn, General Erich 63
von Stroheim, Erich 61, 62
von Trapp, Georg 49, 182
von Treskow, Major-General Henning 86

Wagner Act 38
Wait Until Dark 171, 181
Walker, Robert 127, 128, 130
Wall Street 15, 36
Walt Disney Presents: Annette 116
"Waltzing Matilda" 147
The War of the Roses 185
Warner, H.B. 34, 36
Warner Bros. 70, 173

Washington, D.C. 10, 21, 22, 28, 39, 80–82, 128, 138, 154, 191, 201
Watch on the Rhine 52, 169
WAVES (Women Accepted for Voluntary Service) 80
The Way to the Stars 55
"The Way We Were" 179–80
Wayne, John 38, 39, 40–41, 54, 100, 115, 177–78, 181, 214, 227, 230–34; *see also Stagecoach*; *True Grit*
Weimar Republic 16
Welch, Joseph 128
Welles, Orson 11, 97, 99
Wellman, William 20, 22
Wendkos, Paul 210
West, Mae 171–73, 175, 187
West Side Story 6, 8
Western Europe 153, 156
Western movies 6, 9, 11, 38–39, 50, 53–54, 227–34
Westward Ho the Wagons 116
Westward the Women 170
Wheeler, Burton K. 51, 71
When Ladies Meet 170
"Where Have All the Flowers Gone" 159
Where the Boys Are 214
White Russians 119
Whitfield, Stephen J. 142, 152
Whitty, Dame May 65, 67, 171
Widmark, Richard 152, 158, 160
Wife Dressing: The Fine Art of Being a Well-Dressed Wife 201
Wife vs. Secretary 187, 191
Wild Boys of the Road 20, 27
The Wild One 212
Wilde, Lee 179
Wilde, Lyn 179
Wilder, Billy 50
William, Warren 30, 31
Wilson, Dooley 75, 76, 79
Wilson, Elizabeth W. 204
Wilson, Woodrow 46
The Wind and the Lion 185
Wings 50
Winters, Jonathon 162
Wister, Owen 228

Withers, Googie 65
The Wizard of Oz 10, 11, 21–22, 39
Woman of the Year 174
women 1, 5, 6, 9, 15–19, 22–25, 27, 34, 37, 43, 49, 79–80, 85, 91–92, 100, 131, 138, 140–44, 148, 151, 155–57, 169–234; and work 17, 18–19, 52–53, 60, 80, 82, 89, 121, 124–25, 129, 140–44, 153; *see also* motherhood; Women's Movement
The Women 21–22, 179
Women Strike for Peace 145
Women's Army Corps 80
Women's Movement 143, 178–81, 184, 191, 220, 227, 230; *see also* motherhood; women
Wood, Natalie 183, 230
Wooden Crosses 49
Woods, Edward 22, 24
Woodward, Joanne 228
The World, the Flesh, and the Devil 117
World War I 2, 11, 16–17, 27, 45–47, 49–50, 55, 61–64, 65, 70–74, 76, 109, 111–12, 205; veterans 27, 28
World War II 1, 3, 12, 15, 38, 51–57, 62, 65–66, 76–79, 80, 84–88, 104, 106, 109, 127, 130, 151; post-war 60–61, 91, 93–97, 99, 111–14, 116, 123, 126, 131, 153–54, 159; veterans 88–93, 129, 205, 231; women 176, 180, 195–96, 199, 205–6, 211, 221–22, 229
Wray, Fay 20, 210, 215
Wright, Teresa 55, 88, 90
Wuthering Heights 21, 179
Wycherly, Margaret 70, 72–73
Wyler, William 55, 61, 88, 89, 93
Wylie, Philip 141, 143
Wynn, Keenan 149
Wynter, Dana 131, 132

Yalta Conference 94, 97–100, 113–114
York, Alvin 2, 11, 50, 70–74
You Can't Take It with You 19, 34–38, 43
Young, Loretta 196
Young, Terence 153
Young Mr. Lincoln 21, 39

Zedong, Mao 114, 200